MW01281988

# Sikhs, Swamis, Students, and Spies

# Sikhs, Swamis, Students, and Spies

## The India Lobby in the United States, 1900–1946

### Harold A. Gould

**Sage Publications**
New Delhi • Thousand Oaks • London

First published in 2006 by

**Sage Publications India Pvt Ltd**
B-42, Panchsheel Enclave
New Delhi 110 017
*www.indiasage.com*

**Sage Publications Inc**
2455 Teller Road
Thousand Oaks, California 91320

**Sage Publications Ltd**
1 Oliver's Yard, 55 City Road
London EC1Y 1SP

Published by Tejeshwar Singh for Sage Publications India Pvt Ltd, photo-typeset in 10 pt Palatino by Star Compugraphics Private Limited, Delhi and printed at Chaman Enterprises, New Delhi.

**Library of Congress Cataloging-in-Publication Data**

Gould, Harold A. (Harold Alton), 1926–
    Sikhs, swamis, students, and spies : the India lobby in the United States, 1900–1946 / Harold A. Gould.
        p. cm.
    Includes bibliographical references and index.
    1. Lobbying—United States—History—20th century.  2. East Indian Americans—Politics and government—20th century.  I. Title.

JK1118.G64        324'.408991411073—dc22        2006        2006023058

**ISBN:**  10: 0-7619-3480-4 (HB)        10: 81-7829-627-6 (India-HB)
            13: 978-0-7619-3480-6 (HB)        13: 978-81-7829-627-2 (India-HB)

**Sage Production Team:** Vidyadhar Gadgil, Shweta Vachani, Rajib Chatterjee, and Santosh Rawat

To the memory of
Professor Robert I. Crane (1922–1997),
a dear friend, loyal colleague, and
the inspiration for this work.

# Contents

# List of Illustrations

# List of Abbreviations

| | |
|---|---|
| ACLU | American Civil Liberties Union |
| AFL | American Federation of Labor |
| CBI | China-Burma-India theater during World War II |
| CIA | Central Intelligence Agency |
| CIO | Congress of Industrial Organizations |
| FDR | Franklin Delano Roosevelt |
| FFI | Friends for the Freedom of India |
| INS | Immigration and Naturalization Service |
| NWFP | Northwest Frontier Province |
| OSS | Office of Strategic Services |
| OWI | Office of War Information |
| SHAEF | Supreme Headquarters Allied Expeditionary Force |
| UNRRA | United Nations Relief and Rehabilitation Agency |
| VOA | Voice of America |

# Foreword

In July 2005 the Prime Minister of India, Manmohan Singh, made a visit to the United States that was heralded in the press and applauded in speeches by representatives of both countries as a triumphal expression of the long-enduring friendship that has prevailed between "the world's two greatest democracies". The symbol selected for this amity was a splendid dinner hosted by President Bush. This was especially memorable since the president rarely gives such elaborate dinners to visiting heads of state. And in this case, the prime minister was technically not even head of the Indian state in the conventional sense of the word. Clearly, the rhetoric and the actual state of affairs notwithstanding, there has been a sea change in Indo-US relations, especially when one recalls the atmosphere of pique that prevailed during a great part of the past half-century.

Remarkable in this regard was the Joint Statement issued by the two leaders, which was interpreted by the Indian public as a pledge that the United States "would help India become a major world power in the twenty-first century." Reporting this, one leading Indian newspaper, not noted for its friendly treatment of the United States, declared in a headline that the two countries were "natural partners" and that agreements had been reached which provide for joint weapons production, cooperation in missile defense, export of sensitive military technologies from the United States to India, encouragement of American investment in India, and nuclear cooperation (Pant 2005). This was once again remarkable when seen against the background of previous American policies, which disdained "Non-Alignment," supplied arms to Pakistan, and impelled India to seek compensatory military assistance from the Soviet Union throughout the Cold War.

Harold Gould's fascinating, multi-layered study of the South Asians' quest for social justice in the United States and Canada, meticulously researched and at the same time very readable, scarcely mentions post-2002 events because it deals not with the contemporary state of the Indo-US relationship, but with its historical roots dating back to the turn of the century. His book, for this reason, should be required reading for journalists and politicians who talk glibly of "natural partnerships" and the inevitability of friendship because of shared values between India and the United States. How little the complexity of the relationship between the two countries is in fact understood is glaringly apparent in the almost idyllic reporting on India recently undertaken by the American reporter, Thomas Friedman (2005). In his widely-read and influential book, *The World is Flat*, he rightly makes much of India's technological achievements and their meaning for both countries. But as already suggested, it was not always that way. There is, however, yet little recognition of the relevance of India's history and the power of nationalism, and the forces that determined Indo-American relations throughout much of the twentieth century and are almost certain to continue shaping them in the twenty-first. Perhaps because Gould is an anthropologist whose professional career has been located in the intensive study of Indian society and civilization—something that is always close to the surface in his book—he provides some of that wider and deeper social-historical perspective that is indeed frequently lacking, but sorely needed, in contemporary journalistic perceptions.

In the early decades of the twentieth century, South Asian Indians—mainly Sikhs, but Hindus and Muslims as well—began to trickle into Canada and the United States, in search of economic opportunities and advanced education; but they also met with racial prejudice and obstacles to immigration and the attainment of citizenship rights. Gradually the Indians mobilized to resist white assaults on their civil rights, and in the process came to the realization that British colonialism was a major reason why Indians were held in such low esteem throughout the rest of the world. This culminated, by World War I, in the so-called Ghadr movement. Created primarily by Sikhs from the Punjab who had migrated to California and British Columbia and established themselves there in a modest way as farmers and lumbermen, its aim was to supply manpower, money and ammunition to groups in India that were seeking to overthrow the British Raj. The young, educated Indians who also came to the United States, usually to study, received financial and moral support from this crystallizing Sikh community; and in exchange the Ghadrites and other revolutionaries and reformists got new and more articulate leaders for their cause. This was a link which subsequently enabled South Asian Americans to interface with the emerging freedom movement in India.

Gould gives an extensive account of the Ghadr, or revolutionary movement, because he sees it as a crucial prelude to mobilization and representation processes that ensued in both American and Canadian South Asian communities. The emphasis in his book, however, is on the American side of the border. By the end of World War I, for example, because Ghadr had received funding from the Imperial German Government during the war, some young men of Indian origin were tried and sentenced to prison for allegedly attempting to start an uprising in India in order to achieve freedom from its British rulers.

The response of American opinion, insofar as one can generalize, was probably reflected by an editorial in *The New York Times* on April 13, 1917. "Every day", it declared in language reminiscent of post-9/11 days, "some new conspiracy or espionage in the United States, or directed against the United States from outside its territory, comes to light .... The hospitality of the country has been and is being abused to its damage and its danger."

Then in 1923 another issue faced Indians resident in the United States, when the Supreme Court ruled that Indians, like other Asians, were not entitled to American citizenship because, while they could perhaps be classified as "Caucasian", they were not "white". Gould quotes a commentator of the time on this decision as "a racist edict which dismissed scientific veracity in favor of the prejudices of the uneducated mob" (Jensen 1988: 258). It immediately threatened the status of the few Indians who had previously become citizens. One of them, Taraknath Das, who later taught at Columbia University, was a prominent leader in the ultimately successful struggle to retain his own citizenship and that of his compatriots. It was a victory that pointed to others to come.

From this point on, the effort of young Indians, including Taraknath Das, his compatriot, Har Dayal, and others who had come to the United States as part of the student influx, turned their efforts toward garnering support from influential Americans for the struggle that was gaining momentum in India itself for

Indian independence. The major part of Gould's book examines—
more clearly, more convincingly, and in greater detail than has
been done before—how a small group of Indians in the United
States became remarkably successful lobbyists with Congress, with
journalists, and with other influential groups, for American
support—in effect, for Indian freedom writ large as well as their
own domestic civil rights. "Lobbying" is a word often used pejora-
tively; but here Gould shows how essential a part it is of the
American political process, and how it can be effectively used by
small, dedicated groups.

He does not claim to be impartial and uninvolved: his sym-
pathies with the Indians in their quest for freedom are proudly
displayed; but at the same time he makes clear the factionalism
and internal quarrels that characterized their efforts. The freedom
fighters were by no means a monolith!

This lobby became especially important during the World
War II, when the British government used its very considerable
propaganda skills in the United States to undercut the activities
of the Indian lobby by arguing that Gandhi, Nehru, and the other
advocates of independence were undermining the war against the
Axis powers. They believed that the continuance of rigid British
control over India was essential, especially for the war against the
Japanese, and were determined to exercise that control at almost
any price. Their methods of accomplishing this, of course, were of
great concern to the Americans. The lobbyists were especially concerned that the American government refused to be swayed by
humanitarian considerations and the declared principles of the
Atlantic Charter to alter its see-no-evil policy toward their British
ally. They scrupulously avoided public comment on criticisms of
British rule in India, especially the imprisonment of Mahatma
Gandhi, who had come to be seen as a Christ-like figure in the
eyes of many American churchmen. In this wartime environment,
the British concern was to prevent the Americans, especially
President Roosevelt with his known anti-imperialist stance, from
interfering in India by supporting the Indian National Congress
in its struggle for Indian independence.

One of Gould's most lively chapters concerns the activity of a
mole in the State Department, who supplied evidence of British
duplicity in dealing with the American administration to Drew
Pearson, the influential political columnist, who was sympathetic

to the Indian cause. The incident generated a furor in Congress and in the media. Gould writes about how British arrogance, that had always rubbed Americans the wrong way, reviving memories of the American Revolution, ignited a storm of rhetorical abuse by members of both Houses in the aftermath of the Pearson revelations.

Gould's revelation of who the mole was, why he jeopardized his own career to help the Indians, and how J.J. Singh, the most active of the latter-day Indian activists, used the information, adds a new dimension to the story of the lobbying efforts of the Indian patriots.

Gould concludes his study by noting that the contributions of the Indian lobbyists bore fruit by 1946, when by an act of Congress, signed by President Harry S. Truman, Indian citizenship rights were restored and new Indian immigrants to the United States were welcomed under a quota. Many of them achieved and continue to achieve high positions in business, and in the academic and scientific worlds, on a scale that no other immigrant group has.

In the light of their successes, it is sobering to look back on the racism to which Indians were subjected forty years earlier. India and Indians found a new place in the nation that once treated them with contempt. The change in status recalls what is probably the first mention of Indo-American relations. It is found in a remarkable address given by Ezra Stiles of Yale College in 1783. He was thinking of the Yankee ships that sailed under the new flag, "the thirteen stripes and new constellation at Bengal and Canton, on the Indus and the Ganges," and would bring back, not just material goods, but also "the wisdom and literature of the East." In America this wisdom would be digested and carried to its highest perfection, and then, refined and transformed, their wisdom and ours, would "reblaze back from America to Europe, Asia, and Africa and illumine the world with truth and liberty" (quoted in Embree 1994).

Harold Gould has given us a significant chapter in that saga, more significant perhaps than the current image of cooperation in missiles and military technology.

**Ainslie T. Embree**
*Emeritus Professor of South Asian History*
*Columbia University*

# Preface

The seeds for this book were planted by a conversation that took place in the Graylin Hotel in London in the summer of 1996. It concerned the course of events which in 1943 led to a confidential memo prepared by Ambassador William Phillips, the US special envoy to pre-independence India, addressed to his boss, President Franklin Delano Roosevelt, falling into the hands of Drew Pearson, the godfather of all contemporary investigative reporters (and the intellectual father of Jack Anderson!), whose syndicated column appeared regularly in the *Washington Post* under the title "The Washington Merry-Go-Round." The point is that Ambassador Phillips's memo was highly critical of British policy toward India, so much so that Phillips believed that the war effort in Asia had been placed in jeopardy by what he viewed as British arrogance and intransigence. At a time when American differences with the British over their refusal to negotiate in good faith with the emerging nationalists in order to get India whole-heartedly into the war effort were being swept under the rug in the name of "Allied unity," Pearson's disclosure of the ambassador's comments caused a sensation in Washington, and proved to be a PR windfall for the proponents of Indian freedom and South Asians' civil rights who were active in the US.

The hunt was on for the culprit who blew the lid off. There was much speculation around Washington as to whom it might have been, but "Deep Throat" was never unearthed, until now. It turned out that he was the person with whom I was conversing that day at the Graylin. He had been "Deep Throat," and had managed by the skin of his teeth to escape detection! As was the case with the Woodward and Bernstein informant, this early incarnation of "Deep Throat" also ironically turned out to be a source for the *Washington Post*. His identity had remained a secret for twice as long as had Mr Felt's. How he succeeded in remaining anonymous for so long is a part of our story that will be related at the appropriate time.

My interest in this event and my determination, with the now-deceased narrator's permission, to eventually tell this story, inspired me as a prelude to take a look at the plight of what were officially called "South Asian Indians," who had begun filtering into the United States and Canada around the turn of the twentieth century, and who, as the years passed and their numbers grew, evolved a kind of political consciousness in response to the shabby manner in which racist Canada and the United States had treated them. Sikhs formed the vanguard of the initial migrants. They began showing up in Vancouver, Seattle, and San Francisco as the 1900s dawned. Many were ex-servicemen from the Indian army; almost all hailed from the Punjab. They were essentially peasants who wanted to acquire land for cultivation. They were neither rich nor desperately poor; just salt-of-the-earth Jat Sikhs who were used to hard work, and who knew how to make things grow under the harshest of conditions if given half a chance. Like the Chinese and Japanese before them, they ran into colossal resistance and humiliation from indigenous Whites. The Sikhs, for obvious reasons, were called "rag heads," and viewed as racially inferior, culturally alien, and "strike breakers" who would undercut union labor.

Although their numbers were never great compared to other migrant groups (at no time were there more than 5,000 in the United States, and around 10,000 in Canada), leaders emerged in their midst to champion their cause and gradually link it to the rising tide of nationalism in India. The character of that leadership changed over time, as we shall see. It reflected the lessons these leaders learned from their encounters with the White majority, the historic changes that were taking place in social and political conditions in America, and the impact which World War I, the inter-war years, and World War II were having on everybody. The most striking changes in personnel and modus operandi which the South Asian activists experienced occurred as their level of sophistication in dealing with the political establishment evolved through time. By the run-up to World War II, a coterie of South Asians and their American supporters existed, who had acquired a considerable amount of media savvy and mastery of the art of lobbying the US Congress and other agencies of government. It is for this reason that I have called them "the India Lobby."

By 1946, their efforts had paid the ultimate dividends. They had engineered legislation that confirmed the citizenship rights of "South Asian Indians" resident in the US, gained an immigration quota for their brethren who wished to migrate here, and had made their contributions-at-a-distance to the achievement of Indian independence. In short, these South Asian Indians were pioneers who, like all pioneers, paved the way for the multitudes who would follow. Perhaps, even without their perseverance and their sacrifices, the influx would eventually have taken place anyway—it had to come sooner or later, but by acting sooner the door was opened much earlier than otherwise might have been the case.

A considerable number of scholars produced works of excellent quality on various aspects of the South Asian migration story prior to my project. In some respects I see myself as being no more than a vehicle through which their manifold marvelous contributions to this subject have been infused with a renewed visibility and appreciation. I refer here to the work of scholars like Janet Jensen, Emily Brown, Tapan Mukherjee, Karen Leonard, Acharna Varma, Hugh Johnston, Ruth Price, Susan Bean, M.V. Kamath, Kushwant Singh, Nirode Barooah, N. Gerald Barrier, and Leonard Gordon, to mention only the most notable of those whose work came within my ken. Without them whatever contribution I have made would have been impossible. Citations of their works are sprinkled through the pages of this book. Perhaps what I have primarily done is to weave the various strands into a reasonably coherent social-historical picture of a remarkably interesting but sparsely recognized segment of the South Asian legacy.

Many debts are owed to many persons who generously gave of their time and expertise in order to facilitate my work.

A special debt is owed to the Library of Congress and especially to Dr Allen Thrasher, Senior Reference Librarian, Southern Asia Section, Asian Division, whose generosity and grace, not to mention his vast expertise, played a vital part in whatever I may have produced. Many long hours were spent in the Jefferson and Madison Buildings perusing *Modern Review*, the *Voice of India*, *India Today*, innumerable books and documents, and reams of Congressional testimony and commentaries, dating back to World War I. I learned how to feel completely at home in that incredible facility so beautifully organized and served by such a dedicated and friendly band of public servants.

Another special contributor to my scholarly endeavor was Professor Philip McEldowney, the South Asia Librarian at the University of Virginia Library. His knowledge of the relevant literature and his skill in unearthing and reproducing obscure documents was special and invaluable to me. I shall forever be grateful for all he did to facilitate my work.

I must express a special note of appreciation to Professor T.N. Madan, retired director of the Institute of Economic Growth in New Delhi, India, who undertook a detailed critical reading of my manuscript and made enormously valuable suggestions regarding everything from content to the arrangement and consolidation of chapters. He was a much appreciated, stern taskmaster.

Two other readers merit recognition and thanks as well. They are Professor Ainslie T. Embree, retired Professor Emeritus of South Asian History, Columbia University, who has kindly written a foreword for this book, and Major-General (Retired) Inderjit Rikhye, former military advisor to two UN Secretaries-General (Dag Hammarskjöld and U Thant), commander of the UNEF in the Negev during the 1967 June War, and currently Visiting Scholar, Center for South Asian Studies, University of Virginia.

I would like to acknowledge the friendship and collegiality I enjoyed for many years with "Deep Throat," whose name I do not wish to reveal prematurely—it will be found in Chapter 10. He and I spent many a day during the 1970s and 1980s trudging the halls of the US Congress, endeavoring, not unlike the India Lobby who are the stars of this narrative, to persuade its members to support and fund NDEA VI, the Smithsonian PL480 SFC allocation, and other appropriations designed to keep international education and research alive when there was scant official sympathy for "area studies."

Finally, I would like to thank my wife, Ketayun, herself an Indian, for the love and support that everyone needs if they are going to make it through the day.

Also, I must thank India, with whom it was a case of "love at first sight" that has now endured for over 50 years. This book is a small token of my appreciation for all that this wonderful country and her wonderful people have done for me, professionally, spiritually and personally. An Indian friend, many years ago, once introduced me to an audience as a "brother-in-law of India." The term s*aala*, as those who know Hindustani are aware, can have a pejorative connotation. But not in this case. My friend was merely groping for some way to classify me as worthy of being a kinsman of India, even if by marriage. I proudly and gladly accept this appellation.

# 1 Introduction
## The Drew Pearson Affair

On July 24, 1944, the investigative reporter Drew Pearson published an article in his syndicated column, "The Washington Merry-Go-Round," which created a sensation in Washington, London, and New Delhi. It generated a crisis in relations between Great Britain and the United States right in the middle of World War II. His *Washington Post* article revealed the contents of a private letter which the US Special Envoy to New Delhi, Ambassador William Phillips, had addressed to President Franklin D. Roosevelt on May 14, 1943. In this letter, Phillips had strongly criticized Great Britain's reluctance to settle its differences with the Indian nationalists so that the latter could be persuaded to cooperate wholeheartedly in the war effort. With India's strategic importance growing almost by the day, political conditions there really mattered to the Roosevelt administration. Despite much speculation, the identity of the person who enabled Pearson to obtain access to this vitally important document was never revealed. This book will, in due course, make that identification for the first time and in the process tell the fascinating story of what led up to these dramatic events and the role played in them by a diverse group of courageous and dedicated Indians residing in the United States, who were determined to do whatever they could to bring about an end to British colonialism in India and achieve full civil rights for Indians living in America. To this end, we must explore the historical context and the dramatis personae that culminated in this little-known sideshow to the main event that was at the time consuming the energies and resources of the entire world.

Our narrative commences with a brief survey of the political situation existing in India in 1939 at the outbreak of World War II and subsequently at the point of America's entry into the war on December 7, 1941. As a prelude, we must learn how Indians got to the US in the first place. This story reaches back to the turn of the century and depicts how they eventually employed whatever resources were available to them to pursue their perceived interests and make them count in high places. This was not an easy trek; it never rode on the wings of a large-scale popular movement. There were never enough Indians in the country to form a substantial enough ethnic base for large-scale concerted political action. They did it instead by building networks that reached into a variety of institutions and social enclaves where Indians had established a presence; they did it through the efforts of a handful of committed, socially conscious leaders who tirelessly moved about the country building contacts with fellow Indians and with sympathetic Americans in the press, in academia and in the political establishment.

Let us first turn, however, to the colonial situation in India that was the immediate precipitant of the Drew Pearson affair. It will be remembered that Lord Linlithgow, acting in his capacity as viceroy, arbitrarily committed India to the war without so much as notifying, much less consulting, the country's indigenous political leaders. London, in turn, accepted his action without a murmur. The result was public outrage at British high-handedness and, ultimately, escalating resistance to British rule itself by the country's principal nationalist figures, especially Mahatma Gandhi, Jawaharlal Nehru and the other leaders of the Indian National Congress. There were en masse resignations from the country's provincial legislatures, which had recently been reformed and upgraded under a new and painfully negotiated "constitution" known as the Government of India Act of 1935. In the general election held under its auspices in 1937, the Congress had achieved a majority in most provincial assemblies and the country appeared headed for an unprecedented spell of representative government, based at the provincial level upon a broad (though not universal) franchise, party-structured legislative bodies and ministerial responsibility. All this quickly evaporated following Linlithgow's action and in its place emerged an atmosphere of civil disobedience led by Mahatma Gandhi and Jawaharlal Nehru. This seriously challenged the ability of the colonial government to effectively mobilize India's resources on behalf of the Allied cause, and resulted in the wholesale round-up and incarceration of political dissidents.

In the face of the mounting Axis peril to the Western democracies, the US government expressed alarm over the near–civil-war atmosphere that had erupted in India, which obviously had become a critical strategic factor in the widening world conflict. It led to American efforts to persuade the British to do something about the Indian political situation while there was still time. These urgings greatly intensified once the United States entered the war, especially after the Japanese conquest of Southeast Asia and their stunning advance through Burma to India's eastern borders. These events made it clear that major commitments of American forces and resources would eventually have to be made to the region, both in order to help Britain defend the sub-continent and to maintain a tenuous lifeline to the Chinese nationalists now headquartered in Kunming. This being the case, the Americans were eager for India to become a politically stable platform for the conduct of what were envisioned to be increasingly comprehensive military operations throughout South and Southeast Asia.

In the name of the larger picture, however, Roosevelt and his advisors wanted to keep their representations to the British low-key and as much as possible out of the public limelight. Winston Churchill, an old imperialist curmudgeon, was hypersensitive on the subject of India and blanched at any suggestion of compromises with the Indian National Congress that would accord that party anything approaching a co-equal political status in the war effort. In the words of Secretary of State Cordell Hull:

> We kept our public statements general, without making specific reference to India. But in private conversations the President talked very bluntly about India with Prime Minister Churchill as I was talking with British Ambassador Halifax. While for the sake of good relations with Britain we could not tell the country what we were saying privately, we were saying everything the most enthusiastic supporter of India's freedom could

have expected, and we were convinced that the American people were with us (Hull 1948: 1483).

It was largely in response to these American preoccupations that the British government agreed to send a Cabinet Mission headed by Sir Stafford Cripps out to India toward the end of March 1942, in the hope of reaching a satisfactory agreement with nationalist groups (most particularly, of course, the Indian National Congress) concerning their sharing political responsibility for India's participation in the war. To demonstrate the US administration's deep concern for the outcome of these negotiations, Roosevelt dispatched a trusted advisor, Colonel Louis Johnson, as his personal representative and advisor. Colonel Johnson made a hit with the Indians when he evinced considerable sympathy for their point of view and was not shy about expressing his feelings. The British, of course, were less than pleased with what they regarded as his brash and outspoken ways and exerted pressure to have him withdrawn from India. This happened automatically when the Cripps initiative failed on April 11, amid intimations that the deck had been stacked all along to make sure that nothing came of it—that it had mainly been a ploy to placate the Americans.

Another factor which had provided impetus for the Cripps mission was the ideological spin-off from the Atlantic Charter which Roosevelt and Churchill had authored during their conclave in Placentia Harbor, Newfoundland, in August 1941. Even though it was intended to bolster the morale of Europeans oppressed by the Axis, its phraseology had quite unexpectedly struck a highly responsive chord in the hearts of colonized peoples around the world. It had reverberated with special poignancy in India where nationalism and anti-imperialism had already become an extremely powerful political force. As Robert Sherwood commented, the Atlantic Charter "turned out to be incalculably more powerful an instrument than the officers of the British Government intended it to be when they first proposed it. They discovered indeed that *when you state a moral principle, you are stuck with it, no matter how many fingers you have kept crossed at the moment.*" For it was "not long before the people of India, Burma, Malayasia and Indonesia were to ask if the Atlantic Charter extended to the Pacific and Asia in general" (Sherwood 1950: 362–63, emphasis added).

The Roosevelt administration, however, was unwilling to let matters rest there. The president continued to chide the British at every opportunity about their treatment of the Indian National Congress leadership, especially Mahatma Gandhi, both directly through his conversations with Churchill and indirectly through State Department channels. His advisors urged Roosevelt to also dispatch another personal representative to India in the wake of Colonel Johnson, this time with superior diplomatic rank and a clear mandate to keep alive the US government's belief that efforts should continue to solve the political stalemate that was in effect denying Indian nationalists their civil rights, their political dignity and a meaningful say in the conduct of World War II on their own soil.

The man whom Roosevelt designated for this daunting task was William Phillips, a Boston Brahmin, a close personal friend and a very senior diplomat. Around the turn of the century, in fact, Phillips had been a major State Department player in America's open-door policy formulations concerning East Asia (see Griswold 1962). In Hess's words:

> Phillips did offer more prestige to the Delhi post than Johnson. He was intimately associated with Roosevelt and carried impressive diplomatic credentials .... He had worked in England, China, the Netherlands and Canada and as an assistant secretary of state under Wilson. For Roosevelt, Phillips served as under secretary of state and later as ambassador to Italy. His appointment to the Delhi post underlined the importance that Roosevelt assigned to India (Hess 1971: 96).

At the time of his appointment, the British expected Phillips, a Boston Brahmin, to be less brash and more Anglophilic than Louis Johnson. While symbolizing a heightened American concern for the Indian question, it was nevertheless anticipated on both sides of the Atlantic that William Phillips would not "rock the boat." This expectation was very apparent on the British side. En route to India, he was accorded VIP treatment in London. During a luncheon with Churchill at No. 10, Downing Street on December 16, shortly before his departure for India, Phillips describes an encounter which bespeaks an assumption on the prime minister's part that this was an American who could be relied on to see things the British way—he was fully accepted as an insider. Their conversation ranged across the entire gamut of the problems of the day—the North African campaign, Churchill's estimation of Roosevelt and Stalin, the problems of opening a second front in Europe, etc. Despite this warm acceptance, however, Phillips manifested some discomfort. He felt constrained to observe:

> When the Prime Minister got around to the subject of India, it was difficult to fathom his mind. In one phrase he reiterated his public assertion that he would never part with any portion of his Empire. Yet in another phrase he referred to the offer of freedom which has been made to the Indians, meaning, I suppose, the ill-fated Cripps mission to India (Phillips 1952: 346).

While remarking on "what an outstanding personality Churchill is," the foregoing exchange and one earlier on in their conversation concerning Wendell Wilkie alerted Phillips to the rigidity that the prime minister could display on certain topics. When it proved impossible to disabuse Churchill of the hostility he felt toward Wilkie (even with the help of two other luncheon guests, one of whom was Anthony Eden) as a result of critical remarks the American politician had made about British imperialism during his round-the-world tour, Phillips declared: "… I realized that once Churchill had made up his mind nothing could change it. *Later I was to discover the same uncompromising attitude about India*" (ibid., emphasis added).

A few days later, Churchill sent Phillips a somewhat tattered copy of a delightful book entitled *Twenty-one Days in India* which Churchill said he had been advised to read when he "went out as a subaltern to India in 1866" (ibid.: 347).

While touched by this "courteous gesture," Phillips nevertheless com-ments in his memoirs, "I could not help thinking that *the Prime Minister and Eden expected a good deal of me and might be disappointed*" (ibid., emphasis added). Phillips might also have com-mented on the symbolic poignancy of Churchill's gesture—a tattered relic of a past era to which he continued to sentimentally cling. But he did not.

At any rate, it would not be long before his British host at that luncheon, as well as Anthony Eden and many others, would indeed feel much disappointment with Ambassador Phillips. For despite his establishment credentials and aristocratic demeanor,

William Phillips turned out to be a man of independent mind and high integrity. He would not be, as things turned out, co-optable.

Phillips reached India on January 8, 1943. Nothing happened during the first few weeks to contradict the British government's estimate of him, since for a while the ambassador decided to lay low and develop a feel for his new assignment. Both British officialdom and the Indian press seem to have viewed him in these terms during this period. Upon his first meeting with Lord Linlithgow, he characterized him as a person "of a certain austerity of manner" who was nevertheless "disposed to be friendly." The Viceroy "assured me that India was wide open to me and that I could go wherever I willed and talk to whom I wished" (Phillips 1952: 349). In sum, Phillips concluded, "My first contact with the ruler of India was exceedingly agreeable and reassuring, *although I doubted that in his heart he welcomed the intrusion of an official representative of the President*" (ibid., emphasis added). He would soon discover, in fact, that those nagging doubts he sensed in Linlithgow's heart were very real and would indeed affect the degree to which in reality his host's assurances that the president's emissary had carte blanche to meet and talk with whomever he chose would be honored in actual practice. This became clear when finally he sought permission to meet with some of the incarcerated Congress leaders.

Even though there turned out to be de facto restrictions upon his latitude for meaningful contacts with significant segments of the Indian nationalist leadership, Phillips, no doubt with valuable guidance from the professional foreign service personnel already in place (most particularly Consul General George Merrell), did not take long to begin to grasp the true situation. While he was able to say that in some respects the "official British position was not unreasonable" when they disparaged the Indians' ability to settle their communal differences and thereby pave the way for the achievement of orderly nationhood, Phillips could nevertheless see that "certain inconsistencies were apparent." He declares:

> The British insisted that the Indians show a willingness and ability to get together, yet they were holding incommunicado the Indian leaders, Gandhi and Nehru, the two spokesmen of the All-India Congress Party, the most important political party in the country. The news from India as read in England, gave

people the impression that no agreement was possible between the Hindus and Moslems. *Yet it was the British themselves who were permitting the impasse to continue rather than using their good offices to bring the opposing parties together* (Phillips 1952: 352–53, emphasis added).

He noted that "Hindus and Moslems alike took no stock of London's promises of eventual freedom for India" in the absence of any gesture on Britain's part to prove their good faith. Such a gesture, they told Phillips, would be to "grant a degree of freedom without delay." In a letter written to Roosevelt exactly two weeks after reaching India, Ambassador Phillips had fathomed the root of the impasse. "The Viceroy represents England of the old school, of the tradition of Empire, of British responsibility to govern backward peoples." He was supported by "six hundred British Indian civil servants who are devoting their lives to India and who know little of what is going on in the world outside and who in their hearts want to preserve the status quo, since their livelihoods depend upon it" (ibid.: 354). Gandhi and Jinnah, Phillips saw, were the anchors of another axis of countervailing power that stood in the way of achieving any settlement. Muslims and Hindus were as suspicious of each other as each of them was of the British.

It was also not long before Phillips began to grasp the exploitative and other economically debilitating implications of British rule as well. On his tour of South India the Ambassador visited Bangalore, where he got a chance to look at an aircraft factory and repair facility, which had been established in that city by two American brothers, William and Edward Pawley, for the purpose of maintaining Allied military aircraft in India. "I was anxious to see this large and modern industrial plant under American management," he says (ibid.: 371). He discovered, of course, that under dynamic management Indian workers, contrary to impressions given by the British, performed extremely well. William Pawley told him that "although they were slow in comparison to American workers when they first began, they quickly picked up speed and accuracy which equaled that of our top skilled labor" (ibid.). Phillips goes on to comment that "many months thereafter I heard that British interests and the Mysore State government had bought out the Pawleys and taken over the plant." And, he wonders, "Did the British object to this display of American success... [?]" (Phillips 1952: 372).

This experience led Phillips to comment, in a letter he wrote to President Roosevelt on April 7, 1942, upon the economic dimensions "of increasing anti-British sentiment." Said he:

In those states where there is much natural wealth, the discontent arises from the impression that the British do not welcome full development of the states' natural resources if there is any danger of competition with British industry. As an example, the state of Travancore owns and controls an important rubber factory. While the factory produces many articles required by the Indian army, it is not permitted to produce automobile tires. This is particularly galling to the authorities of the state because the raw rubber obtained within the state has to be shipped to Madras and turned over to Dunlop Tire Company, British owned, which has the privilege of tire manufacture in India (ibid.).

In political terms, William Phillips's assignment to India, and its repercussions for developing relations between India and America, assumed an added poignancy when it turned out that it coincided with Mahatma Gandhi's decision to undertake a "fast to capacity" commencing on February 9, just one month after the ambassador's arrival. It is conceivable, of course, that this was no accident, given the Mahatma's instincts for political timing. But whether this was the case or not, the effect would be the same, for it would place the ambassador in the center of a new confrontation between Congress and the Raj, which the American government would find itself unable to ignore. Realizing that this would inevitably be the case, Phillips requested permission from the Viceroy to visit Gandhi. But with Gandhi on the threshold of initiating a new round of non-violent confrontation with India's foreign overlords, Linlithgow "could now more easily deny the request," which he was no doubt anyway disinclined to sanction if a plausible way could be found to do so. This refusal clearly irked Phillips, an annoyance which grew as Gandhi's fast began to unfold and with it corresponding demands in the Indian press and from the public that the United States attempt to break the impasse before it was too late to save Gandhi's life. As Hess observes:

To Phillips, the government's inflexibility was incomprehensible. On the first day of the fast, his attitude toward the British crystallized. After meeting with two members of the Birla family and Devadas Gandhi, Phillips wrote to Washington: "Reluctantly I am coming to the conclusion that the Viceroy, presumably responsive to Churchill, is not in sympathy with any change in Britain's relationship to India" (Hess 1971: 101, emphasis added).

Phillips became convinced that the British were prepared to let Gandhi die in preference to making any concessions to the Congress that might induce him to break his fast. The viceroy, declared Phillips, "has remained adamant." There seemed little hope of changing the tragic course of events without some kind of American intervention, which Phillips now clearly favored. "I realize perfectly that neither you nor the Secretary [of State, Cordell Hull] could do much," Phillips said in a letter to Roosevelt, "but I had hoped that the Secretary's talks with Halifax might bear fruit in some way." Something needed to be done, he felt, to *avoid the impression here, signs of which have already appeared, that by the presence of our forces in India and my own presence we were openly encouraging the British to retain their hold over India.*" Understandably, Phillips believed, *"they turn to us to give them help because of our historic stand for liberty"* (Phillips 1952: 360–62, emphasis added).

Noting that "the whole episode has brought the United States prominently into the picture," Phillips complains, "I have been literally besieged by callers and overwhelmed by telegrams from all parts of India, asking whether there could not be something done from Washington or by me to relieve the present deadlock." Almost despairingly he concludes:

I fear that the Office of War Information in India have been too active in advertising in the press, under the caption of the American flag and the Statue of Liberty, that the president "has declared the extension of these fundamental liberties to all men [to be] the case of the American people's war aims ...." Certainly the Indians look to us for the help in their struggle, which presumably it will be difficult for us to give during the war. And after the war they believe any such help will come too late, since whatever persuasion we can exercise over the British can be done better now than when the general scramble begins for post-war settlement. That is their view, I think, and one cannot live here without having a great deal of sympathy for it (Phillips 1952: 360–62).

Against this wall of orchestrated public ignorance, Ambassador Phillips and the many other friends of Indian nationalism both within and without the government proved powerless. Phillips's personal communications to Roosevelt could not stir him to decisive action in the absence of any public outcry. Nor could a cable from V.K. Krishna Menon on behalf of Indians living in Great Britain to the American President urging him to intervene before it was too late. Equally futile were representations from such American notables as Pearl Buck, E. Stanley Jones, Harry Emerson Fosdick, John Haynes Holmes, Richard Walsh and Reinhold Niebhur. "Another group of fifty-six Americans pressed their demand for intervention by means of a sympathetic fast." Even Kwame Nkrumah, then a student in the US, appealed to Mr Roosevelt on behalf of African peoples (see Hess 1971: 103). But this too had little effect.

In India, of course, public awareness of the true feelings of President Roosevelt's special representative and of knowledgeable Americans generally was almost as non-existent as was the American public's awareness of the true situation in India. The diversions of global war, the timorousness of an American president and the autocratic proclivities of an Indian viceroy had all tragically conspired to rob the United States of still one more golden opportunity to establish its moral bona fides in the eyes of the Indian people and of the men who would lead those people to nationhood and a position of great influence among the Third-World group of nations following the war.

In a sense, William Phillips was destined, as we shall see, to have his greatest impact on US–India relations following his departure from India. While in India, his attempts to make real contacts with the Congress leadership had been wholly unsuccessful. The viceroy had effectively barred his access to both Gandhi and Nehru despite repeated efforts to persuade and pressure him to afford such access. During Gandhi's 21-day fast, which ended on March 2, 1943, his efforts to get the US government to respond sympathetically in some public fashion to this political holy man's compelling endeavor to call mankind's attention to British intractability and hypocrisy had failed. And it must be said that Ambassador Phillips's lack of the kind of flamboyance displayed by General Louis Johnson may also have hampered his ability to get the public's attention even on those occasions where he actually tried.

His contacts with Muhammad Ali Jinnah and other Muslim League leaders were, of course, more extensive because their hostility to Congress and willingness to cooperate with the Raj had kept them out of jail. But these contacts also bore little fruit, in part because of the freeze that post-Cripps British policies had imposed on the normal political process in India, in part because of the depths of communal antipathy that prevailed between Hindus and Muslims, and in part because Phillips himself found the League's passion for separate Islamic nationhood unpalatable. In Hess's words, "while finding Jinnah to be courteous, charming and brilliant, Phillips remained skeptical of the Pakistan scheme" (Hess 1971: 107). At one point in his memoirs, Phillips very clearly reflects that skepticism, and an amazing prescience about its long-term strategic implications:

> On the Pakistan issue the League members whom I met [during a visit to the Punjab] were all ardent followers of Jinnah and insisted they would accept nothing less than complete separation from Hindu India ... [T]he more I studied Jinnah's Pakistan, the less it appealed to me as the answer to India's communal problem, since to break India into two separate nations would weaken both, and open Pakistan, at least, to the designs of ambitious neighbors (Phillips 1952: 359, emphasis added).

This latter observation turned out to be spectacularly prophetic! Ambassador Phillips returned to the US in May 1943, ostensibly for the purpose of reporting to the president and other government officials directly on the Indian situation as he perceived it.

The implications were that he would return to India after his sojourn in Washington to resume his duties there. But the fact is that his departure from the subcontinent would be permanent. William Phillips himself would recommend to his superiors that he not be sent back "under the existing political conditions."

Recounting a long, private conversation with Roosevelt "in his upstairs library," Phillips says:

> I told him that in my opinion I should not return to Delhi unless the existing political deadlock was broken .... Otherwise I could not see any contribution which could be made, and I personally disliked the idea of resuming my life in New Delhi merely for the pleasure of eating hot curries in the houses of British and Indian friends (1952: 391).

The obviously suppressed premise in this declaration was that all was useless unless the president was prepared to actively intervene to break this political deadlock. "I added," says the disillusioned Ambassador, "that *all India was looking to him for help* and that my continued presence in India would put him in a false position unless the British attitude shifted" (ibid., emphasis added). And unless, of course, Mr Roosevelt resolved to force a change in that attitude!

The closest Roosevelt could come to doing this was to ask Phillips himself to go and talk with Prime Minister Churchill, who was staying at the British Embassy at the time. Phillips went to him on May 23, but the encounter was, in the Ambassador's words, "hopeless." Churchill had reacted angrily to Phillips's urging that talks be reopened with the nationalists and some kind of interim government be established. He concluded that Phillips was recommending an immediate withdrawal of British forces from India. Phillips was "puzzled by this attitude." It seems to have afforded him the final proof that the Tory Prime Minister had a genuine "hang-up" over India. "Never had I mentioned the sudden withdrawal of British power and yet he insisted upon assuming that was my proposal." Phillips concluded, therefore, that it "was only too clear that he had a complex about India from which he could not be shaken" (ibid.: 390).

Summing it all up, Phillips declared, "I have never understood the British position" (ibid.: 395). In his view, the British had deluded themselves into believing that because their Congress party adversaries were locked away in jail, the cause they represented had gone into decline and public restiveness could be managed indefinitely. "I left India discouraged by the attitude of the British Government and fearful of the consequences of the delays caused by the continued imprisonment of the Congress Party leaders" (Phillips 1952: 385).

In this state of discouragement, Ambassador Phillips had on May 14, 1943, addressed a long letter to President Roosevelt which "was in fact a short memorandum rather than a report of my mission," and which was inadvertently destined to have a greater positive impact on US–Indian relations than anything that either he or Louis Johnson had been able to accomplish in India in their respective official capacities. This is because it eventually found its way into the hands of what I shall call the "India lobby," which had over the years been crystallizing in the US, especially in New York and Washington and a few other cities around the country. That communication essentially summed up Phillips's impressions of the Indian question, including a stinging indictment of imperial conduct and policies toward the subcontinent.

"At present," stated the memorandum, "the Indian people are at war only in the legal sense as, for various reasons, the British Government declared India in the conflict without the formality of consulting the Indian leaders or even the Indian legislature." As a consequence of this, "They feel that they have nothing to fight for as they are convinced that the professed war aims of the United Nations do not apply to them." *After all, was it not the Prime Minister of England himself who "has stated that the provisions of the Atlantic Charter are not applicable to India"* (emphasis added)? Can it be surprising under the circumstances that "the Indian leaders are beginning to wonder whether the Charter is only for the benefit of the white races[?]" The result of this hypocrisy is not difficult to fathom. "The attitude of the general public toward the war" is one of "indifference and made all the worse as a result of famine conditions, the growing high cost of living and the continued political dead-lock." Generally speaking, "The peoples of Asia ... cynically regard the war as one between fascist and imperialist powers."

What must be done? To Phillips the answer was clear:

There would seem to be only one remedy to this highly unsatisfactory situation in which we are unfortunately but nevertheless seriously involved, and that is to change the attitude of the people of India towards the war, make them feel that we want them to assume responsibilities to the United Nations and are prepared to give them facilities for doing so, and then the voice of India will play an important part in the reconstruction of the world. The present political conditions do not permit of any improvement in this respect.

Concluding that it is "time for the British to act," Phillips goes on to recommend:

I feel strongly, Mr. President, that in view of our military position in India we should have a voice in these matters. It is not right for the British to say, "this is none of our business" when we alone presumably will have the major part to play in the future struggle with Japan. If we do nothing and merely accept the British point of view that conditions in India are none of our business then we must be prepared for various serious consequences in the internal situation in India which may develop as a result of despair and misery and anti-white sentiments of hundreds of millions of people (1952: 387–88).

What made this eloquent statement to the president of the United States an important milestone in the evolution of relations between this country and India was not so much the effect that it had upon Mr. Roosevelt (for it appears to have had very little) but the fact that the document fell into the hands of the famous and controversial investigative reporter, Drew Pearson, who published long, commented excerpts in his syndicated column, "Washington Merry-Go-Round," on July 24, 1944, more than a year after it had been written. In Phillips's words, "Its publication created a great commotion in England, a favorable impression here, and a burst of enthusiastic acclaim in India" (ibid.: 389).

Indeed it did! The British were outraged. Sir Olaf Caroe, Minister for External Affairs of the Government of India, demanded that William Phillips be declared *persona non grata*, meaning he could not resume his diplomatic mission to India—a moot point, of course, since Phillips had already decided not to return to India. The British ambassador to the United States, Lord Halifax, who had himself once been viceroy (as Lord Irwin), demanded a formal apology for the comments Phillips expressed in his memo. He held this to be essential in the name of "inter-Allied harmony."

While regretting the chain of circumstances which led to the publication of Ambassador Phillips's confidential report to

President Roosevelt, the US government refused to go this far. In a cable to Foreign Secretary Anthony Eden on July 26, 1944, Sir Ronald Campbell recounts his meeting with Secretary of State Cordell Hull. The secretary made no attempt to defend Drew Pearson, whose articles he said he "never reads." He reminded Campbell that the president himself had publicly described Pearson as a "chronic liar." Hull blamed the leak on Assistant Secretary of State Sumner Welles, claiming that the relationship between Welles and Pearson "had been particularly close," so much so, in fact, that "Welles used to show Pearson documents and with him concoct attacks on Hull himself" (Manserge and Moon 1944: 1120, document 602). Hull nevertheless declined to publicly repudiate Phillips, as the British demanded, and privately urged Roosevelt to stand firm, thus making it clear that even in the name of inter-Allied harmony the United States was not prepared to become publicly identified in any fashion with policies toward India with which it was in fundamental disagreement. Declared Hull to Roosevelt:

> It is the Department's feeling that it would be impossible to issue a statement satisfactory to the British inasmuch as we share in general the views expressed in the Ambassador's letter. Unless you feel we should comply with the British request, I would appreciate having your permission to tell the British that we consider it preferable to make no public statement on the subject (*Foreign Relations*, 1944, Vol. V, p. 242).

There is every indication that at least some State Department officials , who had been involved in India policy, took considerable delight in the discomfiture which the Pearson bombshell inflicted on their British allies. Disclosure of Phillips's letter, the visible pique which the British were expressing over the American government's heretofore private estimates of the British Raj, and Roosevelt's unwillingness to publicly repudiate those estimates, made it easier to persuade the Indian public that America was not by any means committed to a defense of British imperialism. It also, as we shall see, strengthened the hands of Indians residing both in the United States and England who were doing their utmost to get the nationalist message across to woefully uninformed publics in both countries.

The full story of how this classic "leak" occurred around 60 years ago at the height of World War II, and particularly the social and cultural milieu which made it possible, is a fascinating one that has long needed to be fully told. It involved a host of improbable characters in all three camps: the American, the British, and the Indian. The full details of how it occurred, and who "Deep Throat" was, will be provided at a later point in our narrative. Its historical roots actually reach all the way back to the turn of the century, to the first influx of South Asians into the United States and their inevitable entanglement in this country's sad legacy of racism and ambivalence about the civil rights of the country's immigrant populations. It consummated in a David-and-Goliath propaganda war waged in the press and on the podium between the mighty British Empire in defense of decaying colonialism on the one hand, and determined groups of Indian patriots on the other, who, along with their American sympathizers, were dedicated to convincing the White House, the US Congress, and the American people that both colonialism and racism contradicted the principles upon which the American republic was erected, as well as the ideals for which World War II was allegedly being fought. It correspondingly brought into focus the moral struggle which the United States was in those days beginning to wage with itself over how, on the one hand, to reconcile the *realpolitik* which as an emerging global power it believed was necessary in order to sustain Allied unity in the international struggle against the Axis with, on the other, the genuine sympathy which the Roosevelt administration and a growing (though as yet by no means massive) number of Americans felt for downtrodden peoples languishing in tyranny and colonial servitude on *both* sides of the battlefront.

## The Context

Today there are almost 2 million persons of Indian ancestry living in the United States. During the period when our story takes place, however, there were never more than a handful of Indians in this country. Although precise figures are not available, at no time did the number in all categories (legals and illegals) exceed five or six thousand. Racist immigration policies then in force had seen to this! Yet out of this fragile reed there gradually crystallized a *mélange* of dedicated and talented individuals from many backgrounds and walks of life who would have a significant impact, at least on how some Americans in high places viewed India's freedom struggle as well as the right of Indian migrants to the US to enjoy the same constitutional and human rights that Whites took for granted.

The number and variety of persons who specifically took part in what we are calling the "India Lobby" naturally fluctuated through time. Much depended on who happened to be in the United States at any given point of time, in what capacity, on what sorts of contacts they developed both with Indians who were already here and with sympathetic Americans, and on how effectively their efforts to represent Indian interests played out in organizational terms. Inevitably, during the pre-war period they mostly inhabited the fringes of political society.

On the American side were a smattering of journalists (predominantly with liberal leanings), a scattering of academics, a sprinkling of government servants, some members of the US Congress, a number of persons with missionary backgrounds, plus a few individuals like Pearl Buck, Henry Luce and his playwright wife, Congresswoman Clare Booth Luce, who enjoyed a measure of celebrity in mainstream American society. As our narrative proceeds, much will be said about these Americans who supported the Indian freedom movement and South Asian civil rights in this country throughout the inter-war years.

Almost all of the politically active Indians present in the United States enjoyed a precarious immigration status which inevitably affected their freedom of action, especially in the political domain. These factors will be alluded to in due course. Some were engaged in business enterprises or held positions as technicians in the corporate community; some were in the professions. There were students matriculating in colleges and universities around the country. There were a scattering of scholars and scientists who held positions as faculty members in colleges and universities. Throughout the inter-war years there were visits to the US by many notables in the Indian freedom movement, like the poet and patriot, Sarojini Naidu, Nehru's famous sister, Vijayalakshmi Pandit, and the great Rabindranath Tagore. Their presence infused vitality and hope into the work of political activists in the US. Also, by the 1940s, there were several Indians serving on the staffs of various liaison missions pertinent to the war effort and in quasi-diplomatic positions. There was as well the occasional journalist working for the Indian press. However, it is not widely known that the majority of Indians present in the United States during the pre-war years were mainly Sikhs, plus a few Hindus and Muslims who had begun migrating via the Pacific to the West Coast of Canada and the United States. Commencing from around the turn of the century, they came in search of improved economic opportunities. Most of these early migrants were, in fact, Jat Sikh farmers from the Punjab, who sought opportunities to acquire employment and land in the agricultural regions of British Columbia on the Canadian side of the border and in California, Washington and Oregon on the American side. The story of how they got here and what they endured in the process of establishing roots on American and Canadian soil is at the heart of the background story that must be told in order to make sense out of what took place in Washington decades later during the war years.

There were as well, however, a number of Indians who were only temporary sojourners in the US, with little or no intention of remaining permanently there. Some had come in search of their fortune, others on a patriotic or spiritual mission. Among these were persons representing various schools of Hindu and Muslim religious and philosophical thought, such as the Vedanta Society, who appealed to Americans with a mystical bent or a thirst for "Oriental culture and civilization." They would have their roles to play in acclimatizing many Americans to the Indian way of life and thought as well as India's struggle for independence. As early as 1911, a very noted activist named Har Dayal (concerning whom much will be said in the course of this study) was to declare that the original Indian influx into America consisted of "Sikhs, Swamis, Students, and Spies!" By the last of these he meant the agents whom the British authorities employed to try and stifle the growth of nationalism and anti-colonialism among South Asian immigrants (*The Modern Review*, Calcutta, July 1911). I found this slogan to be an irresistible title for my book.

In all, these categories of residents, migrants, and sojourners constituted a kind of implicit "manpower pool," from which members and supporters of the "India Lobby" were eventually drawn as the political climate developed over the years. However, before identifying the individuals from both sides of the world who were the significant players in this poignant melodrama, something must be said about the wartime atmosphere in Washington where their energies would eventually be concentrated.

As already suggested, generally speaking the stage was set by the events leading up to America's entry into the war. Not long before Pearl Harbor and following the failure of the Cripps Mission in early 1942, measures were taken that reflected growing American concerns, one might even say alarm, over the security threat to South and Southeast Asia arising from Japanese military successes in these regions, coupled with British intransigence over resolving political unrest in India.

One result of this concern was the establishment of a quasi-separate diplomatic status for India, initially through the appointment in 1941 of an "Agent-General" of the Government of India who would be responsible for things specifically Indian. At first this representative was designated as a member of the ambassador's staff. He was not empowered to deal with political matters. However, by early 1942, Ambassador Halifax "reported that, as developments in the Far East had greatly increased the number of political questions arising between the Government of India and the United States, he had instructed [designated Agent-General] Sir G. Bajpai to handle these questions direct with the State Department, with the result that he had come to occupy a position similar to that of the Dominion Ministers in Washington" (Manserge and Moon 1944: 915–20, 475: *War Cabinet Paper W.P. (44) 221*: Indian Minister at Washington, Joint Memorandum by the Secretary of State for Foreign Affairs). Obviously reacting to pressure from the US government to afford India some semblance of meaningful national identity, Halifax declared that he wanted the Agent-General to be "freed from the suspicion fostered by certain circles in America [i.e., the White House] that in his arguments and expositions of conditions in India, the Agent-General simply echoed the views of His Majesty's Government."

It took time to establish this new diplomatic identity for India because India's viceroy, Lord Linlithgow, and Prime Minister Winston Churchill, the consummate old-line imperialists, opposed it on the grounds that India, as a British colony, "can have no foreign policy of her own." Therefore, it "might not be safe for her to have her own independent diplomatic representatives." In the end, however, by 1944, Halifax had prevailed and Sir Girja Shankar Bajpai, as Agent-General, achieved the status of a de facto ambassador. To solidify this new status, Halifax conceded numerous responsibilities to Bajpai. He "signed the United Nations Declaration on behalf of India, represented the country at Hot Springs and on UNRRA, held conversations in regard to Indian disabilities under the Asiatic Exclusion Act," and took part "on behalf of India in discussions about reciprocal Lease/Lend." With regard to the latter, as already noted, the Agent-General's office in Washington had been created in April 1941, technically for the purpose of facilitating the flow of US military assistance to India after it had been determined that India was eligible to receive such assistance under the Lend-Lease Act. But from the American standpoint its implicit purpose had been to create the aroma of differentiated sovereignty, upon which subsequent sovereignty-building measures could be crafted.

For the US government, in other words, this was a political foot in the door, so to speak, because it enabled the administration to request permission to reciprocally establish an office of comparable authority in New Delhi, since Washington "found it highly unsatisfactory having to deal with the Government of India through the Consulate General in Calcutta, nearly a thousand miles away from New Delhi." With the growth of US involvement in India, "the United States wanted easier access to British authorities and Indian nationalist leaders." It was this, of course, which ultimately led to the de facto ambassadorship of William Phillips and its aftermath (Kux 1993: 8).

On the Washington side, it was important that the position of Agent-General had been awarded to an Indian, Sir Girja Shankar Bajpai. The US had urged the British not only to accord some kind of diplomatic recognition to the Government of India, as distinct from the British government in London, but to do so in a manner that projected Indians as an integral part of that government and of the war effort. Seeing the handwriting on the wall in the circumstances which World War II had brought about, the British themselves, in fact, suggested the appointment of an Indian as a mechanism for placating American sensibilities. The initiative actually killed two birds with one stone: not only did it establish a basis for having an Indian of near-ambassadorial rank stationed in Washington, with all its symbolic implications, but it also opened the door for the United States to obtain reciprocal, explicitly American political representation in New Delhi which, as we have seen, enabled President Roosevelt to dispatch a senior diplomat like William Phillips there with de facto ambassadorial rank. The British themselves recognized that this concession implied a kind of de facto "Dominion status" for India as well. This gave India, in Lord Halifax's words, "an independent diplomatic voice." Since it was mainly a grudging concession designed to placate American sensibilities, Halifax adroitly converted necessity into a virtue by putting a paternalistic gloss on it. It is better, he rationalized, "to take the present opportunity to train Indian diplomatists under British guidance and to direct Indian thought from its present introvert tendencies towards foreign affairs" (*War Cabinet Paper W.P.* (44) 221, R/30/1/4:ff 56–0: Indian Minister at Washington, Joint Memorandum by the Secretary of State for India and Secretary of State for Foreign Affairs, April 24, 1944).

From the British standpoint, then, Sir Girja Shankar Bajpai was the ideal man for this position if indeed it had to be created. He was an elitist to the core, highly Anglicized, a peer, and an appointed member of the Indian Central Legislative Council in Delhi. The British clearly saw Sir Girja as "safe." Yet he was not a monolith. He was a "patriot" in his own way, without however being sympathetic toward the activists and radicals on the colonial issue. In this sense he embodied one of the many different forms that nationalism could take in a multicultural world where British colonial overlords had for two centuries manipulated the minds and destinies of the Indian people. He definitely espoused some kind of political autonomy for India, more or less in the form of "dominion status." But he did not want it to be achieved by violent confrontation with the Raj or by other forms of revolutionary action aimed at the kind of comprehensive political separation from British rule and pervasive domestic political reform which he believed the Indian National Congress and other political groups that he deemed "radical" wished to achieve.

This is evident in a pamphlet he published in 1944 under the title of "India and the United States of America" (Bajpai 1944). Concerning the Cripps Mission in 1942, he rejects any allegation that the Churchill Government deliberately undermined the negotiations with the Congress. Not unlike the tactics one encounters from today's American right, he attributes such claims to "liberals and leftists." "Only radical weeklies," he averred, "like the *Nation* and the *New Republic* blamed London for the breakdown." By contrast, the "majority of papers laid the blame upon Congress" (Bajpai 1944: 4). He contended that Jawaharlal Nehru's reaction to the critics of the Congress was "petulant," and that Mahatma Gandhi's advocacy of "non-violence as the only weapon which India could use against Japan" revealed "a lack of realism" or even "covert sympathy with the Japanese." He justified Britain's arrest of members of the Congress party following their decision to engage in civil disobedience after the Cripps Mission failed as a "regrettable necessity." He claimed further that "faith in the statesmanship of the Congress party has almost disappeared" (ibid.: 5).

Bajpai was genuinely a nationalist in the sense that he advocated some form of political autonomy under the imperial diadem. Most particularly at this point in time, Sir Girja Shankar placed "co-operation" between the US and Britain during the war above pressing America to directly intervene in Indo-British politics. Ironically, this was a position not unlike that which President Roosevelt himself had taken! In his pamphlet, Bajpai acknowledged that the "revolutionary tradition inclines the average American to be sympathetic towards peoples who, in their opinion, are struggling for freedom from foreign domination." However, in the name of the "maintenance of world security," he did not believe that "Indian nationalism [should] look to active or direct American aid for its fulfillment." The most they should hope for was "sympathy and moral support." This, of course is precisely the viewpoint which his British overlords wanted to hear from their handpicked Agent-General!

Sir Girja's critics in the nationalist community heartily agreed with this latter estimation of his diplomatic talents, and strongly disparaged his worthiness to be a spokesman for contemporary Indian political aspirations. They accused him of using his office to help promote anti-nationalist, pro-British propaganda in the United States. Even more, it was claimed that Sir Girja ratted on political activists who were in the US combating British propaganda and trying to promote the cause of Indian freedom, even to the point of attempting to get them deported and sent back to

India for prosecution. An Indian journalist, Chaman Lal (1945), working in the US at that time, claims that this was the case. Although his allegation was called a "black lie" by Sir Sultan Ahmad, a sycophantic member of the Central Legislature in New Delhi, Lal declares that "Sir Girja Shankar did so in my case and definitely tried to get [Dr. Krishnalal] Shridharani, the famous writer, sent back to India to be locked up in prison" (ibid.: 13).[1]

Once established, however, the Agent-General's Office also became a kind of intelligence conduit for the activist nationalists in the US. It was not a monolith. Many of the Indians brought over under its aegis were sympathizers and even closet activists in the nationalist cause. From their vantage point as insiders, they made important contributions to the activities of the "India Lobby," as we shall see. One informant stated that even Sir Girja's military aide-de-camp, Colonel Altaf Qadir, and the High Commission's Press Officer, Obaidur Rahman, were surreptitiously pro-Congress. They regularly shunted documents and the content of confidential conversations to the outside dissidents. Qadir quipped that it was extremely easy to spirit material out from under the Agent-General's nose because he was such an elitist that he regarded it be "beneath his status to look down at a document!"

Without question, Pearl Harbor, the stunning expansion of Japanese power right up to India's eastern frontier and the consequent establishment of the China-Burma-India (CBI) theater of war, which brought substantial American military forces to the sub-continent, clearly added great saliency to American public awareness of South Asia. This, in turn, apart from the Drew Pearson episode, made it much easier for the proponents of Indian self-determination and immigration rights to promote their cause in Washington and indeed throughout the US.

As we shall see, what is being called the "India Lobby" was no monolith. It had no formal charter or other organizational mechanism for promulgating tightly disciplined political activity. Its ethnodemographic base was a *mélange* of South Asians who had found their way to the United States by diverse routes. They were scattered all across the country but, as noted, the bulk of them at first were concentrated on the Pacific coast, in California, Oregon and the state of Washington. Most were Sikhs but there were also Hindus and Muslims plus a few Parsi Zorastrians and Indian Christians as well. In addition to the peasant farmers and manual laborers, there were students or more advanced scholars from middle-class backgrounds, most of whom came to the US via Europe in search of higher education and/or technical training. A few even found their way on to the faculty of American colleges and universities. Most of these were Hindus with a smattering of Muslims. There were also the so-called *"swamis,"* who came to purvey versions of the Hindu tradition to a select body of Americans who had acquired a fascination for Eastern religions and philosophies. And, of course, interspersed among all these more educated sojourners from South Asia were political activists of varying degrees of fervor who wished to rally their fellow Indians and American sympathizers to the cause of anti-colonialism and Indian freedom. Finally, there were a smattering of "spies" who had been recruited by the British to infiltrate the South Asian community and report on the activities and undermine the effectiveness of the dissidents among them.

A comparative handful of individuals will receive a major share of attention in this study. They are the ones who stood out, who tirelessly endeavored to light ideological fires under their diverse countrymen and eventually enabled significant numbers of South Asian immigrants and sympathetic Americans to actively support the freedom movement in India and Indian civil rights in America. However, every effort will be made to depict the social context in which they operated, both that which existed among the South Asians and that which existed in America from the turn of the century through World War I until the end of World War II. Before probing more deeply into the specific political exploits of these individuals, we must first explore in some detail the forces and factors that drew Indians to US soil over the previous five decades. It was they who gradually established the social parameters and subcultural infrastructure within which activism evolved. The cultural resources that Indian migrants brought from their homeland were, as we shall see, a crucial factor in this process. The manner in which they interfaced with American social, economic and political institutions is obviously just as important. Basically, the dynamic interplay between Indian and American traditions *on American soil* fueled the Indians' struggle to try and convince the "Land of the Free" that it must live up to its proclaimed political ideals, with respect to both citizenship rights and the evils of colonialism.

## Note

1. Lal says, "I had brought with me [en route to America] a copy of Sir Girja's letter admitting that fact, but that document was seized by the police Officer who arrested me at Karachi" (1945: xiii). We shall hear more from Chaman Lal later on in our narrative.

# 2 The Yankee Traders

Contacts between India and America actually have a surprisingly long history, even though the magnitude of these contacts was never great until recent times. They were significant enough, however, to play an important role in enabling both parties to have at least some awareness of each other once the immigrant encounter began. Against great odds, they found ways to make their presence felt both in economic and political terms, even in the earliest stages when they were facing vicious harassment by state and local authorities, by White-dominated labor unions, and even judiciaries that were permeated with racist jurisprudents. This is important for our story because it meant that the creators of the "India Lobby" never operated in a vacuum; they had access to "traditional resources" (intra-community networks) and "indigenous resources" (sympathetic outsiders) upon which they could draw to fuel their perseverance and sustain their resilience. And as more and more South Asians themselves found ways to accumulate property and other material and financial resources in America, their legal and political effectiveness grew. By World War II, the assets that they had collectively accumulated, while not by any means massive, nevertheless enabled them to develop political sinew sufficient enough to attract some measure of attention in high places to their personal plight, and to the plight of India.

Even prior to the establishment of this demographic and material beachhead, however, a surprising number of contacts between South Asia and the United States had taken place. As we shall see, these clearly laid the foundations for the more substantial interactions which occurred once immigrants began to arrive in significant numbers after the turn of the century. Enough contact had already occurred by then so that India was far from being an unknown quantity, at least among educated and more cosmopolitan Americans in the northeastern quadrant of the country.

The principal source of this incipient awareness was the impact which the mercantile world system had on America. This was the first genuinely "global economy." It was born in the wake of the Age of Discovery which superseded the Middle Ages. It was driven by the revival of economic life in the West, and by the concomitant rise of the state systems, which were from the sixteenth century onwards crystallizing into modern Europe as we now understand it. One of the main impetuses behind the great voyages of Columbus, Da Gama, Sir Francis Drake and many others was the desire of European commercial interests to gain access to the great markets of Asia. The overland routes to China, India, and Southeast Asia had for centuries been denied to European traders by Muslim domination of the Middle East, northern Africa, and Central Asia. The only solution was to "outflank" the Muslims by developing maritime technologies which enabled European entrepreneurs, increasingly subsidized by royal courts in search of resources to pursue their ever-widening political ambitions, to skirt the regions of Muslim dominance by sea. It was this emergent new nexus of maritime-driven commercialism that created the "pre-adaptive" pattern of relationships between the newly-independent American nation and India and paved the way for the more substantial encounter that occurred from the beginning of the twentieth century.

The first meaningful interaction commenced in the late eighteenth century during the age of sail. However, the motivation for these contacts was trade, not cultural *Gemuetlichkeit*. Its magnitude proved great enough, over the two generations following the attainment of American political independence in 1776, for a substantial quantum of South Asian religious and philosophical content to filter into the salons of America's literati and on to a few elitist university campuses like Harvard and Yale. These intellectual strands, which preceded even the early physical presence of emigrant Indians in America, were important: they would play a catalytic role in facilitating cultural receptivity toward subsequent Indian sojourners, especially those whose path to America led primarily through England and other Western European countries. The principal locus of what may be called this "pre-adaptive" phase of the American–South Asian interface were the parlors, pulpits, and classrooms of New England middle-class society. This came about because the so-called "Yankee traders" who established mercantile commerce between India and America during the era of the "mercantile world system"—the first "global economy" in modern times—were mainly New Englanders who sailed eastward from the Massachusetts ports of Salem and Boston, New Bedford, and Nantucket. Some also came from New York, Philadelphia and other East Coast ports, but in far fewer numbers.

These clipper ships, of medium tonnage and greater speed in comparison with their European counterparts, sailed outward across the South Atlantic, usually pausing briefly in the Azores and Cape Verde Islands, then around the Cape of Good Hope and onward to Bombay, Madras, and Calcutta. Often they stopped in Sri Lanka as well. In the words of Dr Susan S. Bean, "Yankee vessels typically between 250 and 350 tons were manned by crews of 25 to 45. By comparison, typical vessels of the British East India Company were 800 to 1000 tons with crews upwards of 100" (2001: 37).[1]

The first American ship to make this voyage was named the *United States*. It actually sailed from Philadelphia and reached Pondicherry in December 1785. Another ship, pointedly named

**Illustration 2.1**
**Old Yankee sailing ship that plied the India trade in**
**the first half of the eighteenth century**

*Source:* Courtesy of the Peabody-Salem Museum.

*The Empress of Canton*, left around the same time from New York and reached Canton in 1784, thereby opening the "China trade," which would parallel, and indeed ultimately exceed in magnitude, the "India trade."

A global war was raging at this time among the Western nations whose maritime technologies and post-medieval political upsurges had created the mercantile world system. The Revolutionary War which brought independence to the United States was not an isolated event; it was in fact only a single theater of this expansive conflict between the British, the French, the Dutch, the Spanish and the Portuguese. Had this not been the case, it is doubtful whether the comparatively meager American forces could have successfully defeated the much more professionalized British army and navy after 1776. Fortunately for the Colonies, British forces were spread thin—they were widely dispersed around the world, combating the French and the remnants of the decaying Moghul imperium in South Asia, the Dutch in Southeast Asia, the Spanish both on the Continent and in the New World, and the Portuguese all over Asia and Africa. Even then, the final defeat of Cornwallis at Yorktown had to be achieved with the help of French naval forces.

Following independence, the new American nation found itself in a highly favorable commercial situation. For most of the ensuing half-century, it was able to maintain a tremulous neutrality among the principal combatants. Because of this "interstitial" status, its mariners and commercial entrepreneurs were able to move cargoes and conduct trade throughout the world with relative impunity. In fact, the Yankee traders often functioned as go-betweens who could safely transport cargoes for one belligerent or another. This reduced the risk of interdiction by warships and privateers that were roving the sea-lanes in search of enemy prizes. The India trade was a major by-product of this unique situation in which the new American nation found itself from the 1780s onwards. It was also a major source of income for American commercial enterprises, and of tax revenues for the fledgling US government. Speaking generally, Bean declares that "the years of the European wars were immensely prosperous ones for Americans, trading across the globe in their small, maneuverable, armed vessels," so much so that "Between 1795 and 1806, US exports rose from $67 million to $108 million," most of it "derived from the re-export of foreign goods" (Bean 2001: 68).

"Trade with India was a key component of this commercial expansion," says Bean. The spin-offs were considerable and important. A lot of the capital amassed by the Yankee traders soon found its way into investments in "fledgling industries, establishing the financial foundation for the American industrial revolution" (ibid.: 69).[2] A report authored by an East India Company official (and cited by G. Bhagat) declares that the American trade surpassed "everything of the kind recorded in the Commercial History of British India. Seven years before, this trade did not exceed S.Rs. 6,718,992 [approximately $3.5 million] or Sterling 839,784," but in the "year under Report" it had risen to "the enormous sum of S.Rs. 20,020,432 [roughly $10 million] or Stg. 2,502,554, exceeding the total amount of Private Trade with Great Britain" (Bhagat 1970: 43–44).

The India trade was by no means a monolith. Its magnitude and character changed through time in response to international political developments, changes in the world economy and domestic developments within the United States. In the atmosphere of global war that prevailed from the American Revolution until the end of the Napoleonic wars in 1815, the Yankee clippers, despite ups and downs, enjoyed their most clear-cut and comprehensive prosperity. As neutrals in a world gone mad, American ships were able to maneuver through the interstices of the international maritime nexus with relative impunity. Yes, American shipping was periodically harassed and interdicted by the combatants. The British waylaid American ships and impressed members of their crews who were deemed to be British nationals into their navy. The French too preyed on American shipping. The British reserved the right to confiscate the cargoes being transported by neutral vessels if they deemed them to be enemy contraband. To prevent encroachment on existing trade monopolies, a so-called "rule of 1756" promulgated by British courts "obliged neutrals to abide by existing restrictions," which meant that trade closed to foreign shipping in peacetime remained off limits in wartime" (ibid. : 67). In the combative atmosphere prevailing from the latter part of the eighteenth century through the first quarter of the nineteenth, this measure and others that followed, like the Jay Treaty negotiated by John Jay in 1795 when he was ambassador to the Court of St.

James, managed by the slimmest margins to prevent the United States and England from going back to war with each other. In the end, of course, war could not be avoided. British harassment of American shipping grew so bothersome that James Madison, the fourth US president (1809–1817) declared war on Great Britain in 1812. Similarly, as the French Revolution gave way to the Napoleonic era, animosities with the French over the same issues frequently approached the brink of open hostilities but never managed to go over the edge. In all instances, the principal issue was the preservation of American maritime commerce, from which a lion's share of the tax revenues needed for operating the US government were derived. Thus the India trade was perennially held hostage to the political vicissitudes associated with the mercantile world system. At the diplomatic level, one of the chief roles of the US government in those times was the attempt to formulate laws, rules and policies which confronted challenges from abroad in ways which kept trade alive and generally redounded to the fiscal benefit of the American nation and its citizens. The point is that despite all the impediments, the India trade pressed on.

In addition to the international factors affecting the commercial environment encountered by the Yankee traders were the problems that they faced at home. This resulted from the rise of competing visions of what the resources and energies of the new nation should be committed to. As President George Washington's administration wore on, differences between major socio-economic interests began to surface and influenced the political dialog. Washington himself noted their prevalence within his own cabinet. While he "successfully implemented executive power and quieted fears and suspicions of executive tyranny," the president "regretted the rivalry between Thomas Jefferson and Alexander Hamilton which led to the birth of political parties ... Washington feared that allegiance to 'factions' would someday eclipse the guiding light of patriotism" (*The New York Times Almanac* 2000: 99). Washington's sentiments were touchingly naive, of course. Eroding patriotic fervor was an inevitable consequence of the achievement of independence. With a democratic constitution in place and free elections made the basis for determining representative government, post-independence politics by definition ceased being a freedom movement. In its place came multiple interests manifested

by competing factions, which ultimately crystallized into ideologically differentiated political parties (see Gould 1994).

The original factional cleavage between followers of Alexander
Hamilton and Thomas Jefferson laid the foundation for party-
structured competition in post-independence America. It occurred
when Hamilton led his followers out of the Democratic-Republican
Party and established the Federalist Party as its rival for power.
"Hamilton's Federalists supported a strong central government
that would play a major role in the national economy and *represent
the commercial interests of the north*. Jefferson's Republicans advocated states rights and the agrarian interests of the south" (*The
New York Times Almanac* 2000: 102, emphasis added). The dimensions of this cleavage over the fundamentals of public policy have
been vividly described by Chernow. "For Jefferson and his followers," he declares, " wedded to their vision of an agrarian Eden,
Hamilton was the American Mephistopheles, the proponent of
such devilish contrivances as banks, factories and stock exchanges"
(Chernow 2004: 3). Viewed in historical perspective, of course,
Alexander Hamilton was ahead of his time. He had grasped the
inevitable contours of the modern state as well as the structural
implications of the global economy and the impending industrial
revolution. He wished to position America to take maximum
advantage of these processes.

Understandably, the New England traders mostly identified
with the Federalists. Indeed many were significant players in the
new party's activities. Not only were they directly affected by the
political establishment's attitudes and policies toward the maritime trade, the resulting policies also affected the flow of capital
they had amassed from this trade into the nascent factory-based
textile industry whose origins lay in New England. Alexander
Hamilton of New York, the chief protagonist for these interests,
especially when he was serving as Treasury Secretary from 1789
to 1795 in Washington's administration, and afterward when he
strove for the presidency, was their hero.[3] It was he, Bean states,
who "shaped national policy to protect property and to support
commerce and industry" (Bean 2001: 69). It has already been noted
that Federalist policies greatly strengthened the viability of the
US government through the tax revenues that were generated from
overseas trade, especially with India. It was these policies and the
prosperity they yielded which had a cultural impact as well. They

stimulated the development of a cosmopolitan middle class, which helped create a milieu of receptivity towards India and Indians once the influx of South Asian emigrants commenced.

When Jefferson won the presidency in 1800, maritime interests were indeed negatively affected. The irony is that he won because among the Hamiltonians there were factions within factions. A tie in the electoral college between Jefferson and Aaron Burr was resolved in Jefferson's favor when Hamilton and his followers broke ranks with Burr and supported Jefferson. This arose mainly from the personal enmity existing between Hamilton and Burr rather than over high principle.

A Southerner himself, a slave-holder, and a member of the rural gentry, Jefferson, predictably ran on a pro-agrarian platform that opposed the Federalist vision of a strong central government financed by tax revenues garnered from international trade. With executive power in his hands, Jefferson limited the power of the central government by slashing the budget and reducing taxes. He initiated the Louisiana Purchase, which doubled the size of the United States and tilted the balance of power toward the agrarian interests whom he favored and who wanted to orient America toward intra-continental expansion. In what became essentially a zero-sum game, this inevitably meant attenuating America's commercial and political involvement in the global economy and the politics of mercantilism.

However, fortunately for the India trade, Jefferson turned out not to be a total monolith in these matters. Even before he became president, he had revealed an ambivalence which arose both from his own attachments to Europe, especially to France, and his instinctive reverence for the democratic principles which had spawned the Declaration of Independence. This was amply evident in a letter he wrote to John Jay from Paris on August 23, 1785, while he was the designated representative of the US Congress to France. "Cultivators of the earth are the most valuable citizens," he declared. "They are the most vigorous, the most independent, the most virtuous, and they are tied to their country and wedded to its liberty and interests by the most lasting bands." In his own way, Jefferson, like Hamilton, sensed that major technological changes were in the wind, but he had a different take on their implications for the America of his dreams. Eventually, and regret-tably, he believed, there will occur "a surplus of hands" that will have to turn to other means of subsistence. He thought this would take two forms: mariners and "artificers." Between the two, Jefferson preferred mariners, which boded well for the preservation of some semblance of the maritime industry after he became president. "I consider the class of artificers as the panders of vice and the instruments by which the liberties of a country are generally over-turned." But he was prepared to honor alternative vocations in the name of liberty, and freedom of choice, even those he person-ally found unsavory. "I think it a duty," he averred, "in those en-trusted with the administration of [the people's] affairs to conform themselves to the decided choice of their constituents ...." This especially applied to maritime commerce: "... we should in every instance preserve an equality of right ... *to the transportation of com-modities*, in the right of fishing, and the other uses of the sea," despite the fact that the consequence "will be frequent wars with-out a doubt" (Wilson and Stanton 1999: 20–21, emphasis added). Certainly these political values guaranteed at least modest scope for a continuation of the India trade during his presidency. And this of course proved to be the case.

In the international arena, one of the major factors was the inter-play between the East India Company, the British government, Yankee traders, and the American government. The relationship with the East India Company was understandably an ambivalent one. It was a huge monopoly, after all, until Parliament terminated its exclusive hold on the India trade and let other entrepreneurs into the game on an ostensibly equal basis. This occurred in 1813, followed by the abolition of its entire commercial operations in 1834. Prior to these openings, the goal was to establish a balance between the things that the Yankee traders could do which en-hanced Company interests—such as importing silver as payment for commodities acquired in Indian ports and providing "neutral bottoms" for the transport of goods which otherwise, under the prevailing conditions of global war, might be at risk if transported in ships flying the Union Jack—and those which got in the way of the Company's most lucrative commercial undertakings in the sub-continent. In Bean's words, "The powerful East India Company actively sought to prevent American trade with India from com-peting directly with its own interests and for providing a means for British residents in India to evade regulations and get their property to England" (Bean 2001: 69).[4] Notwithstanding these parameters—and this is the important point—enough latitude still existed for both parties to prosper. So much so, in fact, that five years after his surrender at Yorktown in 1783, Lord Cornwallis's next assignment was as Governor-General of India, where he showed considerable deference toward his recent nemesis. Bean cites a book by Girish Chunder Dutt, published in 1868, which declares that because American ships brought with them silver specie with which to conduct transactions, Cornwallis decreed that "the vessels belonging to the citizens of the United States of America should be admitted and hospitably received, in all the sea ports and harbors of the British territories in the East Indies." The Governor-General stated that Yankee vessels "should be treated at the Company's settlements in all respects as the *most favored foreigners*" (Dutt 1968: 35, emphasis added). Here then was an earlier manifestation of the "most favored nation" concept now prevalent in US commercial dealings with the world!

At whatever levels the India trade took place in face of the aforementioned political vicissitudes and impedimenta, it did persist, and never on an insignificant scale. Yankee traders were irrepressible! Commencing towards the end of the eighteenth century and through the first quarter of the nineteenth, Jacob Crowninshield (1770–1808), member of one of the families that founded the India trade, claimed in 1806 that an estimated 30–50 ships per year were voyaging to Calcutta and Madras. Following this peak, sailings tapered off to about 14 per year through the 1820s and then picked up again toward the middle of the century. If true, given the times, even with these oscillations this was clearly a persistent and formidable commerce. Let us make allowance for such periodic variations in the frequency of voyages, and take as a rough average the figure of an even 20 cruises per year over the first half of the nineteenth century, and assume crews averaging 35 seamen per ship. This would mean that each year something like 875 Americans, mostly from New England and the northeast, were having interactive contacts of some kind with the South Asians whom they encountered in ports like Calcutta, Madras, and Bombay. Admittedly this figure would include many individuals who had made the voyage more than once. Even then, if one projects this level of commerce over the half-century, it would still mean that Yankee clipper crewmen had as individuals experienced no less than 43,750 contacts with Indians and brought back to America their impressions of India, however varied in quality and quantity these might be, which they then inevitably disseminated among their fellow countrymen in the pubs, parlors, churches, schools, and colleges where people met and interacted. As Bean puts it, Yankee businessmen "maintained a steady connection between New England and India that carried in its wake *an encounter transcending commerce*. Hundreds more young New Englanders had first-hand experiences of India and returned with stories, souvenirs, books and pictures" (Bean 2001: 181, emphasis added).

Taken together, Susan Bean's (2001) and M.V. Kamath's (1998) books present vivid images of the evolving interplay between American seafarers and the Indians whom they encountered when they reached the shores of Bengal, Gujarat, Maharashtra, Malabar, and Tamil Nadu. Round-trip voyages consumed about a year. The clipper *Belisarius*, for example, left Salem en route to Calcutta in the latter half of 1799 and had returned to Salem by September of 1800 after—according to the log kept by the ship's "supercargo," Dudley Leavitt Pickman (1779–1846)—traveling 14,220 miles going out and 13,950 miles coming home, equivalent to circumnavigating the globe![5]

Clipper ship logs provide the first "ethnographic" insights into how American mariners perceived India in the decades immediately following the attainment of independence. What they brought back with them from a cross-cultural standpoint was as important in the long run as what they brought back materially was in the short run. Most valuable were those portions of the captains' and supercargoes' narratives which revealed some measure of intellectual curiosity about the civilizations they were encountering. Pickman was one such acute observer. Not only does he address "the procedures and prospects for trade," says Bean, "but he also describes architecture, politics and society" (Bean 2001: 90).

Apart from her own historical discourse, Bean presents long excerpts from the logs of six clippers that made this voyage over the span of half a century. These show in considerable detail the nature of the men who undertook these voyages, the impressions which India made on them, and most of all, what they brought home with them by way both of commodities and ideas to dispense among their fellow countrymen. Kamath, more than Bean, documents the aspects of this encounter which most interest us here, namely the India-consciousness which gradually diffused through the more educated circles of New England and northeast society.

The six excerpted clipper logs are from the *Ruby* in 1779–1780, the *Belisarius* in 1799–1800, the *Derby* in 1803–1804, the *Tartar* in 1817–1818, the *Apthorp* in 1833–1834, and the *Rockall* in 1854–1855. They chronicle over half a century of maritime commerce from which the earliest American perceptions of India emerged. As we have said, the importance of the pattern of cross-cultural inter-action which they document pertains mainly to the impact it had on middle-class social circles in New England, New York, and Philadelphia. On the Pacific coast, of course, a considerably different pattern of cultural interaction unfolded, which we must allude to separately.

From their inception, the initial point of contact for the clippers following their arrival in Madras, Calcutta, and Bombay (or indeed any other Indian port) was with a "broker," known in Madras as a *Dubash*.[6] These brokerage houses provided a "cultural beachhead" for incoming mariners. Especially in Calcutta, which handled the bulk of the maritime trade, relationships often endured for years and took on a personal quality far exceeding mere accountancy and the particulars of merchandise and cargoes. This is because the American sea captains, supercargoes and crews were depend-ent on these brokerage houses' cultural resources, as much as their strictly managerial and pecuniary capabilities, to mediate between them and indigenous society across a broad range of matters. Housing had to be arranged while ships were in port. Food, cloth-ing, drink, recreation and all manner of other creature comforts had to be provided through their interlocutory capabilities, since the moorings in India would normally last several weeks. Refitting and the unloading and loading of cargoes took time. In Bean's words, "For a commission of a few percent, Indian middlemen would sign custom house bonds, find buyers for incoming cargoes, purchase and deliver commodities for export, arrange housing, and supply *circars* or *concicopolys* (clerks) and domestic servants" (Bean 2001: 39).

In their commercial and social dealings with the Indians, the Yankee traders differentiated themselves as much as possible from the British East India Company operatives. "The Americans," said Pickman in the log for his voyage aboard the *Derby* (1803–1804), "have very little to do with the English at Calcutta." They settled on a handful of brokers who were not exclusively under the thumb of the East India Company. Pickman mentions "Ramdulalday" (i.e., Ram Dulal Dey), "who is also banyan to the very respectable English house of Fairlie, Gilmore and Co." He characterizes Dey as "very shrewd and capable, extremely avaricious, and possesses great talents for business." Also, there is "Ram Chunder Banorjea [i.e., Ram Chunder Bannerji], a Brahman, who does some southern and a considerable proportion of northern business," and who is "a very smooth tongued man." Then, "Collisunker" (i.e., Kali Shankar) and "Doorgapersaud" (i.e., Durga Prasad) Ghose, who also do some southern and more northern business. "The latter is a shrewd man and industrious when pressed by business" (Bean 2001: 111). These were ties that often endured across generations, unfettered by the social prejudices prevalent in Calcutta's English-dominated circles. The brokers, says Bean (2001: 71) were "specialists in bridging the commercial, linguistic, and cultural gulf between American merchants and local practices."

"Besides pioneering the Asia trade for the United States," says Bean (2001: 40, emphasis added), *Yankee mariners also became the conduits for the beginnings of distinctively American perspectives on India.* What were some of the specific impressions garnered by these American seafarers during their sojourns in the Indian subcontinent? Many "saw themselves along with the natives of India, as fellow victims of British colonial power" (ibid.: 41). Due as much to their own social backgrounds as what they found in India, there were strong perceptions of the various racial divides that socially vivisected the country. Dudley Leavitt Pickman, on his first trip to India in the *Belasarius* in 1799–1800, found that every social group largely inhabited their own, separate ethnic bailiwick. In all the port cities there was a "black town" with narrow streets, small shops, "wretched buildings" and great crowding. The British and East India Company employees had their own quarter, with wide streets, greenery and capacious residences. In Madras, he found Armenians and Portuguese living amongst the "natives" (i.e., "those descended from native parents") in "large and handsome houses with considerable gardens adjoining," while nevertheless retaining their "national appellations." Although "natives" are "very dark," the "writers and accountants" (i.e., *Dubashes*) are "very neat and correct." He provides a reasonably accurate description of the essential ingredients of the caste system, noting especially the effects of its ritual hierarchy, including untouchability. Brahmans, whom he labels "Brahmineys—minister cast," are at the pinnacle, and "will not touch any not of their own denomination, without immediately washing themselves entirely after it" (Bean 2001: 91).

With respect to Hindus of "loose caste" or "outcaste" status, Pickman describes a personal experience he had with this extreme manifestation of ritual pollution. Untouchables, he declares, "are held in such horror by the Brahmins, that on one occasion when I wished to enquire out a store in Black Town, a Brahmin in company refused to ask information, even as interpreter, from one of this description. He spoke to a Gentoo [the word frequently used by Westerners for Hindus] who asked of the loose cast—and finding him acquainted with the object of our search, and that a direct communication was necessary, *the Brahmin obliged him to turn his face from him to give the description we needed*" (ibid.: 96, emphasis added).

Regarding "religious ceremonies, I can say but little." Hardly a day passed, Pickman declared, in which some sort of ritual or ceremony was not taking place. Processions were "always accompanied by music, and large concourses of people, and great respect and obeisance was paid, some even to prostrating their faces in the dust." He witnessed animal sacrifice among Muslims, whom he called "Moormen." He saw a "fanatic, who professed to have devoted himself entirely to god." This *sadhu* was "dancing, etc., before the image, and applying fire to different parts of his body, apparently without effect" (ibid.: 98). Pickman was a guest in a Brahman's household where they were celebrating the induction of a son into the Brahman caste (i.e., performing a sacred thread or *Upanayana* ceremony). "The merchant to whom he was dubash was present with his family, and this attention seemed very gratifying to our host, who filled us with garlands of flowers, sprinkled us with rose water and perfumes, and at parting presented each of us a piece of muslin" (ibid.).

Pickman noted that the natives live on curry and rice "almost entirely"; that the curries are "extremely hot"; that they consume "great quantities"; and that they "eat with their fingers from a leaf." He observed that natives "universally chew betel nut and leaves and chunam [i.e., areca nut, betel leaf, and lime], the former of which gives the teeth and mouth a very red and disagreeable appearance." He claimed that natives "have very little bodily strength." Yet, inconsistently, he declared that palanquin bearers, working for only four *annas* a day, "travel fast and hold up well" (Bean 2001: 97).

"The rich live well and at great expense," he remarked. They employ large staffs of servants. Their cuisine is extensive. They consume "a great variety of dishes on table, and drink much wine." English claret is "most fashionable," although "Much Madeira is also drunk." Pickman's Western cultural and religious sensibilities appear to have been somewhat ruffled by the fact that "almost everyone has his palanquin"; that there "is no theater, or other public amusement"; that "Sunday appears totally disregarded by the Europeans as well as natives"; and that "Business goes on as usual ... I saw nothing to distinguish [Sunday] from any other day" (ibid.: 99).

Pickman endeavored to describe the British imperial establishment in India as he viewed it from his obviously limited vantage. He estimated that there were "about 15,000 Europeans and 60,000 sepoys at present on the India establishment." The sepoys "live almost entirely on rice ... wear short breeches ... short cloth coats, with hats," but "No stockings and generally no shoes." He rated them as "good soldiers," and "when conducted by brave officers and supported by some European troops, will stand as long as any troops whatever" (ibid.: 102).

He encountered the occasional American who had found a niche of some kind in the country and had established residence there. "At Madras, I met very few Americans, and, except in business, formed no acquaintance with the English residents." He mentions one American whom he met, a "Captain Cheevers, born at Danvers [Massachusetts]," who had been in India for "twelve or fifteen years." He was "master of a country vessel," would "probably never return to America," and, rather unflatteringly, "is deaf and not very intelligent" (ibid.). He also met a variety of Europeans who had settled in coastal India, such as a Danish community at Tranquebar on the Coromandel coast, 160 miles south of Madras. "The whites have a Danish church, and one for Roman Catholics, where blacks are admitted after the whites have finished their devotions" (ibid.: 104).

By the second decade of the eighteenth century and thereafter, the early stages of the industrial revolution were already affecting the nature of the commerce being transacted between India and the West. The emerging factory-based textile industry in the latter was delivering the first lethal blows to the "cottage industries"–based economy of the former. The great variety of finely crafted, hand-woven cloth products was one of the main impetuses behind the India trade; and when the cheaper-priced machine-made cotton and woolen textiles pouring out of American, British and Continental textile mills hit the Asian markets, the economics of overseas trade underwent radical changes which affected not only India's economy but inevitably its social and political systems as well. Put simply, in the twilight of the mercantilist global economy, the flow of manufactured products was reversed. "The textiles so admired in the West ... were rapidly being superseded by industrial manufactures ... India was reduced from a provider of coveted wares to a source of raw materials" (Bean 2001: 24).

Yet, as this transformation from the old global economy to the new one proceeded, and societies on both sides of the world underwent massive demographic and cultural changes, the India trade persisted. It merely changed its character.[7]

One of the most unique new turns which Yankee ingenuity took during the nascent stages of this great transformation in Indo-American commerce was the ice trade. It came into existence in the 1830s, when Frederick Tudor developed a technology which enabled ships to insulate their holds so that they could successfully cart ice anywhere in the world. In a sense, the transporting of ice to India by the Yankee clippers was analogous on a smaller scale to the East India Company's opium trade. In both cases, one important purpose was to fill what would otherwise be empty ships' holds "going out" with a commodity that could be sold in the country of destination. The income thus derived helped defray the costs of what was purchased for shipment back to the home country. The crucial difference, of course, was the nature of the "outgoing" cargo. The opium loaded in Calcutta and offloaded in Canton (in order to assure the East Company a favorable balance of trade with the Far East) had disastrous consequences for the Chinese people, and led to the Opium War in 1840.[8]

The ice shipped from Boston to Calcutta by the Yankee traders, by contrast, merely "cooled Indian throats," as Kamath (1998: 68) delightfully puts it. What was most important, however, was what was being shipped back to America in those now-empty holds. They were the commodities—jute, indigo, hides, and saltpeter—which symbolized the fundamentally altered economic relationship between East and West. They were feeding the steam-driven machines of factories instead of the culinary and aesthetic appetites of the New England gentry.

Inevitably, the pervasive structural changes that were taking place in the global economy were also, as already suggested, producing concomitant changes in other domains of both Asian and Western societies. Aside from the enormous increases in the demographic scale (exponential population growth) and social structure (rapid urbanization) in all societies which became entwined in the industrial revolution was the social and political ferment which this alteration in the human condition ignited. Thoughtful people on both sides of the world were driven by rapidly changing material circumstances to undertake a critical examination of the time-worn assumptions underlying traditional society, and to demand changes not only in the political and economic status quo but in the moral and philosophical status quo as well.

In India, the infusion of Western technology had come at the price of military conquest, political domination and the systematic degradation of indigenous cultural and religious institutions. William Rogers saw this clearly as early as 1817–1818, when he sailed as supercargo on the *Tartar*. "Rapacity, thirst for conquest and the worst evils of war," said he, "have followed [British] entrance .... Their public officers have been tyrants, their [private] individuals extortioners. They have overrun the peninsular of Hindoostan and extermination has been the order of the day ..." (Bean 2001: 167). As mid-century approached, British political and economic conquest of India had largely fulfilled itself. The 1850s were especially pivotal. With the consolidation of political control over the subcontinent, the production of cash crops and raw materials now demanded in the West was increasingly rationalized. Railroads and the telegraph were being constructed, which linked inland India to its coastal entrepots, thereby enormously speeding up the flow of commerce and fundamentally altering the country's technological infrastructure. With these changes came opportunities, indeed the demand, for increasing numbers of Indians to enter the world of modern occupations and the educational qualifications needed to fill them. As the depredations from these radical alterations in the "cultural infrastructure" ramified across the sub-continent, this led both to violent social upheavals, such as the Great Uprising of 1857, which for a brief time threatened the very survival of British hegemony over India,[9] and to growing doctrinal and political challenges to the relevancy, viability and justice of the country's traditional way of life. Simultaneously, it sowed the seeds of nationalism, challenging the right of a foreign power to appropriate the country's wealth, exploit its labor, and subject its people to a demeaningly subservient status in their own land.

In the United States as well, the scope of the West's massive economic transformation was spawning unease in the hearts and minds of many spiritually sensitive intellectuals. Along with the rise of factories and industrial towns, railroads and the telegraph were spanning the continent. The transcontinental railroad was completed in 1869. Territorial expansion, which had commenced with the Louisiana Purchase, had continued apace with the absorption of the southwest through Texas's independence in 1836 and statehood in 1845, the Mexican War (1846–1848) and the Gadsen Purchase (Arizona and New Mexico) in 1853, and California's accession to the United States (Treaty of Guadalupe Hidalgo) in 1848. In the eyes of this next generation of reflective thinkers, all this was posing a dire threat to the "simple virtues" upon which the American nation had allegedly been founded. This, after all, was Jefferson's concern, as we saw, even at the dawn of the Republic. Now, they believed, America was increasingly being driven by a doctrine of remorseless laissez-faire capitalism which apotheosized acquisitiveness for its own sake. In their view, the emerging industrial revolution was tearing at the characterological fabric of American society and must be counterbalanced in some manner. It was displacing simple householders from their land and congregating them around factories in towns and cities where squalor and crass materialism increasingly dominated and defined their lives; or else it was uprooting them and propelling them westward in a reckless, headlong pursuit of riches. These doubts were inherent in the religious and philosophical viewpoints being articulated by Unitarianism and by the Transcendentalist movement, the latter inspired especially by idealistic New Englanders like Ralph Waldo Emerson (1803–1882) and Henry David Thoreau (1817–1862), about whom more presently. At one point, Henry David Thoreau had encapsulated these concerns in a quip he made about the recent addition of newer, more "modern" passenger cars by the Boston to Worcester Railroad. "So they made a better railroad car," he remarked. "But have they made better people to put in it?"

From the Indian side, moral-intellectual responses to the West's troubling impact on India's ancient civilization were also emerging. On both the Asiatic and the Western sides, in fact, thoughtful men, each in their own way, had become alarmed over the same underlying trends toward industrialism and materialism, and were groping for antidotes to what they believed were their most morally corrosive ramifications. Thanks to the India trade, channels of communication had come into being through which these mutual concerns could cross-fertilize one another. This was crucially important in setting the stage for the pre-adaptive diffusion of aspects of Indic civilization into the American cultural milieu prior to the actual arrival of South Asians in the United States in the flesh.

In India, the earliest manifestations of social and religious ferment growing out of Western contact were centered on Calcutta for the simple reason that this is where contact and impact on a significant scale first occurred. Soon the effects were reaching into the surrounding countryside. One can say, in fact, that a religio-philosophical revolution was underway right under the noses of the American seafarers and merchants who were plying their trade in the city. Most, of course, were not sophisticated enough to perceive and fully understand what was occurring. Some, however, were indeed aware enough to carry back home with them accounts and artifacts pertaining to these stirrings. This was especially the case once those members of the New England intellectual elite who were themselves mounting a comparable challenge to established values got wind of it. From this point on, specific requests were being made of supercargoes, ship captains, missionaries and other culturally sensitive crew members and sojourners to acquire religious texts, locate scholarly treatises (particularly by learned Englishmen in the Company's employ), and make personal contact with Indians whose reputations had become prominent enough in cosmopolitan circles to be readily identifiable.

Sociologically speaking, what had happened in the course—indeed in part as an outcome—of the mercantile global economy and, subsequently, the nascent capitalist world system, and within it the India trade, is that the basis had been created for a syncretic interface between these two very different cultural worlds. Understanding the circumstances which led to this requires, in part at least, a Marxist perspective. That is, the impact of the scalar change in technology and economic organization had set in motion processes of structural transformation at the material level of both American and Indian society, which in turn had a ramifying impact on both countries' cultural systems. In India, because Calcutta became the first, and remained one of the principal, hubs in the dawning modern economy, Bengal also soon found itself in the forefront of the political and cultural ferment which inevitably accompanied this pervasive transformation that was beginning to reshape human society everywhere.

Specifically, it led to what Kopf (1969) has termed the "Bengal Renaissance." This process commenced during Warren Hastings' second term as Governor-General of the East India Company (1772–1785). He was, says Kopf, one of the few Englishmen "who acquired an intellectual appreciation of Indian civilization" (ibid.: 15). As Smith et al. (1958) put it, "He found Calcutta a counting-house and left it a seat of empire,"[10] mainly because he grasped the need not only for politically and economically integrating India into the British system of power but also for culturally and linguistically blending them together. Hastings, and those of similar intellectual bent who both were associated with him toward the end of the eighteenth century, and who followed his lead into the first decades of the nineteenth century, particularly under the stewardship of his most notable successor, Lord Wellesley (1798–1805), played a critical, yet an often insufficiently appreciated, role in creating a basis for the intercultural communication network through which Indic thought flowed via the Yankee traders into the drawing rooms and on to the campuses of New England society. This, in turn, prepared the ground for the later contact between Americans and the first South Asian Indians to physically set foot on American soil. Paving the way for social and religious reform in the United States was hardly their intent. It was rather a fortuitous outgrowth of the broad forces of change then active all over the world.

The roots of this remarkable conjuncture lay in the "discovery of India" by a generation of men who achieved paramountcy in the East India Company near the turn of the eighteenth century, at the very time that America was attaining independence from Great Britain, and whose motivations for making this discovery had more to do with politics and economics than with cultural *Gemuetlichkeit*. Warren Hastings indeed fell in love with Indian civilization and with the languages (especially Sanskrit, Persian, and Bengali) which he believed contained the keys to its comprehension and appreciation. He provided a supportive environment for the gestation of serous and comprehensive scholarship on India by insisting that for Company employees, "the key to advancement, in most cases, was linguistic proficiency" (Kopf 1969: 27). Admittedly, Hastings was driven as much by political, administrative and strategic considerations as by reverence for scholarship per se. But the depth and sincerity of his own commitment to the latter set in motion irreversible intellectual processes whose reverberations were felt on both sides of the cultural divide. "Between 1813 and 1823," declares Kopf, "as a result of unprecedented experiments in cultural fusion, Calcutta became the earliest of Asian cities to develop the qualities necessary for what Daniel Lerner has described as the transformation of a traditional society" (ibid.: 178; see also Lerner 1964: 62). By the end of Wellesley's term as Governor-General in 1805, the door which Hastings opened in 1772 had secured a permanent place for Indic studies both in India and in the world of international scholarship. The values of the Enlightenment had, as it were, for the first time found fertile soil in Asia.

Making linguistic contact with India meant making cultural contact with and acquiring respect for a non-Western civilization. "In the era of Hastings, and for some time thereafter, the mastery of Indian languages opened the way to both professional advancement and the literary treasures of an Oriental civilization"(Kopf 1969: 27). The interplay between scholarship and administration was a crucial by-product of the Orientalist bent given to Company rule. From an administrative standpoint, it led to the need for translations of official documents, memoranda, etc., in both directions— from Bengali, Urdu, Persian, and Hindustani into English, and from English into Bengali, Urdu, Persian, and Hindustani. To accomplish this, resources for language training had to be created. This began with Hastings developing in the 1770s "a coterie of selected aides whom he personally inspired with a love of Asian literature" (Kopf 1969: 19). These fragile beginnings had within three decades led to the rise of a vernacular press, to the publication of Indian literature, and to the establishment of academic institutions devoted to the teaching of Indian languages and Indic subject matter. The intellectual foundations for Banaras Hindu University were laid in 1791 by Jonathan Duncan, a close associate of Hastings, who wished to establish a "public university" devoted the study of the laws, literature, and religion of India. By 1800, under the guiding hand of "the Wellesley clique," the Asiatic Society of Bengal, originally inspired in the 1780s by the father of Sanskrit studies Sir William Jones (1764–1794), had been rejuvenated, and the College of Fort William had been established. The latter, along with the Serampore Mission, an institution created by the missionary community, were crucial factors in preparing the ground for the collection, publication and dissemination of the Hindu classics, and the study both of classical civilization and of the vernacular languages and cultures of India. It was through institutions such as these that Jones and other classical scholars found the means and the opportunity to discover the Indo-European roots of Sanskrit. This connectedness between Indian and Western civilization, along with the availability of the Indian classics and the commentaries and histories being written by the Orientalist scholar-bureaucrats and missionaries who were responsible for making these classics available in the West, were what made it possible for the New England literati to accord a place to the speculative wisdom of the East in their own quest for a more universalistic conception of divinity. What trickled to the US via the Yankee traders smoothed the transition. It helped New Englanders "pre adapt" to the incoming Bengali and other "modernity seeking" Indian students and sages who filtered over here via London and Paris at the beginning of the twentieth century. It helped these emigrants to adjust in this country by providing at least a semblance of congeniality and sympathetic understanding, at least in the culturally sensitive sections of American society.

From a moral-philosophical standpoint, then, the so-called Bengal Renaissance was to India what Unitarianism and Transcendentalism were to America. They became counterpart movements. In India, it resulted in what is called "Orientalism": the attempt by a group of Englishmen in the employ of the East India

Company, and reformist Bengali Hindus to create a syncretic culture which would, on the one hand, enable the Company to rule India with an enlightened administrative touch and, on the other, enable Indians to make Hindu society and religion compatible with emerging modernity. In America, it led to religious and philosophical essentialism which drew on Indic thought and resulted in the meeting of East and West in ways that would make the transition of emigrant Indians to the United States far more feasible and congenial than might otherwise have been the case.

The sources of disquiet among the Indian elite emanated from the formal critique of orthodox Hinduism, and the implicit critique of Western Judeo-Christian doctrinal chauvinism and its imperialist sponsors, begun in Bengal by the Brahmo Samaj, and later in the Punjab and elsewhere by movements like the Arya Samaj and the Hindu Mahasabha. In America, an assault on both puritanical Christianity and machine-age materialism was mounted by Unitarians and Transcendentalists. The Indian side endeavored to disaggregate the moral and philosophical core of Hinduism from the welter of ritualism and superstition with which it had become encrusted over the centuries, and infuse it with an essentialist dynamism that could hold its own against the muscle-power of politically subsidized Christian evangelism and the imperialist rationales of British colonialism. In the course of these philosophical ruminations, the American side endeavored to broaden the scope of divinity and morality to embrace all humankind out of a belief that it would be possible to enable all religions to, in Thrasher's[11] words, "eventually converge on the essentials" and produce a more socially just, less violence-prone world. It was in this context that the Bengal Renaissance and New England transcendentalism proved to be made for each other.[12]

It is not within the purview of this book to undertake a lengthy exposition of the very substantial body of literature that flowed between India and the West as an intellectual by-product of the India trade. It is important, however, to acknowledge its scope and recognize some of the figures who took intercultural interaction to the next level, thereby paving the way for the favorable reception (at least to the northeastern quadrant of the United States) awaiting early South Asian immigrants and sojourners. It can be safely said, I believe, that Raja Rammohun Roy (1772–1833) was the single most important figure who enabled this process to go forward. It was he and his Bengali cohorts, founders of the Brahmo Samaj in 1828, who transfigured Indian religious beliefs and practices into idioms which resonated with the quest for fresh thinking that was taking place in New England at the same time. "There is some truth to the belief," declares Kopf, "that Rammohun was an original thinker and that his early associations, which led ultimately to the formation of the Brahmo Samaj ... were without precedent in Indian history." At the same time, however, "Rammohun owed far more to his British Orientalist contacts and to the ideas of other Bengalis than is generally acknowledged" (Kopf 1969: 197).

We have noted that Unitarianism and Transcendentalism were the principal mechanisms through which Hindu thought was injected into America's religio-philosophical blood stream. Centered in New England, it was most certainly the major intellectual spin-off from the India trade. Works like the Bhagavad Gita, the *Laws of Manu*, the *Vishnu Puranas*, the Vedas, *Shakuntala*, and the Upanishads, as well as other translations of the Hindu classics and treatises on Indic thought by European scholars like Sir William Jones became part of educated Americans' (especially East Coast Americans) intellectual portfolios. It must be realized that the social relationships which Yankee supercargoes, sea captains and other more sophisticated crew members built up with Calcutta middlemen were the principal avenues through which whatever awareness they acquired of the cultural revolution that was brewing in Bengal occurred. In many instances, these Americans spent significant periods of time living and working in Calcutta between voyages, and especially those who visited the city several times over the years developed real acquaintanceships and friendships with their *Dubashes* and *Banians*. While these Indians came primarily from the mercantile castes and were normally not themselves central players in the socio-religious ferment that was taking place, they were all practitioners of Hinduism and variously aware of and involved in its ritual and domestic practices, and indeed variously affected by the controversies being stirred up by reformers like Rammohun Roy.

According to Kamath, knowledge of Indian religion and culture was widely enough disbursed around New England that Sir William Jones's translation of *Shakuntala* had been published in Boston by *The Monthly Anthology* in 1805. Other works already available in Boston included a translation of the *Ramayana* produced by the Serampore Press and also a two-volume work, *A View of the History, Literature, and Mythology of the Hindus*, by William Ward (1769–1823), later published in London in 1822.[13] Kamath says that a book by Henry T. Colebrooke, one of Wellesley's original circle of Orientalists, entitled *Remarks on the Husbandry and Internal Commerce of Bengal* (published in 1804), was "available to students" (Kamath 1998: 27). A noted philologist, no doubt other writings of Colebrooke dealing with Sanskrit and Bengali found their way to America at this time. Bean says that the brother of Frederic Tudor, who established the "ice trade" with India, was responsible for introducing Rammohun Roy's ideas to America in 1818. William Tudor had a Harvard degree, and when he was editor of the *North American Review* published an article in that journal entitled "The Theology of the Hindus, as Taught by Ram Mohun Roy." The article was inspired by his reading of Roy's *Defense of Hindu Theism*. "Although there is no record of how Rammohun Roy's writings first reached Boston," declares Bean, *"it is most likely they were brought directly from Calcutta on Boston vessels"* (Bean 2001: 192, emphasis added). This was happening around the time that William A. Rogers was demonstrating, during the voyage of the *Tartar* (1817–1819), through his log how far many of these Yankee traders had progressed as cross-cultural observers. Due mainly to the impact Roy was having on the Unitarians by the 1820s, "At least half of the religious journals published in the United States ... made some reference to him" (ibid.). One of Roy's essays entitled "The Precepts of Jesus" had a special impact for the obvious reason that he, as a reformist Hindu, endorsed the teachings of Christ. In 1923, it inspired *The Christian Disciple and Theological Review* to publish a compendium of "The Writings of Rammohun Roy, based on sixteen works in the author's possession" (ibid.). By this time, Roy was corresponding with kindred souls, both in America and England, on a regular basis. In 1833 Roy was in England, "as the titled ambassador from the Mughal emperor to represent the demands of Indians for equal treatment under East India Company rule" (ibid.: 193). While there, the American artist Rembrandt Peale painted his portrait, which today hangs in the Peabody Essex Museum in Salem, Massachusetts.

The point here, of course, is that the Indic world had struck roots in the intellectual, philosophical and theological world of the American literati. Apart from the general awareness of things Indian, which the East-West trade had made possible at a very early point in American history, it also resulted in the emergence of serious scholarship on Indian society and civilization in many centers of learning. As the nineteenth century wore on, several American universities like Harvard, Yale, Columbia, Pennsylvania, Chicago, and Berkeley established professorships of Sanskrit and departments of Oriental Studies which stressed Hindu-Buddhist studies. These drew students into their scholarly orbit, even inspiring some to journey to India to pursue their quest for a deeper understanding of Oriental thought and South Asian civilization. The principal conduit for the original importation of these streams of thought had been the India trade conducted by the old Yankee clippers. The significance of all this for our purposes is that it shows how the encounter between Americans and incoming Indians, when it began, did not occur in a vacuum; and that there was indeed some awareness of the civilizational roots of India among certain segments of educated American society, most particularly in the northeastern quadrant of the United States, which paved the way.

Let us now turn to this influx of South Asians that commenced around the turn of the twentieth century. There were actually two separate streams that were very different from each other. One came via the Pacific coast of Canada and the United States and consisted primarily of Sikh peasants in search of manual jobs through which they could accumulate money to remit back to their natal communities in the Punjab and with which they hoped to find a secure place in the agricultural economies of Canada and the United States. The other stream came via England and Europe from essentially middle-class families in Bengal and other regions of India, in search of higher education, technical training, opportunities to pursue religio-philosophical interests and, in some instances, a desire to pursue political agendas generated by emerging anti-colonialist nationalism. Soon these two streams would conjoin to produce a composite, ethnically structured subculture of South Asians in America, who, like all other ethnic groups before and after them, found themselves increasingly concerned with defining and representing their perceived rights and interests in a society which did not at the outset make their transition easy.

# Notes

1. This volume is a definitive work on the history of contacts between the United States and India from the latter part of the eighteenth century through the first 60 years of the nineteenth century.
2. Bean draws on the work of Prof. Holden Furber (1938).
3. See Chernow (2004) and Ferling (2004) for a thorough description of the political and policy differences between the Federalists and the Republicans which affected overseas commerce.
4. Bean (2001: 13) amplifies this point. Employees, she says, "were permitted a certain amount of private trade in company vessels. Many of them exceeded the allowance and accumulated profits in private trade while in India. Foreign ships were useful in bringing this wealth home to England undetected."
5. The "supercargo" was second in rank to the ship's captain, and was in charge of managing the transport and sale of the cargo.
6. Derived from Hindustani (*do bashay*), meaning "two languages." Referred to in Calcutta and Bombay as a *Baniya*. This term derives from the common Hindustani term *Baniya*, which connotes in less than flattering terms a "money lender," a rustic shopkeeper or small-time entrepreneur. In current Hindustani, business persons of this caste are called "Baniyas."
7. This was because the commercial relationship and its cultural spin-offs had persisted for so long. "Despite the decline of Salem and other smaller ports," says Bean (2001: 177), "some of their merchants continued to prosper, frequently landing their ships at Boston or New York." Also, "The business of men like Henry Lee, Joseph Peabody, and Frederic Tudor maintained a steady connection between New England and India that carried in its wake an encounter transcending commerce" (ibid.: 181). And finally, "In the 1840s, after two decades of languishing, Indo-US trade began to grow again" (ibid.: 211). Only the cargos reflected the impact of the industrial revolution: raw materials in place of finished products.
8. In the words of L. Carrington Goodrich (1951: 22), "Opium poppy ... had far-reaching but exceedingly deleterious results" for the Chinese people. "It despoiled great areas of land, ruined millions of homes, fattened the purses of tax collectors and shortsighted officials and landowners, and eventually led to war in 1840."
9. There is a vast literature on the uprising which commenced with the "Mutiny" (*Ghadr*) of East India Company sepoys in 1857. It raged for two years before British reinforcements from overseas and indigenous native allies like the Sikhs were able finally to suppress it (see Kaye and Malleson 1897–1898; Embree 1987; and also Gould 1971).

10. Warren Hastings's ascent to Governor-General of Bengal in early 1772 was a major turning point in both the fortunes and the nature of the East India Company. During his term in that office (1772–1785), the East India Company was transformed from a commercial enterprise into an Indian state which became a major player in the dynastic politics of the Indian sub-continent. As it did so under Hastings, the foundations were laid for the intermingling of South Asian cultural traditions with the Anglo-Saxon West. This process could not be described better than it has been by Smith et al. (1958):

> Warren Hastings became Governor of Bengal early in 1772. He was then not forty years old, and had first gone to India twenty-two year before. Unlike Clive, he had risen regularly up the rungs of the civilian ladder from the position of writer.... His apparent task was the consolidation of the Company's rule in Bengal....But destiny had reserved for him a far greater one. It was the preservation of the British possessions from deadly danger from without and bitter schism within. He found the Company a commercial corporation turned revenue farmer; he left it one of the great powers of the Indian sub-continent (p. 502).

and further:

> His long residence in Bengal in the shadow of the Mughul cultural tradition had kindled oriental tastes and allowed time for the acquisition of oriental learning... his cultural interests, and his understanding of the people, came nearer to the heart of India than any of the other pre-mutiny rulers. His name became a legend.... He sought to understand Indian culture as a basis for sound Indian administration.... He found Calcutta a counting-house and left it a seat of empire ... (pp. 513–14).

11. Allen E. Thrasher is Senior Reference Librarian, Southern Asia Section, Asian Section, Library of Congress.
12. Structurally speaking, this was not unlike the convergence that took place in medieval India between monistic Hinduism and orthodox Islam through the medium of *Bhakti* and *Sufi'ism* (see Zaehner 1960).
13. Ward "... built the earliest and, for decades, the most important printing and publishing house in the world for books in the oriental languages ..." (Kopf 1969: 72).

# 3 The Early Pioneers

The first demographically significant concentrations of Indian immigrants in the North American continent occurred along the western coasts of Canada and the United States. They started coming late in the nineteenth century and into the first decade of the twentieth. Most of them came from the region of India known as the Punjab. They were predominantly Sikhs but included a smattering of Hindus and Muslims as well. For this reason, we shall at times use the more generic term "South Asians" when it is necessary to identify the full range of Indians who found their way to America.

The Punjab is in many ways a highly distinctive region within the Indian commonweal. Situated astride the gateways leading into India's heartland from Inner Asia, it was for several centuries a perennial battleground between invading tribes from the Inner Asian heartland, bent on pillage and conquest, and the people of the Gangetic plain who were their targets.[1] It was, and remains today, a region where political and cultural turmoil constantly challenge the sanctity and stability of traditional social, cultural and religious institutions. Many ethno-religiously driven political forces have vied, and continue to vie, for control of its rich economic and strategic assets.

The British incorporated the Punjab into its "Crown Territories" in the nineteenth century after a bitter military struggle with the last indigenous dynastic state established there by the Sikhs. Its ruler, Ranjit Singh (1780–1839), known as the "Lion of the Punjab," was a brilliant soldier, a crafty politician, a gifted administrator, and an enormously charismatic leader, who in his day captured the imagination of his Sikh brethren and even to this day stands as an embodiment of the community's martial traditions and national identity. At the height of his rule, he controlled most of the northwest portion of the sub-continent, including Kashmir.

He gave the British fits before they succeeded in subduing him.[2] So admiring were they of Sikh military prowess that following their victory over Ranjit Singh's successors, and their absorption of his state into the Crown Territories, the British recruited Sikhs en masse into the Indian army and relied on them not only to help subdue political opponents in other parts of the sub-continent, but overseas as well. They and the Gurkhas of Nepal were the main basis for characterizing certain ethno-cultural communities in India as "martial races." The Muslims of this northwestern region were also incorporated into this category. Sikh units served widely in the Far East, the Middle East and Africa, and even in Europe during World Wars I and II, as part of various Imperial military undertakings. These facts have much to do with why it was that Sikhs rather than other Indian ethno-cultural communities became the vanguard of substantial Indian immigration into Canada and the United States.

Demobilized Sikhs who had served in British military units in East Asia, particularly Singapore, Hong Kong, and Shanghai, formed the vanguard of the first Indians to arrive in significant numbers on the West Coast. Their largest concentrations were established first in British Columbia and later in California and other West Coast states, particularly Washington and Oregon. It is said that the Boxer Rebellion (1898–1900) was an important stimulus for making Sikh soldiers in the British-Indian army aware of potential economic opportunities on the opposite side of the Pacific after "they came into close contact with men of other nationalities who had worked in America and who probably painted a rosy picture of economic opportunities in both [Canada and the United States]" (Chandrasekhar 1944: 139).

According to Hugh Johnston, "The first of these Sikhs had come to Canada in 1904, encouraged by the Hongkong agents of the Canadian Pacific Railway (CPR), who were seeking to replace steerage traffic lost after the Canadian government had raised the head tax on Chinese immigrants." The principal attraction, of course, was economic opportunity. Far more money could be earned in the New World than could be acquired under the social, political, and economic conditions prevailing in the Punjab at the turn of the century. Jobs in the lumber yards and saw mills in

British Columbia were comparatively abundant and paid $1.50 to $2.00 a day, several times what labor was paid in India. "Lumber companies and railway contractors wanted them; the fruit growers of the Okanagu wanted them ..." (Johnston 1979: 2–3).

These original migrants have been called "pioneers" who came to western Canada and the United States by sea. They were in a sense the counterparts of the Whites who migrated westward overland by rail and covered wagon, and were gradually able to establish a socio-demographic "beachhead" there during a period when the rapid expansion of agriculture, mining, and railroad construction on both sides of the border created a favorable economic environment.

Five Sikhs, "bearded and turbaned, and wearing light cotton European-style clothes," arrived aboard the *Empress of India* in March of 1904; "ten came on the *Empress of Japan* in May and each succeeding month brought two or three more" (Johnston 1979: 3). Soon Indians had become a socially visible enough demographic category to attract "official notice." The census of British Columbia for that year listed 258 "Hindus." Lumping them together in this fashion, of course, reflected local cultural ignorance about India since over 90 percent were Sikhs, the same proportion as subsequently found their way to the United States. By the autumn of 1906, according to Khushwant Singh and Satindra Singh, more than 1,500 Punjabi laborers were working in or near Vancouver. At this stage, "Canadian employers were eager to engage Punjabis, who were not only willing to work for less and, not being members of trade unions, were also willing to work longer hours." Moreover, "The Punjabis were hardier than the Chinese, the Japanese or even the so-called Caucasian races" (Singh and Singh 1966: 1).

Initially, this period of economic ferment played into the hands of the migrants who had managed to gain entry into the country (by whatever means). Jobs were reasonably obtainable, and to a certain extent even opportunities to purchase, rent or share-crop agricultural land could be found. This facilitated the gradual creation of a fragile economic base upon which the material foundations for domestic and community institutions could be built. The frugality and organic solidarity of Sikh migrants, traits they had imbibed in Indian peasant society, were important assets in their quest to put down roots in Canada. In the lumber yards and saw mills of Victoria and Vancouver, declares Johnston, they could accumulate savings on wages of $1.50 to $2.00 a day by "living frugally, three and four to a room, on a sparse but adequate diet," thus saving "most of what they earned." They didn't deposit the money they accumulated in banks but instead "invested in real estate and in this way some had accumulated $3,000, $4,000 and $5,000 since arriving in Canada." While ostensibly their purpose was to send remittances back to their kin groups in India, and ultimately to return to India themselves, many invested their accumulated capital in agricultural and mercantile enterprises in British Columbia and eventually across the border in the United States as well (Johnston 1979: 2–3). This would form the material foundation for their eventual political ascent.

Karen Leonard says that Indian men "were not barred from owning and leasing land until 1923." By this time, however, a backlash had set in, which reflected the innate racism of the region's Caucasian population. After this, legal restrictions were gradually imposed that slowed the flow to a trickle. In the United States, according to Leonard, "Before 1907, fewer than 10 percent of applicants for admission were rejected; but in 1909, 1911, and 1913, 50 percent or more were rejected. The Immigration Act of 1917 was the final blow, with its 'barred Asiatic Zone' and literacy provisions; and the National Origins Quota Act of 1924 confirmed the earlier exclusionary principles" (1997: 45).[3] The nature of these legal obstacles and their repercussions will be discussed in more detail at a later point in our narrative.

At any point in time, getting established in a foreign land is far from easy. The obstacles facing the Sikhs were accentuated by manifestations of inter-cultural estrangement. But to some extent, these obstacles would prove to have a positive as well as a negative side. Prejudice, bigotry and open hostility, as is so commonly the case, inspired these early Indian migrants both in Canada and the United States to fight back and to fashion counter-measures that sharpened their sense of ethnic self-awareness and aroused their political sensibilities. This would play a significant role in the struggle that Indians increasingly waged both for their own civil rights in North America and on behalf of the freedom movement in India. It would become manifest when these grassroots Sikhs eventually developed relationships with men "who attacked British rule and preached revolution—men who could not return to India for fear of

the police and who waged war from abroad ..." (Johnston 1979: 7).
These were men like Taraknath Das, Har Dayal, and M.N. Roy.

Who, then, were these so-called "Hindus" who undertook the
arduous trek from northwestern India to northwestern Canada,
and subsequently the American Northwest as well, in search of a
better way of life for themselves and the kin they left behind in
the sub-continent? The fundamental question, of course, is what
motivated Sikhs and other Punjabis to migrate from their
home region to a world thousands of miles away inhabited by
Whites who did not welcome their arrival and indeed did whatever
they could to obstruct their social progress on Canadian and
American soil.

As their numbers increased, so did their social visibility and
they soon found themselves to be objects of the same racism which
had confronted the Chinese and Japanese before them. Punjabi
migration to the New World was an aspect of a general Indian
diaspora that co-terminated with the rise of the Industrial Revolution and with it colonialism and imperialism. This was the other
side of the coin of the ferment and disruption which had led to
the Bengal Renaissance and "Anglicism" in the Indian domestic
social environment. Economic opportunities abroad for menial and
artisan labor increased markedly, especially after the abolition of
slavery by Great Britain in 1834. This created occupational gaps
that were increasingly filled by indenture and other forms of
contract labor. It deposited non-Western peasants and menials in
the midst of Caucasian populations that were already deeply
infected with racial self-consciousness, born to an important extent
from their military successes against the native populations they
encountered in the process of European expansion. In the case of
Indians radiating outward from the sub-continent along the
politico-economic networks established by the British Empire, "the
battle lines had already been drawn," according to Janet Jensen.
"The very characteristics which made Asian workers attractive to
employers—their willingness to remain separate, to maintain their
own cultures, and not to assimilate European work attitudes—
made them less acceptable to [other] workers and to Europeans
less directly interested in their labor" (Jensen 1988: 10).

What were the logistics involved in journeying so far from their
homeland and establishing themselves in a "new world," whose
inhabitants did not by any means welcome them with open arms?

What were the cultural resources they brought with them, and what role did these play in adapting to the social and material conditions that awaited them? Their discovery of the West Coast indeed may have been the fortuitous outcome of colonial military service, but once these demobilized soldiers and others of their countrymen entered this new environment and, via the grapevine, informed their Punjabi kinsmen and cohorts of its economic promise, the flow of migration commenced in earnest.

The conventional explanation is that economic hardship drove them to it. It turns out, however, that for the most part the Punjabis who undertook the journey to North America at the turn of the century did not fit the conventional stereotypes. While not wallowing in the lap of luxury, they were by no means suffering from abject poverty either. On the contrary, they were a moderately prosperous peasantry who saw migration not as an escape from starvation but as an opportunity to increase their agricultural wealth and enhance the social status of their kin groups. The fact that many early Sikh migrants themselves characterized their emigration as a response to abject poverty must be taken with a grain of salt, according to Archana B. Verma. She believes it was in fact a kind of self-congratulatory validation of their transformative quest. "The 'poverty' assertion," she declares, "was 'mythologizing' their experience." This was a view that "fitted in with the assumptions of their Canadian audience, and it made sense to Punjabis themselves when they contrasted what they had before emigration with what they gained from it." The fact is, however, that "economic advantage, not economic desperation, was the reason they had emigrated." It was really seen as a "chance to enhance their position at home by bringing back foreign savings" (Verma 2002: 85).

Although not themselves Hindus, Sikhs are a historical offshoot of Hindu civilization, who, since their parturition from the parent faith, have enjoyed a symbiotic coexistence with both Hindus and Muslims in the multiplex cultural environment of northwestern India. The Sikh religion and the socio-cultural milieu in which it evolved was founded upon doctrinal divergences both from orthodox Hinduism and fundamentalist Islam. It rejected many of the formalisms of the caste system and embraced principles of social egalitarianism derived both from Islam and *Bhakti*; it rejected orthodox Hindu polytheism and adopted a form of denominational monotheism based upon the authority of a succession of gurus. Its emphasis was, in Madan's words, "anti-ritualistic, anti-idolatrous, and social egalitarian" (1997: 80).

Sikhism also rejected Islam's anthropomorphic version of ultimate being on the one hand, and its messianic fanaticism, especially coercive conversion to the faith, on the other. At the same time, caste-like social formations persisted in Sikh society, although in far less extreme form as far as concepts of pollution and minutely delineated status hierarchy are concerned. This must be seen as an inevitable consequence of having evolved out of Hinduism (much like Protestantism in the West) on the one hand, while being compelled to share its cultural world with encompassing, demographically dominant Hindu society on the other. Under these circumstances it is not realistic to imagine that all vestiges of the caste system could have been eradicated.

Yet, the differences were an important aspect of the Sikhs' ability to cope with Canadian and American society. Sikh social stratification clearly was less pervaded by preoccupations with ritual pollution, occupational orthodoxies and rigid endogamy. This made it easier for them to undertake necessary adaptive transformations in their social organization that would enhance their capacity to survive and prosper in the Canadian and American social environments.

Verma provides an excellent picture of the early years of Punjabi emigration in her recently published work, *The Making of Little Punjab: Patterns of Immigration* (2002). She concentrates her attention on the history of the members of a comparatively small caste group, called Mahtons, from a single village named Paldi, located in Garshankar *Tahsil* of Hoshiarpur district, thus making them a kind of "case history" of the larger whole that is ultimately her central concern. Paldi is in the heartland of a cluster of Punjab districts (Gurdaspur, Amritsar, Jullundur, Ludhiana, Ferozepur, and Hoshiarpur) from whence a large portion of the early Sikh migration both to Canada and the US emanated. What makes them particularly interesting is that these Paldi Mahtons established a village in British Columbia with the same name. This made it possible to show how "Punjabis sustained themselves in Canada as a community, centered unmistakably on the Punjab" (ibid.: 15). From the standpoint of understanding the development of the settling of Indians along the western coasts of Canada and the

United States, this allows one to comprehend some of the details and complexities of the emigration-immigration processes in sociological terms. It shows that this process was far from being random, episodic or ego-centric, but in fact displayed systematic characteristics that help explain how South Asians became an institutionalized presence in both countries, able to provide a stable life for themselves there, to enhance the lives of the kinsmen and castemen they left behind in India, and acquire the material and cultural resources needed to fight for their civil rights.

Mahtons are a Punjabi caste whose traditional occupation was/ is, in Verma's words, "market gardening." They are what today is called in India a "middle" or "backward" caste, structurally analogous to the Murao caste in Uttar Pradesh (Gould 1994). Their specialty was cultivating vegetables and other leguminous products. As such they formed an integral part of the traditional division of labor. They contrast with the Jat Sikhs in that the latter are not only far more numerous, but also specialize in a different aspect of agricultural production. Jat Sikhs are "crop farmers" who cultivate the major foodgrains such as wheat, rye, oats, and barely.

Decisions to emigrate to Canada or the United States were rarely individual or idiosyncratic. They arose from collective deliberations by the kin and caste groups to which individuals belonged. Essentially these were the type of extended kinship units which anthropologists know well as basic functional units of social structure in Indian society. This was especially the case in agrarian society at the turn of the century. The authority structure of extended families provided the immediate social framework within which decisions were made concerning what members would be permitted to migrate. Known as *baradari* in its broadest manifestation, this group also acted as the principal source of funding for and legitimiser of such migrations. Since the cost of a journey half way around the world, even in steerage, was substantial, the money had to be raised from among supportive kinsmen who saw the undertaking not simply as a "cost" but as an "investment." It was a matter of *izzat* (family honor), "a key element in the emigration process." It was seen as a way not only to "make money in a short time ... and improve the living standards of their families," but also a way of enhancing status (*izzat*), "not only in the village, [but] also within the *baradari*" (Verma 2002: 65–66).

Another factor that made emigration more than just an individual matter pertained to the retention of property rights (*haq shuda*). In keeping with the rules of inheritance that are commonplace in most of India, each male consanguine in a joint family is entitled to an equal share in the land at the time of partition. This was true then and it remains true today. Until actually divided, the share to which a male member is entitled depends upon how many male members there are at any given time. In the case of Sikh migrants at the turn of the century a decision to migrate to America could affect one's *haq shuda*. If an individual decided to migrate against the wishes and without the permission of his kin-group elders, he would lose his coparcenary rights, which meant being denied access to or inheritance of his inherent share of the joint-family patrimony. This was a material (*haq*) and status-related (*izzat*) blow which few men could endure.

The point is that emigration was in most instances not an abrupt severance of vital ties between kinsmen but an extension and elaboration of traditional ties in order to take advantage of perceived opportunities to participate in the new economic order which the industrial revolution had wrought. This was not solely the case for the Mahton and Jat Sikhs whom Verma studied, but also for Sikhs, Hindus, and Muslims who became emigrants in general. As we shall see, however, all Sikhs did not return to the Punjab after they had "made their fortune," so to speak, but stayed on in America, got married there, often to non-Indians, and eventually became citizens. Detailed data do not exist on the proportions who retained Punjabi *izzat* and *haq shuda* and those who, undoubtedly for a mixture of reasons, eventually cut themselves loose from their primordial ties and their attendant material and status perquisites.

As already noted, the trip to Canada by Sikhs who assembled sufficient resources and the requisite blessings to undertake the journey was by no means a picnic. By urban and international standards their wherewithal was very meager. They were peasants who had simple tastes, minimum education, and were accustomed to physical hardships. In keeping with the *baradari*-structured mode of determining who went, the journey normally commenced as part of a group that had kinship and caste credentials in common. In this manner, travel and maintenance costs could be shared and mutual protection could be provided as they moved in a world filled with strange customs and many perils. Also, such groups, called *kafilas*, had the names and addresses of kinsmen, caste-mates, fellow villagers, etc., who resided in towns along their route, not only in India but in places like Singapore, Hong Kong, and Manila as well. And, of course, they brought with them the names of the persons with whom they must connect after arriving in British Columbia or America.

*Kafilas* seem to have numbered from 15 to 30 individuals. For Hoshiarpur Sikhs the nearest railway station was Jalandhar, about 65 miles away. Verma quotes a passage from one of the interviews she did with an informant who was either 80 or 92 years old (her data are not clear on this point), which provides a nice insight into how their journey began:

> Our men began their journey for Canada at about three or four a.m. in the morning and after covering about two and a half miles from the village to Mahilpur *thana*, they walked on the Garshankar-Hoshiarpur road, reaching Hoshiarpur city by 8 or 9 o'clock, in the same morning, when *kachheri* (Courts) opened in the District Commissioner's office. It took them about a day and a half or maybe more in those days to reach Jalandhar station from the Hoshiarpur city. People took rest in the villages on the way (Verma 2002: 100).

They had to obtain permission from the Hoshiarpur District Commissioner to travel abroad. Passports were obtained in Jalandhar, from where one caught the train to Calcutta. "Travel to Canada was cumbersome: it required official approval and documents, and for new emigrants the routes ahead posed daunting prospects. Within the group that formed a *kafila*, however, all this was manageable" (ibid.). In those days there were no direct passages from India to America via Calcutta. One was compelled to sail from Calcutta to Hong Kong and then board another steamer from there to Vancouver. The stay in Hong Kong while awaiting onward passage could be managed by staying with fellow Sikhs who were living there (a by-product of Sikh military service) or could be arranged through the *gurdwara* which had been established in the city to serve its Sikh residents. Aboard ship and during the layover in Hong Kong, which could last "an infinite number of days," the value of one's *kafila* was self-evident. It was in essence a mobile version of the primary group structures which governed their lives in the village and enabled them to maintain social cohesion and attend to basic needs throughout their journey. "Punjabi emigrants adjusted with equanimity to the hardships of the journey, to the problems associated with food and to the snubs of their upper-class fellow passengers on the ship route from Hongkong to Canada" (Verma 2002: 102).

The statistical data assembled by Verma from three sources show that 45 "entrants of Indian origin" came in 1904–1905; 387 in 1905–1906; 2,124 in 1906–1907; and 2,623 in 1907–1908 (*Canada Year Book* 1905–1908; Das 1923; Buchignani et al. 1985). After 1908, restrictive measures kicked in and the numbers dropped precipitously from that time onward. Those who made it, however, ranged over British Columbia searching for economic opportunities that would fulfill the dreams which brought them to this new land. They were, as stated earlier, "pioneers" who laid the social foundations of the Indian presence in North America. Many did indeed succeed in establishing secure patrimonies, which included business enterprises, and through their accomplishments gradually created a significant material and cultural base upon which an authentic lifestyle and effective political action could be fashioned.

## Migration to the United States: The Rise of the Indian-American Constituency

In the United States, a comparable process of immigration and assimilation was simultaneously taking place. It was not identical, of course, because real differences existed between Canadian and American society, which affected the details of the South Asian experience in each. Yet there were extensive demographic and social interconnections, which soon acquired political significance once civil rights concerns and Indian nationalism reverberated through both communities.

As in the case of Canada, what especially paved the way for the Punjabi influx into the United States was the availability of manual work in the lumber industry and railroad construction, plus the rise of vigorous farming economies in the San Joaquin,

Imperial and Sacramento valleys of California just before and after the beginning of the twentieth century. It was catalyzed by the effects of Canadian racism, especially after it eventuated in restrictions on Indian immigration. As Jensen observes, "By 1861, farm-ing fever replaced mining fever in many California communities" (1988: 33). Farming had become highly mechanized by 1875, as agricultural lands "passed from the hands of their original owners [recipients of Mexican land grants] into the hands of Euro-Americans interested in agro-business" (ibid.). Irrigation projects ramified this process ever more widely through the arable portions of the state. In this context, "specialized large-scale vegetable and fruit ranches were developed at a time when local Euro-American workers and business people" were driving out the Chinese who had been the principal labor supply and replacing them with Japanese workers. However, the Japanese were not numerous enough to fill the gap. This created an opening for still another genre of imported labor, namely, Punjabi farmers. "Expansion brought increased competition for wage labor and increased wages" (ibid.). Given their peasant roots and the simi-larities of the agricultural environment to that of their homeland, Sikhs proved to be highly adaptable to this increasingly special-ized ecosystem. In Leonard's words, "Punjabi laborers and farmers [fitted] into California's regional economies at several levels, although they had to battle ethnic stereotypes to do so" (1997: 21). About 85 percent of the Indian immigrants were Sikhs and 10 or 12 percent were Muslims, according to Leonard (ibid.: 43).

Most South Asians who found their way into the West Coast agrarian system were the same Jat Sikhs who had been in the van-guard of the Canadian influx. Their predilection for farming and their reputation as hard workers coincided well with a period of rising demands for cheap labor, a convergence of circumstances which for a time afforded scope for considerable immigration, both legal and illegal. The pattern is reflected in immigration statistics over the first two decades of the twentieth century. "Before 1907," says Leonard, "fewer than 10 percent of applications were rejected" (ibid.: 45). During this period there was what Leonard calls an "agricultural ladder" from farm worker to tenant to owner, along which, "until the agricultural depression of the 1920s, men could establish themselves and move up those steps in response to a combination of energy, determination and luck" (Leonard 1997: 21). By the 1920s, however, racial discrimination was replicating the Canadian model. In 1909, 1911, and 1913, rejection rates increased to over 50 percent.[4]

"The Immigration Act of 1917 was the final blow, with its "barred Asiatic zone" and literacy provisions, and the National Origins Quota Act of 1924 [which] confirmed the earlier exclusionary principles" (ibid.: 45). The demographics favored this outcome, of course, as had been the case north of the border: The greater the numbers, the greater the social visibility; the greater the social visibility, the greater the racially driven resistance to immigration. The legal obstacles that emerged naturally slowed the adaptive process down to a crawl, although never stopping it completely. I think this is mainly because, during the brief span of competitive openness, a demographic critical mass was achieved which facilitated the establishment and consolidation of a socio-economic infrastructure that became too deeply embedded in the wider society to any longer be uprooted. This in turn acted as the basis for further socio-cultural elaboration and eventual political mobilization.

By the time the Canadian "refugee influx" commenced, the American Sikhs had already established a considerable network of enclaves, which had become socially interconnected and had developed a corresponding sense of ethnic identity. *Gurdwaras* had been erected, the first one in Stockton, and cultural organizations established that were, as in Canada, able to acquire a political dimension once White resistance to the Indian presence started to get ugly. This nexus, with California as its hub, acted as a "catch basin" for the subsequent trickle of incoming Sikhs and other Indians from Canada and abroad. However, by the mere process of increasing their demographic density and therefore their social visibility, their ingress intensified the problems with racial prejudice that already existed for Indians on the American West Coast.

One of the most important challenges to the adjustment process was the search for ways to develop a functional kinship nexus that could provide a measure of grassroots stability to their ongoing social life in America. With respect to Canada, Verma shows how the institution of *haq shuda* (inherent male consanguine entitlement to a share in the joint property) sustained formal ties between emigrants and their extended families back in India. Marriage was the key. She implies that most Sikhs either arranged marriages with caste- and *baradari*-appropriate women before they migrated, or returned later to undertake such marriages, or in some instances remained unwed, in order to preserve their coparcenary rights (*haq*) of inheritance. No data appear to be available on how many men broke their traditional social contract, thus forsaking their inherent property rights, by marrying non-Indians. Presumably there were not many such cases in Canada.

There seem to have been some differences in the way many Punjabis who settled in the United States dealt with the desire to establish stable domestic units. Many strayed farther outside the traditional fold than did their Canadian brethren. A significant number of the Punjabis who settled in America created what Leonard picturesquely calls "biethnic communities ... by marrying women of Mexican ancestry." Initially, she says, Punjabi immigrants simply cooked and cleaned for themselves, and augmented their domestic chores by hiring local women. "They also formed relationships with local women. [However] those who wanted a stable family life in the United States began to marry" (Leonard 1997: 62). Doing so must have resulted in the termination of their *haq shuda* rights and must for this reason be seen as having constituted a decisive break with formal structural aspects of their Indian heritage. As Verma says, "an unsanctioned absentee was likely to lose his *haq shuda* ..." (Verma 2002: 97).

In three important ways, this undoubtedly constituted what Talcott Parsons (1952) has called an "adaptive transformation." First, it overrode many of the strictures about socio-religious exclusiveness and caste endogamy that were pervasive aspects of South Asian social organization. Second, it circumvented racist-driven indigenous American barriers to intermarriage with White women. Third, it compensated for the gap which racial exclusionism created in the normal operation of the traditional Punjabi kinship system.

Until 1904, there were less than 100 Indians known to be resident anywhere in the United States. Between 1901 and 1910, 5,762 Indians legally came to American shores. The number of immigrants dropped to 1,562 in the next decade (1911–1920), further to 1,177 in the next (1921–1930) and to a mere 131 in 1931–1941. This factors out to an average of 577 Indians per year in decade one (1901–1910), 156 per year in decade two (1911–1921), 118 per year in decade three (1921–1930), and a mere 1.3 per year in decade four (1931–1941). This is a total of 8,572 tabulated from the official Immigration and Naturalization Service (INS) database. In the words of demographer S. Chandrasekhar (1944: 138), "immigration policy resorted to ... selection at first, restriction later, and finally ... exclusion."

This being said, however, these statistics do not express the entire magnitude and characteristics of the Indian population on the US West Coast. In addition to the officially recognized legal immigrants, there were many others who eluded the radar screen. Some men found ways to later bring wives in from India; most intermarried with indigenous women, as already noted, thereby increasing the overall size of the Indian community through a kind of "natural accretion" as children were born and in turn married, etc. Then came the secondary influx from Canada for already adumbrated reasons. On top of this, of course, there were inevitably uncounted and uncountable "illegals" whose numbers cannot be calculated but who undoubtedly contributed some additional demographic weight to the overall total. As Leonard observes, "[Despite impediments] men from India continued to arrive in the Imperial Valley." By 1918, she avers, "the press worried that the Hindus were becoming 'a menace' because they were no longer content to be day laborers—*they were interested in farming for themselves.* Soon, in the Imperial Valley, they began to settle into local society more permanently" (Leonard 1997: 48, emphasis added).

By 1924, 88 percent of the ranches in the Imperial Valley were being heavily farmed by Indian and other Asian tenants. In the Indian case, and no doubt in the case of other Asians as well, their ability to accept a high measure of hardship was an important factor. But just as surely, aspects of their traditional social organization were equally decisive. Indians were accustomed to functioning in "feudal" agrarian systems, employing corporate kinship structures (what in India are called *baradaris* and "joint families") as their basic productive units. By establishing extended family structures analogous to those which they had known in India through adaptive transformations (viz., intermarriages with Hispanic women and other non-Indians) they were able to establish viable productive units well suited to the manpower and cost requirements of a labor-intensive agrarian system. These assets enabled them to utilize family labor at a "no-wages" cost, pool money to lease land, and invest savings in more land. "Kinship, village relationships, and even regional origin," Jensen rightly declares, "formed the basis for living groups and for the trust upon which their business relationships developed." These solidarities enabled Indians "to prosper in a highly competitive agricultural market" (Jensen 1988: 30–40).

Most Sikhs initially settled in the Sacramento, San Joaquin, and Imperial valleys. The Imperial Valley was apparently a particular locus for the "compromise kin groups" that conjoined South Asian men with Hispanic women. The process commenced in earnest in 1916, declares Leonard. Legal South Asian immigration had been virtually terminated. An alternative source of demographic infusion was sorely required. "Mexican families displaced by the Mexican Revolution were moving across the border, finding work in cotton fields from Texas to California." This was the grassroots solution. "Thus, the labor markets and the Punjabi-marriage networks developed in tandem, from El Paso, Texas, to California's Imperial Valley. One marriage to a Punjabi led to others ..." (Leonard 1997: 48–49). Networks sprang into existence. Wages ranged between $1.20 and $1.30 per day for agricultural labor, wood-cutting, land-clearing and laying railroad track. The Sikhs, being sons of the soil, obviously preferred farming, were good at it, and constantly searched for ways to acquire parcels of cultivable land on a rental or ownership basis. The latter rarely proved possible, at least at the outset, but leasing arrangements, often by small groups, proved to be more feasible. "Many became successful farmers, and leases recorded in the county courthouse show many Punjabi farmers and partnerships, some of them linking the more numerous Sikhs with Muslims and Hindus" (ibid.: 49).

Here aspects of the Sikhs' traditional social organization gave them an edge, especially as they migrated southward into the Imperial Valley. Having entered the region as lemon-pickers and ranch hands, the Sikhs progressively turned to farming when Anglo farmers proved to be less adaptable to the ecosystem and agrarian structure that existed there in the first decades of the twentieth century. White ranchers were cultivating land in a semi-arid environment by leasing plots to small cultivators who faced very narrow margins between resource inputs and market returns. It was in effect a de facto share-cropping operation. Combined with the physical hardships of eking out an existence under these circumstances, most Anglo farmers proved unable to make the grade. In a sense, this was the opening that Punjabi farmers hoped for. Unable to purchase land outright, they were able to acquire de jure and de facto rental and leasing opportunities that gave them access to cultivable land on an entrepreneurial basis. Their skills and adaptability did the rest.

Jensen cites the case of a Professor E.E. Chandler who taught chemistry at Occidental College and bought a ranch in 1909 at Brawley. He rented it to what he called "Euro-American" farmers and lost money. He concluded that the area was suitable only for Asian workers and declared: "I do not believe the Imperial Valley is a white-man's country and am willing to hand it over to the Hindus and the Japanese" (Jensen 1988: 36).

Although some Sikhs returned to India and invested their profits in their home region, most stayed on and became small-scale agricultural entrepreneurs. Others, of course, in time, exceeded the "small-scale" label, and became quite well off. Between them, which is the point of this study, they created "socio-economic beachheads" in White-dominated California, and to a lesser but not inconsiderable extent in Washington, Oregon, Texas, Arizona, and other Western states as well, which in turn provided an important resource base upon which political representation could gradually evolve. The upshot is that Punjabi immigrants along the Pacific coasts of America and Canada were able, against all odds, to achieve a critical mass of resources and numbers, whereby they could organize and mobilize to defend themselves against hostile Whites in their immediate grassroots environments, against racist-driven local governments seeking to deprive them of access to agricultural land and established domesticity, and, in the end, even against state and national governments that sought to exclude them. Ultimately, their presence and staying power, however tenuous at first, became unbeatable.

As Leonard (1997: 82–83) puts it, "The Punjabi men formed local organizations which typically bridged the lines of religion in rural and urban California." They also "formed statewide political organizations ... loosely based on religion or regional origin." The latter were focused on the Indian freedom movement (i.e., anti-colonialism) and demands for civil rights in their adopted country.

As their socio-economic base expanded, Indians showed up in all corners of California. According to the 1919 census, Indians occupied more than 80,000 acres of land in California, 52 percent of this in the Sacramento Valley. The Death Index of the California Department of Health showed wide dispersal of Sikh farmers as well. Between 1905 and 1929, it listed 258 persons with the surname "Singh." They died in 29 counties, indicating that "many went their own way" after reaching California, "and lived away from the majority of their countrymen" (Jensen 1988: 33). This was probably the tip of the iceberg since so many Punjabis had intermarried with mainly Mexican-American women and altered their surnames and other aspects of their identity—or at least their offspring did—to reflect their assimilation into the American agrarian subcultural environment. In time, of course, with education and the adoption of middle-class life-styles, it led to penetration of the urban social environments as well.

Leonard published an extremely insightful study of the Indians' grassroots adaptation to American life which she entitled "Pioneer Voices from California: Reflections on Race, Religion and Ethnicity."[5] In addition to publicly accessible statistical data, Leonard undertook detailed interviews with 65 informants. These included "a few members of the dominant Anglo culture and Punjabi men, their Hispanic and other non-Punjabi wives, and their sons and daughters, most of whom were called 'Mexican Hindus'" (Leonard 1997: 121). Most of the couples lived and worked in the Imperial Valley. This is where the majority of the mixed marriages took place (see Table 3.1), no doubt because of the region's propinquity to Mexico and the Hispanic population which had long populated the American Southwest. Among the 378 spouses she culled from the entirety of her data, she learned that 304 (80.4 percent) were Hispanic, 48 (12.7 percent) were Anglo, 15 (4.0 percent) were Black, 9 (2.4 percent) were Indian, and 2 (0.5 percent) were American-Indian. Clearly, the racial barrier remained in place.

It was, as already noted, the general practice to refer to the Indians as "Hindus" in spite of the fact that the overwhelming majority were Sikhs. Some also called them "Mexican Hindus" because of the extent to which they had intermingled with Hispanic culture by acquiring Mexican wives and themselves learned Spanish. Clearly this was a by-product of cultural ignorance,

**Table 3.1**
**Spouses of Asian Indians in California, 1913–1949**

| Counties | American | | Hispanic | | Anglo | | Black | | Indian | | Total | |
|---|---|---|---|---|---|---|---|---|---|---|---|---|
| | No. | % | No. | % | No. | % | No. | % | No. | % | No. | % |
| Yuba/ Sacramento/ San Joaquin | 45 | 50.6 | 25 | 28.1 | 9 | 10.1 | 8 | 9.0 | 2 | 2.3 | 89 | 23.6 |
| Fresno/ Tulare/ Kings | 38 | 76.0 | 11 | 22.0 | 0 | 0 | 1 | 2.0 | 0 | 0 | 50 | 13.2 |
| Imperial/ Los Angeles/ San Diego | 221 | 92.5 | 12 | 5.0 | 6 | 2.5 | 0 | 0 | 0 | 0 | 239 | 63.2 |
| Total | 304 | 80.0 | 48 | 12.7 | 15 | 4.0 | 9 | 2.4 | 2 | 0.5 | 378 | 100.0 |

*Source:* Leonard (1997: 51, Table 2.1).

which, incidentally, few of the Punjabis bothered to contest. Almost none of the wives converted to Sikhism or any other Indian religion. "Almost all of the men," Leonard (1997: 126) says, "allowed or actively encouraged their children to be brought up Christians." Fathers did, however, encourage their children to take an interest in their Indian cultural heritage, but the problem was that most were uneducated and were compelled to work long hours in the fields. There were no religious specialists among them to provide systematic spiritual input. The result was that religious indoctrination was left to wives who were Hispanic Catholics. There were exceptions, however. The farther Indians were from the Imperial Valley, the less the proportion of Hispanic wives and the more often one found spouses who were Anglo and even Indian. The more this was so, the greater was the tendency for the father's religion and culture to be emphasized. "In the northern and central valleys, where Anglo and Black wives diluted the Hispanic domestic culture characteristic of life in the Imperial Valley, and where the few real Indian wives lived, one heard slightly more about Indian beliefs and practices" (ibid.: 127). These latter tended to view "hispanized families" with disdain. Even in the Imperial Valley, Leonard declares, households with Anglo and Indian wives looked down upon those with Hispanic spouses (ibid.: 127).

On the whole, however, the Punjabis who settled in America experienced a social-organizational meltdown as far as traditional caste and kinship standards were concerned. The internal differentia that characterized caste society in India lost much of their saliency in the crucible of American egalitarianism. This was especially evident not only in their marital decisions but in many other lifestyle choices as well. Cross-ethnic marriages, says Leonard, "simply reflected the men's decision not to return to India and the families they may have had there" (Jensen 1988: 52). The net outcome was that the West Coast South Asians were transformed from a "caste community" on the Indian model to an ethnic category on the American model. The critical factors were the decision of immigrant Sikh men to implicitly forsake *haq shuda* by adopting exogenous marriages, and their abandonment of the ritual orthodoxies that ordered social interaction in their homeland. Thus, "the Punjabi-Mexican families formed a distinctive community," which outsiders labeled "Hindu" or "Mexican-Hindu" (ibid.: 53). One important consequence of this internal homogenization process is that the religious basis of cultural identity be-came, as we shall see, secondary to a primarily politicized form of ethnic identity.

## Notes

1. Many of the decisive battles between incoming invaders and indigenous polities occurred at a place called Panipat, well inside the Punjab, north of Delhi. This seemed to be the point at which the force-levels on both sides reached their "critical mass" and resulted in a final military showdown. Years ago, two young Englishman, recent graduates from Oxford, and off on their world tour, whom I met aboard a P&O liner en route to India in 1959, upon reading about this interesting historical phenomenon, remarked, "One gets the distinct impression that every new invader sent a message down to Delhi saying, 'I'll meet you in the usual place!'"

2. Ranjit Singh ascended to political power at Lahore in the Punjab in 1799, having been confirmed in that position by Shah Zaman during his last visit there in 1798. At the age of 19, his charisma, political acumen and military skills enabled him within a short time to establish a Sikh state north of the Sutlej River, which by 1809 included Ludhiana and Amritsar and by 1834 embraced Multan, Kashmir, Ladakh and, Peshawar. Primarily as a result of his wise decision to limit his conquests and his control within the parameters of British East India

Company power to his south and Afghanistan to his north, his state survived until his death in 1839. Ranjit Singh's principal instrumentalities of conquest and consolidation were in part his highly disciplined army, officered and trained by European military specialists, and in part by his genius for practicing a type of consensual politics that accommodated the diverse interests and ethno-cultural characteristics of the Muslims, Hindus, Buddhists, and other groups who inhabited his realm. His army, of no less than 75,000 soldiers, was built into a highly disciplined force. In the words of Smith et al. (1958: 14), "These forces constituted the material strength of the Sikh power and as long as they held together and were capably led, they had no superior in the sub-continent." In political terms:

> The Panjab state was neither a traditional Indian territorial state and monarchy, nor merely a dictatorship of one community over another. They were... the leading partners in the state.... There was an element of partnership with other communities, even if it was only subordinate partnership, and included the Muslims as well as various kinds of Hindus (ibid.: 613).

3. Leonard refers to Harold S. Jacoby (1958).
4. Leonard obtains these statistics from Harold S. Jacoby (1958: 35–40).
5. Published as Chapter 5 of Barrier and Dusenbery (1989).

# 4 The Politicization of Punjabi Immigration

Through World War II, the number of Indians from all sources residing in the United States and Canada probably never exceeded 10,000 in either country. In the American case, despite their relative paucity of numbers compared to other ethnic minorities, it was nevertheless sufficient, given their concentration in fairly compact demographic pockets along the West Coast, and a few Eastern cities, especially New York, Chicago, Detroit, Philadelphia, and Washington, to provide an ethnically structured base of operations for the numerous proponents of Indian freedom and civil rights who either rose directly from their ranks or entered the fray after reaching America's shores as students, lecturers, religious figures, businessmen, journalists, or even in quasi-diplomatic capacities. This was the case because, in spite of the fact that the West Coast Indians were by and large workers and peasants who had experienced a high measure of assimilation into their cultural surroundings, significant numbers of them had nevertheless, as much out of necessity as by conviction, retained a significant measure of ethnic self-consciousness to enable them to socially assert themselves.

Unquestionably, White racism was the crucial variable here. It had placed implicit limits on how far assimilation could proceed. In the last analysis, it left Indians no alternative but to cling to some semblance of who they were culturally and historically. This hierarchically structured sense of "difference" between Indians and Whites kept issues in play that otherwise in time probably would have almost entirely dissipated. Along with the Indians' growing economic viability, it set the stage for increasingly organized confrontation and conflict between them and Whites over several crucial issues, among the most important of which were, of course, immigration and citizenship rights in America, plus nationalism and British colonialism in India. In the American and Canadian contexts, "being Hindu," says Leonard, "meant politics more than religion, for the men had a passionate interest in both U.S. and Indian politics." So much so, she declares, that "They took their wives and children to political rallies where Syed Hossain and Madame Pandit, and other figures from the Indian independence movement spoke" (Leonard 1997: 57).

Immigration and citizenship rights progressively became the defining issues for grassroots Indians on the West Coast, and indeed throughout America where Indians were concentrated in any number. It was the portal through which all the other strands of dissent and mobilization entered the mix and gave some measure of coherence to the Indians' quest for a dignified and legally secure place in American society. The simple fact was that America, like Canada, was a racist society. Indeed, when viewed in the larger historical context, it was undoubtedly more so. Whites had a pure and simple aversion to dark-skinned people. Most Indians were "colored," had a different "look" (turbans and beards), had "strange" social and religious customs, spoke incomprehensible languages, and, perish the thought, hailed from a British colony that ranked low in the hierarchy of imperial esteem. On top of this, there were the objections of Caucasian blue-collar workers with whom the incoming Indians competed in the labor market, something which the conservative labor unions left no stone unturned to exploit by invoking racism. Also, there was the pernicious role being played by the imperial authorities, who were anxious about the politically disruptive feedback implications of large numbers of ordinary Indians becoming "infected" with the democratic doctrines and practices prevalent in open societies such as Canada and the United States. They did not want Indian immigrants to come here in large numbers and "get ideas" which might snowball into "sedition" (i.e., demands for political freedom) back in India, especially among Sikhs, who along with the Gurkhas formed the backbone of Britain's colonial armies. The lengths to which authorities were prepared to go to keep tabs on and, where possible, subvert South Asians' efforts to politically mobilize and assert their civil rights would, as we shall see, assume dramatic proportions.

In Canada, and later in the United States, the Sikhs, with their distinctive turbans and beards, who formed the bulk of this new immigrant population, were highly "socially visible" in ways that distinguished them both from Africans and Orientals. They were commonly labeled "rag heads." With their physical appearance, along with their rustic life-style and vibrant Punjabi culture, they came to incarnate in the eyes of White Canadians and subsequently in the eyes of White Americans as well, still another breed of dark-skinned, alien intruders into the imagined pristine purity of their Caucasian-Christian social world. As had been the case with their East Asian predecessors, British Columbian society (and subsequently all of Canadian society) mobilized to try and halt this latest influx of brown-skinned outsiders and do whatever possible to make life as unpleasant and tenuous as possible for those who had already gained entry.

British Columbian authorities faced a particularly vexing dilemma as they searched for ways to exclude Indians. India was a member of the British Commonwealth. Indians were therefore technically British subjects, legally entitled to all the rights and privileges associated with this status. This included the legal right to emigrate wherever they wished within the Commonwealth without being discriminated against on the basis of race, religion or ethnicity. Devising means to exclude them required especially elaborate and devious subterfuges and collusion between Vancouver, Ottawa, London, and Calcutta. This was accomplished by the time-tested method of creating draconian rules and regulations that excluded Indians while not explicitly ordaining that Indians *qua* Indians were the targets of such measures. "Legal restriction," says Jensen, "based on a social rather than a racial characteristic was a favorite of moderates who hoped to avoid conflict between the peoples of different cultures attracted to the same areas by the pull of the international labor market" (Jensen 1988: 10).

By 1908, as racist-driven machinations were rapidly falling into place, there were officially 5,179 Indians in Canada, plus an uncounted and uncountable number who were there as illegal aliens. According to Emily Brown, 6,656 South Asian Indians had been admitted into the United States by 1913 (Brown 1986: 41). Johnston contends that by 1913 there were "three times as many Sikhs in the United States as in Canada, but this is a doubtful figure in the light of data compiled by Chandrasekhar (1944), Brown (1986) and others, at least as far as legal immigration is concerned.

Inevitably, as the numbers grew, racial prejudice, repression and exclusion gradually caused simple economic interest to merge with crystallizing ethnic self-consciousness and consequent intensified political awareness. Attempts at exclusion and deportation started the political ball rolling, as it were. One kind of backlash led to another!

The battle commenced in Canada with the British Columbia State Legislature passing several ordinances designed to prevent the hiring of "Orientals" in certain industries and restricting their immigration. However, since human rights in Canada were framed under Anglo-Saxon law, and since Canada had a democratic constitution and open political system, laws designed to bar immigration and deprive South Asians of their civil rights never went unchallenged. A number of Sikhs, for example, who were convicted of illegal entry under the 1908 Immigration Act successfully got their convictions vacated through habeas corpus writs. This in itself shows that in the short span of years since Indian immigration began, South Asians had already achieved enough solvency and social cohesion to successfully employ the legal system to fight for their rights. Outcomes like this impelled the Canadian government to appeal directly to the Government of India for some kind of relief. This in turn brought to the forefront the matter of the civil rights to which all members of the British Commonwealth were purportedly entitled. There was clear ambivalence about this, which drove the British Columbian White establishment to seek ways to circumvent principle in the service of expediency in the case of South Asians, and in turn drove the South Asian victims of this obfuscation to seek redress both by legal and political means.

The ambivalent feelings about Commonwealth status were apparent all the way to the top. Sir Wilfred Laurier, the Prime Minister from 1896 to 1911 raised the issue himself, when he initially expressed doubts as to whether British subjects of any race could be excluded from Canada. He later backed away from this position under pressure from British Columbian Whites, and also when "the government of British India ... were afraid that Indian nationalists would find a way to exploit the issue" (Johnston 1979: 4). So, in the end, Laurier resorted to the widely asserted allegation that Indians were "unsuited to live in the climatic conditions of British Columbia and were a serious disturbance to industrial and economic conditions in portions of the Dominions."[1] Sir Wilfred told the British Viceroy, Lord Minto: "Strange to say, the Hindus ... are looked upon by our people in British Columbia with still more disfavor than the Chinese." This was because "They seem to be less adaptable to our ways and manners than all the other Oriental races that come to us" (Quoted by Singh and Singh [1966] from Morse [n.d.]). A strange conclusion indeed in the light of his original position, and the Indians' recently proven ability to successfully enough "adapt" to the legal system by employing the mechanism of habeas corpus!

Predictably, the British-run government of India pledged to do whatever it could to oblige their Canadian brethren. This was a vivid example of the moral bankruptcy of colonialism. You had the spectacle of the Government of India, which was constitutionally obliged to see to the welfare of its own citizens, colluding with a fellow Commonwealth government that was determined to deny one group of these citizens the civil and human rights to which they were formally entitled! The Government of India responded, in fact, by issuing warnings to potential immigrants that there was no employment available in Canada (a lie, of course) and by ordering steamship companies to stop advertising travel accommodations and economic opportunities there. They also "invoked the provisions of the Emigration Act (XXI of 1883), originally passed to safeguard the interests of indentured labor. Under the Act, emigration was only allowed to countries which had passed legislation to protect the interests of emigrants and were listed in the schedule" (Singh and Singh 1966: 7). However, since Canada was not listed in the schedule and had no wish to encourage Indian immigration, even for the sake of "limiting" it, it was unwilling to pass the legislation to which Act XXII applied. The Canadians had, in short, hoist themselves by their own racist petard!

In its quest to circumvent the moral issues, the Canadian government turned to further subterfuges. In 1908, two Orders-in-Council were passed (and incorporated into the Immigration Act of 1906 by amendment) which ordained that Indians would be admitted into the country only when they met two conditions: (1) They must have come straight from India on a single direct ticket, and (2) upon arrival they must show officials that they had in their possession at least $200 in cash. These rules proved not only to be offensive to Indians in and of themselves, but also in terms of the invidious comparisons they evoked vis-à-vis other immigrant groups. "The 'continuous journey' regulation," says Harish Puri, "had no relevance to the immigration from China and Japan because direct steamships from ports in both these countries to Western Canada had been running for a long time." Moreover, the authorities "were also fully aware that the requirement of 200 dollars imposed on Indians was discriminatory because that did not apply to the Japanese who were covered by 'treaty right'" (Puri 1983: 30). Chinese and Japanese immigrants, pointedly, needed only $20 to meet this qualification!

The first requirement was obviously an outright gimmick designed to make entry for Indians into Canada virtually impossible on any account for the simple reason that no ships sailed directly from India to Canada, and direct tickets were therefore unavailable from anywhere. Lord Minto concluded that these measures "are likely to prove effective" and reassured the Canadian Premier that British imperialism was firmly on Canada's side. "We raised no objections to the methods adopted by Canada," said he, "and we have no intention of raising any questions regarding them" (Singh and Singh, 1966: 8; Morse n.d.: 40–41).

In March 1908, the first test of the new Orders-in-Council was set in motion. The ship *Monteagle* arrived in Vancouver port with 200, mostly Sikh, passengers aboard. Eighteen who had caught the ship in Hong Kong were summarily refused entry because they had not come directly from India as the law now stipulated. Another 105 were turned back, even though they had boarded the *Monteagle* at Calcutta, on the grounds that they could not prove they were the actual persons who had originally purchased the tickets issued in Calcutta. Among these passengers were, however, Balwant Singh and Bhag Singh, who, accompanied by their wives and children, would prove to be an early test case for the newly honed directives and the efforts of the Sikh community to challenge them. A detailed account of the relevance of these two men to the wider politicization process will be presented at a later point in our narrative. For the present it is sufficient to note their presence on the *Monteagle* in Vancouver Harbour in 1911.

Bhag Singh was the president and Balwant Singh the priest of the Vancouver *gurdwara*. Balwant Singh had returned to India in 1909 and Bhag Singh in 1910 for various business reasons, but also with the intention of attempting to return to Canada with their wives and children, clearly in order to test immigration policy. With their families in tow, the two men left Calcutta in 1911, seeking to obtain passage back to Canada from Rangoon or Hong Kong after their attempt to do so from Calcutta failed to pan out. Attempting at one point to try and get back via America—through the "side door," as it were—they were refused entry at San Francisco and Seattle. Later that year they were back in Hong Kong, where Bhag Singh's wife gave birth to a child which had been conceived during their travels. Significantly, "Their attempts to enter at American ports had been supported and publicised by Taraknath Das and other agitators and Indians in North America *who were well aware of their situation*," says Johnston (1979: 10, emphasis added). (As with the other parties in this saga, Taraknath Das will be more precisely identified in due course.)

Finally, at Hong Kong they managed to get passage aboard the *Monteagle* along with the other South Asian passengers already aboard after receiving assurances that a delegation to Ottawa led by Teja Singh, a prosperous Sikh entrepreneur (also to be described presently) had persuaded the Minister of the Interior to permit the entry of wives and children of admissible Sikh males. Teja Singh's alleged achievement proved to be chimerical. When *Monteagle* reached Vancouver, says Johnston, "The two men, having been in Canada before, were landed." Their wives and offspring, however, "were detained and ordered deported, and released on $2,000 bail pending an appeal to the Minister" (ibid.: 12).

This confrontation between the Canadian immigration authorities, representing White society, and the now demographically significant Sikh/South Asian community was noteworthy for what it revealed about the nascent political process that was taking place among the latter. Put simply, they were acquiring some political clout. Despite representations by various White groups, like the Women's National Council, "claiming to represent 400 local women, and the Ministerial Association of Vancouver, both opposed to the admission of Indian women" (ibid.: 13), plus the bulk of the labor unions and the local politicians, enough commotion was generated by the emerging South Asian activists to force the government to back down. A CID agent, William Hopkinson, who, as we shall see, became a major player in the attempt to thwart Indian political aspirations, recommended that the wives and children of Balwant and Bhag Singh be allowed to land, while making it clear that this was a one-time concession made to important religious figures in the community. It was regarded as a tactical maneuver whose purpose was to neutralize the radicals by taking the steam out of their agitation. As part of this "gentlemen's agreement," the two men took their case to the Supreme Court, where, in the face of this challenge, the Immigration Department "relented" and permitted the women to remain in Canada "as an act of Grace, without establishing a precedent" (House of Commons debate 1912 No. 2457, cited by Singh and Singh 1966: 11). Less well-connected Sikhs, of course, suffered a very different fate. Families were shattered and hopes of a stable domestic life in the New World were dashed. Over the ensuing two years, only five wives, one mother and 13 children were allowed to disembark. These cases undoubtedly undermined the structural linkages between some immigrants and their kin groups in India, and in the end undoubtedly paved the way for some biethnic marriages.

However, Johnston declares, this outcome did not defuse the anger and discontent in the Sikh community because "the issue had already dragged on for six months and in the meantime Bhag Singh, Balwant Singh, and their friends had cut into the ranks of the conservatives and uncommitted" (Johnston 1979: 13). Tensions escalated further when in the summer of 1913 a Sikh revolutionary name Balwant Singh Jakh slipped by immigration officials and managed to linger in the country for weeks while the authorities tried to deport him. He was an effective speaker and "began lecturing at weekly meetings in the *gurdwara*, urging his listeners to adopt the *Bande Mataram* ... greeting of the Bengali extremists as a mark of unity with other Indians" (ibid.: 17). In this atmosphere, a Japanese liner named *Panama Maru* docked in Victoria on October 17 with 56 Indians on board. After prolonged litigation between the lawyers for the immigrants and the immigration authorities, the chief justice ruled that the orders-in-council were flawed and ordered the release of all of the Sikhs except four that were rejected on medical grounds. But even they "ran away after they were brought back to the immigration Hall" (ibid.: 21). Eventually, this led to the final ordinance which barred all skilled and unskilled laborers of any race or nationality from landing in British Columbia. The Canadians had used a sledge-hammer to kill a fly!

The Bhag Singh/Balwant Singh, Balwant Sigh Jakh and *Panama Maru* incidents had been setbacks. But the Canadian authorities were undaunted. They immediately rushed back to the drawing board, and concocted the fateful rule that all "artisans or laborers, skilled or unskilled" regardless of place of origin were prohibited from entering Canada "at any port of British Columbia." This language did the job, of course, because "Orientals" alone entered Canada through British Columbia. Since the Japanese "were exempted by virtue of a 'Gentlemen's Agreement' with their Government," and the rule "was not invoked in the case of the Chinese ... the Canadian Government again succeeded in discriminating against the Indians without having to use the word" (PC 2642 of 1913 and PC 23624 of 1914, cited by Singh and Singh 1966: 12, fn. 19). In Singh and Singh's (1966: 12) words, "This time the door to Canada was firmly shut and bolted with a notice in invisible ink reading 'Only Indians not allowed' printed on the outside."

Even in the face of this seemingly insurmountable wall of obstructionism, Indian resistance nevertheless persisted. Racism was, in fact, a made-to-order recipe for sharpening political consciousness among the Pacific Coast East Asian immigrant communities. Speaking of this transition, Adhikari declares: "[Punjabis] settled on the Pacific Coast ... were working mostly in the lumber industry. Most of them were nonpolitical in the beginning; but their own difficulties abroad, the refusal of the Canadian authorities to allow any further immigration, the refusal of permission to ships carrying Indian emigrants to land in Canadian ports, etc., soon brought them to the realization that these arose because India was a colony of the British imperialists and not an independent nation" (Foreword by G. Adhikari, in Josh 1970: viii). As Johnston (1979: 6) declares, the Sikhs "were mostly peaceful men .... Yet they were aware of Canadian hostility, and they saw evidence of persecution, not just in the immigration law which prevented their friends and relatives from entering the country, or in the speed with which the British Columbia provincial assembly moved to deny them their right to vote, but in their daily encounters with the authorities." Racism was fueling anti-colonialism and nationalism. Their treatment laid the foundation for eventually enlisting their overseas support for the nascent freedom movement in India, including the soon-to-be created Ghadr Party.

Driven by the increasing restiveness in the Sikh community, leadership emerged when it was needed. This leadership came from both within and outside their ranks. By the second decade of the century, enough Sikhs had acquired sufficient material well-being to contribute time and money to organized legal and political resistance to White bigotry. Moreover, in Johnston's (1979: 7) words, "In British Columbia and other colonies overseas, Sikh emigrants mixed with men who attacked British rule and preached revolution—men who could not return to India for fear of the police and who waged war from abroad." Another thing that was going for the Sikhs and other South Asians both in Canada and the United States was that these were countries with viable, independent judiciaries and open polities which provided scope both for the legal redress of grievances and collective action. It was this that enabled Balwant and Bhag Singh to generate public support and successfully employ habeas corpus to get their wives and children off the *Monteagle*.

Typical of emerging indigenous Sikh leadership was "Professor" Teja Singh from Amritsar. Teja Singh arrived in Canada in 1908 and instantly caught the imagination of his fellow Sikhs. He is a type-case of how indigenous political leaders evolved in Canada and subsequently in the United States as well. He was born in 1878 in the small village of Balawali located about 60 miles from the birthplace of Ranjit Singh and his great general, Hari Singh Nalwa. Although of peasant stock, Teja Singh's kin group had found their way into the professions, in part through service to the Sikh state. His father was a physician and surgeon, and Teja Singh received a good education. Despite a phase of youthful indiscretion which caused his father for a time to cut off his allowance, Teja Singh eventually returned to the straight and narrow path and completed his education, obtaining an M.A. in English and an LL.B. Part of his maturing process involved a moral transformation inspired by Swami Vivekananda. "He read and re-read," says Saint Nihal Singh (1909: 109), "until the great truths of the master were seared into his soul." The next step in his regenerative process was to come to terms with his identity as a Sikh. This occurred following a few desultory years of practicing law and working in government service, when he decided to pursue a career in education. He offered his services to Khalsa College and was appointed Vice-Principal and Senior Professor of English Language and Literature, and also Superintendent of the Boarding House attached to the institution.

Until then, he declared, his education had been strictly secular, a Sikh in name only. All this changed at Khalsa College. "Within his soul was born the desire to lead the spiritual life .... He was uplifted into a sphere of love, devotion and service and thus converted, he was baptized a Sikh ..." (Singh 1909: 108). Until then his name was actually Niranjan Singh Mehta, but, with the baptism that was administered by Sant Attar Singh, his name was changed to Teja Singh. His mother, wife and little son were also baptized with him. Afterwards, he pledged to go forth and preach the religion of Guru Nanak, "and also to study the educational systems of the occident in order to evolve a sound scheme of education for his people" (ibid.). In his view, doing so required that he journey to the West.

Departing on September 8, 1906, from Bombay to Marseille en route to America, the "born-again Sikh" tarried in London while he attended a three-month course of lectures at University College. Then, in June 1908, he sailed for America, reaching New York City on July 7, one of the few Sikhs of this era who entered the US via the East Coast. In this he was following the path which many a middle-class Indian from Bengal and other parts of Hindu and Muslim India was also beginning to follow. Not unlike the latter, once in the US he was admitted to an American academic institution, in this case Columbia University Teacher's College. He attended summer school and actually delivered two public lectures.

This opened the door to Teja Singh's next incarnation. When one of his lectures was published in a Punjabi newspaper to which Canadian Sikhs subscribed, he was invited to come to Canada. The networking process had begun! He toured Sikh communities in Vancouver, Victoria, Portland, and San Francisco before returning to New York on September 22, ostensibly to resume his studies. Less than a month later, however, he returned to Canada for good "to engage himself in uplifting his countrymen in Canada and the United States" (ibid.).

Teja Singh rapidly emerged as a major player in the cadre of leaders which the Canadian Sikh community was casting up. As his contemporary, Saint Nihal Singh put it, "He has been engaged in this [community] work ever since, labouring with a remarkable singleness of purpose" (Singh 1909: 108). Most important, he combined his ideological commitments with a not inconsiderable measure of business acumen. This was an area in which he stood apart from the general run of young migrants from the Indian middle classes. He did, however, display the organizational and activist qualities which would be characteristic of several other individuals who would indeed emerge from the pack to articulate the concerns of their fellow Indians and lead them in their struggle to achieve the social equality and respect which both Canada and America offered *in principle*, but not *in fact*, unless they were fought for.

Within months after his arrival, Teja created a vital economic resource for his and the community's undertakings by founding the Guru Nanak Mining and Trust Company. With an authorized capital of Rs 150,000, he purchased 180 acres of land for Rs 96,000. He organized the Sikh community in Victoria and acquired land to build a *gurdwara* there. In 1909, he was arranging to purchase a plot in Seattle upon which was to be built both a *gurdwara* and a Guru Nanak Home for Students. "But this is not all that he is interested in doing," exclaimed Nihal Singh. "*He is planning to organize his people and establish them on a sound religious, moral, social, educational and economic basis*" (ibid., emphasis added).

This is a crucial event because Teja Singh was an early manifestation of a different breed of migrant to the United States, viz., Indians from educated, middle-class backgrounds. They would come not across the Pacific in steerage, but across the Atlantic to New York via sojourns and stopovers in London, Paris, and other European venues. Many had explicit political agendas by the time they reached the United States, or would acquire one soon afterward. Many of them had become politicized in varying degrees before they left India, especially the Bengalis, Maharashtrians, and Punjabis who had been influenced by the emerging nationalisms in those regions. Others imbibed it during their transit through England and France en route to America. This was, of course, in marked contrast to their Punjabi Sikh brethren who preceded them. The latter were essentially peasants in search of economic opportunities in the agrarian and manual-labor domains, which was what their cultural and educational qualifications equipped them for. Teja Singh himself was clearly not radical in the strict sense of the word, but his class and educational backgrounds were typical of what was coming down the road, viz., a more educated, socially sophisticated and politically aware type of person with developed or developing activist propensities.

Teja Singh rose to prominence in 1908, shortly after his arrival in British Columbia, by playing a major role in rallying his Sikh brethren to oppose an attempt to round them up and ship them en masse to British Honduras. This undertaking was initiated, says Nand Singh Sehra, by "the Dominion Government in consultation with the Imperial and Indian Governments who decided to transport the entire Indian community to British Honduras" (Sareen 1994: 217). The authorities tried to sugar-coat the move by claiming that in Honduras the Sikhs would find a climate and an environment more compatible with what they had allegedly known back in the Punjab. Brigadier-General Swayne, the Governor and Commander-in-Chief of British Honduras, who was interviewed in Winnipeg by a reporter for the *Vancouver World* (December 11 and 14, 1908) stated that the move must be an "entirely voluntary matter with the Sikhs." General Swayne, who had served as an officer in the Army of India for 16 years, believed that he understood the psyche of Indians and enjoyed their trust and that he could therefore successfully persuade Canada's Indians to join him as "pioneers" in Honduras. He told the *Vancouver World's* correspondent, "I think my offer to them is too tempting to be refused." He aspired to be the Pied Piper of Indian extrusion from Canada!

To convince the Sikh community of the government's sincerity, two Sikhs were included in a delegation headed by J.B. Harkin, private secretary to the Minister of the Interior of the Ottawa government, along with the CID man, Hopkinson, that was sent "to see the country." They were expected to confirm Swayne's assurances that the Sikhs would make the "right choice." However, "immigration officials warned the Sikhs that if they did not go, and were found vagrant, they would be deported" (Johnston 1979: 6).

The Sikhs were neither duped nor intimidated. They saw through the scam at once, mainly due to leaders like Teja Singh. They understood that this was nothing more than a sugar-coated scheme to ethnically cleanse Canada of its Indian population. They denounced it as a policy in which the Sikhs had no voice; "the whole scheme being one-sided and shaped on false grounds .... The country of Honduras is very arid, barren and altogether an undeveloped region. There is no arrangement for artificial irrigation when there is no rain; the little water that is stored is kept for drinking purposes" (Jensen 1988: 144). Honduras was an utterly inhospitable environment both for the Sikhs' style of agriculture and for the quality of life to which they aspired. The climate was terrible. On top of this, the Indians found that the wages they could expect to receive for their labor were a fraction of what they were already earning in British Columbia. In Sehra's words, "The whole scheme was to reduce them from free laborers to the level of indentured coolies" (ibid.). The remuneration offered was $8 per month plus a packet of food stuffs worth about $4 a month; in British Columbia, on the other hand, the prevailing wage for Indian laborers was $30 per month! In the aftermath, despite the anger and frustration which the authorities felt, Swayne himself was compelled to admit that the Indians were actually better off in Canada. *"During my two days' investigation in Vancouver I have not found more than six indigent East Indians."* He concluded that "we certainly would not for a moment entertain any idea of taking away those Hindus (Indians) from British Columbia who have steady employments here, for they can earn four times as much in this country as we could offer them in British Honduras" (ibid.: 145, emphasis added).

Then what was this maneuvering all about? In the process of rejecting the Honduras proposal, things were said that revealed with remarkable clarity what was really bothering the imperial establishment. *It was the fear that Indians living in open societies like Canada and the United States were undergoing social and ideological changes which had revolutionary implications for the perpetuation of British rule in India!* The British were eagerly searching for ways to prevent such Indians from "getting ideas."

As far as British Columbian Sikhs and other Indians were concerned, it was their *prosperity*, rather than their *poverty* and "inadequate cultural sophistication," that was the real cause for concern. Improving life-styles, education and economic development were eroding caste differentiation, Swayne declared, which was enabling the Indians to achieve a higher order of political unanimity. He noted how the "speedy elimination of caste in this Province" is evident *"by the way all castes help each other."* In fact, said the *Vancouver World* (December 14, 1908) reporter, "this elimination of caste was looked upon by the Governor as one of those grave issues which resulted from the familiarity with whites acquired by East Indians in countries heavily populated with white people" (Jensen 1988: 145, emphasis added). This was the real basis for Swayne saying he was "unalterably opposed to the deportation of any East Indians indigent or otherwise, *as this would aggravate the situation in India."* "These men go back to India," Swayne continued, "and preach ideas of emancipation which if brought about would upset the machinery of law and order." While conceding that "emancipation may be a good thing at some future date," it was already proving to be "too premature" under present circumstances (ibid.: 145–46, emphasis added).

Teja Singh, who had from the start preached a doctrine of community solidarity which helped his fellow Sikhs mount effective resistance to the Honduras scheme, had come to exemplify the social developments that the Imperial authorities at all levels feared. One can say that his success "smoked out" the bottom-line agenda of British rule in India, which the budding nationalists increasingly came to refer to as *"Divide et Impera"* (Divide and Rule)!

What counted most was a level of political awareness born from exposure to the new forms of political ideology associated with rapidly accelerating Westernization. Revolutionary doctrines inspired by the emerging radical movements in Europe (which included terrorism) were finding their way into India and entering the minds of the country's youth—especially in those regions, like Bengal, Maharashtra, and Punjab, which had long histories of political unrest. In the cities and towns, which were the principal loci of radicalism, were to be found, in Sareen's words, "mostly educated young men who believed fanatically that ... constitutional methods for achieving concessions—political, social and economic—from the British were ineffective ..." (Sareen 1994: 2). Increasing numbers of these politically restive students, as well as more mature revolutionaries, were finding ways to emigrate to America via England, France, and Japan, ostensibly in search of modern education and occupations but also in search of opportunities to pursue radical nationalism beyond the reach of the British imperial apparatus and its agents. Gradually these nascent activists and revolutionaries connected with the South Asian immigrant peasantry on the Pacific Coast who were struggling for economic survival against racial bigotry and denial of their civil rights. This convergence became, as we shall see, a vital aspect of the social nexus that would ultimately make the "India Lobby" possible.

By the second half of the first decade of the twentieth century, Teja Singh was by no means the only activist of note moving among the Sikh immigrants on both sides of the border. This was fortunate because in the aftermath of the *Monteagle* affair Teja Singh had lost much of his political legitimacy among the Canadian Sikhs and had returned to India. By then, there were already a number of activists at work in the South Asian grassroots movement; and most of these were far more radical in their political orientation. There were Taraknath Das and Har Dayal, both of whom, as we shall see, became major players in the confrontations that were to come. Guran Dutta Kumar was another who entered the fray. Hailing from Bannu in the Northwest Frontier Province, he had been a photographer's apprentice in Rawalpindi who gravitated to Calcutta where he became an instructor in Hindi and Urdu. He stayed in a boarding house at Maratha College where he met Taraknath Das, who radicalized him. With the latter's encouragement and help he was able to migrate to Victoria in 1907, where he set up a grocery store. With this foot in the economic door, Kumar then had enough resources to move into Vancouver, where in 1909 he established Swadesh Sevak House (Service to Country), "a meeting place and shelter for revolutionaries masked as a night school in English and mathematics for Sikh immigrants" (Johnston 1979: 8).

Still another activist was Chagan Vairaj Varma, who had entered Canada in 1910 and had "eclipsed" Teja Singh by 1913. He hailed from Mahatma Gandhi's home state, Porbandar. He was an older man, already 48 when he entered Canada, and had lived for several years in Japan before coming to the New World, after encountering unspecified "financial trouble" and "absconding" to Honolulu under the name of Husain Rahim. From there he made his way to Vancouver, "with a first-class rail ticket to Montreal." Upon returning to Vancouver, Rahim went into business and petitioned to remain in the country; instead he was arrested and ordered deported. He fought the deportation order in the courts and won despite determined efforts by Hopkinson and others to prevent it. Rahim established the Canada India Supply & Trust Company, which traded in suburban real estate. "His clients were Sikh mill-workers, and like other Hindu businessmen—storekeepers and contractors—who had set up shop in Vancouver, he had a stake in the community" (Johnston 1979: 9).

Another "moderate" on the Jagjit Singh model who achieved some measure of importance was Dr Sundar Singh, who originally gained access to Canada via Halifax in 1909. After reaching Vancouver he had founded an English language newspaper called *Aryan* that had a brief existence in 1911. He also established an organization called the Hindustanee Association, "of which he seemed to be the only member" (ibid.: 11). This is an interesting point, in fact, because it was standard procedure for Indian activists in this era to create on-the-spot organizations, regardless of how small and tenuous, as a means of affording themselves some sort of political legitimacy. At times there was almost a "Wizard of Oz" quality to it. The rationale was clearly that if you were the president or secretary of a named organization, you could then claim standing as a leader. In another instance, Sunder Singh teamed up with a Presbyterian missionary named L.W. Hall, who had purportedly become a convert to Sikhism, and together they established the Hindu Friend Society of Victoria.

Rahim, Kumar, Taraknath Das, and Har Dayal exemplified the emerging interplay between the Sikh, Hindu and Muslim South Asians, who faced harassment on a daily basis, and the revolutionaries who could organize, publicize and lead resistance to White racism. This interplay would never be a monolith, however. The revolutionaries were "clean shaven, educated, Westernized Hindus far removed in outlook from the Sikh immigrants with whom they worked," says Johnston (1979: 11). But responsive chords were struck in many corners of the Sikh community over time, despite these differences, especially as confrontation and conflict escalated with each new outrage.[2]

Even though there admittedly never arose a single charismatic leader or organization who captured the imagination of the entire Sikh community, these four activists and many more lesser-known figures whom they attracted to their standard over the years leading up to World War I helped create an environment that heightened Sikh and South Asian political awareness and provided vital avenues for expressing their grievances.

## The *Komagata Maru*

The Honduras incident and repeated confrontations over attempted landings by new immigrants had demonstrated that the demographic weight of the South Asian presence in Canada and the US had reached a level where the machinations of scheming White bigots could not be pursued with impunity. The so-called *Komagata Maru* incident, which erupted in Vancouver and ramified across the border into the United States in 1914, was a crucial turning point in the politicization process among South Asians on both sides of the border. It occurred after the founding of the Ghadr Party in 1913 in the United States, and was indeed, as we shall see, interconnected with it. The Ghadr Party was the first revolutionary movement in modern times to be created outside India for the purpose of fomenting a military uprising within India. From the South Asian immigrants' standpoint it was a breakthrough-level convergence between Sikhs and other grassroots East Indians toiling on the West Coast on the one hand, and the incoming trickle of middle-class intellectuals with revolutionary proclivities on the other.

The *Komagata Maru* was a Japanese ship chartered by a well-to-do Sikh entrepreneur named Gurdit Singh Sarhali. The purpose was to transport a large contingent of Sikhs directly from India to Canada in order to test the "direct passage" clause of the orders-in-council before the immigration door would finally be closed by the ordinance (which followed the *Monteagle* fiasco) barring all Asian workers from entering Canada via British Columbia, which was scheduled to go into effect by June of 1914.

The career and fortunes of Gurdit Singh were a prelude to this dramatic turning point in immigrant history. Like so many of his Sikh brethren, his life began in a Punjabi agrarian family. His father, Hookam Singh, was a farmer who owned a few acres of irrigated land. This "was what Gurdit Singh knew for the first eighteen or twenty years of his life." Due to a conflict with the priest who ran the religious school in the vicinity of his village, at the age of six he left it and refused to return. Realizing by the age of 12 that he was so illiterate he could not even write a coherent letter to his father, who had gone to Malaya in search of work

**Illustration 4.1**
**Headquarters of the Hindustan Ghadr Party, San Francisco**

*Source:* Kamath 1998.

during a period of drought in the Punjab, Gurdit Singh "got hold of a primer and taught himself." Eventually he too went to Malaya, trailing after his brother who preceded him there, after he had been rejected for military service on the ground that he was too thin in the chest. There his life clearly turned around. He proved to have considerable entrepreneurial talents. "He worked for a Chinese pork-dealer in Taiping, learning Chinese and Malay in the process, and then started a dairy supplying the Sikh regiment stationed there." On the side, he imported cattle from the Punjab, "where they were cheaper," and also "made money out of railway contracts and by planting rubber." It is said that he became an influential person in the local Sikh community and was "remembered as a litigious man, frequently seen in the law courts" (Johnston 1979: 24). Clearly good preparation for what was to follow in his life!

It was while living in Singapore that a trip to Hong Kong in connection with a lawsuit turned his attention toward the plight of his fellow Sikhs who were trying to migrate to Canada. He had been compelled to set up an office in the *gurdwara* in Hong Kong, where he inevitably became "aware that here were several hundred men hanging about, desperately looking for a ship to Canada—illiterate helpless men who had been up to two years in the Far East unemployed or taking what work they could and unwilling—having mortgaged family property—to go home until they had a chance to earn good money" (ibid.: 25).

Being an older man (55 years old) and having accomplished much already, Gurdit Singh had an inspirational impact on his fellow Sikhs—both by example and through talks he gave at the *gurdwara*. Several approached him and asked them for his help. One of them was a young Hindu, Behari Lal Varma, who had unsuccessfully tried to charter a boat to transport fellow Indians to Vancouver. It was at this point that Gurdit agreed to do what he could. In effect, Gurdit made the definitive transition from businessman to political activist at this time. "He saw it as an act of patriotism which, win or lose, would win him recognition among nationalists in India; and, before he left for Singapore, he promised, however difficult it was, to get a ship on his own" (ibid.). In the process, he took on two young Sikhs as his assistants: Bir Singh from Amritsar district, and Daljit Singh from Ferozepore. The latter had been associate editor of a Sikh newspaper in Amritsar, and became Gurdit's personal secretary; Bir Singh became his assistant secretary. "They organized a passenger's committee and, on Gurdit Singh's instructions, began corresponding with the Khalsa Diwan Society in Vancouver" (ibid.).

What this shows, of course, is how far network formation had gone by 1913. Sikhs were mobilizing their resources throughout the Pacific Rim—"rag-head" Sikh peasants struggling for pennies in the backwaters of British Columbia and West Coast America were far from being the entire story.

The strategy, as noted, was to deliver a shipload of Punjabis to Vancouver and through them challenge the stipulations (the 1906 and 1910 Immigration Acts, the orders-in-council) which the Canadian government had created to thwart South Asian immigration into British Columbia. The ship would disgorge its passengers in Vancouver and then carry a cargo of lumber back to Calcutta to help defray the costs, and incidentally, also make a tidy profit for Gurdit Singh. Gurdit had gotten intimations, or at least he said he did, from his contacts with the Khalsa Diwan Society that the $200 landing fee required of each Indian immigrant would be raised by the Sikh community in British Columbia, a fact in itself indicative of the growth of the South Asians' resource base. Ultimately, he and his committee were able to charter the Japanese ship, *Komagata Maru*, for six months. The craft was a 2,900 ton freighter with a Japanese crew of 40 men. But the course leading to this outcome was by no means a walk in the park. According to Johnston, "The committee at the *gurdwara* in Hong Kong wanted the ship to start at Hong Kong," which eventually they were forced to do "because [Gurdit Singh] could not get a shipping company in Calcutta that would deal with him" (Johnston 1979: 26).

Returning to Singapore, he contacted the assistant manager of the Straits Steam Ship Company, "a Chinese he knew well." He was shown two ships, the *S.S. Hong Moh* and the *S.S. Hong Bee*, "which did not cost very much," but were "very old and unfit for a Pacific crossing." While this was going on, significantly, "he was receiving impatient messages from Daljit Singh who was trying to raise money and having problems because everyone wanted to see the ship first" (ibid.). So Gurdit returned to Hong Kong with his 7-year-old child, Balwant, in tow, all that remained of his immediate family since both his first wife and younger second wife had died. There, he tried to acquire a ship, the *Kut Sang*, through a British firm, Jordan Co., for $9,000 a month; but this fell through when at the last minute the company refused to sign the papers. "He was certain the British government was responsible for this" (ibid.). He was probably correct. Finally, he met a German shipping agent named A. Bune, "who offered him a small steamer which was being used to carry coal. Named the *Komagata Maru*, the ship had been built in Glasgow in 1890 for a German company in Hamburg and registered under the name of *Stubbenhak*. Having gone through other ownership permutations, the ship was currently owned by a Japanese company, Shinyei Kisen Goshi Kaisa, to which they had given the name, *Komagata Maru*. The cost was $11,000 per month, "the first month to be paid on signing, the second within a week; the third and fourth within two weeks; and the remainder within two months of the commencement of the charter." It was agreed that the owner would provide the captain and the crew (Johnston 1979: 27).

Due to the efforts that Gurdit and his "committee" were making to raise money and sign up passengers for $210 HK, the British authorities got on their tail and attempted to thwart the enterprise. They almost succeeded, but Jagjit had signed a contract just in the nick of time that was deemed legal.[3]

The prices they were charging for tickets were more than double that of a third-class fare on a Canadian Pacific liner from Hong Kong, but this was what circumventing the direct passage rule would cost. Singh then used the proceeds from the advanced ticket sales, and melded them with his own resources. This would follow the smaller-scale attempts which had preceded it, such as the *Monteagle* and the *Panama Maru*, the latter having also, as we saw, occurred the previous year when 39 passengers aboard had ultimately been allowed to remain in Canada after a writ of habeas corpus was upheld by the Chief Justice of the Supreme Court. Ultimately, the ship boarded a total of 376 Indians, 346 of whom were Sikhs, including wives and children. In conformity with the rule that the carrier must commence its voyage from an Indian port in order for its passengers to gain legal entry into Canada, the *Komagata Maru* would depart from Calcutta and terminate at Vancouver, making stops en route to take on mainly Sikh passengers in Hong Kong, Shanghai, Kobe, and Yokohama. It left Calcutta with 165 Sikhs aboard and picked up passengers en route. The final complement of 376 passengers was achieved by accretions at the ports of call along the way. A final group of 14 who had been left behind at Hong Kong caught up with the ship at Yokohama, making the final total of 376. When it left Kobe the *Komagata Maru* was carrying 340 Sikhs, 24 Muslims, and 12 Hindus, all Punjabis. The British decided not to meddle in the enterprise until it reached Canada. "At Hong Kong, [Gurdit Singh] ... consulted a leading firm of English solicitors who had given assurances that there was no bar to the admission of the Indian immigrants to Canada" (Singh and Singh 1966: 22).

Balwant Singh had wanted Gurdit Singh to accompany him on another liner that would enable them to reach Vancouver ahead of the *Komagata Maru*, but the passengers insisted that Gurdit remain with them. Cabins were allocated to Gurdit and his young son; to the medical officer, Dr Raghunath Singh, who was traveling with a wife and young child; a man named Sundar Singh, whose wife and two small children were accompanying him; and to the persons who had organized the voyage, Daljit Singh, Bir Singh, Harnam Singh, and Amir Muhammad Khan. "These men paid nothing extra and it was in the nature of this ship that no one complained" (ibid.: 34).

The British correctly believed that the Ghadrites had infiltrated the passengers. "At Shanghai and Moji, Gurdit Singh and his lieutenants had brought aboard bundles of the *Ghadr* [the movement's monthly newspaper] and other revolutionary literature. As the ship got underway, at gatherings aboard ship, poems from the *Ghadr* or from a revolutionary anthology, *Ghadr di Gunj*, were read, recited, explained, paraphrased, and deliberated upon" (Johnston 1979: 32). Here was further testimony to the degree of politicization which had taken place in the South Asian communities that were lapping against the shores of the New World.

The journey of these immigrants turned out to be a poignant, tragically ill-fated attempt by the Sikh and other revolutionaries to once and for all mount a decisive challenge to Canada's racist immigration policies. From the instant it set sail from Yokohama, on May 2, 1914, for the trans-Pacific leg of its voyage, the *Komagata Maru* created a public furor in Vancouver. The activism of the Sikh community in Victoria and Vancouver, along with the press and officialdom, played no small part in raising public consciousness in both camps. Balwant Singh had reached British Columbia as planned and had immediately swung into action. He addressed a meeting at the Victoria *gurdwara* on May 20 and followed this up with a similar meeting in Vancouver. When the *Komagata Maru* made landfall, Husain Rahim and Rajah Singh (the latter was secretary of the United India League in Vancouver) swung into action, revealing once again how far the Sikh community had come in organizational terms. They had learned through their lawyer, J. Edward Bird, that the orders-in-council contained a loophole which the *Komagata Maru* might be able to exploit. The port of Alberni was the only one not mentioned as a place where the landing of laborers was forbidden. Frantically they attempted to get word to the ship that this is where they should berth; but they were unsuccessful in this endeavor and the *Komagata Maru* ultimately anchored "on the far side of Burrard Inlet, opposite Vancouver" (Johnston 1979: 37).

There the ship inevitably faced a direct confrontation with Canadian immigration law. The local Member of Parliament, H.H. Stevens, a passionate opponent of East Asian immigration, obtained a renewal of the government's ban on artisans and laborers. The White population in general ardently backed Stevens and threatened to engage in the kind of violence which had occurred in 1887 and 1907. Local newspapers reported on the ship's every move, some calling it a "mounting Oriental invasion." When the ship reached Vancouver harbor, a two-month standoff ensued. On the day of her arrival, news reporters boarded her and interviewed the passengers while immigration officials were on hand

**Illustration 4.2**
**Gurdit Singh (with binoculars) aboard the *Komagata Maru* in Vancouver Harbor, May–June 1914**

*Source:* Courtesy of the Vancouver Public Library.

to undertake required screening and negotiation procedures. Interestingly, the journalists could find no evidence that these Indians
fit the ugly stereotypes by which the White racists had characterized them. A reporter for the *Vancouver Daily News Advertiser* found
the men to be in "good health," "certainly clean," "well set up
and handsome men." The *Victoria Times* correspondent noted that
most had served in the British army and "are a handsome lot ...
superior to the class of Hindus which have already come into the
province ... stand very erect and move with an alert action ... their
suits are well-pressed ... their turbans are spotlessly clean ...," and
"Most of them know a little English ... some of them converse in it
remarkably well" (cited by Singh and Singh 1966: 23).

Supporters of passengers' rights, such as the lawyer, Bird, and
the Reverend L.W. Hall from the Hindu Friend Society of Victoria
who attempted to board the vessel and commiserate with the
immigrants were turned away. Johnston (1979: 37) provides a
vivid description of the on-aboard scene after the ship moored at
Bullard Inlet:

> At dawn the passengers were out on deck, with tree-covered
> mountains rising behind them and the city across the water in
> front. They were dressed in their best with their bags packed,
> ready to go ashore. At 8 A.M. a launch came out with customs
> officials, a medical inspector, the shipping agent to whom the
> *Komagata Maru* had been consigned, and a party of immigration
> inspectors, Hopkinson and Reid at their head.

Based upon the legal advice Gurdit Singh obtained in Hong
Kong, the Indians claimed that their passage from India and their
eligibility to gain entry into Canada conformed fully to the stipulations of the 1906 and 1910 Immigration Acts. Therefore, it was
contended, there could be no legal or moral basis for denying them
entry. However, the sojourners were not allowed to disembark!
In a footnote, Singh and Singh suggest that the Hong Kong solicitors likely "did not know of the Orders-in-Council passed after
the Chief Justice [rendered] his decision in *Re. Narain Singh*" (Singh
1966: 22, fn. 27). This turned out to be the critical factor that doomed
the *Komagata Maru* enterprise. The Canadians had concocted a legal
artifice while the *Komagata Maru* was still on the high seas stipulating that even direct passage and the $200 entry fee were in effect

invalid bases for entry, thus nullifying the 1906 and 1910 Immigration Acts!

When Stevens returned from the Parliament session in Ottawa on June 14, he stated that he had strongly urged the government to develop a comprehensive immigration policy that would place control of East Indian immigration to Canada in the hands of the Government of India. He assured his constituents that authorities are absolutely determined that the law with reference to the admission of Hindus shall be strictly enforced. Then he engaged in a bit of demagoguery by blaming the victims. It was the Hindus themselves, he declared, who by their belligerent attitude in attempting to evade the regulations were the cause of the problem.

Even though the stalemate lasted for 45 days and ended with the immigrants being sent back to India, the socio-political impact was formidable. For all practical purposes the *Komagata Maru* had been "impounded" in Vancouver harbor. It could neither disgorge its human cargo nor leave Canadian waters! It sat in the harbor for eight weeks, a provocative embodiment of the simmering animosity that Canadian racism had wrought. It was an incident which is to this day remembered by politically conscious Indians everywhere as one of the early milestones in the crystallization of anti-colonialism and the struggle for human rights by South Asians in North America. It elevated political consciousness among the immigrant population to a new level.

The plot thickened in Vancouver in late June when the Ottawa government got directly involved in the stalemate. Responding to the public outcry and legal maneuvering by both sides, they decided that the passengers should be allowed to land and then test their right of entry in the courts. Predictably, H.H. Stevens immediately declared that he would oppose any such move. He claimed the landing of these "Hindus" would be more likely to cause riots than if they were left where they were. He predicted that Vancouver's citizenry would try and forcibly prevent such a landing. There were a series of "spontaneous meetings" around the city and the surrounding area; and on the night of June 29, the City Council adopted a resolution introduced by Alderman McHeath protesting the ship's passengers' landing. The Court of Appeal had reinforced the objections when it ruled on a test case on behalf of one passenger, Munshi Singh, that he could not disembark to enter Canada. The grounds were: (1) he was a native of

India and did not possess the necessary $200 landing fee; (2) he had not come to Canada on a "continuous journey" as mandated; and (3) he was an unskilled laborer. In effect, the decision of the Court of Appeal meant the end of Asiatic immigration into Canada for half a century.

Meanwhile, four activists connected with the United Hindu League attempted to board the *Komagata Maru* and commiserate with the passengers. They included Bhag Singh, head of the League, a "priest" named Balwant Singh and Rahim Singh. They were foiled in this effort, and the authorities increased their surveillance of the vessel.

When utter stalemate resulted, Gurdit Singh and his "Committee of Safety" aboard the *Komagata Maru* decided to abandon the effort and return to India. The passengers had become disenchanted with Gurdit Singh, who charged them $100 for a voyage for which the Canadian Pacific Railroad steamers charged only $65. Supplies were running low. It was costing $200 per day to maintain the passengers; a burden that was falling upon the Vancouver Sikh community; a debt of $18,000 had already been amassed. At the last minute, as the departure date approached, the passengers mutinied and took control of the ship from its captain, Yamamoto, and his crew on July 18. Yamamoto sent a letter to the Vancouver authorities asking them to help him regain control of his ship.

The Canadian authorities responded by attempting to forcibly remove the Punjabis from the *Komagata Maru*, place them aboard a British liner, the *Empress of India*, and shunt them to Hong Kong. When officials and police approached the ship aboard a tug named *Sea Lion*, "The Indians," declares Jensen "had other plans." They were armed "with bamboo poles, stoking irons, axes, swords, wooden clogs, and a few firearms," as well as "stacks of bricks and piles of concrete and scrap on the deck." They fiercely resisted. They hurled their missiles and cut the grappling hooks. "Police then turned a water hose on them." Since the *Sea Lion* was a smaller vessel, the Sikhs actually occupied the high ground, which made the missiles they hurled at their adversaries highly effective. There were 125 Vancouver policemen and 33 immigration officials aboard the *Sea Lion*, plus a contingent of local militia waiting on the wharf. Several policemen suffered cuts and bruises, "one was knocked down ... another was knocked overboard," and three

Illustration 4.3
**H.H. Stevens (center) meets the press on board the tug *Sea Lion*,
with Malcolm Reid (standing third from left) and Hopkinson
(second from right), May–June 1914**

*Source:* Courtesy of the Vancouver Public Library.

shots were allegedly fired from the *Komagata Maru's* deck. These apparently came from Harnam Singh, who allegedly retained a pistol from his military days. In 15 minutes, the battle was over when the *Sea Lion* withdrew from the fray to lick its wounds (Jensen 1988: 134).

The Vancouver Punjabi community rallied in support of their beleaguered brethren in the harbor. A meeting was convened on May 31 at Dominion Hall in Vancouver by the Khalsa Diwan Society and the United India League. It drew between 500 and 600 Indians plus around 20 Whites, along with two reporters and the ogreish Hopkinson along with his stenographer to record what was being said. Rahim chaired the meeting and Balwant Singh harangued the crowd in Punjabi. As Johnston puts it, "Even with Hopkinson there, he was pretty daring." He continues:

A man who had used some striking similes in Lahore was not going to be too careful in Vancouver. *He spoke of a changing mood in India, a return to the spirit of 1857,* a new unity against the

English, and *the inevitability of revolution if Indians did not get home rule within the next few years.* He talked about the exclusion laws in the white dominions and of the weakness of the Indian government within the Empire. Then, finishing with a reference to Sikh warriors of the past who fought three times with the English, he called on his audience for funds for the *Komagata Maru* (Johnston 1979: 40, emphasis added).

Seth Hussain Rahim spoke, as did J. Edward Bird, the lawyer who had successfully won reprieve for the 39 Sikhs in the *Panama Maru* case in 1913; and also a Socialist named Fitzgerald who "made a particularly violent attack on the racial policies of his countrymen." At one point, he cried: "Get up and arm yourselves and fight to regain your liberty. Inspire your countrymen to return and sweep all the whites from India."[4]

Rahim ran a tight meeting. After Balwant Singh finished speaking, when others wished to speak, he cut them off and declared that this was not an occasion "for talk" but for business. "What was needed was hard cash: enough to keep the ship in Vancouver ..." (ibid.).

The main reason for narrating these events is to emphasize the point that the *Komagata Maru* had taken on a symbolic significance well in excess of its purely material proportions; it produced a quantum leap in the degree of community organization and political consciousness among Indians situated along the West Coast, no more than a decade after their original arrival.

Ordinary Sikhs acting through mobilizational groups that had been steadily springing up on both sides of the border struggled to raise the $22,000 needed to take over the charter of the ship from Gurdit Singh. But this was only part of the challenge confronting them. A flow of funds was needed to meet the terms of the charter as well as to keep provisions flowing to the 350-plus passengers who were in effect marooned aboard the *Komagata Maru* while negotiations, confrontations and stalemate dragged on. Gurdit Singh appears simply to have run out of money, which meant that the Shore Committee was compelled to pick up the tab if the agitation was to continue. While this meant great hardship for the supporters ashore, it also shows that a not insignificant resource base now existed. Still, it was a finite base and this fact put pressure on the South Asians to make concessions to the authorities regarding the timing of a final legal showdown.

During this period, there was a flurry of appeals and petitions, some of which carried all the way to Ottawa and London. Even King George V refused to intervene. London basically ignored the petitioners, and endorsed whatever the Canadian government elected to do. The Government of India also unsurprisingly blatantly sided with the Canadians. Lord Hardinge noted that the *Komagata Maru's* voyage had been undertaken without the Government of India's approval and, in any event, contravened Canada's immigration laws. "He spoke of the generosity of the Canadian Government for supplying the *Komagata Maru* with $4,000 worth of provisions" for its return voyage! (Singh and Singh 1966: 24–25)

Litigation finally came to a head toward the end of June 1914. Both sides had tired of the stalemate and agreed that the way out was for a test case to be presented before the court. The government had been reluctant to litigate for fear that it might lose and then be compelled to admit the immigrants via habeas corpus. The Indians had wanted to stall as long as possible in the hope they could mount enough popular support to pressure the government into rescinding the draconian rules that barred Indian immigration into British Columbia. The compromise was that Malcolm R.J. Reid, the Vancouver immigration agent, would select two passengers to be brought from the ship where the Indians' lawyer, J. Edward Bird, would select one of the two to become a test case. This was the point at which the Munshi Singh test case was heard and resulted in a final judgment against the immigrants.

Finally, on July 23, 1914, the "hungry and humiliated immigrants" were compelled to return to their homeland. Even their outward passage was tainted by further duress and humiliation. There was a dispute to be settled over how $7,000 invested by the Sikh temple to help cover the cost of the charter would be retrieved. The Shore Committee believed it was entitled to offload cargo which the inbound ship had carried and sell it on the open market as a means of accomplishing this. It also demanded that they be allowed to send cargo back to India to be sold in order to defray expenses incurred en route. There were issues about who would provide provisions for the return voyage. This was settled when the government, in their eagerness to get rid of these troublesome adversaries, agreed to supply them, provided the Indians agreed to return at once to Hong Kong. Fifteen men from the Vancouver *gurdwara* came to verify that the provisions had indeed been provided. "They were forced to pass between troops with bayonets to inspect the provisions," declares Jensen (1988: 135). But the fact that the final act occurred in this form attests to how far the Sikh community had come in the assertion of its political presence.

At 5 pm on July 23, 1914, the *Komagata Maru* sailed out of Vancouver harbor escorted by the *Rainbow,* an old tub of a Canadian naval vessel taken out of mothballs specifically for the occasion. World War I broke out while they were at sea. What awaited them in Calcutta was in some respects a more horrendous fate than the one they had just experienced in the New World. These dauntless pioneers had challenged and indeed humiliated the British Empire, and now they were going to be made to pay the piper for their temerity in having done so.

It was when the ship reached Yokohama that the passengers got the news that World War I had erupted. This heightened tensions considerably, as the passengers learned that the British planned to arrest any of them who tried to land at Hong Kong. In the light of this revelation it became clear that the emigrants would have to be transported non-stop all the way back to India. This would require more provisions than the *Komagata Maru* carried. At Yokohama, therefore, Gurdit Singh appealed to the British consul for the necessary supplies. The request was turned down. At the next stop, Kobe, Gurdit Singh once again appealed to the British consul for assistance. This time the request was granted with the proviso that the ship not discharge passengers at Singapore but sailed directly from Kobe to India. In the end, however, the *Komagata Maru* did lay over in Singapore for three days (September 16–19), but the authorities refused to allow anyone to disembark.

The *Komagata Maru* arrived in the mouth of the Hooghly River on September 26, 1914. Various officials began boarding the ship as it moved up river. In Johnston's (1979: 97) words:

On Sunday morning, the ship had three high-ranking visitors: James Donald, magistrate and chief administrative officer of the surrounding 24-Parganas, F.S.A. Slocock, from the office of the Director of Criminal Intelligence for the Government of India, and R. Humphreys, a Deputy Commissioner from

Hoshiarpur District in the Punjab. These men were accompanied by a number of Punjabi constables, a Punjabi Deputy Superintendent, Sukha Singh, and two European Punjab police officers. The police were not in uniform, and, for a moment, Gurdit Singh thought they were friends. He had hoped that a delegation of Indian spokesmen would meet the ship to publicise the grievances of its passengers, but the telegrams he had tried to send from Singapore had apparently not been received.

The ship reached Budge Budge on September 29, two months after it set sail from Vancouver, and after another flurry of official activity, it was moored at a floating pier adjacent to the railway station. The plan was to load the passengers on to a waiting train and transport them to the Punjab. In those days, the buzzword for suspected plotters against the state was "sedition." During the prolonged ordeal of the voyage of the *Komagata Maru*, the British authorities had gradually convinced themselves that native provocateurs lay behind this undertaking and that their sinister machinations must be neutralized. The authorities were not entirely mistaken in this view, as we shall presently see. Therefore, getting these Sikhs out of Calcutta in as "sanitary" a manner as possible was deemed essential. For this reason, "The British," says Jensen (1988: 137), "had made special provisions for the arrival of the men because they wanted to return them directly to the Punjab before they could spread their discontent to other Sikhs."

Many complexities arose in the course of this undertaking, much of which exceeds the compass of this study. There were, for example, factional cleavages among the passengers which the British authorities found it possible to exploit as a means of paring down the size and clout of the core hardliners. "Muslims from the Shahpur district who claimed that they had been bullied by Gurdit Singh and his gang of Sikhs and robbed of all their money—one made a motion indicating he was afraid his throat would be cut—said they wanted to disembark" (Johnston 1979: 98). The net result of this pruning process was that about 250 Sikhs remained to be dealt with in political terms. Gurdit Singh was the focal figure in what ensued. He demanded that the Sikhs be allowed to proceed in a procession to Calcutta before being compelled to board a train for the north. At the head of the procession they carried the Sikh flag and a copy of the *Granth Saheb*. The Sikhs were by now highly agitated and the authorities were extremely uneasy about their ability to contain the situation. Five miles outside Budge Budge, the Sikhs encountered J.H. Eastwood, Superintendent of the Reserve Police, who held them back until a contingent of Royal Fusiliers could be brought up. At this point, Gurdit Singh engaged in a dialog with Sir William Duke and J.G. Cumming, Chief Secretary to the Government of Bengal. When Duke asked him where he and his followers were going, the following dialog ensured:

> We are going to Calcutta.
> What business have you in Calcutta?
> First to deposit the Holy Book in a Gurdwara and afterwards to seek an interview with the Governor before whom we will lay our grievances.
> The Governor has sent me to hear your case. I am his Commissioner.
> If such is the case, very well listen to me. I will relate to you the miseries and injustices suffered by us.
> Not here. Return with me to Budge Budge station where I would hear your case (Johnston 1979: 101–2).

Upon returning to their starting point, the Sikhs were asked to sit down in a grassy area not far from the Budge Budge railway station. It was at this point that something went terribly wrong. There was agitation whose precise cause is not clear; firing ensued. There was "a series of explosions on the far side of the crowd," at which point, "The Sikhs had jumped to their feet." There were "revolver shots and Halliday could hear the whine of bullets over his head" (ibid.). Eighteen processionists died on the spot, another 25 were wounded. One was drowned in the river while trying to escape. A European police officer, a head constable and two bystanders also died. Gurdit Singh and 28 other passengers absconded. "Almost all of the remaining Sikh passengers were arrested and imprisoned under the new wartime Ingress of India Ordinance, passed on 5 September, to allow suspected subversives to be summarily arrested and held without trial" (Jensen 1988: 134). Statistics provided by Singh and Singh (1966: Appendix-I) indicate that out of the 313 who disembarked at Calcutta, 222 were detained under the Ordinance. The surviving

passengers were rounded up and sent to the Punjab where intern-
ment under the Ordinance was effectuated. It is not clear how
long they were incarcerated. Jensen (1988: 137) claims that 31 were
released after January 1915. The precise fate of the remainder is
unclear. The government subsequently appointed a commission
of enquiry into the shooting at Budge Budge Harbor which predictably "exonerated the police and put the blame squarely on the
passengers of the *Komagata Maru*" (Singh and Singh 1966: 34).

In the process, however, the British had managed to make
martyrs out of the Sikhs who perished in the shooting, a hero out
of Gurdit Singh (who remained a fugitive for six years until Gandhi
persuaded him to surrender to the authorities), and dedicated
patriots of the surviving emigrants whose only "crime" originally
had been a desire to make a new life for themselves in Canada.
This paranoid policy which transformed innocents into "subversives" and patriots would eventually come home to roost both
in India and in the New World. More than many realized at the
time, this incident had played a major role in raising the political
consciousness of Sikhs and other South Asians in the United States
and Canada, and brought the already established Ghadr Party
decisively into the political arena.

Established in Stockton and San Francisco, California, on November 1, 1913, it was the first revolutionary political organization
ever to form outside India whose explicit goal was to bring down
the Government of India by violent means. Its origins, activities
and importance in the nascent political process that was taking
place now that the South Asian population on the West Coast was
achieving a demographic critical mass will be taken up in Chapter 6.

Understandably, the impact of the *Komagata Maru* incident was
most immediately felt in Canada. It got everybody's political attention as nothing had before. The Sikhs discovered that they had
few White friends in Canada, but that they could nevertheless
effectively mobilize their community's resources in defense of their
perceived civil rights. White anxieties and antipathies had intensified, as also the realization that Asian Indians could not be taken
lightly and were not going to go away. The former were energized;
the latter were driven to greater heights of paranoia. But the impact
was far from inconsiderable on the American side of the border
as well.

# Notes

1. Excerpted from *Order-in-Council, March 2, 1908,* by Singh and Singh (1966: 6).
2. Johnston, however, makes a lot out of the differences; more, I would suggest, than the unfolding of events would seem to justify. He says:

> Many were wary of any action that would lead to trouble with the authorities—afraid at one point, to send a delegation to London lest it offend the Canadians. A solid core of veterans looked back on their service with pride and wore their decorations without apology. Rahim dismissed them as "a few of the war dogs' utilized by the British to kill Chinamen in Hong Kong," but their attitude was certainly an obstacle to united action (Johnston 1979: 11).

3. In Johnston's (1979: 27) words, Daljit Singh:

> ... had raised $10,000 before any arrangements had been made for a boat, and someone reported this to the Hong Kong police. They came to the *gurdwara* on the afternoon of 25 March [1913], raided Gurdit Singh's office, and seized his papers. As it happened, he had signed a charter contract the day before, and, although the police brought him before a magistrate, they decided that they did not have a case against him ....

However, the incident did raise serious problems for the enterprise:

> The incident worried a good many timid souls who did not like trouble with the authorities, and they backed out. Gurdit Singh, who had room for over 500 passengers, was left with only 165.

4. See Johnston (1979: 40–42) for a full account of this meeting, including Fitzgerald's remarks.

# 5 Intensification of Community Awareness

Indian organizations dating back to the earlier phases of immigration, which were originally concerned in the main with advancing economic well-being, facilitating religious practices and promoting social cohesion, went through a dramatic transformation. The Khalsa Diwan Society was established in Vancouver by 1907. It established branches in Victoria, Abbotsford, New Westminster, Frazer Mills, Duncan Coombs, and Ocean Falls. A *gurdwara* was erected in Vancouver in 1909 (largely through the initiative and the resources of Jagjit Singh), followed three years later by another in Victoria (also through Jagjit Singh's initiatives), plus smaller ones in other towns over ensuing years. Eventually one was built in Stockton, California, as Sikhs migrated across the border in growing numbers, thereby adding demographic weight to their brethren who were already there. Other organizations came into being, such as the United India League in Vancouver that was founded by Seth Hussain Rahim and a Punjabi Hindu named Atma Ram. About this time, the Hindustani Society of the Pacific Coast was established in Astoria, Washington. More will be said about this latter organization when we come to the exploits of Har Dayal and Taraknath Das.

The point is that with the rise of inter-racial confrontation and conflict, *gurdwaras* and lay cultural organizations became foci of political mobilization. We saw this in spades in the context of the *Komagata Maru* episode. This is, of course, an old story in the history of how ethnicity and religion become bases for politicization. As Singh and Singh (1966: 15) declare: "Since the only places where Indians could meet were the Sikh *Gurdwaras,* and as politics began to dominate the scene in both countries, the Sikh temples became storm centers of political activity." Social consciousness deepened and radiated ever more widely as Indian activists turned to publishing pamphlets, newsletters and other tracts in Gurmukhi, Urdu, Hindustani, and English. Singh and Singh (1966) were able to identify some of these undertakings in the course of their research on the Ghadr movement. They were: *Desh Sewak*, published in Gurmukhi and English by Harnam Singh and Guru Datt Kumar from Vancouver; the *Khalsa Herald*, a Gurmukhi monthly started in 1911 in Vancouver by Kartar Singh Akali; *Aryan*, an English-language journal edited by Dr Sunder Singh with the help of Quaker friends; *Sansar* (1913) edited by Dr Sunder Singh; and *Hindustani* (1914), an English-language journal edited by Seth Hussain Rahim. Dr Sunder Singh was an especially enterprising activist who also created a publication in Toronto called *Canada and India* that survived until 1917. "Kartar Singh also shifted to Toronto for some years and edited the *Theosophical News*." The results of all this intensified activity "were soon visible in the large attendance at meetings and the number of petitions and memoranda sent out" (Singh and Singh 1966: 15).

## White Backlash

In response both to incidents like the *Komagata Maru* and heightened politicization across the board in Indian communities along the US Pacific Coast, the Canadians, the British and subsequently the Americans fell victim to a state of phobia about Indian immigration. On both sides of the border, and in Ottawa and Whitehall as well, more comprehensive countermeasures were devised to cope with what was increasingly termed "sedition." From their standpoint, alarm was called for because the scope of restiveness in the Indian communities clearly seemed to be metastasizing from ordinary expressions of protest and dissent to politically loaded nationalism, anti-colonialism and even calls for violent revolution. The turmoil created by the onset of World War I added to British anxieties. Intensified surveillance followed. Planting moles in Sikh organizations and employing agent provocateurs to subvert and disrupt them, along with the legal harassment already in place, became the weapons of choice of the authorities in both countries.

Attention was no longer focused almost exclusively on local, grass-roots Sikh activists but increasingly on students and intellectuals as well, whom the authorities rightly concluded were a primal source of revolutionary ferment. They saw that class factors were beginning to enter the picture: that the Sikh peasantry was beginning to interface with revolutionary intellectuals.

## Hopkinson

A milestone in the rise of White "counter-insurgency" was the employment of William C. Hopkinson to spy on and, where possible, to disrupt political mobilization in the Indian community, first in Canada and subsequently in the US. Surveillance of this more systematized and sophisticated genre had actually commenced in 1908, following the collapse of the "Honduras scheme." Hopkinson, as we saw, had actually been one of the persons deputed to accompany the delegation that traveled there to look the situation over, obviously to keep tabs on the Sikhs in the party. The Sikhs' refusal to go along with these blatantly Machiavellian games earned them further enmity in the White community and convinced the authorities that "agitators" among the Sikhs were becoming dangerously influential. This is what gave rise to men like Hopkinson. He was engaged in 1909 on a full-time basis as more or less the "point-man" in the effort to head off and undermine Indian attempts to mobilize support both for immigration reform and opposition to British rule in India.

Why Hopkinson? In Jensen's (1988: 163) words, "Hopkinson built his career around the desire of the British to know what Indians were doing to oppose their rule in India." He was peculiarly suited to his arcane game. Hopkinson was born in Yorkshire in 1878, the son of Agnes and William Hopkinson. His father was a sergeant in the British army who had been deputed to Allahabad to serve as an instructor of volunteers. It was in this context that the son revealed a talent for languages. He became fluent in Hindi and developed a working knowledge of Punjabi and the Gurmukhi script. In 1904, Hopkinson became a police instructor in Calcutta and then migrated to Vancouver in 1907. The Canadian government hired him as an immigration inspector and interpreter.

He married an English stenographer who gave birth to two daughters. They lived in a comfortable house in Vancouver.

Hopkinson's position in the immigration department was his pathway into the arcane world of the secret agent. While he maintained his typical middle-class lifestyle in Vancouver, Hopkinson also led another, very different life as well. "In a poor immigrant suburb of Vancouver, he also had a shack where he lived part time under the alias of Narain Singh, leading the life of a penniless laborer from Lahore, wearing a turban and a fake beard." From this vantage point, for at least six years, "Hopkinson attended meetings at local Sikh temples, paid other Indians to tell him about the activities of immigrants he suspected," and fed this information back to his superiors (Jensen 1988: 164). Apart from the specifics of his nefarious career, the fact that he was active for so long is a further testament to how far the South Asians in North America had progressed in demographic, economic, and political terms toward becoming a force to be reckoned with.

One of his principal henchmen was a man named Bela Singh. A former soldier from Hoshiarpur district in the Punjab, Bela Singh's job was to keep tabs on the activities of Indian organizations in and around Vancouver. He was one of a small coterie of henchman whom Hopkinson recruited. While they had for several years spied on the Sikh community and kept the authorities informed about the plotters and agitators in their midst, they had been able to perform their duties with relative equanimity. The *Komagata Maru* affair changed all that. Animosities rose to fever pitch among the Sikhs. This was directed especially against Hopkinson and his circle of informants. It soon led to violence, which eventually engulfed Hopkinson himself. A wave of killings and woundings occurred that were instigated, on the one hand, by Bela Singh's thugs, with Hopkinson's approval, and, on the other, by the targets of their nefarious activities. Harnam Singh, one of Bela Singh's underlings vanished on August 17, 1914 and toward the end of the month turned up dead. Another of Hopkinson's agents, Arjan Singh, was shot dead soon after by Ram Singh, "an elderly, religious man who had not been visible before." He was tried and acquitted, and following the trial, on September 5, Arjan Singh's body was cremated, after which a memorial service was held at the *gurdwara*. There were approximately 50 people in the temple for this ceremony. A man named Bhag Singh was leading the ceremony, and Bela Singh was sitting directly behind him. About twenty minutes into the ceremony, Bela Singh started shooting. Since Arjan Singh was theoretically one of Bela Singh's cohorts, and the audience for this reason presumably consisted of his family, friends and supporters, it is not clear why Bela Singh chose this occasion to fire upon people in attendance. But shoot he did, and nine persons were wounded, while two, Bhag Singh and Bhattan Singh, died. Bela Singh was tried and acquitted for the murders, claiming "self-defense," despite the fact that he had used two pistols in the melee. Hopkinson helped to get him off by supporting his self-defense plea, claiming that he had witnessed the event "at a distance" and could attest that Bela Singh was not the perpetrator.

The cycle of violence reached a dramatic climax when Hopkinson himself was murdered. This occurred in the context of the Bela Singh trial that took place between October and November of 1914. Following his testimony in that trial, Hopkinson himself was assassinated right in the courtroom by Mewa Singh, the priest of the *gurdwara*! Four bullets had struck him—in the chest, knee, and back. Hopkinson had grabbed Mewa after the first shot, but Mewa struck him with the pistol and then finished the job.

Mewa Singh's trial followed. He made a full confession, was convicted and sentenced to be hanged. The statement he made before the court following his sentencing enshrined him in the pantheon of martyred Sikh patriots. "My religion," he declared, "does not teach me to bear enmity with anybody, no matter what class, creed or order he belongs to, nor had I any enmity with Hopkinson. I heard he was oppressing my poor people very much ... I, being a staunch Sikh, could no longer bear to see the wrong done both to my innocent countrymen and the Dominion of Canada .... And I, performing the duty of a true Sikh and remembering the name of God, will proceed towards the scaffold with the same amount of pleasure as the hungry babe does towards its mother. I shall gladly have the rope put around my neck thinking it to be a rosary of God's name."[1]

Unquestionably, the *Komagata Maru* incident had been a crucial turning point in the political awakening of the Punjabis and other South Asians all along the Pacific Coast. Not only was it a culmination of the atmosphere of frustration and anger that had been simmering in Indian communities up and down the West Coast for several years, but it had also led to a certain amount of demographic restructuring, as it also intensified the flow of Canadian Sikhs crossing the border into the US in search of a more congenial civil rights environment. This added social mixing narrowed subcultural disparities between the two populations and diminished the ideological divide between them. Especially important, Indians in America became more aware of the fact that their struggle for civil rights was linked to the anti-colonialist struggle in India. In the words of G. Adhikari (1970: viii), initially most Sikhs were "non-political, but their own difficulties abroad, the refusal of the Canadian authorities to allow any further immigration, the refusal of permission to ships carrying Indian emigrants to land in California ports, etc., soon brought them to the realization that these arose because India was a colony of the British imperialists and not an independent nation." These realizations fed ineluctably into identification with the emerging Indian freedom movement.

The degree of collective response to *Komagata Maru* emanating from both sides of the border also revealed how far social consciousness and political ferment was progressing among the South Asians. The rise of *Ghadr* and the assassination of Hopkinson, plus other incidents of inter- and intra-ethnic violence, like Bellingham, certainly attest to this! The pattern of racial discrimination driving Indians to litigate against US immigration laws was an impetus for broadening the spectrum of political awareness. The situation in Canada was an added ingredient, as news of what was taking place there inevitably filtered into the Sikh communities on the American side of the border.

Students and other intellectuals diffusing around the country played an increasing part as well. They were becoming an emerging presence in the United States and Canada as the twentieth century wore on. As revolutionary fervor intensified in their ranks, educated activists found ways to reach out and make common cause with Indian workers in the fields, factories and mills along the Pacific Coast. As early as 1906, young intellectuals who had been honing their radical perspectives in London, Paris, New York and various East Coast and Middle West locales were discovering that their revolutionary doctrines resonated well in grassroots Indian communities where the quest was under way for leaders who would give voice to their social disabilities and political discontent.

Initially, one of the main impetuses for this interaction between Sikh farmers and other manual workers and the students was economic need. Most of the students reached the US with meager resources and limited opportunities to supplement whatever little they had. Resultantly, they sought employment wherever they could find it. This meant taking menial jobs in the service and production sectors of the US economy, as Sudhindra Bose's and Jagjit Singh's experiences demonstrate. Students wrote home speaking of how comparatively easy it was for the "ambitious" among them to get manual work to help make ends meet.

In those early days, the *Modern Review*, published out of Calcutta by Ramananda Chatterjee, was a treasure trove of writings on every conceivable aspect of Indian society and civilization, from antiquities to politics, from poetry and literature to the South Asian diaspora. At one time or another, almost every Indian and Western journalist, scholar, philosopher or religionist concerned with things Indian or international contributed articles to its pages. One of the most frequent topics appearing in *Modern Review's* pages, from its founding in 1906 through the inter-war years, was the "American experience," especially concerning what, in 1909, one author called "The condition of Hindu students in America" (*Modern Review* 1909, Vol. 5: 53). In general, there was much enthusiasm and optimism about the prospects of studying in the United States. The US, despite admitted obstacles and problems arising from racial prejudice and cultural ignorance, was genuinely seen as "the land of opportunity" where suitably dedicated and ambitious young Indians could acquire the technologies, the advanced education, and even an appreciation of what a genuinely secular society was all about, which India's trek into the modern world required. Every detail of what this experience entailed, from how to prepare for it and how to handle oneself after arriving in the United States, was addressed by various contributors. One article written by Sarangadhar Das in the December 1911 issue asks the question, "Who Should Come Here?" His answer: "The graduates of Indian universities with due credentials will be taken as post-graduates in their own lines for the Master's and Doctor's degrees." Indians coming at the undergraduate level "who have passed or read up to the Intermediate Standard can easily enter the American universities as regular students and follow the classes." For specialized disciplines like engineering, chemistry and agriculture, it is recommended that the student first matriculate for a year or two in a high school. "Without this preliminary training they cannot at all understand the lectures in these subjects in the university." Even students at the secondary school level were encouraged to come if they seemed to posses the necessary social and intellectual credentials.

The writer gives advice on what items of dress and grooming would be appropriate both for the long voyage to Seattle (in this case via Japan and the Pacific), and when the emigrant takes up residence on an American campus. He tells the reader that in "Yankeeland" one should adopt informal dress. "Whatever stylish clothes you may bring from Calcutta, Bombay or Madras, they are all English styles and [here] a man looks ludicrous with these tight trousers and short coats ...." If you are traveling as a third-class passenger, you must provide your own bedding. Just "bring some of your old beddings ... for the voyage and throw them away at Seattle." He advises the potential sojourner to contact the American Consul General in whichever city is closest to "get a recommendation letter from him to the Immigration Inspector at Seattle ..." and from any organization that may be sponsoring the student in whole or in part. When passing through Immigration, he says, there are things to be aware of: "The Immigration Inspector will ask you *whether you believe in polygamy, and whether you will be financially backed from home. The first question requires a negative and the second a positive answer from you" (*Modern Review* December 1911: 604, emphasis in original). This passage provides a delightful glimpse of the prevailing American stereotypes of the day!

A listing of individuals whom students may contact for assistance en route and when they reach the US shows that by 1911 the Indian community had built a network capable of handling the basic requirements of incoming students. He mentions Maulvi Muhammad Barakatulla who resides at 40 Daimachi, Akasaka-ku in Tokyo, as a contact en route. This was a man who himself later on came to the US and became highly involved in political activism, including the Ghadr movement. In Seattle, we are told, one must write the Secretary of the New India House at 45414, 8th Avenue, NE, and also Mrs Evelyn Burlingame Covington at 707, 13th Avenue in North Seattle so that they can receive you at the dock and put you up until you are ready to move on to Berkeley, where the writer of this article himself will receive you and help you get you settled in.

These instructions show, of course, that sympathetic Americans were very much a part of a social pattern already in place, and also that some of the Indians who were playing roles in these structures were more than just transient matriculates. They were persons who had been able to develop a more viable presence in the United States.

The existence of Americans in these networks, especially around university campuses, was to a not insignificant degree a dividend derived from the century-long channels of intercultural interaction which the old Yankee traders had pioneered. By now there were a scattering of Americans all across the country, especially those who had access to or lived in the major urban centers like Boston, New York, Philadelphia, Chicago, San Francisco, Los Angeles, Seattle, etc., who were familiar enough with Indian philosophies and religions, about India's colonial plight and about her people's growing political consciousness to offer a sympathetic and supportive hand to Indians who had come on a shoestring from afar in search of Western education and the keys to social parity for themselves, and political freedom and social uplift for their country. There was a clear line of diffusion from the Bengal Renaissance, through New England Unitarianism and Transcendentalism, to a substratum of contemporary Americans with humanistic inclinations who could identify with the needs and aspirations of these young Indians adrift in the Western world. Many, but by no means all, were on college campuses. Sarangadhar Das essentially validates this viewpoint. "I have been helped to a great extent," he states, "by my American friends *most of whom are either Theosophists or Vedantists*, or have known something of Hindu philosophy in one way or another. Such friends also make it a point, while meeting people ignorant about India, to remove their ignorance ..." (*Modern Review* December 1911: 610, emphasis added). Das singles out Mrs Evelyn Burlingame Covington of Seattle as a stellar example of the kind of caring and sympathetic Americans who help look after Indians and make them feel welcome and wanted here. "My dear Brother Sarang," she writes in a letter to him, "You only know too well that I love and cherish every Hindu, whether laborer, student, priest or prince; and my heart and home, wherever I may be, will always be open to each and every one of you."

We know who the rustic Punjabis who came to Canada and the United States were. But what of the students who made the long trek? We have learned that the Punjabis were predominantly Sikh peasants, plus a smattering of others from the Punjab. Verma, Jensen, and Leonard show that economic destitution and social deprivation were far less factors in their decisions to migrate than met the eye. It was driven, they say, more by a desire to augment and enhance their already decent but not affluent material circumstances. One commentator, Saint Nihal Singh, who during this period was a frequent contributor to *Modern Review*, augmented this perception to some degree. He contended that paucity of cultivable land did indeed play a role. He saw the Indian peasant "with small or no holdings" as one of two sections "which evolves men who migrate"(*Modern Review* 1909: 204). This does not necessarily negate the conclusions of the other aforementioned commentators, however, who also implicitly concede that *perceived* land insufficiency, blended with status pretensions, played a role.

Singh's other category, especially its social psychological aspects, was obviously pertinent. They were the demobilized soldiers from the Indian military. He believed that the "military races in North-western India, more than any other single class, constitute the favorite breeding ground of the emigration germ." Once uprooted from their natal villages, Singh avers, these young men found it difficult to re-adjust to the slow pace and stilted routines of rural life. It reminds one of an old World War I ditty which plaintively asks, "How ya goin ta keep em down on the farm after they've seen Paree [Paris]?"

"Life in the village is without excitement," Singh declares. "When the soldier returns to his plough, after serving a term of years in the native army, he finds it difficult to resume the thread of life where he left off .... He prefers to go to some distant land where, perchance, he may receive better wages and probably find genteel work to do, such as policing the streets and wharves, of standing sentry at bank gates, store entrances and exits" (ibid.). These restive men undoubtedly formed the vanguard of emigrating Sikh peasantry, who were then followed along the trails they blazed by the kind of men whom Verma, Jensen, and Leonard describe.

The students were cut from very different cloth. Many were already imbued with political consciousness when they left India.

Most had at least a modicum of higher education. They had come from urban communities and from middle-class families. Sarangadhar Das, during his Berkeley days, compiled a list of 46 of these students, which, as a committed activist, he had compiled from his vantage point at the University of California. Among the 34 for whom accurate regional identifications could be made, 22 were Bengalis, five were Punjabis, and one each was from the United Provinces, Bombay, Maharashtra, and Madras. One was a female and two were Muslims. All had come to the United States between 1904 and 1910. Nine had attended West Coast high schools before going on to college, 20 had attended the University of California at Berkeley and one the Southern California University in Pasadena. Three had attended Stanford. Seven had gone to the University of Washington in Seattle. Others had wandered farther afield. Two attended the University of Illinois, one the University of Wisconsin, one the University of Iowa, one Cornell University, and one the University of Nebraska. Some had found their way to smaller, more specialized institutions such as Oregon State Agricultural College, Oakland Polytechnic, Washington State Agricultural College, and Utah State Agricultural College. A common thread obviously running through these matriculations was the pursuit of what we would today call "high-tech" skills. The majority appear to have been interested in the agricultural sciences and botany. Chemical, electrical, and mechanical engineering were popular choices, as was mine engineering. Some pursued commerce and economics curricula. Very few were into liberal arts. This selection of students was clearly oriented toward the hard sciences.

According to the very brief bio-sketches which Sarangadhar provided on each student, it can be said that most of them succeeded in achieving the principal goal which brought them to the American shores. With some there seem to have been false starts which required curriculum adjustments along the way. Most eventually returned to India and found careers consistent with the education they received here. Some obtained positions in other overseas countries where they either took up residence or merely remained to work for a while before returning to their native land. Satish Chandra Basu, for example, started at Berkeley in 1907, moved on to the University of Nebraska where he did a masters degree in Economics, and eventually became a Professor of

Economics at Kooch-Behar Raj College in Bengal. Naresh Chandra Chakravarti came to Berkeley from Calcutta University in 1903. After attending high school for his first year (to prep for the college curriculum), he enrolled in the College of Mining and obtained a B.S. degree in 1908, got a job as an assaying chemist in a big copper mine in Mexico and went on from there to become superintendent of another copper mine in Peru. Kunapureddi Ramasastrulu left India when he was in the 4th class in India. His patron discontinued his allowance when he left Japan. When he reached America he worked in a shipyard until he earned enough money to attend the University of California. Later on, his patron also resumed helping him, and he obtained his B.S. degree in the College of Agriculture in 1910. He found employment in a "small state in Madras."

These examples are typical of the careers of the first wave of Indian students. For the most part, they were young men in their late teens and early to middle twenties. Most had to pinch pennies to make it. Most were certainly conscious of the nationalist ferment that was becoming ever more prevalent in India, and along with the Sikh peasants they experienced the racial tensions prevalent in America. How intensely they were involved in the ideological ferment occurring around them clearly varied according to the individual and the orientations they brought with them from India or acquired through contacts after they reached America.

Noteworthy in Sarangadhar's list were Sarangadhar himself and Taraknath Das. Both of them turned out to be committed activists who emerged from the pack and took on leadership roles. They formed part of what I would call a "resource pool" of politically aware, young, middle-class Indians who were by 1910 centered around the Berkeley campus. As time passed, they would form links with other activist Indians who were appearing on the scene from abroad and emerging out of the Sikh communities in the rural hinterland, as the material base of the latter kept growing.

One important cluster of committed Indians was a group of Bengali students, including Taraknath and Sarangadhar, who, by pooling their resources, lived cooperatively in a rented residence which they named "Nalanda House." Another group that came slightly later had in part been made possible by the Nalanda House set. They consisted of six students who had been selected for scholarships through a competition in India to come to the University of California by a committee on which Taraknath Das sat.

Called the Guru Govind Singh Saheb Educational Scholarship, funds for this undertaking had been raised from Sikh farmers in the Stockton area. Although the details of this interface between students and peasants must await further elaboration of the politicization process occurring among South Asians in America, it is important to note that such an interface was underway well before World War I. Political consciousness among the students was clearly present. "The heart of Young India is throbbing with the passionate desire of service to the mother," declared Sarangadhar in *Modern Review* (December 1911: 609). "The nationalist movement has infused a new life into our people and everyone is desirous of doing something or other in his or her own way." The point of coming abroad, the *raison d'être*, is finding the appropriate means to do one's duty, "... but it is impossible for us to serve unless we are fully equipped with the best knowledge of how to serve." He clearly believed that this vital knowledge existed in the West and that he and his fellow Indians must come here and imbibe it.

Many of the students who had migrated, from whichever direction, all the way to the West Coast found that they could take advantage of employment networks which had already been forged by their Punjabi predecessors, not only in agriculture but generally in the domain of manual labor. Itinerant work gangs operated by "Hindu boss men" moving about the region in response to the seasonal cycle were an especially fertile source for the kind of part-time work which fitted the needs of students on summer holidays from colleges and universities. This fact itself testifies to the network development and social differentiation that was taking place among South Asians. In Leonard's (1997: 84) words, "Those who could enter legally, university students from India, used to do farmwork during summers in Punjabi crews under Punjabi bosses .... Meanwhile, Indian lawyers and other professionals living in California's cities invested in farmland and employed Punjabi crews." These conjunctures deepened and filled the nascent South Asian nexus that was forming in the United States. An ethnic resources base was being formed, upon which political activists could increasingly build as social consciousness, community awareness and demographic density increased.

Understandably, the *Komagata Maru* incident was a catalyzing force. But there were also defining incidents which contributed to the process. One of the most notorious occurred in Bellingham,

Washington, on September 4, 1907. A mob of four to five hundred Whites raided an Indian enclave located on the outskirts. Many of the Sikhs were beaten up; many fled their homes wearing only their night-clothes. Some of those were then arrested by the local police. The victims were treated as the culprits! "During the course of the disturbance, the indignation of the crowd was fanned to action by speakers who addressed impromptu audiences on the street corners and incited citizens to 'help drive out cheap labor'."[2] There were other ugly incidents of this kind at Marysville, Stege, Live Oak and many other California towns where Sikh workers were located. These events had especially profound repercussions in Indian communities up and down the West Coast—all the more so because the aftermath of the *Komagata Maru* and other incidents which occurred north of the border resulted in an increased flow of Canada-based Indians. More and more came in the mistaken belief that a better racial deal awaited them in America.

One important effect of this demographic shift was that it heightened the awareness of Indians in the United States that a connection exists between the way they were being treated in the New World and the evils of British colonialism. In the words of G. Adhikari (1970: viii), initially most Sikhs were "non-political, but their own difficulties abroad, the refusal of the Canadian authorities to allow any further immigration, the refusal of permission to ships carrying Indian emigrants to land in California ports, etc., soon brought them to the realization that these arose because India was a colony of the British imperialists and not an independent nation." Their awareness of this fact was sharpened by what seemed to be the more favorable outcome of Japan's efforts to ameliorate the condition of their emigrants. Because Japan was an independent state that was able to project a powerful political image, especially after their victory in the Russo-Japanese war (1904–1905), both Canada and the United States showed far greater deference towards it and a willingness to negotiate on the immigration rights of its nationals. For example, the entry fees charged for Japanese immigrants were always kept lower and were sometimes waived altogether, while such fees were increased to prohibitive levels on Indian immigrants for the express purpose of trying to exclude them. The Indians soon saw this, and their emerging leaders were emphasizing the connection between the condition of Japanese immigrants who were being represented and defended by a sovereign government towards whom the American and Canadian governments were compelled to show some deference, as opposed to the colonial Government of India which treated its nationals more as chattel and potential sedition- ists rather than valued citizens of the Indian state.

## Notes

1. The quote appears in Chadney (1989: 188). Chadney took the quotation from Khushwant Singh (1966: 179–80).
2. *Echoes of Freedom: South Asian Pioneers in California, 1899–1965.* University of California Library, Berkeley: Chapter 4. This is an archival document for which page numbers are not available.

# 6    Ghadr

Another major turning point in the politicization of South Asians in America was the formation of the Ghadr Party on November 1, 1913. It was the first manifestation of politically institutionalized resistance to colonialism and indigenous racism emanating from overseas Indian immigrants. In its ideology and mobilization patterns, the party mingled traditional images of rebellion derived from Indian history and social experience with modern images and models of revolutionary nationalism imbibed from its experiences in the West.

There was a clear catalytic relationship between the circumstances surrounding the *Komagata Maru* incident and the emergence of this movement. As we shall see, some of the same activists were involved in both. *Komagata* in particular had in many ways become the last straw that transformed what had up to then been a rather desultory and disjointed pattern of social protest against grassroots racism into a militarized assault upon the Indian state itself. Ghadr had taken the next step by actually creating a politically structured, formal organization whose declared purpose was to overthrow what was perceived to be the root cause of South Asians' duress—viz., the British-Indian government itself—and replace it with native rule.

Even in the pre-*Komagata Maru* period, as we have seen, political ferment with revolutionary overtones was congealing throughout the West Coast South Asian communities on both sides of the border. These clearly played their role in leading up to *Ghadr*. In the United States, out of this general restiveness there emerged several political formations with revolutionary agendas. There was the Indian Association of the Pacific Coast, formed by G.D. Kumar in 1912 and the Hindustan Association formed by Ram Nath Puri.

Especially important was the Hindustani Workers of the Pacific Coast. Formed in the Stockton area in the summer of 1913 by so-called "Hindese patriots," it was a strictly grassroots undertaking that raised money through donations from ordinary Sikh farmers and other manual workers all over the region. It would prove to be the direct precursor of *Ghadr*.[1]

With Ghadr's emergence, declares Haridas T. Mazumdar, "strictly political activity on behalf of India's freedom was launched in the United States ...." Like the Great Mutiny, from which it drew its inspiration and its name,[2] Sikhs (who were the overwhelming majority), Hindus (mainly small shopkeepers), and Muslims (with backgrounds comparable to the other two communities), combined their talents and their resources in a coalition that would raise a military force, consisting of ex-soldiers and indeed any able-bodied believers from anywhere they could be found, and dispatch them to India to raise the standard of rebellion (*Ghadr*) (Mazumdar 1960: 7).[3]

The most important groups in the period leading up to World War I that consummated in the Ghadr Party obviously were the grassroots Sikh communities scattered across California, Oregon, Washington, and British Columbia. Ironically, in the original Great Uprising that occurred in 1857, it had been Sikhs' "loyalty" to the East India Company which had saved its bacon! As the movement grew, the Ghadrites exploited their international networks as well, consisting particularly of Sikh communities located along the Pacific Rim in Shanghai, Hong Kong, Canton, Manila, Singapore, Rangoon, and Japan. As we shall see, ties were even developed with imperial Germany when World War I commenced in August of 1914. Supportive of the Sikhs, of course, and in some ways helpful to them in terms of ideological and strategic input, were the growing number of students, scholars, and intellectuals who were diffusing across the North American continent, and more and more making common political cause with the Sikh farmers. But these students simply lacked the manpower to add any significant demographic muscle to the undertaking. Outside the US, prior to its founding in California, precursors of Ghadr had sprung up, all of which shared a growing belief that a military challenge to British rule in India was essential. The Seventh Report of the Senate Fact-Finding Committee on Un-American Activities in California (1953) asserts that Ghadr was established in Lahore in 1907, "as part of a movement to emancipate India from British control and to establish a free united states of India." This was an oversimplified view, of course, worthy of the intellectual shallowness characteristic of the anti-Communist witch-hunting bodies that operated during the McCarthy era. But there was nevertheless a grain of truth there. In Tokyo, Singapore, Hong Kong, Shanghai, Canton, Manila, Bangkok and Indonesia, as well as in India itself, groups of Sikhs had emerged in recent years to promote revolution in India, many of which were subsequently transformed into Ghadrite cells once the parent organization came into being in California from 1913 onwards. Let us turn to some of the principal personalities who were instrumental in creating this party.

## Key Figures in the Formation of Ghadr

### Har Dayal

Apart from the general run of students and agrarian Sikhs, there were a number of other individuals who entered the fray and played special roles in awakening the political consciousness of South Asians in Canada and the United States. Some were ideologically developed activists who had acquired their political agendas before coming to the United States and who after their arrival molded followings out of the "raw material" they found here, or co-opted formations that already existed in nascent form, or built organizational structures virtually from scratch. Others were well-established leaders or proponents of causes that already existed in India or in England, Paris, etc., who came to the US "on tour," as it were, and then lent their celebrity, rhetorical skills, and organizational capabilities to indigenous organization- and movement-building. We must now begin factoring some of these persons into our narrative. We start with the rise and fate of Ghadr.

Essentially, it must be understood that Ghadr was born among a few thousand Sikh peasants, living a tenuous existence in a foreign land, among whom literacy and education levels were comparatively low, economic resources were scarce, and cosmopolitanism was not highly developed. Even as they were becoming more politically conscious—or at least conscious enough to conceive of such a movement as Ghadr—they were still sorely in need of higher-level, more sophisticated leadership if their aspirations and their endeavors were to bear fruit. At the propitious moment, there did indeed appear on the scene a savior of sorts. This was a young Punjabi radical named Har Dayal. He proved to be the person needed to consolidate various nascent political formations scattered around western America and Canada into a more comprehensive and coherent political movement with a revolutionary ideology, printing presses, money, organization, and broad membership base.

Har Dayal did not come to America as a "student." He made his way here in 1911 by a complicated route that had taken him to England, back to India, and then to Paris, Algeria, Morocco, Martinique, Hawaii, and finally San Francisco. By the time he reached here, he had evolved the skills to become a seasoned, effective organizer and ideologue—or "propagandist," as he termed himself. He was a new breed of leader on the American scene, the kind whom the restive elements among both the students and the Sikhs were by now longing for.

Har Dayal would be the first to provide major organizational focus, combined with ideological zeal and direction, to the crystallizing South Asian political subculture struggling to be born on the West Coast. Although his talents and impact would in the long run be matched, indeed even exceeded, by Taraknath Das and others, it was he who in many ways started the political ball rolling.

After Har Dayal reached San Francisco, he immediately plunged into the task of organizing the Indians he found there. As we shall learn, he did not exactly arrive in San Francisco out of the blue; the door had been pointed out to him by a friend and supporter who preceded him. And it must be said, moreover, that by 1911 some of the political space he sought to occupy was already being taken up by Taraknath Das, Gobind Behari Lal (Har Dayal's first cousin), and others. But this does not detract from Har Dayal's importance. In his own right, he had arrived in California as a dedicated revolutionary determined to try and change the world as he perceived it. In a sense, in fact, when he reached the United States, you could say that he was a leader in search of a following, searching for a vehicle that could propel him into the international political limelight to which he aspired. The harried Sikhs and other

South Asians he encountered in America were a made-to-order constituency for him, especially inasmuch as they had already been "softened up" by predecessors, and by the objective conditions that existed on the West Coast.

He had a brilliant mind. He was multilingual. He was a scholar of formidable proportions, knowledgeable in Sanskrit and Persian; in Hinduism, Buddhism and other Eastern religions; and also in Western social and political thought. He was a gifted speaker and an indefatigable toiler for the cause of Indian freedom. He had a big impact on the Indian community because in their humble eyes he had all the ingredients of a political redeemer, especially when it became known that through his erudition and eloquence he was having a significant impact among enlightened segments of the White community.

At an Indian Association meeting in 1912, with his notoriety spreading, a member suggested that Har Dayal be invited to address them. Pandit Kanshi Ram, a fellow Hindu, agreed to write him a letter of invitation. Har Dayal replied that he would come in the last week of December. But he did not in fact show up until March of 1913. When he did finally come, the political conjunction between the grassroots and the intellectuals in the context of formal organization took a giant leap forward. The Ghadr movement was the scalar increase in political awareness, organizational capability and mobilizational commitment that resulted.

Office space was purchased on Wood Street in San Francisco and a printing press was acquired, largely though the connections which Har Dayal had established in the wider community. They called their building "Yugantar Ashram" (New Age Retreat) and began publishing two weekly newspapers, both of which were titled *Ghadar* (The Revolution), one in Punjabi (i.e., in Gurmukhi script) and the other in Hindustani. In time, the organization adopted the name of its publication as the name of the movement and called itself the Ghadr Party.

Who, then, was this man? Har Dayal (1884–1939) was born and brought up in Delhi, the youngest of four sons of Lala Gauri Dayal, a member of the Kayastha caste, "a Reader in the District Court of Delhi and, as such, an employee of the British" (Brown 1975: 11).

He arrived in the United States in February 1911, ostensibly planning to carry on his studies of Buddhism at Harvard University. But this never seems to have been his bottom-line agenda, because Har Dayal was nearly 30 years old and already politically preconditioned by the influences which had played on him both in India and in Europe prior to his emigration to the US.

In India, Har Dayal was the scion of a well-off, well-placed, socially conscious "old Delhi" family for whom learning and public service were everything. His birth, position and upbringing were the diametric opposite of the simple peasant folk with whom his life became intertwined in the New World. He was the youngest of Lala Gauri Dayal's four sons. Dayal was a *baradari* name within the Kayastha caste. Thus, he called himself "Har Dayal." He mastered Persian and Urdu as well as Latin and English as he was growing up. This was a natural outgrowth of the fact that he was the member of a caste whose traditional occupation was as specialists serving in administrative and managerial capacities for the country's rulers. When India was ruled by the Mughals, Persian was the court language and Urdu the Muslim vernacular; when India was under the British, it was English with Latin and Greek as the classical languages of the Western literary tradition. In addition, as a Hindu, he learned Sanskrit, which was the classical language of traditional Hindu civilization. And he of course learned Hindustani, which was and remains to this day the street language of northern India.

He attended Christian missionary schools, where he mastered English and got early exposure to Western thought. He matriculated at St. Stephens, where he stood first in most subjects. However, when a boy from Lahore topped him in overall standing in his class, he went to Lahore to pursue an M.A. There he racked up records for intellectual performance and caught the eye of many prominent figures in that city's rich intellectual environment. When he was 17 years old and still a student at St. Stephens, one of India's towering political-intellectual figures of his time, Sir Tej Bahadur Sapru, was introduced to him and was deeply impressed. This recognition was only a sample of what was in store for him as his intellect and ideological awareness matured.

The shift to Lahore was critical from a political standpoint. While reminiscences of Delhi's past glory rang in the ears of its contemporary residents, social discontent was fairly benign, confined, in the words of Gobind Behari Lal (Har Dayal's first-cousin and contemporary), to "progressive pother" about the good and bad side of the caste system, the *zenana* system, *purdah* and

vegetarianism versus meat-eating, etc. In all this "Christian reformism and a sort of Westernism in general ... there was as yet no
animus against the British ...." It was a different story in Lahore.
That city was a hotbed of political ferment. "It was combative, in-
tolerant, intense, even ferocious." There was "much more awareness and dogmatism of different religious faiths, the Hindus and
the Moslems and the Sikhs were powerful and clashing systems."
There were also Hindu, Muslim, and Sikh reform movements but
"much more rancorous and active." The Punjabis themselves
seemed "physically more virile and emotionally more ebullient,"
more prone to "love and enjoy warlike expression and moods, if
not violence" (Sareen 1994: 24–25).[4] In short, Lahore was all at the
same time a cauldron of cultural revivalism, reformism and nascent nationalism into which this brilliant young man was plunged.
Its challenges and distractions did not impede his intellectual
development—instead, they planted new seeds which would
profoundly affect its eventual direction.

He acquired many role models at this stage of his life. One was
Romesh Chander Dutt (1849–1908) who had risen to become a
professor of history at London University. R.C. Dutt combined
scholarly stature with political commitment. He was elected
President of the Indian National Congress in 1899 and Har Dayal
said of him that he was "the ideal civil servant" who "never gave
up love of his country." Another was R.P. Paranjpye (1876–1966),
whom he saw as "the ideal academician." Paranjpye attended
Cambridge University under a government scholarship where he
amassed a brilliant academic record. But he was another one of
those privileged young Indians who combined his devotion to
learning with an awakening and ramifying commitment to nationalism. "Should I decide to enter the field of education," Har
Dayal declared, "I would model myself after this man who, in
1899, became the first Indian to be bracketed senior wrangler at
Cambridge, which he attended under a government scholarship."
What was ideologically important was the fact that Paranjpye
"could have had his pick of government jobs," including appointment to the Indian Education Service, "until then virtually closed
to all but Europeans," but instead became principal of Fergusson
College at a paltry salary of Rs 75 per month (Brown 1975: 16).

Paranjpye's independence of mind clearly made a deep impression on Har Dayal because he was willing not only to assert his

patriotism in his dealings with the British but also his intellectual independence with respect to his fellow Indians. Paranjpye had at one point angered Bal Gangadhar Tilak, for all practical purposes the father of right-wing Hindu nationalism, by refusing to close his college "on the day after the solar eclipse and then defended his position in an article entitled, 'Is Religious Education in India Necessary?'" (Brown 1975: 17).

Apart from its relevance to Har Dayal's political maturation, this incident, of course, reveals things about the mentality of the emerging "far right" in Indian nationalism after the turn of the century—things, incidentally, that still characterize the mentality of the more extreme adherents of *Hindutva* in the present day, i.e., the admixing of what at the time passed for modern political activism tinged with cultural revivalism. This was playing on the minds of the young men in whom political consciousness was dawning, including many of those who were journeying to America for further education.

Others who contributed to Har Dayal's formative phase in India, where not through personal contacts then by reputation, were the well-known array of political, religious and philosophical figures of the period. Lala Lajpat Rai (1865–1928), the so-called "Lion of the Punjab," was first encountered during his Lahore days. Har Dayal at first revered him for his outspoken patriotic nationalism but then cooled somewhat toward him when he later realized that while Lajpat was a tough political activist, he was not all that intellectually deep, nor a master of classical languages and philosophies like himself and the great thinkers whom he so much admired. We will have occasion to consider Lajpat Rai's importance further when we address his contribution to the freedom movement during the period from December 1914 to December 1919 while he was marooned in the United States during World War I. Dayanand Sarswati (1824–1883), founder of the Arya Samaj and creator of the network of DAV colleges dedicated to the promulgation of his Vedantic (or "Back to the Vedas") version of Hinduism, had an impact on him, as did the opposite genre, the Brahmo Samaj of Raja Rammohan Roy, which, as we have seen, propounded an Indian modernism that clashed with those aspects of traditional Hinduism which Roy, the Orientalist, believed impeded India's march toward gaining cultural parity with the West.

Others in the Lahore milieu included Hans Ras, the principal of DAV College (whom he called "Mahatma") and an Arya Samaj missionary named Bhai Parmanand (1876–1947), regarded as "a man of the people" whose friendship literally accompanied him to the New World. Bhai Parmanand turned out to be special because of this. Bhai Parmanand was a dedicated Arya Samajist who became a staunch opponent of the caste system, so much so that he founded an organization, the Jat Torak Mandal, dedicated to this end. He advocated widow remarriage and deplored untouchability. He wanted Hindi to be the medium of instruction in the schools. He wrote a "History of India," employing sources that were banned by the British. Ultimately, he was arrested and sentenced to death for alleged participation in the Ghadr movement during the Lahore Conspiracy Case. His sentence was commuted at the last minute to life imprisonment in Port Blair in the Andamans, the Raj's version of Devil's Island. After serving from 1914 to 1920 he was released on a clemency plea by Mahtama Gandhi and Lala Lajpat Rai. The point is that Bhai Parmanand was a major role model for Har Dayal in his activist political incarnation.

Gobind Behari Lal, however, believed that the notables in whose midst he moved had less direct, personal influence on Har Dayal's early political development than did the Christian missionaries whom he encountered at St. Stephens College. Emily Brown quotes him as saying that "most people overlook the fact that Har Dayal was profoundly influenced by the Christian missionaries at St. Stephens College .... They influenced him by their sincerity, by their earnestness, and by the way they lived ... devoted, thorough gentlemen ..." (Brown 1975: 15–16).

Har Dayal reached his zenith as the fair-haired embodiment of what the imperial Raj expected good and "loyal" Indians to become when he was selected for a State Scholarship. This was the penultimate honor that could be conferred on a young Indian scholar. He was the first "inlander" to be so honored. All previous awards had gone to students from Bombay, Calcutta, and Madras. A state scholarship putatively guaranteed permanent status to the recipient in the upper echelons of India's bureaucratic elite.

Although there were no stipulations as to where in England he would matriculate, or what he would study, Har Dayal selected St. Johns College at Oxford. He enrolled in the Honour School of Modern History, "taking as his subject the later period of European history and British India as his special study." When he was at the University of the Punjab, "he had been an Aitchison-Ramrattan Sanskrit Scholar, and he continued his studies in this language at Oxford" (Brown 1975: 19). The upshot is that he made his mark at Oxford and seemed well on his way to a successful academic and/or bureaucratic career.

During that initial year in England, however, something snapped. Gobind Behari Lal says that his cousin "had a most profound psychological change, a deep conversion, a self-conversion, the sort of experience that new prophets go through." Out of London's fog, he declares, "*Har Dayal discovered patriotism.*" It grew out of an amalgam "of Delhi civic pride, Lahore propagandism, reawakened Indian [and] historic consciousness ..." (Sareen 1994: 23–24, emphasis in original). It was also no doubt the influence of the nationalist ferment that in those days was centered on London's India House, and a plethora of Indian students and intellectuals who were moving in and out of London and Paris. "In addition to participating in campus life, Har Dayal joined other Indian students in visits to London to attend meetings on behalf of Indian nationalism" (Brown 1975: 21). Among the nationalist stars who shone in London at this time were the great political moderate, Dadabhai Naoroji (1825–1917), and the notorious radical extremist, Shyamaji Krishnavarma (1857–1930). The latter ruled over India House and controlled its political agenda. In Paris, the Indian contingent was led by a Parsi from Bombay named Madam Bhikaji Rustom Cama (1861–1936), who, at the 2nd International Socialist Congress in Stuttgart in 1907, dressed in a *sari*, unfurled the first flag of independent India on foreign soil.

Without warning, Har Dayal showed up in Delhi in the summer of 1906 during the vacation term in England. He told Gobind Behari Lal that he planned to "work for our country. I am not going into Civil Service but don't tell anybody" (ibid.: 20). He would return to England but would take with him his wife, Sunder Devi, to whom he had been married off by his parents. The couple were in love. Sunder Devi's family were high-ranking officials in Patiala state. Since both sides were socially conservative, the idea of Sunder Devi accompanying her husband abroad was inconceivable. Har Dayal was determined, however, and his wife was willing; "therefore, Har Dayal was going to break the centuries old, strict *purdah-zenana* law which forbade the emergence of a secluded woman from the four walls of the house" (Brown 1975: 24–25).

The effort to take Sunder Devi back to London with him turned out to be a "mini cloak-and-dagger operation." With both sets of parents adamantly opposed, recounts Gobind Behari Lal, "Har Dayal, with the aid of my elder brother and some other intimates, contrived to get his wife, in a man's disguise, smuggled out of the *zenana* and safely placed in a reserved train compartment. So the couple 'escaped' to Bombay, and then sailed for England" (ibid.: 25)

As Gobind Behari Lal puts it, "That was Har Dayal's first deed of revolt—a revolt against his own community tradition." Because of Har Dayal's notoriety, the event was actively reported in the British-Indian press. His act also inspired one of his friends and fellow Oxford student, Lala Chandu Lal, to behave accordingly. He too returned to Delhi, liberated his wife from the *zenana* and smuggled her out of India. In Gobind Behari Lal's words, " Mrs. Chandu Lal and Mrs. Har Dayal became closest friends. Chandu Lal apparently had ample means, because, says Gobind Behari, his friend's generosity and love ... saved Har Dayal and his wife from economic troubles which soon descended on them, many times" (ibid.).

Upon his return to England, Har Dayal resigned his state scholarship. He resisted all efforts to dissuade him from doing so, and thus plunged himself and his wife into very precarious circumstances. He transformed himself into a "political saint," adopted an ascetic life-style and he took to wearing Indian dress (*kurta-dhoti*) in 1906–1907, "long before the days of Mahatma Gandhi" (ibid.). When his wife became pregnant in the spring of 1908, Har Dayal and Sunder Devi returned to India. There was a tearful and recrimination-filled reunion with the parents in Delhi. Sunder Devi thenceforth remained in Delhi with her newborn daughter, dividing her time between the two parental domiciles, while her husband essentially became a wandering political saint. He never again saw his wife and daughter. He abandoned them completely and spent the rest of his life immersed in his patriotic causes and personal pursuit of notoriety.

After obtaining the backing of an old and dear friend, a teacher of history at St. Stephens Mission High School, Har Dayal commenced his new mission to teach and propagandize in the cause of Indian freedom. He began acquiring a following as he moved in nationalist circles. He went to Kanpur, a city in the then United Provinces (subsequently Uttar Pradesh), where a Kashmiri Brahman gentleman-of-means, Prithinath Chak, sponsored him and allowed him to use his residence, "*Chak Haveli*," as a meeting place for his followers. Among them were Tarachand, who in later years became ambassador to Iran, plus "a Peshawar student, a couple of Lahore and Allahabad students, and I [i.e., Gobind Behari Lal]" (Brown 1975: 26). Later Har Dayal returned to Lahore where it is said that he had some contact with Lala Lajpat Rai following the latter's release from detention in Mandalay. He began to publish political tracts and gain a wide reputation as a revolutionary. Gobind Behari Lal credits his cousin with mobilizing the Hindustani language to make it more understandable to ordinary people. He used it as a rhetorical weapon. One example he gives is his ridicule of Indians who seek favor and approval from the British. He characterized them as, "*Safed patang ki kali tang*" (the black tail of a white kite).

When Bengali terrorists resorted to bombs in 1908, the British decided to crack down on "extremists" and simultaneously cultivate political moderates like Gokhale and Dadabhai Naoroji. Two English women were killed in this explosion when the bomb missed its intended mark, the magistrate of Muzaffapur. Har Dayal was one of a number of radicals for whom the British issued warrants in the aftermath of this turn toward terrorism, even though it was never established that Har Dayal himself ever went so far as to be implicated in political murders. Emily Brown (1975) refers to Hanwant Sahai, who claims that a Muslim member of the Viceroy's Executive Council sent word to Lala Lajpat Rai that the "topmost authorities" had "malevolent designs" on Har Dayal and suggested that he be sent abroad "to save his valuable life" (Sahai 1957, quoted in Brown 1975: 58). Gobind Behari Lal states that after the warrant was sworn out on Har Dayal, "one of his admirers in the Punjab Government tipped him off just in time" (Brown 1975: 29). Har Dayal caught a train out of Lahore and in a few days reached Colombo. From there he reached Italy and then went to Paris, where he made contact with Madam Cama. Not long after his arrival in Paris, Madan Lal Dhingra, a follower of the radical nationalist, V.D. Savarkar, shot dead two officials at India House, from the office of the Secretary of State for India. Essentially this meant that it was not safe for Har Dayal to go to London. He readily fitted into the Paris set. He mastered French and plunged into studies of the entire range of revolutionary literature that was circulating at that time.[5]

But Har Dayal was never able to remain very long in one place. There were always reasons why he felt the need to move on, sometimes out of necessity because the colonial authorities or their allies were on his tail, and sometimes, it seems, because he was an incurable peripatetic political saint who was forever simply searching for a new cause to champion (I will comment further on this trait later on). When he contracted pneumonia in Paris, he moved to Morocco because of the warmer climate and because living costs were lower. He drifted to Algeria but did not remain there very long because living costs were too high. He next went to the Caribbean and ended up living in Martinique. He found it "culturally dead" and eventually decided to move on to America.

This latter decision was influenced by his hero and old friend from the Punjab, Bhai Parmanand, who showed up in Martinique by a circuitous route. According to Emily Brown (1975: 81), *Bhai-saheb* returned from England in 1909 and was "arrested, tried and made to furnish security for good behavior for three years." In order to avoid causing his friends to lose their bond money, Bhai Parmanand decided to leave India. He went to America with the intention of taking a degree in pharmacy. He missed meeting Har Dayal in Paris because the latter had moved to Algiers. So he continued on to Philadelphia, arriving in October 1909. "I took a second-class berth in a Dutch steamer, the Amsterdam, to New York," says Parmanand (1982: 41) in his autobiography, *The Story of my Life*.

His description of the seven-day voyage vividly captures the flavor of what immigration to America was like shortly after the turn of the century. (It really has not changed all that much even today!) Because there is "great competition among the steamer-lines between Europe and America," he declares, "one can command every sort of convenience in these vessels." In the second-class accommodation there were two or three hundred chairs and tables in the dining hall. "There were also arrangements for various kinds of games aboard ship." It was a "sociable experience: In each class hundreds of travelers made one another's acquaintance almost the very next day after starting." He observed

**Illustration 6.1**
**Bhai Parmanand**

*Source:* Singh and Singh 1966.

that most of the passengers were German, Austrian, Dutch, and French, who could not speak English. However, "Even on board ship they were making efforts to learn and speak English." Upon reaching New York, Bhai Parmanand captures the flavor of being suddenly cast adrift in an alien land. He complains of having been compelled "to pay a large sum for night charges." And he laments that "A new arrival in a foreign land naturally shrinks from kicking up a row, and these fellows can really pick out new arrivals" (Parmanand 1982: 42). New York has changed very little since then!

His encounters with racism convinced him that "the United States of America is no happy land for 'coloured'." Lodgings were hard to acquire if one were not White. Lodgings which in an English town or village could be had in a few minutes ... had in America to be sought for days. In restaurants and hotels, "the contempt for colour is transparently seen." He conceded that maybe the English too have racist feelings, but there "the good manners of the English people never allow them to exhibit it to the world" (Parmanand 1982: 43). In all fairness, however, Bhai Parmanand saw that there was also "another school of opinion," which he attributed to the teachings of Theosophy and Swami Vivekananda. This is "very courteous, and being in love with Hindu religion and philosophy, not only does not treat Indians with contempt but exhibits toward them great affection and regard" (ibid.). Here we see still another illustration of the cultural diffusion which the Yankee traders helped make possible.

When he reached Philadelphia in late October to enroll for his pharmacy course, Bhai Parmanand discovered that he had arrived too late. The term had already begun and he would be compelled to wait until the following year to sign up. Faced with the racism and the social isolation, Bhai Parmanand decided to spend the year touring British Guiana "and other lands" in search of his fellow countrymen. "In Africa I had learnt that a considerable number of Indian labourers used also to go to South America" (ibid.).

He went to British Guiana where he engaged in Arya Samaj missionary work among the substantial community of indentured Indians residing there. He describes the situation he encountered. Cut off from viable contacts with their homeland, the Indians appeared to him to be experiencing a gradual cultural melt-down. Many had been converted to Christianity. Upon reaching Georgetown, "I did not know where to go." He encountered a "Negro missionary" and asked him where the Indian laborers could be found. They went by tram car about two miles outside the city, got down, walked a short distance and "we came to a line of small houses with a canal in the middle and rows of houses on both sides." Bhai Parmanand was told that Hindus lived here. "He took me to a small temple of theirs.'

There was a big room-like structure inside an enclosure. An idol-like thing lay in one quarter of it and two or three mats were spread in the remaining portion .... An Indian priest with his hair grown long presently came and asked me where I had come from and who I was. I said I was a Brahman and had come from the motherland. He then asked me if I had come as a cooly and if a new steamer had arrived. I replied that I had come just as I was (Parmanand 1982: 46).

Gradually, Bhai Parmanand established an identity for himself as a lecturer dedicated to reawakening the Hindu faith among this backwater branch of South Asian civilization. "I toured and gave lectures throughout the colony," he declares. "The Christians were much perturbed .... In British Guiana, the great majority of the educated people had turned Christians," to a high degree because "the state placed all [education] funds in the hands of the mis-sionaries and all schools were inside the churches" (ibid.: 48).

Undoubtedly, the most important outcome of Bhai Parmanand's Caribbean sojourn was the opportunity it provided to meet Har Dayal in Martinique. En route down from the US, his steamer had stopped at Port de France in Martinique, and, knowing that Har Dayal was living there, Bhai Parmanand searched him out. Har Dayal was living the ascetic's life. He said he had chosen this place in order to prepare himself "by discipline and study for his great mission .... He used to sleep on the hard ground, eat some boiled grain or potatoes and be engaged the whole day, except for a short time devoted to study, in meditation." He said he planned, like Buddha, to found a new religion that would transform mankind. "We slept side by side on the bare floor and ate the same food, with this difference that I began to add salt and chillies to my dietary, on which he remarked that I could cook much better than he" (ibid.: 44–45).

It was Bhai Parmanand who talked him into coming to America, thus dissuading Har Dayal from putting all his eggs in the basket of trying to be become another messiah. Bhai Parmanand seems to have instinctively distrusted prophets. "My own view," he averred, "is that all religions and creeds are a kind of fraud upon mankind." He quoted Frederick the Great to the effect that all three of the world's greatest prophets—presumably Christ, Muhammad, and

Buddha—were "three great imposters." Bhai Parmanand contended that "adding one more great fraud to those already existing ... would only multiply the number of creeds." *It would be better "to go to America and propagate the ancient culture of the Aryan race"* (Parmanand 1982: 45, emphasis added).

Har Dayal sailed for America and showed up in Boston. At Harvard University he established contact of some sort with some of the classical scholars on the faculty, especially Professor J.H. Woods, the Sanskritist. "He was impressed," says Bhai Parmanand, "by the fact that Dr. Woods had studied in India and expressed both pleasure and surprise that Harvard students were working on translations of Patanjali's *Yoga sutras*" (ibid.: 85). He never enrolled in any courses, however, and was not taken into the academic program in any capacity. But he elicited enough respect on an informal basis to be allowed to use the university library's research facilities.

The next step in Har Dayal's march of destiny occurred while he was in Cambridge. Bhai Parmanand notes that "Sardar Teja Singh who had gone there to take his degree after staying some time in California told him that California would suit him better" (ibid.: 45). Bhai Teja Singh made him aware of "the literally thousands of Sikhs and other Punjabi laborers working in the fields or factories on the west coast of the United States who lacked leadership in their struggle for social acceptance and economic equality." He agreed to go there, says Bhai Parmanand, "in the interest of patriotism," but probably also because "the prospect of a milder climate was appealing" (ibid.: 85).

After staying a while in California, Har Dayal impulsively dashed off to Hawaii. Bhai Parmanand attributes this to ideological backsliding. It revealed a streak of moral and intellectual ambivalence that seems always to have inhabited Har Dayal's psyche. "The old ideas ... again got the uppermost in his mind ... and he ... went to Honolulu to practice his ascetic life" (ibid.: 46). There, he did indeed resume the lifestyle of a *sadhu*. According to his cousin, Gobind Behari Lal, he "started living in a cave on Waikiki Beach, where Japanese workmen often listened to his talks and gave him food." He talked to them, apparently, about Buddhism. His reading included Shankaracharya in Sanskrit, and the German political philosophers—Kant, Hegel, Marx, etc. It seems to have been his intellectual entrée into socialist thought. "He wrote an

**Illustration 6.2**
**Lala Har Dayal**

*Source:* Singh and Singh 1966.

article for the *Open Court* magazine, published in the United States by an American Buddhist, which aroused much interest among thinkers in the United States" (Sareen 1994: 30).

This Hawaii digression did not last long. With Har Dayal's final arrival in San Francisco in February 1911, the circle was somehow closed, as it were. Brains and brawn had found each other. Bhai Parmanand also reached San Francisco from Guiana around the same time and decided to enroll in the College of Pharmacy there rather than in Philadelphia in order to stay close to his friend.

Har Dayal had traveled far, both physically and intellectually, in the five years or so since he sailed off to Oxford with his coveted state-sponsored scholarship in hand. In the end, the Sikhs were to find their political savior, and the would-be political messiah was to find a flock to lead, at least for a comparatively short while. Neither would be quite the same afterward.

He was an instant hit on the West Coast thanks largely to the fact that he quickly gained what we would today call "media access." One reason was that Bhai Parmanand was also present in the San Francisco area and seems to have developed a number of network connections with the Anglo community. These apparently grew out of his Arya Samaj–Vedanta Society activities. It seems that Bhai Parmanand was instrumental in putting Har Dayal in contact with Dr Starr Jordan, the president of Stanford University at Palo Alto. It resulted in his being given an opportunity to lecture on Indian civilization and philosophy at the university and also created opportunities to meet and develop relationships with other noted intellectuals and journalists in the area. "The University of California invited him to deliver a series of discourses on Buddhist and Sanskrit philosophies," says Gobind Behari Lal (Sareen 1994: 30).

"At one of his public lectures," Behari Lal continues, "two very important Americans heard him speak." One was Fremont Older, the editor of the *San Francisco Bulletin*, and his wife. According to Lal, "Har Dayal simply overwhelmed them." This acquaintance-ship opened the door to "Older's writers and colleagues, especially John D. Barry, a Harvard graduate, who wrote a daily column," as well as Paulin Jacobson and others, who "became fast friends and admirers of Har Dayal." John Barry then published a number of articles "about Har Dayal, the Indian scholar, saint, fighter for the freedom of India" (ibid.). Barry clearly built Har Dayal up in the public eye, and put him in contact with a host of other social reformers, progressives and liberals. This even included Emma Goldman (1869–1940), the illustrious anarchist/socialist,[6] and other American leftists of the day, including Irish nationalists, who believed that violent revolution was the way to emancipation of the masses.

The net result of this experience was that "He was able to influence the Indians who were living in California because he had been made prominent by the [*San Francisco*] *Bulletin*" (ibid.). This was, in effect, the breakthrough that enabled him to rise quickly to the forefront of West Coast South Asian Indian politics and indeed to actually shape its course as World War I was approaching.

Building what may be called "intellectual infrastructure" played an important role in Har Dayal's political stratagems. This meant developing connections with Indian students in the West Coast colleges and universities—especially, of course, in Berkeley and Stanford, where so many of them were matriculating. The goal was to facilitate an increase in their numbers, assure their economic survival, and steer them toward building solidarity with the grassroots laborers and farmers in the region who could supply the demographic muscle and a major share of the funding for revolutionary activity. Pursuant to this goal, says Gobind Behari Lal, "Har Dayal, Teja Singh (of British Honduras fame in 1908), Taraknath Das and Professor Arthur U. Pope, then a member of the faculty of the University of California, formed a committee to send for a number of scholars from India for higher education at Berkeley" (Sareen 1994: 31). Once again indicative of the growing resource base of West Coast Indians, they were able to persuade Bhai Jwala Singh, "a Sikh farmer of Stockton... and his friends, all exceptionally patriotic and pious men" to fund the creation of six Guru Govind Singh Scholarships.

The composition of this committee is significant because it shows that between 1906, when Taraknath Das established himself in America, and 1912, after Har Dayal made his debut on the scene (1910–1911), a considerable interface had developed between student activists located mainly on the Berkeley and Stanford campuses and emergent leaders among the South Asian laboring and entrepreneurial groups dispersed in the grassroots. In addition to Taraknath Das, Gobind Behari Lal mentions the names of Sarangadhar Das, H.K. Rakshit, Bhai Parmanand (now studying pharmacy at Berkeley), and Dhan Gopal Mukerji (1890–1936). The latter became, according to Gordon H. Chang (Chang et al. 2002: 2), "the first author of Asian Indian ancestry who successfully wrote for American audiences about Indian life."[7] There are scant data on how much interaction occurred between these young men in the broad context, but there can be little doubt that all were roughly on the same page as far as working for the overall causes of civil rights and Indian freedom was concerned. It is an open question just how closely Taraknath Das and Har Dayal, clearly the premier actors as far as visible political activism was concerned,

coordinated their actions. One gets the impression that their strong
egos, individualistic personalities, and thirst for social prominence
imposed significant limitations on the depth of their relationship.

The first batch of six scholarship students came over from India
in 1912. Gobind Bihari Lal lists them as: (1) V.R. Kokutnur—Poona,
Bombay University graduate in chemistry; (2) S. Sharma—Madras,
B.A., LL.B in political science; (3) Mahmud (first name unknown)
—Anglo-Islami College, Aligarh; (4) Nand Singh Sihara—Khalsa
College, Amritsar in civil engineering; (5) Panday (first name
unknown)—Madrasi Christian; and (6) Gobind Bihari Lal (Har
Dayal's first cousin)—Delhi, studied in St. Stephens College,
Punjab University.

The students entered in the Fall term, in September 1912. "I
was the only one of the scholars who knew Har Dayal intimately
at home," Gobind Behari Lal says, adding that Har Dayal was six
years older than he, which means Lal was 22 years of age. When
the other students met Har Dayal, he declares, "they were practically hypnotized by him." Professor Pope offered hospitality to the
Indian students and facilitated social contacts with other members
of the Berkeley faculty and student body. The boys were lodged
in a rented house where they were expected to be "a self-managing
boarding house and fraternity." Nand Singh, "being a Sikh (*sic*)",
was selected as the administrator. "Foodstuffs were provided, and
each scholar did a turn in cooking a simple meal—usually Indian
food of a very simple kind: rice, dal, milk, vegetable or meat."
Har Dayal stayed in the house when he was in town, sharing a
room with Gobind Behari Lal. This afforded the students plenty
of contact with him and solidified his status as a role model. Whenever Har Dayal gave a public lecture, the story was in the papers
the next day, "*and the students were thrilled to read about their great
compatriot* .... Everybody called him 'Lalji' ..." (Sareen 1994: 31–32,
emphasis added). There seems to be no question that Har Dayal,
in comparison to Taraknath, enjoyed the greater notoriety at this
point in time.

Gobind Behari Lal presents a picture of a rather diversified
mix of Indian students who were studying in the University of
California in those days. Wherever their numbers were sufficient,
and as much as possible, they appear to have residentially differentiated themselves in accordance with their ethnic backgrounds.
The Bengalis apparently formed the most preponderant group of

"self-supported" students and formed a "fraternity" of their own which they called the "Nalanda Club," named after the purportedly oldest Indian university dating back to the days of Emperor Ashoka. Members at one time or another included Taraknath Das, Dhan Gopal Mukerji, Surendranath Karr, and Sarangadhar Das, all of whom, as noted earlier, became revolutionary activists of one sort or another in their own right.

The attempt on the life of Lord Hardinge by a bomb-thrower—as the Indian viceroy was making a "state entry" into Delhi at the time when the capital of India was being transferred from Calcutta to Delhi—created a sensation among the Indian students at Berkeley and Stanford and other institutions, West Coast or otherwise, where Indians existed in any numbers, but especially in the San Francisco area. Har Dayal soared to unprecedented heights of public attention and rhetorical fervor. He was the principal speaker at a rally held at the University of California YMCA. "He attacked British rule in India, and said something to the effect that the Indian people had the right to struggle for their independence, equality and other human rights in any way they were able to" (Sareen 1994: 33). And that included tossing bombs at viceroys! Replying to an attack against him and the Indian students at Berkeley by British-born Professor Henry Morse Stephens (1857–1919), then a prominent member of the University of California faculty, Har Dayal stated in the student newspaper that British Rule in India was "an infamy that must be erased."

This got the attention of the British authorities, and Hopkinson quickly rushed into the breach. Having learned that Master Amir Chand and several of Har Dayal's closest friends over in India had been implicated in the conspiracy, the British authorities implied that he too bore some relationship to the attack on Hardinge. To try and convince the American authorities that Har Dayal was a threat to their country as well as to Britain, they circulated the charge that he was "not only engaged in a speaking tour which would take him through Oregon and Washington, but that he was acting at the same time as an advance agent for the notorious anarchist Emma Goldman" (ibid.: 138. See note 6 in this chapter). This latter was an unsubstantiated allegation perpetrated by one of Hopkinson's informants, which Hopkinson himself was, of course, happy to try and manipulate in any way he could.

These developments would eventually imperil Har Dayal's ability to remain in the United States, or at least give him a legitimate excuse for leaving in search of new political pastures. This distinction is important, as we shall see, because there is some question about Har Dayal's staying power in anything he undertook. But in the short run, they ideally prepared the way for him to fulfill his long-standing craving to emerge as the acclaimed leader of a revolutionary movement.

The England experience and what followed had enabled him to craft his thoughts, feelings and impressions into a broad revolutionary perspective. The doctrines—an amalgam of socialism and nationalism—propagated by Shyamaji Krishnavarma, V.D. Savarkar, Madam Cama, and other hard-line revolutionaries at India House and in Paris, and his restless wanderings in search of a creed to live by and to propagate, prepared Har Dayal, at the age of 26, to come to America with a well-constructed revolutionary mind, the determination, organizational skills and literary ability to translate words into actions, and the charisma to attract followers. "He belonged to that group of fearless Indians who were struggling to achieve the freedom of their country by organized rebellion," declared Gobind Behari Lal (Sareen 1994: 8). The immigrant Sikh peasants and other Indians on the West Coast were the principal objects of this improbable conjuncture between a young Indian freedom fighter and the yearnings of an emigrant, predominantly Sikh peasantry for political freedom in their country of origin and civil rights in their adopted land.

Haridas Mazumdar (1962: 7–8) speaks of having met Har Dayal in New York City in 1938–1939, years after his role in the Ghadr movement, and found him to be "an urbane gentleman, deeply devoted to philosophic research, [and] burning with a desire to serve mankind." Har Dayal built the Ghadr Party "from scratch," asserts Mazumdar. Its membership included Sikh, Hindu, and Muslim farmers from California along with several "intellectuals" such as Dr Taraknath Das, Bhagwan Singh Gyanee, Ramchandra, and a "romantic figure" named Raja Mahendra Pratap, who "seems to have had something to do with revolutionary activities on behalf of India's freedom in America, Japan and China" (ibid.). By 1916, even the peripatetic Comintern revolutionary M. Roy had become involved.

Har Dayal came along at the right moment to take advantage of a rising tide of social ferment pervading the South Asian communities along the West Coast, generated by the racist immigration attitudes and policies that were increasingly imperiling economic opportunity and basic civil rights for the South Asian minority. He helped build the Ghadr Party by parlaying the favorable public image he had achieved, in the journalistic and academic communities and among the general public following his arrival in the Bay Area, into high visibility among his fellow Indians. He convinced many that an authentic leader had arisen in their midst who had clout in important sections of White society, and who possessed the talent to provide vigorous leadership to his fellow Indians in their struggle for human dignity both in India and in America. "The mood had changed," says Brown (1975: 138). "The stage was set for Har Dayal."

It has to be reiterated that activists like Har Dayal pre-dated the rise of Mahatma Gandhi with his doctrine of non-violent resistance (*satyagraha*) to colonialism and social injustice. They were also by and large ideologically at odds with the political moderates of their own day like Gopal Krishna Gokhale (1866–1915) and Dadabhai Naroji (1825–1917), whom they regarded as being political wimps, excessively obsequious to the Raj. At this stage of overseas Indian political evolution, they believed that militant action alone (including terrorism) was needed to achieve political independence for India. The role models for young, would-be Indian radicals and revolutionaries were Maharashtrian religio-cultural revivalists like Bal Gangadhar Tilak (1856–1920), V.D. Savarkar (1883–1966), and Shyamaji Krishnavarma (1857–1930); radical Bengali extremist nationalists like Bankim Chandra Chatterji (1838–1894) and Bipin Chandra Pal (1858–1932); and Punjabi revolutionary nationalists and Arya Samajists like Lala Lajpat Rai (1865–1928) and Dayanand Saraswati (1824–1883).

The modus operandi Har Dayal selected was a direct outgrowth of "a plan which he had conceived even before his resignation from Oxford." It was, says Brown "an organizational pattern which had been established by Vinayak Savarkar when he formed the Free India Society in England," a pattern which Savarkar had in turn derived from his reading of Mazzini's Young Italy (Brown 1975: 142). This in itself reveals how much Indian revolutionaries were blending their own culturally rooted political ruminations with Western political doctrines. Essentially, this involved gathering up existing organizations and factions scattered among the American and Canadian Sikhs, then trying to meld them into some semblance of a coherent organizational structure, imbuing the members with systematic infusions of radical propaganda, pointing them toward the designated adversary, and waiting for the propitious moment for revolution to explode on to the scene, much as it had in the days of the Indian Mutiny (which the radicals called the Great Indian Uprising) in 1857.

There were many scattered groups to work with. Two major ones that were ripe for consolidation were the Hindu Association of the Pacific Coast (HAOPC) and the Hindustan Association. As noted earlier, the HAOPC had been formed in January 1912 by G.D. Kumar. Sohan Singh Bhakna became its first president. The Hindu Association was created by a small entrepreneur named Ram Nath Puri. Har Dayal himself was active in the Radical Club, the IWW, and the Fraternity of the Red Flag, the latter being an organization of his own creation. In all three of these latter it was essentially socialist-style class warfare that was the central theme.

One of the most striking of these grassroots activists was Pandurang Sadashiva Khankhoje. Prior to his coming to America, Khankhoje, a Maharashtrian Chitpavan Brahman, was a devotee of Bal Gangadhar Tilak who urged him to go abroad and acquire military training so that he could return to India and help promote armed rebellion against the Raj. He first went to Japan but there ran afoul of the Anglo-Japanese Alliance of 1902, which prevented the Japanese from enabling Indian dissidents to acquire weapons technology for use against their British ally.[8] Although "still a young man" when he reached California in 1908, Khankhoje rapidly became "a veteran in West Coast nationalist activities" (Brown 1975: 136). He established relationships with Indian students at Berkeley but failed to interest them in pursuing military training in the US. They preferred to remain focused on their studies and on earning money with which to support themselves. Khankhoje himself did manage to enroll in a local military academy and, in Brown's words, "was stunned to discover that technology, with chemicals and weapons developed on principles of modern science, had put warfare beyond the scope of the untutored and unskilled Indian" (ibid.). He wanted to enroll in West Point in order enhance his military capabilities but discovered that only

American citizens were eligible. He then applied for American citizenship but was turned down.

Nevertheless, Khankhoje persisted with his agitational activities among the West Coast South Asians. He shifted his emphasis from attempting to directly create a body of armed combatants to building a mass political base that might one day yield an army of freedom fighters. "Without securing this mass support, no revolutionary movement would succeed," he declared, "I, therefore, decided that with what I had acquired, I would be able to do much in India" (quoted by Brown 1975: 137, but source not mentioned). With this goal in mind, he established the Indian Independence League in California, but moved it to Portland, Oregon, when it failed to attract many members there. It was a different story in Portland once he garnered financial support from Pandit Kanshi Ram, "a wealthy entrepreneur in the lumber labor market," who also served as the organization's treasurer. "Membership soon jumped to 500, and grew further as the region's immigrants experienced increasing duress from officials of the USINS, and as Khankhoje himself found ways to import illegals from Mexico and Canada" (ibid.). As immigration restrictions grew ever more draconian, on both sides of the border, particularly from 1910 onwards, Khankhoje shifted the focus of his operations back to the Bay Area. In effect, this positioned him for the political developments that would catalyze Har Dayal's entry into the local arena.

The principal outcome of this concatenation of events and personalities was Har Dayal's emergence as the leader who had the charisma, intellect and legitimacy needed to weld South Asian immigrants into some semblance of a coherent political force. The fact that the Indian community was now prepared to support and sustain a leader with these qualities is in itself a testament to the extent of their demographic expansion and social consolidation, their adaptation to the American and Canadian political cultures, and to the magnitude of economic resources they had collectively accumulated since their original, tremulous ingress into the New World.

The immediate result of this scalar increase in political ferment was the formation of the Ghadr Party. The Hindu Association of the Pacific Coast became the staging base, as it were, for this development. This was, as Brown (1975: 140) puts it, "an uneasy coalition between Hindu intellectuals and Sikh farmers, peasants and lumber mill workers." Although in the end it proved to be a fragile reed, lasting no more than four or five years in its original form,[9] it clearly set the stage for more sophisticated forms of political awareness and interest representation by South Asians in America down the road. Most of all, however, Ghadr marked the point where different strands of Indian immigration to North America politically converged and began to cross-fertilize one another in an unprecedented manner. It was this combination of growing identification with the freedom movement in India and the civil rights concerns of South Asians in America that gave it political impetus. But achieving this early synthesis of interests required the emergence of bold, articulate and charismatic leadership. Har Dayal and Sohan Singh Bhakna were moving spirits behind the creation and organizational strengthening of the Ghadr movement; Taraknath Das, as we shall see, was the catalytic force whose example, peripatetic energy, revolutionary fervor and political staying power helped keep the flame of political awareness and commitment burning throughout the South Asian community during the inter-war years and especially in the years that followed, after Har Dayal's abrupt departure from the scene.

The key meeting which led to the creation of Ghadr occurred in Portland, Oregon, on May 8, 1913. Pandit Kanshi Ram had been the driving force in bringing brains and brawn together under the rubric of the Hindu Association of the Pacific Coast. Sohan Singh Bhakna (1870–1968), a Sikh peasant who had risen to prominence among his countrymen following his arrival in America in 1909 (and whose relevance will be described in the next section) was selected as president, while Har Dayal was chosen as secretary. Har Dayal was obviously the power behind the throne. He supplied the needed ideological fervor, organizational brains and public image. He was in charge of establishing the organization's publications agenda in his status as editor and publisher of *Ghadr*, the monthly magazine that would be distributed far and wide to propagate the movement's revolutionary political agenda. Har Dayal wished to establish a headquarters in San Francisco and call it Yugantar Ashram (New Age Center). He wanted to purchase a house on a hill in order to symbolize the movement's "high ambitions." Such a place was found, "on the very top of a hill in Mission District, at 436 Hill Street. It faced the famous Twin Peaks to the north. It was a gray colored two-story wooden house, which had escaped destruction by the great San Francisco earthquake and fire" (Gobind Behari Lal, in Sareen 1994: 35–36). That too was deemed to be "symbolic."

To celebrate the commencement of Ghadr, says Gobind Behari Lal, a gathering was held "of very selected guests, almost all distinguished Americans," at the Shattuck Hotel in Berkeley. They included Mr and Mrs Fremont Older, Austin Lewis (lawyer and reformer), John D. Barry (*San Francisco Bulletin* columnist), Winston Churchill (an American novelist who wrote *Inside the Cup*), and "several progressive and noted University of California Professors." The latter group included Dr Thomas Reed (Professor of Political Science), Arthur U. Pope (Professor of Philosophy), Drs Riber and Lewis from the Philosophy Department, Dr Carlton Parker (Economics), Mrs Cornelia Stratton Parker, Professor Arthur Ryder (Sanskritist, translator of *Shakuntala*), and also, "several Berkeley officials" (ibid.: 36). The gathering exemplified the success which Har Dayal had in projecting the South Asian cause into the liberal-intellectual community of San Francisco.

The first issue of *Ghadr* came out on November 1, 1913 in Gurmukhi (Punjabi), Devanagari (Hindi), and Urdu. It enunciated the political intentions of this new organization. "Today," it read, "there begins in foreign lands, but in our country's language, a war against the British Raj." Their work, their cause, it went on, was to reach the point "when rifles and blood will take the place of pen and ink" in their contemplated revolution. They declared themselves the "Enemy of the British Government" and, on the eve of World War I, heaped praise upon the Germans whom they obviously foresaw as potential partners in their country's liberation (Singh and Singh 1966: 19). There was a set feature on its lead page which read: *Angrezi Raj Ka Kachha Chittha* (Balance Sheet of British Rule in India). The choice of the word *"Kachha"* in this title had significance in the Hindustani language. It implied that this "record" was "low-grade," "vulgar," something which British officials and agents would immediately grasp. This is what Gobind Behari Lala meant when he said that Har Dayal wished to mobilize the vernacular languages to the cause. Har Dayal wrote signed editorials that were scathing indictments of the Raj and promised an eventual uprising (*Ghadr*) that would end it. *Ghadr* ran instalments of V.D. Savarkar's famous work, *The Indian War of*

*Independence of 1857*. There were translations into Hindstani and Punjabi of William Jennings Bryan's lectures on "The British Rule in India". And much more.[10]

However, before we consider further the accomplishments and the importance of the Ghadr movement, it is necessary to consider in some detail the roles played by at least two other personalities who contributed to its establishment and to the general atmosphere of political ferment that was abroad in the American and Canadian South Asian communities as World War I was approaching. They are Sohan Singh Bhakna and Taraknath Das. The former was a key figure in developing the linkages between grassroots Sikhs and the middle-class students and intellectuals who together brought Ghadr into being. Das was an intellectual and revolutionary spawned by Bengali radicalism, whose implacable dedication to the cause of South Asian immigrants' civil rights, and whose staying power in the struggle encompassed not only the founding of Ghadr but the entire panoply of the struggle, over a span of more than half a century—from 1906 to 1964, by South Asians in North America to secure their human rights and those of their countrymen in India.

## Sohan Singh Bhakna

Sohan Singh Bhakna (1870–1968) was a product par excellence of the grassroots, peasant aspect of emerging South Asian revolutionism in the American environment. Born in the village of Khutrae Khurd in Amritsar district, he was the only son of Karam Singh, a moderately well-off Jat Sikh peasant farmer, who died when Sohan was only a year old. By comparison with Har Dayal and Taraknath Das, Sohan Singh Bhakna was a rustic, deeply rooted in the Punjabi soil. His family was not impoverished, however. Within the compass of his village, the family was "quite a rich peasant household" with 65 acres of land (Josh 1970: 1). Because Sohan's father died when he was only a year old, his personality was shaped by a devoutly religious mother and other adult members of his extended family. His father, Karam Singh, left a legacy of having been a man who was honest, kind-hearted and sympathetic to the poor, and who disdained the strictures of caste. With little formal education available in rural Punjab, Sohan Singh's early education was at a *gurdwara*. However, he never learned to write the Punjabi language, although when he was 11 his mother got him admitted to an "Urdu school" that opened in their village and provided education up to the fifth class. He was a good student but this was all the education he ever received, since middle school and higher education were available only in the cities. Sohan indeed had the means to go further in school but to do so he would have had to live away from home. "His mother could not stand this separation," writes Josh (1970: 2), so, as Sohan himself put it in a small booklet he published later in life, entitled *Jiwan Sangram* (Life Struggle), "My being the only son stood in the way of my pursuit of education and I was prevented from going in for higher studies" (ibid.).

Somewhat like Teja Singh in Canada, Sohan Singh went through a period of youthful delinquency before getting his bearings. The difference was that Sohan did not emerge from his social miasma by choosing the path of formal education and "enlightenment." Sohan's was what might be called a "folk" transfiguration. It occurred as he was walking past the *gurdwara* while two musicians were chanting *slokas* of the *Bhakti* saint, Baba Farid. "He stopped and then went inside the gurdwara and listened to the hymns. The *slokas* had a profound effect on him" (ibid.: 4).

This spiritual experience led him to seek out another local saint, Baba Kesar Singh, who had once been connected with the *Namdhari* sect but had moved on to promulgate his own version of divinity which emphasized a strong measure of socio-religious egalitarianism. This is what impressed Sohan Singh. "He stood above the rituals and narrowness of sects," he said. "He was an embodiment of unity and he did not discriminate between a Hindu, Sikh, Muslim or Christian .... He did not believe in untouchability" (ibid.: 5). One cannot help but observe that this doctrine was an analog of the ethical values to which his long-deceased father was said to have adhered and which his mother had conscien-tiously imparted to the son.

For the next decade, Sohan Singh devoted himself to a kind of grassroots social reformism that featured the hosting of sojourners and pilgrims passing through his village during religious festivals. The stress was on "social ecumenism": providing hospitality to all regardless of caste or sect. He even initiated an annual festival in his own name (*Bhakna hola*) which celebrated this universalistic theme. It is said that he spent thousands of rupees on these activities until the money began to run out. Eventually, however, this pattern exhausted its appeal and his thoughts turned toward new horizons, catalyzed by political developments in the Punjab. In 1906–1907, an agitation broke out there in opposition to the so-called Colony Bill, whose purpose seems to have been to increase the powers of landlords over their tenants. The agitation was led by several emergent political leaders, the most prominent of whom was Lala Lajpat Rai, a founder of the Arya Samaj, whom Sohan Singh would later on encounter in America. It made a big impression on him mainly because it succeeded. The Viceroy, Lord Minto, in the face of widespread public unrest, vetoed the legislation, and this was viewed at the grassroots "as the first victory of Hindu–Muslim–Sikh unity" (Josh 1970: 11).

It was around this time that Sohan Singh became interested in emigration. "A friend from America had assured him full help and had written that one could earn a lot there and that he should not hesitate to leave at once," recounts Josh (ibid.: 8). Although it is not certain which factors were more decisive in stimulating thoughts about traveling abroad, it is doubtful it had very much to do with expanding Sohan's political awareness. I put it this way because when he migrated to America in 1909 at the age of 40, his stated reason for doing so was primarily to earn enough money through manual labor to pay off his debts back home. Activism may have lurked in the background but had certainly not yet become his *raison d'être*.

Even though Sohan Singh expressed no overt political reasons for emigrating, it cannot be doubted that in the last years before his departure he had internalized a measure of political awareness upon which circumstances he encountered in the New World would resonate. He landed at Seattle on April 4, 1909. His friend Harnam Singh helped him in his job search until he finally found employment in Monarch Lumber Mill. It was already employing around 200 Punjabis who worked 10 hours a day at a daily wage of $2.50 (Rs 5). Racial animosity simmered between Indian and White workers because the Sikhs were manipulated by millowners in their confrontations with the labor unions. They were socially vulnerable, far removed from their homeland but still attached to it in primordial ways which impeded their assimilative tendencies. "Their standard of life and the level of their wages were very low as compared with the American workers." For this reason, "the organized workers of America disliked them because when [they] fought for raising their wages and reducing the working hours [the Sikhs] stood in their way—they would go back to work on lower wages and thus served as a weapon of the employers in strikebreaking" (Josh 1970: 13).

**Illustration 6.3**
**Baba Sohan Singh Bhakna**

*Source:* Singh and Singh 1966.

The outcome of an Imperial Conference that was convened in London to address the issue of Indian migration proved to be the final straw for most Canadian and American Sikhs, including Sohan Singh. The precipitating event was the refusal of the Colonial Secretary, Lord Lewis Harcourt, to meet a delegation dispatched from Canada under the auspices of the United India League and the Khalsa Dewan Society (Vancouver) and listen to their grievances. They made public appeals to the English people; they met members of Parliament and union leaders. They even journeyed to India following their London rebuff and visited Bombay, Madras, and Lahore. All to no avail. They returned to the West Coast in July 1913 and found that their Indian brethren had already been moved to action. The *Komagata Maru* incident was ongoing. A revolutionary organization was already in the process of materializing. Indian workers in the Portland area had met in late 1912 and agreed to organize. They proposed that their organ-ization be called the Indian Association of the Pacific Coast; that an office be opened in Portland; and that a newspaper be published that would be called *Hindustan*. A measure of how far Sohan Singh Bhakna's political awakening had proceeded in the intervening years since reaching America is the fact that he was elected pre-sident, while G.D. Kumar was chosen secretary, and the well-to-do Brahman entrepreneur, Pandit Kanshi Ram, was designated as cashier. Meetings were held every Sunday and were convened in many different locations. It was through the efforts and mone-tary resources of Kanshi Ram, of course, that the next step was taken and Har Dayal was brought into the mix to energize its trans-formation into Ghadr. For tactically self-evident reasons, Sohan Singh was retained as president during this transition: he was the embodiment of the movement's populist roots.

This multiplicity of meetings is an important datum because it attests to the frequently-alluded-to process of ramifying the polit-ical interaction that was taking place. Also indicative of a growing dynamism is the report which British Ambassador Sir Cecil Spring-Rice sent to the American Secretary of State, William Jennings Bryan, on February 15, 1915, about a year after Ghadr came into existence: He speaks of "the recent endeavours to create a revolu-tion in India by means of assassination, dacoity, dissemination of revolutionary literature, suborning of troops, importation of arms, and other means." These "crimes," he asserts, "were *in the main*

**Illustration 6.4**
**Pandit Kanshi Ram**

*Source:* Singh and Singh 1966.

*instigated, and to a large extent perpetrated by emigrants who returned from America after the outbreak of war"* (Josh 1970: 68, emphasis added). He alludes to the modus operandi of the movement's operatives: "Ram Chandra, Gobind Behari Lal, and others go out to the ranches, where poor labourers are working, on Saturdays and Sundays; they preach revolution to them until these poor and illiterate people think they must drive the English out of India or kill them" (Sareen 1994: 72).

## Taraknath Das

The third person who contributed his talents to this developing political brew was Taraknath Das. He reached America in 1906 via the Far East and Japan. Unlike Har Dayal, he had not been a poster-child of the Raj, sent with fanfare to Oxford on scholarship, purportedly destined to scale the heights of imperial fame and fortune. Taraknath's political personality had been shaped almost entirely in the crucible of turn-of-the-century Bengali radicalism and modernism. The political role he played in the American South Asian community complemented that of Har Dayal, indeed intersected with it in many respects, but was never identical to it. It was as though each had his designated role to play in the crystallization of a South Asian identity in the New World. Har Dayal's political style reflected his elitist Delhi and populist Punjabi roots; Taraknath's his middle-class and radical Bengali roots. We saw how Har Dayal reached America after a European sojourn where he had imbibed the "sankritized" radicalism of Shyamaji Krishnavarma at India House in London, and the socialistically tinged, "continental" nationalism propagated by the Madam Cama circle in Paris. Taraknath Das by contrast reached America after having been politically socialized entirely in the Bengali radical tradition and then being compelled to flee India with the King's jailers in hot pursuit.

In Bengal, Taraknath Das was admitted to the Arya Mission Institution and in 1901 passed the entrance exams with first division marks, which gained him entrée into the General Assembly's Institution which later became Scottish Church College. When an essay he wrote on the unsuitability of the British-structured educational system for India won a silver medal and attracted the attention of Pramathonath Mitra, a member of the Calcutta High Court who was one of the judges for the competition, Taraknath was recruited into the "original cadre" of the Anusilan Samiti. Today the Samiti would be called a "paramilitary" organization. Essentially, it was a gymnasium (*akhara*) whose purpose was to train middle-class Bengali youths in the martial arts, including marching drill, wrestling, sword, and *lathi*- (bamboo staves) play. It was established "to counteract historical British contempt for the Bengalis as a physically weak, deceitful and cowardly race" (Mukherjee 1997: 2). The goal of the Anusilan Samiti was "to build a cell of physically strong, brave young men who would eventually form the base of a disciplined national army." Initiation rites included dedication to the goddess Kali. The academic curriculum included classes on the Great Indian Uprising (*Ghadr*) of 1857, treatises on guerilla warfare, and exposure to the indigenous philosophical and ideological ruminations of persons like Surendra Nath Bannerjea, Chitta Ranjan Das, Aurobindo Ghose, and Sister Nivedita.[11]

Taraknath Das quickly gravitated toward the most militant faction of the Anusilan Samiti, which advocated direct forms of action against British rule. This group studied the use of weapons. He himself became skilled at fencing and shooting guns, as well as one of its most energetic propagandists and organizers. He developed a close relationship with Bhupendranath Datta, Swami Vivekananda's younger brother, and thus a link to Sister Nivedita.

His connection with such an anti-government secret society caused consternation in his family, who feared reprisals that would damage their economic condition and social position. This was resolved by his agreeing to leave home and continue his studies at Tangail PM College in Mymensingh district. There he met Ram Dayal Majumdar, who had been principal of the Arya Mission Institution in Calcutta when Taraknath had been a student there. Majumdar was a nationalist hardliner. "By this time," says Mukherjee (1997: 3), "anti-British secret societies were springing up all over Bengal" and Mymensingh had become "an active center for underground revolutionaries." He guided Taraknath Das into the region's secret societies and, in effect, launched his career as a revolutionary nationalist pledged to devote his life to driving the British out of India. He was barely 18 years old when this self-transformation took place. The political turmoil that arose following Lord Curzon's announcement of the partition of Bengal in 1903, leading to the Swadeshi movement, intensified Taraknath's revolutionary zeal. Not unlike Har Dayal in America, he devoted his nascent organizational talents to consolidating a number of cells that were scattered about in his vicinity in order to achieve a scalar increase in the movement's effectiveness. It was good preparation for his political career in America. In order to garner funds for the Anusilan Samiti, he engineered a program of purchasing large boats that could intercept and rob river-craft carrying remittances from British-owned jute mills (Mukherjee 1997: 5).

When factional conflict between the Calcutta and Dacca branches developed to the point that Taraknath decided it was impeding the effectiveness of the Samiti, he opted out and in 1905 shifted his political act to Madras where he "set out to establish a revolutionary base in South India" (ibid.: 6). He acquired a following in the name of the Anusīlan Samiti, which included several young men who eventually became noted freedom fighters in their own right.

By the end of 1905, however, Taraknath Das had acquired enough political visibility to run the risk of being arrested for "sedition." He was warned of his imminent apprehension by a sympathetic police inspector and advised to get out of the country. With passage money obtained from "patriotic wealthy men," a number of young radicals had already left India. When Taraknath Das's turn came, he had to seek "alternate means." The requisite alternate means came in the form of money stolen by a compatriot who worked as a landlord's employee. It funded Taraknath's and a few of his cohorts' flight from India. "In late 1905, 'Tarak Brahmachari,' clad in a flimsy *gerua*, left for Japan as a deck passenger on a livestock-carrying French ship ... During the voyage he suffered a great deal due to cold weather, rough seas, and lack of food" (ibid.: 6–7).

Japan had acquired considerable prestige in the eyes and imagination of Indian radicals by virtue of having been the first indigenously Asian state to defeat a European power in a modern war. The Japanese victory in the Russo-Japanese War of 1904–1905 was seen as the first successful Asian challenge to White colonialism. However, the Japanese were themselves too racist, imperialistic and culturally involuted to fully capitalize on their achievement in ideological and strategic terms. This became painfully evident to young Indian revolutionaries like Taraknath who journeyed to Japan in search of political succor. They found the Japanese difficult to relate to. They found the language differences to be almost insurmountable. Most Indians who went there for technological training or university education were unable to comprehend technical and advanced lectures and discussions in Japanese.

All the while he was in Japan, Taraknath was being monitored by British officials there, who eventually prevailed upon the

Japanese to take coercive action against him. While they were unwilling to extradite him back to India, they "unofficially asked
him to leave Japan as soon as possible," says Mukherjee (1997: 7).
Money was raised from Indian merchants to enable him and a
fellow Bengali radical, Pabita Kumar Roy of Mymensingh, to book
passage for America. They sailed for Seattle in steerage class
aboard the *Tango Maru* on June 20, 1906, and reached their destination on July 12. "He gave his name as Jogendranath Das in the
passenger manifest, a small deception that would haunt him
for many years" (ibid.: 8). His first job in America was as a manual
laborer in Seattle, after which he made his way to San Francisco.

This was only two months after the San Francisco earthquake
and fire of April 18, 1906. Interestingly, the first Hindu temple
ever erected in America, indeed in the New World, existed there.
It had been the brainchild of Swami Trigunatita, the head of
the California Vedanta Society, and was constructed in 1902. It
"miraculously" survived the natural holocaust. Trigunatita acted
as mentor to many of the Indian students struggling to make it
in the Bay Area and at first willingly took Taraknath Das under
his wing. His credentials as one of the founder members of
the Vivekananda Society of Calcutta, as well as other interactions
with members of the Ramakrishna Mission back home, also
helped Taraknath gain entrée. He shared a room in the temple
with another student, Girindranath Mukherjee. But he soon fell
out with the Swami. Taraknath was too volatile a personality
and independent-minded for the Swami's taste. A strict discip-
linarian, in the *guru* tradition, the Swami "demanded unquestioned
obedience to the rules he set for the temple household." Most
important, "He disapproved of Taraknath's extremist comments and anti-British propaganda among the American devotees"
(ibid.).

Like most other student migrants, Taraknath commenced his
American career on the ground floor. He took menial jobs and
lived a Spartan existence. As in so many other instances, his fortunes improved when he caught the eye of a sympathetic good
Samaritan. A Berkeley professor noticed him sitting in a corner
reading a book. Impressed, he arranged for Taraknath to get employment as a laboratory helper at the university. By January 1907,

he was admitted as a special student in the chemistry department. Like the determined political activist he had become, Taraknath hit the ground running as soon as he got his American bearings. Almost immediately, he formed a group and launched into political activity. Once again we see the tendency of the young political activists of these times, wherever they alighted, to immediately undertake to validate themselves by founding some sort of organization that could act as a vehicle for their mobilizational and propaganda activities.

He formed the California Hindu Students Association with a membership of no more than a dozen individuals. By the end of 1906, Ramnath Puri had reached San Francisco. As 1907 wore on, other young radicals arrived from abroad. Pandurang Khankhoje came from Japan. Adhar Laskar, a fellow member of the extremist faction of Anusilan Samiti, showed up. Together, they set about to build links with the grassroots Indian laborers out in the countryside under the rubric of an organization they called the Indian Independence League. In a free evening school started in Oakland, they taught English, American history and whatever else they could think of to help the workers improve their chances of obtaining American citizenship. Puri began publishing an Urdu periodical called *Circular-i-Azadi* (The Freedom Circular).

The organization did not last long. In characteristic Maharashtrian fashion, Laskar and Khankhoje enrolled in Tamalpais Military School; Puri went his own way. Taraknath was having difficulty making ends meet and had to find some sort of steady employment. His experiences with worker's education had heightened his awareness of the one thing that most directly concerned the Sikh and South Asian laboring class in America and Canada at that time: immigration. In 1907, he applied for a position as an interpreter at the Immigration and Naturalization Service (INS). He passed the examination "with the highest rating" and was assigned to Vancouver at a starting salary of $60 per month. This was, of course, a fortuitous move because it materially enhanced his contacts with the Canadian milieu of the South Asian immigrant population.

Even before he became an employee of the INS, he had himself filed for American citizenship toward the end of 1906. In Mukherjee's words, "Expulsion from Japan had taught Taraknath the lesson that without the right to stay in the United States, nothing meaningful could be done to promote revolution in his homeland or to work for the rights of Hindu immigrants" (1997: 9). This initial attempt at gaining American citizenship failed, however, because Taraknath, well prior to the Ozawa case (to be discussed later), was not deemed to be "a free white [Caucasian] male." In any event, there was not at this time a uniform federal policy on citizenship applications. This was left a "local option" matter to be mainly determined by county court proceedings. Nevertheless, the racist predilections of the country as a whole made it virtually inevitable wherever they resided that any aspirant to American citizenship who was deemed to be a person of color would be turned down. Taraknath protested the decision in writing, employing what would soon be the standard line of objection to racist categorizations of South Asians: that the anthropological evidence proved that Indians were a branch of the so-called Caucasian race and were, therefore, "White." Taraknath's day would eventually come, but somewhat further down the road.

Meanwhile, however, his acceptance by the INS and assignment to the Vancouver office laid the groundwork for expanding his political horizons into Canada. At the height of the anti-Indian rioting in Vancouver and Bellingham, and the turmoil surrounding the refusal of the Canadian authorities to allow ships containing Indian immigrants to disembark at Vancouver, Taraknath in 1907 characteristically formed a new organization, the Hindusthani Association, for the purpose of defending Indian rights. By April of 1908, he was publishing a bi-monthly magazine called *Free Hindusthan*, whose declared purpose was to "exert our best energies to get Swaraj" and "make the [Canadian] government hesitate in any policy of exclusion or even restriction by threat of revolt in India."[12] What may be most important about Taraknath's entry into the Canadian political imbroglio were two interconnected factors: (1) It measurably enhanced his reputation and widened his networks as a political activist, and (2) brought him to the attention of the Imperial intelligence apparatus. Convinced that he had something to do with the Vancouver and Bellingham unrest, a Canadian government agent named W.M. MacInnes interviewed Taraknath and concluded that he was "the principal ring leader of Hindu agitation," and, according to Mukherjee (ibid.: 11), "recommended to the Dominion government that Hindu immigration be stopped altogether." To the extent that this was true, it is a strong indicator of how well activists like Taraknath were succeeding in instilling political consciousness among South Asians.

It is remarkable how quickly Taraknath Das had moved from being a mere political refugee and a social nonentity to becoming a significant player in the immigration wars on the West Coast. It is a testament to his energy and his zeal. Clearly, the agitational skills and intensities he had acquired in the Bengal crucible had prepared him well to have an impact on the Pacific coast. It is equally remarkable how touchy the Imperial authorities were about the slightest hint of revolutionary political dissent. Taraknath, Har Dayal and other young activists at this time were hardly persons of major stature in the domain of international politics and social revolution. Mainly they could be characterized as little more than "coffee house radicals," minor players, small potatoes, with paltry resources and minimal followings. Yet they were viewed with enough alarm to draw professional agents like William Hopkinson and MacInnes into the cloak-and-dagger arena. Soon the Canadian and British authorities had created a network of spies and informers in the South Asian community that even included Swami Trigunatita of the San Francisco Vedanta Society, and some of the students whom Har Dayal had arranged to bring over through the Guru Gobind Singh scholarships.

There was, in fact, a kind of gathering of the "usual suspects" along the Pacific Coast by 1907. More of Taraknath's Mymensingh cohorts, such as Surendramohan Bose and Guru Datt Kumar, arrived via Japan. It was the year that Hopkinson became an active player. By the following year, *Free Hindustan's* incendiary rhetoric was generating considerable political ferment in the South Asian immigrant community and consequently considerable alarm in official Canadian and Imperial circles due to their hypersensitivity to what they perceived as "sedition." The declared purpose of his new organization and its publication was unambiguously revolutionary: "Dear brothers of Hindustan," its inaugural issue intoned, "for the sake of humanity, let us be united together, and exert our best energies to get Swaraj—absolute self-government ... sacrifice will be the only genuine test .... Progress will be the path, and education will be the way ...."[13]

When his detractors attempted to single out Taraknath's roles in founding the Hindusthan Association and publishing its

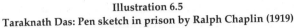

Illustration 6.5
Taraknath Das: Pen sketch in prison by Ralph Chaplin (1919)

*Source:* US National Archives.

bi-monthly newspaper as proof of his anarchistic proclivities, he tendered his resignation from the INS in order to avoid accusations of conflict of interest. This was in April 1908. Hopkinson and his cohorts nevertheless persisted in trying to smear Taraknath in official American circles in the hope of blocking his efforts to obtain US citizenship, which they now knew he was seeking. Their ultimate purpose was, of course, to get him deported and handed over to British authorities where he could be prosecuted, indeed even hanged, for "sedition."

It is to the credit of numerous individuals in the official establishment, academia, the journalistic community and among well-placed private citizens that the opposition to South Asian immigration and to the work of Indian patriots like Har Dayal and Taraknath Das was never a monolith. The spirit of democracy and fair play was alive and well in many quarters of American society. We have already seen that in academia, in particular, several faculty members and administrators at institutions like Berkeley and Stanford actively supported the right of the political activists to publicly champion their causes. Indeed at crucial times many joined them on the podium. They also facilitated their access to the universities' academic curricula so that they could pursue advanced degrees, even while simultaneously pursuing their political agendas, and thereby enhance their educational credentials, which in turn enhanced their intellectual credibility and political staying power. There were journalists, such as John D. Barry, *San Francisco Bulletin* columnist, who publicized their political doings and afforded them personal access to the media. And there were prominent citizens in the local communities, like Mr and Mrs Fremont Older and Austin Lewis, who developed friendships with the most talented of the activists and were valuable sources of financial support and entrée into liberal society.

These were especially important assets for Taraknath Das in his quest for American citizenship. Great efforts were exerted by Hopkinson, MacInnes and other Imperial agents to try and checkmate this undertaking. They importuned all manner of persons both in local government and the relevant federal agencies, even including California members of Congress, trying to convince them that Taraknath Das constituted what was in the McCarthy era of the 1950s termed a "security risk." Due to their efforts, it would be almost six years before Taraknath could realize his ambition to become a bonafide American citizen. The reasons for such determined opposition are patently obvious: If Taraknath Das, or indeed any politically committed Indian immigrant, achieved American citizenship, the rights and protections he would then enjoy would place him decisively beyond the punitive reach of the Raj.

Following this unsuccessful attempt, Taraknath returned to Seattle in May 1908 and soon afterward took an amazing new turn in his career. At the age of 24, he obtained admission to Norwich Military College in Norwich, Vermont. Established in 1818, it was the oldest collegiate military institution in the United States. How precisely he learned about and gained admission to Norwich Academy is not entirely clear, nor why he chose this particular moment to undertake such a radical departure from his ongoing political itinerary. With regard to his decision to seek military training at all, however, there was precedent for such a move in his Indian background. The political idioms of turn-of-the-century Punjabi, Maharashtrian and Bengali radicalism, and his membership in the Anusilan Samiti, all enjoined the acquisition of military prowess with a view to eventually overthrowing British rule in an uprising inspired by the Indian Mutiny of 1857. V.D. Savarkar had, after all, in part gained his fame as a role model for the Indian revolutionaries of this era by publishing a book entitled *The Indian War of Independence*, which for the first time publicly acclaimed this bloody uprising against the British East India Company as a patriotic insurgency. So it is not in this sense surprising that Taraknath Das, like the Maharashtrian Khankhoje before him, endeavored to acquire a military education while in the United States.

It was this orientation, of course, which would soon spawn the Ghadr Party. Taraknath's other reason for breaking away from the West Coast turmoil at this point in time seems also to have had something to do with the fact that by 1908 the draconian laws and regulations put into effect by the Canadian authorities had all but shut down South Asian immigration into that country. For the time being there was little left to fight for in Canada.

Before leaving Seattle, Taraknath persuaded a socialist newspaper in Seattle, the *Western Clarion*, to print *Free Hindusthan* while he was gone. After reaching New York, he made contact with the Irish nationalists and also got George Freeman, the editor of *Gaelic American*, to print *Free Hindusthan* on the East Coast. So you could say that Taraknath was able to simultaneously work both sides of the continent! Surely this too is a testament to his resourcefulness and powers of persuasion if nothing else. This arrangement also signifies the important role which Irish émigrés centered in New York started to play in providing both moral and material support to the young Indian activists who were attempting to secure a political foothold in the New World. The Irish freedom movement, of course, had much in common with the Indian. Like turn-of-the century Indian nationalism, the Irish revolutionaries were militants who believed that violent means would eventually be required to achieve political emancipation from British rule. But the Irish at this time were organizationally much more deeply embedded in American society, both because they had been at it longer and were far more numerous.

His Norwich experience lasted no more than a year. But it was noteworthy in many respects. It was one of the few times that an Indian radical had found his way into an American military-oriented academic institution and succeeded in making a significant mark. Tapan Mukherjee says that Taraknath "lost no time getting involved in various college activities" (Mukherjee 1997: 18). He joined the school debating team; he wrote articles for the student newspaper; he lectured on Hindu philosophy around New England. He presented an essentially Vedantist point of view. This latter was undoubtedly another example of spin-off from the Yankee trader days, which had paved the way for a person like Taraknath to garner receptive audiences for such presentations. The curriculum combined engineering and military science. He got through his first year with flying colors and was promoted to the sophomore class. He was well liked by his professors and developed a long-lasting friendship with William Ellis, the librarian, "with whom he spent many hours discussing religion, history and politics" (ibid.).

Taraknath's past finally caught up with him at Norwich and shortened his time there. His public lectures, his published writings and his private interactions had attracted attention from the authorities. In issues of *Free Hindustan*, for the time being published by the *Gaelic Press*, he called for the Khalsa and the Gurkhas to revolt; he published pictures of Indian rebels being blown from cannons following the 1857 Mutiny; he published anonymous, politically loaded articles in *Bande Mataram*, Madam Cama's Paris-based political journal; he published cadaverous photos of Indian women and children who were victims of the Bengal famine. "Taraknath had cards made out of these pictures and distributed them at his lectures in towns and villages surrounding Norwich University" (ibid.: 20). Taraknath was in communication with various Indian radicals in England and France who were under suspicion for complicity in the assassination of Lord Morley's political aide-de-camp, Sir William Curzon-Wyllie. The murder occurred "at the annual meeting of Dadabhai Naoroji's Indian Association in London and also claimed the life of Cawas Lalcala, a Parsi physician who rushed to the aid of Curzon and caught the sixth bullet from the revolver." Police found a postcard in Madanlal Dhingra's (the assassin's) room with Taraknath's name written on it. He was also in contact at the time with V.D. Savarkar and Madam Cama. Taraknath had traveled to Cambridge, Massachusetts, to meet Sister Nivedita and Bhupendranath Datta who were in town after Datta had fled India out of fear of being arrested and imprisoned because of having edited the publication *Yugantar*, the organ of Taraknath's old radical alma mater, Anusilan Samiti. He had been aided in his flight by Sister Nivedita who obtained a false passport for him.[14]

Hopkinson was soon on Taraknath's trail. His reports were passed along to the British military attaché in Washington, DC (Lt. Col. B.R. James), who contacted Brigadier General W.W. Wotherspoon, chief of the Second Section of the US Army. Col. James was trying to play it coy. He began by saying he was interested, "as a point of information," in the type of military curriculum being taught at Norwich. Then the other shoe dropped. He rather casually requested "confidential information on the character of a student" enrolled there. Displaying his cultural ignorance, the British colonel said the student's name was "Paraknath Mdass"! "It is understood," Col. James wrote, "that this man is a fanatic on the subject of freeing India by the use of physical force, and there is a suspicion that he is preparing himself by military training at your school for ulterior objects." Wotherspoon in turn contacted Captain Leslie A. Chapman, the school's military instructor, who told him that he had been opposed to admitting Taraknath because, "The man is bitterly hostile toward England ... he writes pretty well. He makes every endeavor to speak before clubs and societies .... His topic [is] invariably 'Free Hindustan'.... Personally, I was opposed to his being admitted here ...." President C.H. Spooner, "with whom Taraknath had considerable correspondence before admission," rejected Chapman's advice and admitted him. Chapman lamented that "my personal advice was not well received [so] I dropped the subject." This meant that Taraknath was home free! In the end, however, after successfully completing his final examinations, Taraknath accepted an "honorable discharge" from Norwich at the request of President Spooner, who feared the loss of federal funds supporting the school's military program. He tried to get admitted to Harvard and Columbia universities but was unsuccessful, probably because by now he had a "reputation" (Mukherjee 1997: 22–23).

Nevertheless, the net outcome of his Norwich sojourn once again confirms the fact that the American public was by no means a monolith. There were strong currents of independent thinking and skepticism toward conventional wisdom and established authority, which favored a patriotic young Indian like Taraknath. In addition, in the early twentieth century, especially in New England and the Northeast, there lingered a healthy dose of antagonism toward the British dating back to the American Revolution. Tweaking the nose of the British Lion was still a popular pastime. These attitudes undoubtedly helped to shield Taraknath Das from the machinations of British intelligence. Then, as has been mentioned so many times, there was the romanticism concerning the "wisdom of the East," which Das clearly exploited in his public appearances. Another benefit which Taraknath clearly derived from his Norwich experience was the networking he was able to engage in on the eastern side of the country. He had established a working relationship with the Irish revolutionaries based in New York, to the point of being able to utilize their publishing facilities to keep the *Hindustani* in print. He made contact with other radicals, both Indian and American, in the New York area as well. They included Bhupendranath Datta, "who rebuked him for mixing politics with studies, thus wasting a wonderful opportunity at Norwich and also causing damage to the revolutionary movement" (Mukherjee 1997: 22–23). He also encountered Chandra Chakravarty, who was expert in making pitric acid bombs. He had brought with him from India House in London a bomb-making manual, whose contents he imparted to Taraknath. These were assets which would redound to his and his fellow South Asians' advantage down the road.

By June 1909, Taraknath was back on the West Coast. He seems to have taken Bhupendranath Datta's advice seriously, for the time being at least. He signed up for classes in political science and history at the University of Washington. He got his B.A. degree in1910, then got a fellowship to pursue graduate studies. His subject was "Employers' Liability Law in the United States." To gain "practical experience" for his project, Taraknath went to California to work as a vegetable-picker. But politics was in his blood. "While working on the farm ... *he made frequent visits to Berkeley to organize Indian students to fight for the immigration rights of the Hindus*" (ibid.: 34, emphasis added). Here, of course, was the critical link between the two strands of South Asian immigrants and their respective political concerns!

Another move made by Taraknath around this time was to further pursue his quest for citizenship. He clearly understood that achieving this would make it virtually impossible for his detractors to dislodge him and attempt to ship him back to India where undoubtedly they would find a way to kill him. In January 1912, he filed in Cook County court in Coquille, Oregon. He had moved to Bandon, Oregon, and late in November 1910, registered the Bandon Clay Products Company. He had a deed on 15 acres of wilderness land and control over 60 acres as a gift from Mr and Mrs J.P. Degassen, a couple he had befriended at the Hindu temple (Mukherjee 1997: 38). For reasons that are unclear, this undertaking does not seem to have gotten anywhere, but it does provide more evidence of how assiduously and successfully Taraknath was cultivating relationships outside the boundaries of the Indian community.

Maneuverings by Hopkinson, by Canadian Interior Minister W.W. Cory and a host of enemies on all sides—British, Canadian, and American, including even the British ambassador, Lord Bryce—constantly dogged his efforts. They succeeded in blocking him this time. This was the context in which Lord Bryce, the British Ambassador, was persuaded to intervene at the highest levels, by "raising the issue" with Secretary of State Philander Knox in a "private and confidential memo" promising a "full report with evidence" (ibid.: 34). Nearly four years were to pass before Taraknath finally succeeded. The most remarkable thing, of course, is that in the end he did!

Meanwhile, Taraknath Das was not idle. He completed an M.A. degree with teacher's certificate from Berkeley. Mukherjee cites the *Cosmopolitan Student*, a magazine published by the International Association of Cosmopolitan Clubs, which stated that Taraknath "was the president of the Philosophical Club, member of the Badger Debating Club, and president of the Cosmopolitan Club." Moreover, the *Cosmopolitan* article continues, he started "agitation among two thousand students for a free hospital, yet at the busiest moment in this propaganda he found the time to champion women's suffrage ..." (ibid.: 35). He supplemented his income by performing interpreter services for the Chalis County Superior Court. He was perpetually in difficult financial straits because he funneled so much of what he earned into his causes, including helping Indian students in greater need than himself. He created an organization named the Association of the Promotion of Education of the People of India. Serving as its general secretary, he persuaded six university professors and a federal judge to sit on its board of trustees. "Many prominent American citizens in the area supported his cause. A house was purchased [in Seattle] to provide a residence for Indian students [which] cost four thousand dollars, partly donated by the Gaekwar of Baroda while he was in Vancouver; Taraknath raised the rest." He attempted to acquire a similar facility in Berkeley (Mukherjee 1997: 35).

Clearly, these achievements reveal a Taraknath Das who was making himself a force to be reckoned with, both in the eyes of the South Asian student and laboring communities and, of course, in the eyes of Canadian and British intelligence. Not unlike Har Dayal, and perhaps in the long run even more so, Taraknath's talent lay in incorporating influential and committed Americans into the coalitions he built. This would become evident in the manner by which he ultimately attained American citizenship. It was also evident in the manner by which he mobilized the fight to prevent the imposition of a new set of draconian immigration rules which, if adopted, could have as effectively throttled further Indian immigration into America as comparably draconian measures already had in Canada.

The effort to further close the door to Indian immigration which commenced around 1911 was occurring in the tense atmosphere generated by the *Komagata Maru* crisis in Canada, the formation of Ghadr in the United States, and the approach of World War I. In America, the immigration issue culminated in the already mentioned Congressional hearings of February 1914. Not long after this came conspiracy accusations and trials which led to Har Dayal fleeing the country and Taraknath being sentenced to prison, fortunately after he had obtained his citizenship. One must view this swirl of political ferment as indicative of how far the South Asian communities both in Canada and the United States had progressed in terms of social consciousness and organizational capability in the decade since the first Sikh immigrants tremulously endeavored to establish a foothold and an honorable place on the soil of North America. For, as we shall see, politically conscious Indians were now to be found throughout the country, especially in major urban centers like New York, Philadelphia, Chicago, Boston, and Detroit, and on the campuses of major universities such as the Universities of Illinois, Wisconsin, Chicago, Missouri, Iowa, and Michigan in the Middle West and, of course, institutions like Harvard, Yale, Columbia, and Pennsylvania on the East Coast.

What is difficult to assess, so far removed from the actual events and in the absence of any surviving eyewitnesses, is how much and what kind of coordination of effort occurred between Taraknath Das and Har Dayal. Both were obviously dedicated idealists, deeply devoted to the nationalist and human rights causes. Clearly, they agreed on the ends. But both were very strong personalities, with large egos, whose conception of the appropriate means to achieve their noble ends were not necessarily identical. In any event they were inevitably influenced by their own yearnings for power and notoriety. Their situation was compounded by the fact that there were many other players in the arena who also wanted their share of credit and recognition for whatever political successes might be achieved. We have noted some of these other players: Sarangadhar Das, Gobind Behari Lal, Sudhindranath Bose, G.D. Kumar, Teja Singh, etc. Others will be noted as our narrative continues. It is impossible to disentangle personal ambition from idealism in the character structure of political activists. Differences in the juxtaposition of these two traits are always a matter of degree. It is the net outcome of their actions that count in the long run.

These complexities are evident in the roles that both Har Dayal and Taraknath Das played in the *Komagata Maru* incident, the founding of Ghadr, and the House Committee on Immigration hearings between 1913 and 1914. In his capacity as the driving force behind Ghadr, Har Dayal became involved in the maneuverings that revolved around *Komagata Maru*, but, it would seem, with a certain amount of ambivalence. Overtly, he threw the propaganda weight of the organization behind the marooned Sikhs in Vancouver harbor. Brown says that the party organ, *Ghadr*, issued "the clarion call for mobilization as soon as the *Komagata Maru* was turned back" (Brown 1975: 153). However, Gobind Behari Lal states that Har Dayal, Ram Chandra, and Barakatulla "did not like the situation at all." They feared this would intensify the already strained relations between Sikhs and the Canadian and American labor unions, "who were particularly determined to resist Indian immigration" (Sareen 1994: 46). Once it was clear that they could not stand idly by while this incident was creating a furor among South Asians in both countries, they arranged to get Ghadr literature distributed among the passengers, and to help smuggle supplies, including, the Canadians and the British government charged, even weapons. "Thus," declares Gobind Behari Lal, "the *Komagata Maru* was virtually turned into a [Ghadr] ship on its return voyage; such anyway is my understanding of the affair" (ibid.). This is a perception that is confirmed by Johnston's (1979) account.

While these events were occurring, on June 6, 1914, Taraknath finally succeeded in obtaining American citizenship. This preoccupation certainly affected the role he played in *Komagata Maru*, and may have affected as well the amount and nature of his contact with Har Dayal at this time. Whereas Har Dayal did spend time in Canada and made direct contact with leaders like Harnam Singh, Taraknath was wary of crossing the border out of fear that the INS might deny him re-entry at the very time when his immigration case was pending. He was, however, in touch with the members of the "Shore Committee" and other parties who were orchestrating the affair, but mainly from the American side of the border. "From Sumas [Washington], he was in constant touch by telephone and letters with Harnam Singh Sahri, Husain Rahim and Bhag Singh, counseling them on various alternative steps concerning the *Komagata Maru*" (Mukherjee 1997: 57). Just how much more deeply involved he was in hands-on aspects of the attempts to bolster the endurance of the ship's passengers is problematical. Hopkinson was convinced that there was more there than met the eye. Mukherjee (1997: 45) believes that Taraknath was "the only American Hindu involved in the *Komagata Maru* affair." This is clearly a dubious conclusion since, at the minimum, Har Dayal also was. He does seem to have been implicated in the effort by Harnam Singh, Balwant Singh, and Bhag Singh to smuggle revolvers on board. He was temporarily arrested by American authorities but then released when it was determined that as an American citizen he had violated no laws. Whatever may be the truth about these matters, Taraknath, like Har Dayal, definitely employed his publicity resources to champion the passengers' cause. In the *Hindustanee* (June 22, 1914; reprinted by Mukherjee

1997: 57), he wrote: "Let us voice the sentiments of our people in North America, especially in the United States of America, that we shall not leave any stone unturned to give the Hindustanees on the Komagata Maru a chance to present their case before the courts of justice." Once again, the point of mentioning all these activities is that it affords further insight into how far politicization had advanced among the South Asian immigrants.

The government, undoubtedly prompted by British and Canadian agents, endeavored to the bitter end to try and block Taraknath's attainment of citizenship. They pursued every angle. "The Bureau of Immigration in Washington sent circular letters to field offices with instructions to gather damaging information from people who knew Taraknath" (Mukherjee 1997: 56). But Taraknath had won the hearts and minds of a wide spectrum of discerning Americans. Mukherjee and others found that his principal supporters were persons from academia and the liberal establishment generally. President Spooner of Norwich Academy told an agent that "it would be an offense against simple justice to bar this man from citizenship. He is one of the most mentally able men I have come in contact with as a college student." Congressman Frank Plumley of Vermont said Taraknath had one of the most wonderful minds he had ever come across. Several other university professors similarly praised him for his character and his intellect. Grudgingly, the INS was compelled to grant him his citizenship, and did so on June 6, 1914. Home free, and with Har Dayal gone, Taraknath was able to turn his attention to his version of the battle for American South Asians' civil rights and Indian freedom.

World War I was on the horizon, and Ghadr was busily engaged in its attempt to assemble an invasion force to liberate India by provoking an uprising there on the model of the 1857 Mutiny. With Har Dayal out of the picture, it was logical to assume that Taraknath would take his place. This, however, did not happen. Evidence that the two men were not fully on the same wavelength seems inherent in the fact that Har Dayal rather matter-of-factly designated others as his successor.

We must pause briefly to discuss the reasons why Har Dayal decided at the very moment of his successful ascent to a commanding position in South Asian immigrant politics to abandon it all and take his act elsewhere. Overtly, the precipitating event was an arrest warrant issued by the INS, which alleged that Har Dayal's writings and public pronouncements promoted anarchism and sedition.

Legally speaking, the indictment was a paper tiger. At its inception, the Ghadr Party had pledged "not do anything against the laws of any country where the party might be working." As Brown states: "The Indians in the United States had little difficulty holding to the tenet in view of the fact that no legislation existed under which an alien might be indicted for the kind of activity being carried on by Har Dayal and his associates" (Brown 1975: 152, quoting Chirol 1910b). An attempt had been made in 1912 to tack an amendment (the Root Amendment) on to the Dillingham Immigration Bill, which would have allowed the deportation of any aliens who took advantage of their US residence to conspire to overthrow a foreign government officially recognized by the United States. It was defeated after a flurry of protests by concerned citizens who declared that such a measure would fly in the face of America's traditional support for freedom fighters everywhere.

The trouble was that Hopkinson and other British and Canadian agents were busily at work attempting to circumvent this safeguard by muddying the legal waters in order to get their hands on activists like Har Dayal and Taraknath Das. Their ultimate aim was not so much to get targeted radicals arrested, prosecuted and incarcerated under the American judicial system as it was to get them extradited as undesirable aliens to British jurisdictions where they then could be prosecuted, imprisoned and even executed for "sedition." Their modus operandi was to exploit the ignorance and insecurity about the rules on the part of local-level immigration officials. In the diffuse administrative and political environments that existed in those earlier days, this was apparently not all that difficult to do. This, at least, is what Hopkinson and his cohorts undertook to do in Har Dayal's case. They spent time around San Francisco assembling "evidence" for "immigration inspectors in the field who worked surreptitiously with the British to establish a case against Har Dayal ... even though the commissioner general in Washington was unaware of the fact that his inspectors were making use of the services of a Canadian immigration official" (Brown 1975: 152, quoting Chirol 1910a). It was on the basis of this collusion between spies and local racists that a case had been developed and a warrant issued on March 25, 1914 for Har Dayal's arrest. He was immediately freed on $500 bail.

Har Dayal engaged Charles Sferlazzo as his lawyer. He was, says Gobind Bihari Lal, "an Italian-born, naturalized American citizen," who "regarded Har Dayal as a kind of Hindu 'St. Francis' with modern passions." Although the government did not seem to have a very strong case and many of Har Dayal's American supporters were willing to come to his defense, Sferlazzo told Har Dayal that he could not absolutely guarantee that the Immigration people would fail to contrive some means of doing him in. It was at this point that Har Dayal's fears of "extradition" as opposed to mere "deportation" became acute. This fear apparently haunted Har Dayal, especially since he knew that the colonial authorities suspected him of complicity in the attempt on Viceroy Lord Hardinge's life in 1912. "He recalled that France had extradited Savarkar, a political refugee from Britain," after which "he was taken to India, tried and sent to the Andaman Islands" (Sareen 1994: 38–39).

"Not long after that," relates Gobind Behari,

> I met Har Dayal, and he was looking especially tense and exhausted ... I was worried .... Then he said, "I am leaving the United States, but tell nobody, I am going to Switzerland. The Gadar business can be continued, *the boys have learned how to do it. I have shown the way. San Francisco is a backwater of civilization. Modern culture and Civilization are in Europe* ... I shall maintain the closest contact with the Gadar here, and will go on giving advice and guidance, but in Europe I shall be in touch with our people, with our country more than here" (ibid.: 39, emphasis added).

Gobind Behari says he was "dumbfounded" and greatly disappointed with his mentor. Har Dayal pledged to bring him over to Europe, to the Sorbonne or Cambridge. "The University at Berkeley is for American farmers." Clearly, Har Dayal had somehow grown disillusioned with his three-plus-year political tryst with America. He had decided to move on, and it is likely that his legal problems were as much a rationalization as a cause for doing so. "I put him on the train, the Overland Limited, and he promised to write me from New York and keep me posted from Europe," says Gobind Bihari Lal. "I heard nothing from him, but Ram Chandra remained in contact with him" (Sareen 1994: 39).

Ram Chandra was chosen to succeed Har Dayal as *Ghadr's* editor. Gobind Behari Lal contends that it was he, "for obvious reasons of personal, most close relationships," whom Har Dayal preferred as his replacement. He had misgivings about Ram Chandra because he believed that his marital life would be a distraction. "But the majority of the Council, consisting of wifeless Punjabi boys (*sic*), were deeply impressed by the presence of a married man, with a wife with him, and so chose Pandit Ram Chandra" (ibid.: 42). Ram Chandra was a fellow Punjabi "editorialist," a member of the "Delhi Circle" "by a sort of adoption," whom Har Dayal had invited over from India along with another friend, Barakatullah, the latter designated to take charge of the Urdu edition of *Ghadr*. Gobind Behari says he was actually relieved by this turn of events because he preferred to concern himself "with the ideological, literary, publication aspects of the Gadar operations." He says he continued living in Berkeley, close to the campus, went on taking courses at the university, and performed his *Ghadr* duties on the side (ibid.).

This was not, after all, the first time that Har Dayal had walked away from things, nor would it be the last. This was a consistent pattern in his life. He had abandoned the state scholarship he had received in 1905 for study at Oxford by 1908, after coming under the influence of Krishnavarma and the India House radicals, and after smuggling his wife out of India in order for her to be with him. In 1908, back in India, he had then abandoned his wife and child in order to live the life of a peripatetic radical. He never saw them again. Later in 1908 he left India for good and was in Paris, moving in the Madam Cama circle, until he became disaffected with her "socialist style" of revolutionism instead of the "nationalist and Hindu style" which he preferred. Then it was Algiers in 1909, back to Paris in 1910, and then to Martinique where Bhai Parmanand found him in ascetic retreat. From there he went to San Francisco, then Hawaii (also in ascetic retreat), and back to San Francisco in 1911.

Despite his comparatively brief encounter with the South Asians in North America, and the erratic and complex relations he had with fellow activists, Har Dayal was indisputably a seminal factor in the politicization process on the West Coast. He had helped awaken the Sikhs and give direction to their social restiveness. With Ghadr he had provided an organizational structure for harnessing their political energies. Writing in *Bande Mataram* in 1910, following Savarkar's apprehension, Har Dayal had looked toward America as a fertile recruiting ground for the freedom cause. "We admit for the present all active propaganda among the young men of India with a view to the acquisition of new workers is exceedingly difficult." The place to turn is America and Japan, he declared, where "there are hundreds of patriotic Indian students ... who can be inspired with apostolic fervour if only some capable workers are sent among them" (Brown 1975: 80). He came, he saw, he inspired, and he stirred things up with his rhetorical and organizational gifts. He left a legacy of activism and commitment which energized the American branch of the Ghadr movement. But his own involvement was henceforth marginal. With the immanence of World War I, he would soon have new political fish to fry.

By 1913, an extensive socio-political fabric had formed among the West Coast Sikhs which featured a variety of real and potential players. There were major *gurdwaras* in Stockton, Vancouver, and Victoria, as well as in Hong Kong, Shanghai, and Singapore; in several other places along the West Coast there were minor ones, or at least designated places for worship and socialization; finally, there were numerous socio-political organizations such as the Hindu Association of the Pacific Coast. From this milieu had arisen the leadership of Ghadr, with whom Har Dayal surrounded himself and from whom most of his successors were drawn. Here again was a measure of how far social and political development had proceeded among the Indians. They numbered many thousands by now; their material resources had greatly increased; their networks were widely dispersed; and their interconnections with the White majority had, both for good and ill, become very extensive. "Within a few months the Ghadr Party had the unanimous support of the entire Indian immigrant community of the Pacific Coast and had changed the Sikhs from loyal British subjects to ardent revolutionaries" (Singh and Singh 1966: 21).

What, then, was Ghadr, and what were its actual prospects for fomenting a mutiny-like uprising in India against the British Raj? In historical retrospect, we can only conclude that it was little more than a touching, quixotic fantasy. It produced only a trickle of men, primarily Sikh farmers and laborers, most of whom forsook their comparatively safe havens abroad to try and smuggle themselves and a handful of weapons into India to confront the continental power which had held their country in servitude for generations. It failed, of course, and the eventual cost was the apprehension, imprisonment and execution of many brave revolutionaries. However, in other respects Ghadr had many positive achievements to its credit. One might say that its cultural reach well exceeded its military achievements. It created an organizational structure with wide-ranging tentacles that could safely flourish beyond the reach of effective imperial retaliation. It captured the imagination and garnered the support of hundreds of Sikhs and other South Asians in the United States and Canada, as well as in overseas venues. Through its printing presses, it churned out a torrent of anti-colonialist propaganda, both in English and vernacular languages, which challenged British pretensions about the glories and the "justice" of the Raj. Most important, perhaps, it survived as an institution for almost half a century.

As Ram Chandra was assuming control of the organization, the Sikhs plunged into the task of assembling a fighting force to be dispatched to India. The coming of World War I would add unanticipated dimensions to this undertaking. In the initial stages, however, the modus operandi involved employing Sikh networks throughout the West Coast and along the Pacific Rim of Asia to recruit as many willing combatants as could be found. A great many, it seems, were Sikh veterans of the British colonial army. As early as November 1913, *Ghadr*, the newspaper, was printing the following advertisement in its "Wanted Columns":

Wanted: Enthusiastic and heroic soldiers for organizing Gadar in Hindustan.
Remuneration: Death
Reward: Martyrdom
Pension: Freedom
Field of Work: Hindustan

According to Singh and Singh (1966: 21), "In the *Gurdwaras*," in the United States, Canada, Shanghai, and Singapore, "it became customary to recite poems from *Ghadr* and hold discussions on political problems after evening prayers."

As the Sikhs began making their move, Singh and Singh (1966: 35) say that *Ghadr* published "special supplements" on July 18 and August 4, 1914, "explaining their duty in the event of war." Local newspapers carried their story. A *Portland Telegram* headline on August 7, 1917, read: "Hindus Go Home to Fight in Revolution." Datelined Astoria (Oregon), the article declared, "Every train and boat for the south carries a large number of Hindus from this city, and if the exodus keeps up much longer, Astoria will be entirely deserted by the East Indians" (ibid.). The assumption was that the Sikhs were returning to India via San Francisco as freedom fighters.

The chroniclers of the movement make much of *Komagata Maru*, not only in terms of its symbolic importance as a catalyzer of protest and rebellion, but partisan accounts also imply that by the time the ship reached Calcutta it had become a nest of recruits for the contemplated uprising. This too was the view of British intelligence. A report (*Home Department, Political report #101*) dated September 1915 states:

> That the case of the British Indians who went to Canada in the *Komagata Maru* with Gurdit Singh was made the occasion of fresh activity by the conspirators, particularly by said Balwant Singh and other accused *at Vancouver*, and *these passengers were themselves in large numbers seduced from their the allegiance* to His Majesty the King-Emperor by seditious literature, particularly the *Ghadr*, and by other means and joined the conspiracy for a rebellion in India (Sareen 1994: 75, emphasis added).

Whether entirely accurate or not, it was about this time that Ghadr recruits were infiltrating into India, in most cases after having booked regular passages that were often subsidized by the movement's leaders. They dispersed mainly northwestwards into the Gangetic plain towards the Punjab. Most showed up around army posts where they could make contact with Sikh units stationed there in order to induce them to rebel. Many returned to their native districts and their native villages in search of converts to the cause. Always short of money and supplies, some of the conspirators turned to robbing banks and post offices. Many, if not most, were quickly rounded up and neutralized by the authorities. In the end, the strictly military phase of the Ghadr operation was done in by what can be called a pathetic level of naiveté about the magnitude of what they had taken on.

A further complicating factor in this quixotic undertaking was the onset of World War I. This brought Germany into the political mix. Its eventual effects would radically affect the fortunes of Ghadr and the South Asian political scene generally in the United States. There were already scores of Indians living and studying in Germany, including many with political agendas, much as in the United States. Here was another venue where Indian national-ists could operate beyond the reach of British political repression and garner support from radical and leftist elements in the local population for their anti-colonialist activities. "As tensions in Europe grew and it became obvious that war would see Great Britain and France lined up against Germany, Berlin became the most revolutionary center in Europe" (Singh and Singh 1966: 48). Even before war erupted, at the time Ghadr came into existence some party leaders had contemplated the potential significance of a German connection. "The Germans have great sympathy with our movement for liberty," Ghadr declared on November 15, 1913. "In future Germany can draw assistance from us and they can render us great assistance also." These Indians, in other words, quickly resonated with the old axiom that "the enemy of my enemy is my friend"!

The focal point of the German wing of Indian nationalists was the so-called Berlin–India Committee. This was a shorthand ap-pellation for "a far reaching organization known as the Indian Nationalist Party" whose "chief unit" was called the Indian Com-mittee of National Independence. There is some confusion as to who its original founder was. Some have claimed that is was Virendranath Chattopadhyaya (1879–1937), the brother of Congress party notable Sarojini Naidu, and Abinashchandra Bhattacharya. Others credit Champak Raman Pillai and Har Dayal (Gower 1997). To whomever credit goes, it is clear that all of these individuals were major players in the founding and operation of the committee. It is unlikely that Har Dayal could have been a founder of the Berlin Committee since, according to Brown's sources, "'the famous trio of Pillai, Chattopadhyaya's and Har Dayal' did not actually arrive in the German capital until the com-mittee had been in operation for almost five months" (Yajnik 1950: 317, quoted in Brown 1975: 181). Taraknath Das also became a member of the committee not long after he got his US citizenship, although he never showed any inclination to remain permanently abroad as Har Dayal did. The fact that Har Dayal's name arises in this connection is significant, of course, because it tells us where his travels led following his flight from America. He had shifted from Geneva to Berlin after he had been persuaded to do so by Chandra Kant Chakravarty, who had been sent to Geneva by his German patrons for the specific purpose of recruiting him because they "thought that he would be valuable in recruiting Gadar revolutionaries for insurrections through Western India." The Germans felt that the existing crop of revolutionaries in Berlin was composed of novice students (Mukherjee 1997: 73). Chakravarty, as we shall soon see, was a key link between German intelligence, the Berlin Indians and Ghadr.

We also learn that Maulvi Barakatullah, whom Har Dayal had originally enticed from Japan to become the editor of *Ghadr's* Urdu edition, followed closely on his heels. Barakatullah's passage was paid by funds made available by the German consulate in San Francisco. As a strong advocate of anti-British Pan-Islamism, Berlin was the place to be, given Germany's alliance with Turkey and the interest both countries had in inciting the Islamic world against the British. The prominence accorded to the Islamic factor is attested by the fact that the committee's president was Mohammed Mansoor/Mansur Raham, a philologist, who had originally gotten to Germany on an Indian government scholarship.

The importance of the German factor for our purposes pertains to the impact it had on Ghadr's affairs in the United States, especially with respect to the fortunes of many of the South Asians that became involved in it.

Taraknath Das, despite feeling compelled for political reasons to tacitly endorse it, seems to have felt some ambivalence about Ghadr. He thought the entire enterprise was both unrealistic as a military undertaking and ill-advised from the standpoint of the negative effect it might have on American public opinion. He believed that "without education, self-discipline, proper military training (shades of his Norwich Academy experience and his Anusilan Samiti background!) and sound organization, the revolution was certain to fail" (ibid.: 64). This attitude, plus, Mukherjee believes, a certain amount of jealousy over his having acquired America citizenship, caused some tensions between him and fellow

Ghadrites. His relationship with Chandra Kant Chakravarty was a marriage of convenience devoid of emotional warmth. This seems to have become the case especially once war broke out. "His American friends and acquaint-ances started to distance themselves" from him, so much so that his positions and relation-ships in the Hindusthani Association and the Cosmopolitan Club both suffered. Some disgruntled Indians even circulated rumors that he had become an American spy! Another of his friends, Professor Arthur U. Pope, stated to Captain John B. Trevor on October 31, 1918 that "Das is in a painful position." Apparently, the Ghadrites came to believe that Taraknath had been unwilling or unable to use his American citizenship to effectively assist the movement. "They would pass him on the street and they would say things to him such as 'coward' and 'traitor', until Das asked me, 'what shall I do, it is perfectly intoler-able'" (Mukherjee 1997: 117).

Yet, up until then, Taraknath had played quite an active role in Ghadr, which makes the eventual estrangement somewhat mys-terious. "In September 1914," Mukherjee (ibid.: 66) relates, "he went to Seattle and Vancouver to dispose of the Seattle house, and settle his account with the Guru Nanak Trust." Then, with what money he realized from these transactions, plus that pro-vided by the Germans, who were now systematically funding Ghadr, Taraknath set sail to Europe from New York. He reached Berlin and clearly became actively involved with the Berlin Com-mittee. How much contact he and Har Dayal had with each other is not clear, though there certainly was some overlap. One reason may be that both were preoccupied with their own agendas. In 1914, Har Dayal was in and out of Switzerland organizing some-thing called the Indo-Egyptian Nationalist Congress. Then the German ambassador to Constantinople, Franz Von Pappen, had gotten him invited there to act as an "expert on Indian affairs." When he reached Constantinople he discovered that the political environment in which he was compelled to work was a factional can of worms. The Muslims in the mix were focused on pan-Islamic strategies both for India and the Middle East. The Hindus were primarily concerned with more broadly conceived Indian national-ism with special emphasis on fomenting rebellion in India. The German diplomats and intelligence agents were, of course, mainly preoccupied with manipulating all the factions to the advantage of imperial grand strategy. However, the details of these machinations are beyond the scope and relevance of this narrative.

It was in this context that Taraknath also accepted assignments from the Berlin Committee, which took him to the Middle East as well. He was involved in a scheme, with which Har Dayal was also identified, to try and stage an invasion of India via Afghanistan by inciting the Pathans and other tribal groups in the Waziristan region to rise and invade the Kashmir state and thence the Indian heartland. In the end, none of these schemes got anywhere. The Afghan project fell on its face when the British found out about it after they had obtained a copy of a German decoding manual that enabled them to read all the traffic between Berlin and the German embassy in Washington, "which also included communication between the Berlin Committee and its principal representative in Washington" (Mukherjee 1997: 78). The British countered by doubling the Amir's subsidy and "extracted a pledge from him not to support the German military or Indian revolutionaries." Thus, when the German–Indian party arrived in Kabul they were kept waiting for several months until "the Germans left in disgust and the Indians were left without money or protection." Fortunately, however, neither Taraknath nor Har Dayal were members of this group. The Germans had underestimated the viability and the guile of the Government of India, who were very sophisticated practitioners of the "Great Game." For their part, the various Indian revolutionaries had overestimated their capacity to promote revolution.

Har Dayal continued his political wanderings through Europe and the Middle East during World War I and afterwards, basically because he had for the foreseeable future made it impossible for himself to set foot either in the United States, India or England. Taraknath, on the other hand, managed to keep his American citizenship intact, though not without difficulty, and finally made it back to the United States on July 11, 1916. By he time he returned, he had agreed to make a trip to East Asia on behalf of the Berlin Committee, despite the fact that his relations both with members of the Committee and their German sponsors, and with the Ghadrites at home, were far from tranquil. By 1916, Dr Chandra Kant Chakravarty, "a diminutive and dapper young Bengali," had been sent over to the US with a bundle of cash to take control of Ghadr. He had become for all practical purposes a German agent in Bengali garb, but one whom even the Germans eventually came to regret having taken on. Chakravarty turned out to be corrupt. One commentator depicts him as "a thin-faced, falsetto-voiced Hindu, a native of Bengal, and a speaker of many languages" (Gower 1997: 6). He used the first installment of $60,000 which the Germans sent to him through the Committee to purchase New York real estate for himself. "Thereafter, he fed the German Government with reports of the work he was doing .... The Germans continued to hand out money till they discovered how the smooth Chakravarty had taken them up the garden path. Then they washed their hands of the whole affair and even became insulting in their behavior toward the Indians" (ibid.: 7).

While all this was happening, British intelligence had penetrated Ghadr, the American branch of the Berlin Committee and just about every other revolutionary organization that mattered. They even penetrated the American government. "Exasperated by the State Department's stubborn refusal to restrain the revolutionaries," says Mukherjee, "the British Foreign Office took matters into their own hands by setting up an elaborate intelligence network in the United States." From their headquarters in Ottawa, Canada, they managed to place an agent in the Justice Department; to employ "the unofficial Czech secret-service in the USA to follow the Indian revolutionaries ..." Indians were hired to spy on their fellow countrymen. "The Gadar Party's central committee was penetrated, and student spies, pretending to be revolutionaries, brought news of secret meetings ... and stole correspondence from nationalist student organizations ... British agents went to university administrations inquiring about the Indian students" (Mukherjee 1997: 91). This was a pattern which, in fact, the British would continue to follow all the way through to World War II, until India got her independence. It was the reason for Har Dayal's quip that Indians in America were of four types: "Sikhs, students, swamis, and spies."

Even as the wheels were falling off the great crusade, Chakravarty nevertheless found the means to send Taraknath Das to East Asia. He left for Tokyo, on August 26, 1917, aboard the Tenyo Maru. During this voyage, he met two well-placed American women who would prove to be valuable supporters later on. These were Ellen N. La Motte, the niece of Albert du Pont, president of the du pont de Nemours Company, and Emily C. Chadbourne, the sister of a Chicago industrialist named Charles Crane. He was to visit China and build links with Ghadr-oriented revolutionaries there. There is no need to belabor the results that were achieved, because they were limited. British intelligence consistently checkmated Ghadr's and the Berlin Committee's international operations almost everywhere. What is important for our purposes is to document the peripatetic activity in which America-based South Asian activists engaged themselves, with persons like Taraknath Das, Har Dayal, Barakatullah, Gobind Bihari Lal, Sailendranath Ghosh, Sarangadhar Das, etc., leading the way. During and following World War I, undoubtedly due to the catalytic effects of the Ghadr movement and the war itself, the number and variety of players involved in revolutionary activities substantially increased. If there was one significant personal accomplishment by Taraknath arising from his East Asian junket, it was the impact which a book he had written entitled *Is Japan a Menace to Asia?* had in Japan once it had been translated into Japanese. Because the book advocated that Japan's legitimate interests in East Asia should be understood and honored by the other great powers, it was read and appreciated up to the highest levels of the political elite, including Hideki Tojo (1884–1946), then a graduate from the Japanese Military Academy, who would one day become Japan's Prime Minister and the architect of Pearl Harbor.[15]

The next major event in the saga of South Asian politicization was the Hindu–German Conspiracy Case of 1917–1918. This had grown out of the tangled web of intrigue, conspiracy and corruption which had been generated by the machinations of World War I intelligence agencies, and by the attempts of the Ghadr movement and a host of other Indian nationalists around the world to take advantage of the opportunities that the war seemed to offer to advance the cause of Indian freedom. A key factor in the South Asians' calculations was the willingness of the Germans to incorporate Indian nationalists into their grand strategy for defeating the British Empire, and to throw a lot of money around in pursuit of this end. As long as the United States remained neutral, as it did for the first two years of the war, there was not much interference in the Indians' anti-British activities, providing they did nothing which seemed to violate American neutrality or in other respects contravene US anti-sedition laws.

However, when President Woodrow Wilson declared war on Germany on April 6, 1917, everything changed. War hysteria spread throughout the United States. Rioting, looting, and murder were inflicted on immigrant German populations in New York and other cities; a bogeyman image of Imperial Germany was avidly perpetrated by politicians and the press. As the war dragged on and the Russian Revolution added new dimensions to the struggle, the "Red Menace" was added to the roster of American political bogeymen. In this charged atmosphere, the relationship between the German government and Indian nationalists, and later with Bolshevik communism, came under close scrutiny. Implying a sinister connection between South Asian revolutionaries and these perceived threats to the American way of life quite understandably became a major preoccupation of British intelligence. In pursuit of this aim, the *San Francisco Chronicle* (April 14, 1918) claimed that "about 200 members of the British Secret Service had been in San Francisco for more than two years." The British regarded American tolerance of revolutionaries to be excessive. They decided to take matters into their own hands by goading the Americans into initiating sedition proceedings against South Asian activists. In this manner they hoped not only to politically undermine the nationalists, but also, as already noted, to get them deported back to India or somewhere in the Commonwealth where the imperial authorities could lay hands on them.

Demonstrating that there were connections between Taraknath Das and his Ghadr cohorts, the Berlin Committee and the German government became the principal goal of these maneuverings. It must be said that their strategy succeeded to a great extent once America entered the war. Commencing in early 1917, the US Justice Department, making abundant use of surreptitiously supplied British intelligence data, began rounding up alleged Indian and German conspirators. Commencing in early 1917, a total of 105 persons were indicted for "providing and preparing the means for a military enterprise to be carried out within the territory of the United States against India, the territory and domain of the British Empire with which the United States was at peace."[16] Thirty-seven were ultimately tried. What made this an illegal, indictable act was not the fact per se that the Indian nationalists were engaged in a freedom struggle against a colonialist oppressor. That, after all, was what the American founding fathers had done against this same oppressor in 1776. It was, rather, the fact that Great Britain was now an *American ally* against Germany. By waging war with arms and ammunition against America's ally from American soil, the South Asian revolutionaries had been transformed by legal artifice from patriots into seditionists! Two newspapers, the *New York Times* and the *San Francisco Chronicle*, in particular, sensationalized this alleged conspiracy. The *Chronicle* was, of course, notorious for its anti-Asian racism. The *New York Times's* motives were less blatant. They seem to have been a projection of the anti-German animosity whose roots lay in the presence of so many German immigrant enclaves in New York and other East Coast cities. The inclusion of the South Asians in their conspiratorial perspective—because Ghadrites had been connected to the German machinations—was in the main a matter of "guilt by association." However this happened, the *Times* editorialized on April 13, 1917:

> Every day some new German activity, conspiracy or espionage in the United States, or directed against the United States from outside its territory, comes to light .... The hospitality of the country has been and is being abused to its damage and its danger ... Germany has continually violated our neutrality, broken our laws, exerted an authority and domain here as if she were in occupation of a conquered country (Gower 1997: 6).

The *Chronicle* coverage of the trial was focused on the arcane doings of "the Hindus." A December 13, 1917, headline read: "Former Stanford Girl Lifts Veil from Hindoo Plotters."

> Flames of Oriental passion that burned hatred into the hearts of two Hindoo leaders in the plot to restore independence to India; that brought dissension and threats of exposure which were rekindled before the jury yesterday in the German-Hindoo revolt trial by a woman who in a calm betrayal of both men, made enemies through desire to control her destiny (ibid.).

The trial began on November 20, 1917. The defendants were nine German citizens, four German-Americans, five Americans, and 17 Indians. Among the latter were Taraknath Das, Chandra Kant Chakravarty, Ram Chandra, Gobind Behari Lal, Bhagwan Singh,

and Gopal Singh. The presiding federal judge was William C. Van
Fleet of the US District Court of Northern California/San Francisco.

The trial itself revolved around alleged military collaboration
which had occurred between the Ghadrites and the Germans for
the purpose of invading India using armed, primarily Sikh, volunteers in the hope of provoking a general uprising in the country,
as in 1857. "The trial was said to be the most picturesque scene
ever enacted in an American court" (Mukherjee 1997: 118). It revealed more than just the lineaments of what in the end proved to
be a touchingly naive attempt by a collection of zealously idealistic
Sikhs to bring political freedom to their native country and social
justice for their brethren overseas. It also revealed the effects which
the influx of German money had on the activists' idealism and
political cohesion. Also, it revealed how much Ghadr-driven political mobilization in the context of global war, combined with the
greatly increased monetary resources emanating not only from
the Germans but from the South Asian community itself, had widened the spectrum of political consciousness among South Asians
and increased the scope of their political activism.

Taraknath Das was actually in Japan when the indictments were
being handed down, and there was speculation about whether he
would return to the US to face trial or would, like Har Dayal, flee
prosecution by remaining abroad. Rumors to this effect were circulated by his factional enemies. However, Taraknath, by now an
American citizen, did indeed return, was indicted, and posted a
$10,000 bond. Mukherjee cites excerpts from a letter he wrote to
H.P. Shastry, in which Das displays his Hindu roots by stating
that he is "not at all surprised to hear the insinuations about me.
But, my friend, I am what I am. *I am the imperishable and unchange-
able of Gita* ..." (ibid.: 116, emphasis added).

The trial was a media circus. It lasted 155 days, cost the US
government $450,000 and the British government $2.5 million. The
amount the British spent is obviously a measure of how threaten-
ing they believed Ghadr, in concert with the German enemy, had
become. There were eleven lawyers representing the various defendants. Only Chandrakant Chakravarty refused counsel and
represented himself. The witness list was replete with informers,
opportunists and intelligence agents. Judge Van Fleet was obviously biased toward the prosecution and consistently blocked the
introduction of motions, testimony and evidence favorable to the

accused. Mukherjee (1997: 119) states that, "British agents gathered the bulk of the material evidence against the Indians, and the San Francisco Consulate hired William A Mundrell International Detective Agency to collect information within the United States ... Sir George Denham, chief of the Indian Criminal Intelligence Department came to San Francisco to prepare the case." He brought with him from India "a number of veteran police officers." He and two of his Indian assistants were even allowed by Judge Van Fleet to take active part in the trial!

From a strictly legal standpoint, there was undoubtedly a substantial case that could be made against the defendants. Real attempts had indeed been made to assemble and ship weapons by sea from the United States to India, so as to coordinate with the flow of combatants that were being sent with Ghadr and German money in groups of varying size as passengers on steamers plying the Asia trade. In one attempt to smuggle arms, the Ghadrites purchased 5,000 pistols and had them loaded onto a ship, the *Henry S*, at Manila. But the British intercepted the *Henry S* at sea and arrested the entire crew. This happened, according to Singh and Singh (1966: 49), after an agent named Dr Daus Dekker, allegedly a Japanese national, "who had been taken into confidence by the revolutionaries was arrested in Hong Kong and forced to disclose the code used by the Ghadarites." With this information and further information obtained from a Ghadrite named Jodh Singh, "who had been connected with the revolutionaries in Europe," British intelligence had "all the information it needed."

Following the *Henry S* fiasco, another attempt to purchase arms, this time in Japan, was made by Harambalal Gupta, a member of the Berlin Committee and apparently a protégée of Har Dayal, who had in 1914 been dispatched to America "with German money in his pocket" (ibid.). However, British intelligence was onto him and persuaded the Japanese government to neutralize him. After spending several months in hiding he escaped from Japan and returned to the United States empty-handed. Harambalal was also involved as a money conduit and go-between in a harebrained plot to raise an army of 10,000 men and send them across the Burmese border to attack and capture Calcutta. The principal architect of this quixotic enterprise was the aforementioned Jodh Singh, who would later directly figure in the San Francisco conspiracy trial.

While the Gupta enterprise was underway, still another, and perhaps the most spectacular, attempt to smuggle arms into India was in progress. This one was part of a fairly elaborate logistical operation. It involved a "schooner" named the *Annie Larsen*, and a tanker, the *S.S. Maverick*, the latter originally owned by the Standard Oil Company, "which had been purchased, repaired, and outfitted for the voyage with German funds that also provided the salaries of the crew," an amount estimated to be around $166,000, which shows the magnitude of money being thrown around by the Germans (Brown 1975: 202).[17]

The *Maverick* sailed from San Francisco on April 22, 1915, headed for the Socorro Islands off the western coast of Mexico where it was supposed to rendezvous with the *Annie Larsen* and transfer her arms cargo to itself. The trouble was that the rendezvous never happened. It was another foul-up. Signals got crossed. By the time the *Annie Larsen* reached the appointed place, the *Maverick* had not even left San Francisco! So the schooner hied to Acapulco from where its skipper contacted the German consul in San Francisco. He told the *Annie Larsen* to return to the rendevous point where it lingered until April 10 without making any contact with the *Maverick*. Ultimately, the *Annie Larsen* docked in Aberdeen, Washington, where, Brown says, its cargo was seized by US authorities. What is not clear is what exactly was seized, and indeed what happened to the smuggled munitions, since allegedly they never got transferred to the *Annie Larsen*, on the one hand, while, on the other hand, the *Maverick* ended up in Batavia "without any arms, its only cargo being Ghadr literature stowed in the trunk of one of the five Indians aboard, all of whom were listed as Persians" (ibid.). Meanwhile, the revolutionaries who had made it back to India were left high and dry, and were soon rounded up or otherwise checkmated. Singh and Singh say, "The Germans had planned to send five other ships with arms to India, but the fate of the *Henry S*, the *Annie Larsen* and the *Maverick* plus the quarrels between the Indians somewhat cooled them towards the Ghadar movement" (1966: 50).

What is important about these events is, once again, what they revealed about the scale of political activity which had been achieved in the South Asian community. Brown (1975: 204, emphasis added) concludes: "Nearly all of these ventures—at Djakarta, Bangkok, Shanghai, Manila, Singapore, and Rangoon—were participated in by returned Indians who were members of the Ghadr party. *It was the basis for the later conspiracy trial which was held in San Francisco in 1917–18."* Also, the impact in terms of ramifying political awareness was evident at the grassroots. Gobind Behari Lal provides a colorful picture of this:

> In the fields where Indians worked all day, sowing or cutting crops or plucking fruits for their American employers, strange things would happen at nightfall. These Punjabis would get together in their simple camps, eat their Indian bread and vegetables or meat, and sing and dance about the Revolution. Sometimes they played dhol drums; and chanted revolutionary songs composed in Punjabi or Urdu by the staff poets of the Gadar, including Bhagwan Singh. Pathans would dance war dances .... The movement was truly "popular" (Sareen 1994: 47).

The trial took many twists and turns and revealed much about the inner workings of Ghadr. Perhaps more interestingly for our purposes, it provided a lot of insight into the character of some of the figures who had become significant players in the politicization process now well underway among South Asians in the United States and Canada. Aspects of the personal lives of Taraknath Das and Har Dayal got a lot of press exposure in the San Francisco area as the trial unfolded. This was an outgrowth of what came out concerning the women in their lives. Taraknath had developed a relationship with a woman named Camille de Berri, who by the time of the trial turned informer for District Attorney John Preston. "She was sent to the county jail with instructions to trick Taraknath into compromising himself" (Mukherjee 1997: 115). De Berri had allegedly been born in India, although it is not clear whether she was an Anglo-Indian or of some other parentage, or indeed whether she really did have Indian roots at all. He had met her at the Cosmopolitan Club and appointed her his secretary of social affairs after he was elected its president. He had gotten her "interested in the education of Indian girls in America," and to offer "her home to female students from India coming to the University of California" (ibid.: 62). Because of this personal relationship, prior to his trip to Sumas, Taraknath had entrusted Ms de Berri with many of his personal documents, including the bomb-making materials he had received from Europe via Surendra

Mohan Bose. In her sworn statement before the US Attorney (1917), she declared:

> About a week before he left ... he gave me a bundle of papers to keep for him in my garret. He gave me his confidence and entrusted to me the bundle of bomb pamphlets and some other papers .... He told me that there were lots of Indians on the West Coast and in Canada and scattered about the States who were endeavoring to make munitions for purposes of revolution ... (Mukherjee 1997: 62).

Ms de Berri seems to have had a rather checkered past! The *Chronicle* (January 16, 1918), in an article titled "Mystery Woman Identified," described her as "an Oakland divorcee of a wealthy mining expert who had recently remarried." Her next marriage seems to have been far from idyllic, since it turned out that her new husband "had been suspended from the University of California, immediately after graduating, for petty pilfering from gymnasium lockers." Ms de Berri "had come to his rescue by testifying as an alibi witness for him."

The description of the alleged competition for Ms de Berri's affections make it clear that the reporters had partly confused her with another woman with whom both Taraknath Das and Har Dayal had had some sort of a relationship during their Stanford days. Her name was Frieda Hauswirth (1886–1974), a student who had come from Switzerland at the age of 17 and was working her way through Stanford. In Har Dayal's philosophy course, she met and subsequently married a medical student named Arthur Munger, "in a ceremony which, according to a newspaper account, 'accentuated the social side of marriage and minimized the religious'" (Brown 1975: 104). The implication was that Har Dayal's strong advocacy of women's liberation had influenced their decision. He had become quite well-known publicly for his views on "free love." Her marriage to Munger disintegrated after a year and she returned to Switzerland. But by that time she had established a kind of symbiotic emotional interlock with Har Dayal which endured for many years and in the end generated tensions between him, Taraknath Das, and other members of the revolutionary community. In fact, one of the unacknowledged reasons why Har Dayal chose Switzerland as the initial site of his self-imposed exile may indeed have been the fact that Frieda Hauswirth had returned there. Brown provides extensive excerpts from Har Dayal's correspondence both with her and with mutual friends who knew the whole story. It reveals a man in his late-20s to early-30s, who clearly had had very little experience with women, struggling with his feelings, trying to reconcile the conflict between heart and mind that afflicted him. "I wander about the streets [of Palo Alto] sad and weary, thinking of all that has been, the room where you typed my essays on Hindu philosophy, 127C house where we would sometimes stand talking in the street, till midnight ... the walks by the creek—do you remember?—I think of all those days and my heart is sick unto death" (Brown 1975: 105). It has to be remembered that technically Har Dayal still had a wife and child in India. Despite Har Dayal's entreaties, however, Frieda never returned to the fold. She felt stifled both by his ultra-romantic and ultra-ideological intensities. She told Sarangadhar Das (May 11, 1914): "Somehow I simply do not feel on safe ground with him ... I know today as well as in the past, that I have not, and never will have reciprocal feelings for Har Dayal ...." That these romantic complications caused disarray in the ranks of the revolutionaries is attested to by Surendra Mohan Bose's comments in a subsequent letter to Frieda:

> For some time past I have been hearing various kinds of allegations against Har Dayal .... Some of the charges are very grave and I could not believe them, in fact I cannot yet believe that Har Dayal could have fallen so low. Sometimes back I heard from F.W. [not identified] and he says that he himself saw letters in which Har Dayal had made his immoral proposals (sic). Now I want to know the whole truth from you ... (ibid.: 106).

Frieda Hauswirth eventually married Sarangadhar Das. Having been refused entry to India to accept a teaching position there, despite having a valid US passport, she traveled to Hawaii where Sarangadhar was then living. They were married on June 13, 1917. Eventually she made it to India as Das's wife, although how this helped her to do so is not clear since he himself was on the list of seditionists. She published two books on her life there: "one recounted her experiences and the other reflected her interest in Indian women" (ibid.: 176).

Throughout this period she remained on friendly terms with Taraknath and maintained an extensive correspondence with him. As the conspiracy trial was developing, Naval Intelligence in Honolulu interviewed her about Taraknath and Har Dayal. As a result, says Mukherjee, she destroyed most of her letters, even though some survived and were entered in evidence. "While Har Dayal tried to recruit her for revolutionary work, Taraknath consistently advised against this." Since Frieda "denied any knowledge of Taraknath's activities in the Berlin committee," her surviving letters did no real damage to Taraknath other than, as Preston claimed, "proving" that "Taraknath was associated with Har Dayal and hence was a party to the conspiracy" (Brown 1975: 122). These perceptions, of course, suggest that despite whatever may have been their personal differences, they were able to maintain a working relationship regarding political matters.

The fragmentary information about Taraknath's female connections, garnered from Ms de Berri's testimony during the trial and Frieda Hauswirth's letters and depositions, fueled the *San Francisco Chronicle's* lurid coverage. "The Chronicle played on the mysterious and exotic aspects of these Indian men in an effort to explain the American women's attraction to their movement." It was stated that "the men had each written [de Berri] letters in which 'all the subtle arts of the Oriental were brought into play to force her to break her resolve.' During her testimony, she remained 'unabashed by the dark eyes of Taraknath Das, which never left her face'"(Gower 1997; *San Francisco Chronicle* excerpts from December 22, 1917 edition).

The trial ran its predictable course. The defendants didn't have a chance. As noted, all 15 Indians received sentences. Taraknath's sentence of 22 months in federal prison was the harshest of them all. But the climax of the Hindu–German conspiracy trial was the assassination of Ram Chandra! "On the last day, Ram Singh, one of the accused, who belonged to the faction of Bhagwan Singh 'Gyani,' whipped out a revolver and shot Ram Chandra dead. A marshal then shot and killed Ram Singh. For all practical purposes, this ended the Ghadar conspiracy to foment revolution in India" (Singh and Singh 1966: 52).

It is important to analyze the roots and implications of these factional differences. Clearly, they reflected the fact that the scale of political development among the South Asian immigrants had markedly increased. German money and the catalytic impact of World War I had poured unprecedented financial resources into the coffers of Ghadr and provided the movement with logistical capabilities which for a while gave it international scope. In Gobind Behari's words, "for some three years, the Gadar worked in the matrix of the First World War—and it was transformed" (Sareen 1994: 46). Throughout the war years, there was a "Berlin-Berkeley axis" that provided the means for Ghadr to vastly increase its propaganda output; enabled its operatives to travel all over Asia and the Middle East on revolutionary missions; enabled it, however limited the results, to smuggle arms and men into India; and brought into existence an organizational nexus which enhanced the political focus of many activist groups and individuals throughout the United States and Canada. The negative side, of course, was that this increased demographic scale bred factionalism, while increased infusions of money bred corruption. This underlay the assassination of Ram Chandra. That assassination also brought out the fact that ethnic and class differences between Hindus and Sikhs; between Bengali students and students from other regions of India; and between middle-class students generally and the less educated, more rustic Punjabi farm workers had also become accentuated by the increased political and economic stakes.

Unquestionably, Chandra Kant Chakravarty and Ram Chandra turned out to be unprincipled self-aggrandizers. Chakravarty, as we saw, obtained his money directly from the Germans, and spent a great deal of it on himself. In Ram Chandra's case, through his succession to Har Dayal's position as the head of Ghadr, he "had control of the donations made by the immigrants, the Ghadr papers and the Yugantar Ashram." Meanwhile, "The rank and file, who had staked all they had, including their lives, had nothing" (Singh and Singh 1966: 51). When Bhagwan Singh Gyani, Santokh Singh and Ram Singh openly opposed Ram Chandra, he expelled them from Ghadr on the grounds that "in Canada [they] fleeced the poor of thousands of dollars and spent it on pleasure, mingled themselves with crowds of undergraduates of the same kind as themselves" (*Ghadr*, March 1917). Clearly, it was the pot calling the kettle black!

Yet, in Ram Chandra's case, there were many redeeming features as long as Ghadr remained politically viable. He definitely brought administrative skills to his job, probably of a higher order

than Har Dayal provided. Obviously, Ram Chandra had an entrepreneurial bent which he employed in an attempt to lift the organization out of its rustic milieu and transform it into a major political
force. To the extent that his motivation was service to the cause,
and not to his own cupidity, this certainly helps account for his
determination to augment Ghadr's indigenous sources of revenue
with German money, and expand the scope of the organization
wherever possible. Since most humans are driven by a mixture of
vanity and idealism, there is no reason to suppose that Ram
Chandra was an exception to the rule. Whatever may have been
his personal flaws, he was also able to expand Ghadr's contacts
with other revolutionaries outside of the West Coast. He encouraged Gobind Behari Lal to undertake a six-month tour across the
country to build up the party's networks. "I had letters of introduction from my university professors ... I stayed at a number of
places on my way from San Francisco to New York. At Columbia,
Missouri, I spent a day with Thorstein Veblen, famous American
sociologist." Upon reaching New York, "I had lunch with Walter
Lippman, the columnist, then the editor of the New Republic ...."
His mention of pauses along the way in places like Columbia,
Missouri, where the University of Missouri is located, is extremely
significant. It is another indication of the widening interface between Indian students, scholars and professors on numerous
American campuses, especially in the Midwest. They constituted
enclaves where numerous Indian figures associated with the nationalist movement found hospitable receptions whenever they
visited the United States; as such, they were an ideal environment
for the nurturance of political rapport between Indian patriots and
the liberal wing of the American intellectual community (Sareen
1994: 48).

The visits of Rabindranath Tagore to the United States between
the years 1912 and 1929 are a case in point. This pattern grew
directly from the flow of Indian students onto American campuses.
Rabindranath, believing that the agricultural sciences were an essential need for predominantly agrarian India, sent his son in 1906
to the University of Illinois at Champaign-Urbana. "For Tagore,"
says Kamath (1998: 168), "the important thing for India was acquiring scientific knowledge for agricultural development, and since
ninety per cent of the people lived on the land, he would rather
Indians become better farmers in Illinois than better 'gentlemen'

at Oxford." Illinois was then one of the premier state universities in agricultural research, as it remains today. In 1912, Tagore, accompanied by his son and daughter-in-law, came to the university and sojourned there for several months, while Rathindranath worked on his doctoral degree. During that period, Rabindranath honed his writing skills in English and lectured at cultural societies and other campuses in Chicago, Boston, and New York. In Chicago, he met and established a life-long friendship with Mrs William Vaughan Moody, probably the widow of playwright William Vaughan Moody (1869–1910), of whom he was to say, "This contact led to a much-cherished friendship lasting until death of this remarkable woman, whose house was the refuge of many would-be artists and writers and a great attraction to all persons of eminence visiting the United States"(Kamath 1998: 169).

Tagore spoke frequently at the Urbana Vedanta Society. Some years ago, Professor Blair Kling, the university's now-retired South Asia historian and I interviewed an elderly lady who had witnessed some of Tagore's lectures there. "He was," she said, in a rapturous voice, "the most beautiful man I ever saw in my life!" There is a group photo, titled, "The Tagore Circle," taken at the home of Dr A.R. Seymour, an Illinois faculty member. Seated in the front row, flanking Rabindranath, are several American ladies, and two small children sitting cross-legged at his feet. Standing in the second row are seven Indian students and four American men, one of whom is his host, while the other three are probably fellow faculty members. Tagore returned to the United States in 1916, 1920, and 1929. His 1916 visit generated controversy when he forthrightly denounced the "cult of nationalism." Interestingly, this produced "an incident" in San Francisco, "instigated by some Indian residents in the area," which left Tagore "deeply hurt and mortified." The *Examiner* (October 6, 1916) reported that Tagore had even received a death threat, which resulted in his receiving police protection. His detractors obviously included some Ghadrites who were nationalists par excellence and were at that time engaged in mobilizing their resources for an attack on India. Gobind Behari Lal, significantly, one suspects, makes no mention whatsoever of Tagore's presence in San Franciso in 1916.

Tagore nevertheless returned in 1920 and gave a talk at the Brooklyn Civic Forum on November 20, which had such a large turnout that "hundreds were turned away." This was followed by another visit in 1929 which turned ugly. As he was going though customs, an immigration officer subjected him to racial slurs which were so repugnant that he canceled his engagements and quickly left the country: "His insulting questions and attitude were deeply humiliating." Eventually, he did go to Los Angeles to give some lectures, "But all the time I was impressed by the spirit in the air. The people seemed to be cultivating an attitude of suspicion and incivility toward Indians." He said it was not so much a "personal grievance, as a representative of all Asia peoples, [that] I could not remain under the shadow of such insults" (Kamath 1998: 170).

For good and ill, Tagore's ruminations in the United States illustrate the growing socio-political networks which a comparatively small number of South Asians were developing over time throughout the country. By the inter-war years, this process was well under way. There existed innumerable venues from coast to coast, where Indian activists could find havens and hospitality, and "cultural safe-houses" where Indian notables in the freedom movement coming from abroad could establish political and intellectual relationships with sympathetic Americans in the press, in the universities, in churches, indeed in the liberal establishment generally. As we shall see, by the World War II era, this process had culminated in what we call the "India Lobby".

Returning now to Ram Chandra, it must be said that with all his faults, he was nevertheless an effective editor of Ghadr's publications. In their pages, he was himself an articulate purveyor of the party's platform and ideology. Dr T.R. Sareen in his work, *Selected Documents on the Ghadr Party* (1994), compiled several pages of Ram Chandra's writings in *Ghadr* as well as in other publications. A few excerpts will capture the flavor of his rhetoric, and reveal why he was perceived by the British as a major thorn in their side.

Speaking of allegations by Austin Chamberlain, the British Secretary of State for India, that German money was behind Ghadr from its inception, and that its leaders had known "three years ago about the coming war," Ram Chandra declared: "We wish we had known it." He attributes these accusations to British efforts to depict Ghadr as part of a German conspiracy instead of what it actually is: "The American people will recall that the founders of this great republic, who accomplished exactly what we hope today for India, were stigmatized by the British as 'plotters and seditionists'" (Sareen 1994: 132). Attacking British claims that hegemony over India is a blessing for her people, the headline of one of his articles declares: "Hindus are Starving."

> One-third of India's revenues is spent on armaments and less than one-sixteenth is spent on education and sanitation. If this is the case, how can Hindus live? The Hindus are not living—they are dying. Nineteen million died of famine and 15,000,000 died of plague and malaria ... from 1891 to 1900. Hundreds of thousands died in Bankura, Bengal and Rajputana in the famine of 1915–16; 7,251,257 died from plague during the period of time between the years 1897 and 1913 (Sareen 1994: 133).

The full text of this article was reprinted in the *Philadelphia North American*, the *Detroit Free Press*, and the *New York Freemen's Journal*, which indicates the tireless efforts that were being made by *Ghadr* under Ram Chandra to disseminate its political message throughout the country.

On the use of Indian soldiers abroad by the British military, Ram Chandra vigorously refuted the Government of India's claim that their troops were sent to fight in the war because "the Indian public demanded it." Preposterous, Ram Chandra declared:

> India takes no pleasure in the fact that her sons have been sent to be butchered abroad. The Hindu soldiers do not go willingly .... Mercenary troops have no choice. They, like other Hindus, are brave people. Extreme poverty thanks to British administration, has compelled them to sell their manly virtues—in order to earn $3.00 a month for wife and children. They are giving their lives, not for the British Empire, not out of loyalty to an alien oppressor; but for the sake of their starving children. They are perverted martyrs to domestic virtue (ibid.: 136).

In the *American Independence* (September 13, 1916), a San Francisco publication, Ram Chandra drew a poignant conclusion from a comparison between India's current freedom struggle and America's similar quest a century-and-a-half earlier:

> When the American colonies dumped the British tea over board in Boston harbour rather than pay an unjust tax thereon, King George III wrathfully exclaimed that such anarchy in America

must be suppressed. The arrogance and intolerance which marked British officials of that period has not materially diminished, which may explain the state of mind which prompted Lord Hardinge, former Viceroy of India, to declare in a recently-published interview given to American newspapers that the present discontent in India is "anarchistic rather than revolutionary". The yearnings of the oppressed for a measure of political freedom always appears "anarchistic" to the oppressor (Sareen 1994: 139).

Why did Ghadr fail? Certainly the eventual defeat of Germany in 1918 was a major factor. The principal sources of money and logistical support disappeared. But there was more to it than this. Singh and Singh (1966: 55) provide a concise summary:

> Lack of arms; lack of experience; bad leadership; the notorious inability of the revolutionaries to keep secrets; the tension between the Germans and the Ghadarites; the efficiency of the British Intelligence Service which planted spies in the highest councils of the revolutionaries; the stern measures taken by the Government of India; the brutal methods adopted by the Punjab police which compelled many of the leaders ... to tell on their colleagues ....

As we have noted, while Ghadr was running its course, its tentacles spread widely across the country and energized other revolutionary formations both in terms of marshaling support for or generating opposition to its aims and methods. The distinction is important, because most of the Indians who were reluctant to support Ghadr did so out of concern for its violent methods rather than its declared purpose. Differences revolved around the former, not the latter. With the emerging influence of Mahatma Gandhi following World War I, issues of means and ends began to exert a strong influence on nationalist thinking.

Nowhere were the positive and negative effects of Ghadr more apparent than in New York. By the run-up to World War I, a considerable number of Indians had found their way into New York's political environment. It was a melting pot of contending ideologies which ran the gamut from anarchism to nationalism to communism and socialism.

# Notes

1. The word "Hindese" was created from "Hind," a Hindi word for India. Thus, people of Indian extraction were called "Hindese."
2. *Ghadr* in Hindustani means "disloyal." In this context its implication was that the East India Company *sepoys* had in 1857 decided to be become "disloyal" (i.e., "rebels") against their British masters.
3. Prior to its publication by Central Book Depot, 100 copies of Mazumdar's treatise were produced in 1960 in cyclostyled form as a "Preview Edition" by *World In Brief* of New York. It was edited by William D. Allen, who characterized his service as "intended to help U.S.A. specialists by bringing them, in highly condensed form, the thinking and achievements of modern Indians in their own field .... Copies are not for sale. They can only be obtained as loans via requests from established libraries."
4. I will draw heavily on Gobind Behari Lal's *Detailed Account of the Ghadr Movement*, which has been reproduced by Dr T.R. Sareen (1994). I feel that this document remarkably captures the flavor of the times in which Har Dayal and his cohorts lived.
5. He was clearly a linguistic genius who could learn languages with remarkable speed. It is said that by the middle of his life he was fluent in English, French, Latin, Greek, Swedish, Persian, Urdu, Hindi, and Sanskrit.
6. Emma Goldman was born in Kovno, Lithuania, "in the Jewish Pale of Settlement in the Tsarist Empire." Her parents ran an inn. When her parents lost their business, Goldman was compelled to do factory work from the time she was 13 until she and a sister migrated to the United States after she turned 16. It was during this period that she came under the influence of political radicalism, specifically the Nihilists, who engaged in plots to assassinate politicians and policemen. After reaching the US, while living in Rochester with her sister and a local relative, Goldman married Jacob Kerschner, thereby enabling her to gain American citizenship. Their marriage was stormy; they divorced and then remarried. She shifted to New York City and there met Alexander Berkman, an "anarchist militant, with whom she would develop a relationship of political collaboration that lasted the rest of their lives." She says that a turning point came in her life when she attended a memorial in Rochester to the radicals who were executed in the aftermath of the Haymarket riots of 1886 in Chicago for killing several policemen with a bomb. Her biographical account of what followed is an insight into the birth of a kind of "born again" militancy that would have rendered her and Har Dayal kindred souls. "The next morning I woke as from a long illness ... I had a distinct sensation that something new and wonderful had been born in my soul. A great ideal, a burning faith, a determination to dedicate myself to the memory of our martyred comrades." She became a member of a circle that included Alexander Berkman which culminated with an 1892 attempt on the life of Henry Clay Frick, manager of the Carnegie steel plant in Homestead, Pennsylvania, after company goons and the local police had engaged in lethal violence to quell a workers' strike. In the trial that followed, Berkman was

sentenced to 14 years in prison. Goldman herself was never indicted, "though she admitted her collaboration after she was in exile."

Her exile did not occur, however, until 1919. It resulted from her opposition to America's involvement in World War I. She and Berkman formed a Non-Conscription League in 1917, which ran them afoul of wartime anti-sedition laws. They were prosecuted and sentenced to two years imprisonment after which they were deported to then-Bolshevik Russia. The two had a stormy career in the cauldron of factional conflict which characterized the sorting-out process and consolidation of the Soviet Communist state. They were never purged, however, and Emma Goldman led a peripatetic existence over the remaining decades of her life, which included involvement in the Left's ideological controversies surrounding the Spanish Civil War. She died in Toronto in 1970.

During their overlapping careers, it is not clear how frequently Har Dayal and Emma Goldman crossed paths. There were apparently not that many encounters, and none were that deep; but it seems there was enough contact for Har Dayal, as a recognized Indian revolutionary, to partake of some of the radical contacts which she commanded.

Material for this sketch was garnered from Lance Selfa (2004).

7. According to Chang et al. (2002: 2), "He was a pivotal figure in the trans-mission and interpretation of Indian traditions to literary America in the first several decades of the twentieth century." Dhan Gopal Mukerji's book *Caste and Outcaste* was originally published in 1923 and was followed the next year (1924) by *My Brother's Face*, which was based on his impressions of India following a 1922 return trip to his native land after several years in the West. Other writings accompanied these, and Mukerji established himself as a reasonably successful author who somehow bridged East and West. In the author's own words, "there is a gulf between the oriental and the occi-dental mind: it is as though each were a lighthouse on a separate headland, illuminating the channel on one side and the channel on the other, but leaving in complete darkness the crossing between" (ibid.: 132).

8. This treaty was part of Britain's attempt at the turn of the century "to restore the balance of world power recently upset by her three great rivals," viz., Germany, Czarist Russia, and the United States. "All Asia was feeling the im-pact of Russian imperialism, which threatened to overrun British spheres of influence in China and even the Indian frontier itself .... For a moment England stood alone, friendless, amid the ruins of her once 'splendid' isolation. Then, in a characteristically pragmatic fashion, her diplomats began a search for allies on all three continents, and a systematic effort to re-establish the balance of power wherever British interests demanded it." One solution to her dilem-ma was the Anglo-Japanese Alliance of 1902; another was the *Entente Cordial* with France in 1904 (Griswold 1938: 36–37).

9. It did survive, however, as a pressure group representing Punjabi interests until final disbandment in 1937.

10. Between William Jennings Bryan's 1900 and 1908 unsuccessful runs for the US presidency, he took a trip around the world. In 1905, he reached India. Landing in Calcutta, he declared, "what extremes are here!" While describing in travelogue-like narrative what he saw and experienced, and despite his

well-known fundamentalist Christian biases, Bryan evinced great sympathy and understanding for India's plight as a conquered land being remorselessly exploited by a colonial master. "Let no one cite India as an argument in defense of colonialism," declared Bryan. "On the Ganges and the Indus the Briton, in spite of his many noble qualities, and his large contributions to the world's advancement, has demonstrated as many have before, man's inability to exercise, with wisdom and justice, irresponsible power over helpless people." "Yes," he continues, "he has conferred some benefits upon India, but he has extorted a tremendous price for them. While he has boasted about bringing peace to the living, he has led millions to the peace of the grave." The Briton has engaged, he declared, in the "legalized pillage" of India! Bryan published his conclusions in an article on British India "which has been severely criticized by the government papers in India *and as heartily praised by prominent representatives of the native population. Delegations of Indians called upon me in London, Paris and New York to express their thanks*" (Bryan 1907, emphasis added).

11. "Sister Nivedita" was born in Ireland in 1867, the daughter of "a preacher to whom religion meant service to the poor." Her birth-name was Margaret Noble. In 1895 she met Swami Vivekananda when he was visiting England and they made an impression on each other. She attended his lectures and resonated with his fundamental message that selfishness, ignorance and greed were the evils which brought suffering to the world. She followed Vivekananda to India, arriving in Calcutta on January 28, 1898. The Swami initiated her as his disciple on March 25, 1898, and conferred upon her the name "Nivedita," which means "One Devoted to God." She immersed herself deeply into Indian culture and religion and evolved into a dedicated nationalist. Her fame spread though Bengal and beyond. Through her dedication to the freedom movement and to the condition of women and her work in the Calcutta slums, she became a precursor of Mother Teresa. Through the intellectual, rhetorical and literary skills she brought to her opposition to colonialism, she became an inspiration to young Bengali nationalists. "The conviction grew upon her that until India gained political independence, Indians could never be treated like men." This conviction, of course, was entirely in keeping with the thrust of Bengali radicalism. "All over Bengal, Nivedita's name became a household word. Addressing mammoth meetings in several important places like Patna, Lucknow, Varanasi, Bombay, Nagpur, and Madras, she sounded the clarion call of freedom." This, of course, explains why Taraknath Das acknowledged his intellectual debt to Sister Nivedita, along with the many indigenous figures who made their mark on his political consciousness. Her tirelessness and the privations to which she subjected herself in her quest to help set India free led to her untimely death in 1911 at the age of 44 (quotations are from an online biography entitled *Sister Nivedita*, written by Prabhu Shankara).

12. "Two thousand copies of *Free Hindusthan*," says Mukherjee (1997: 15), "were printed and distributed worldwide. The National Archives of Canada has Taraknath's handwritten mailing list of forty-three Indians in South Africa alone."

13. The full passage may be found in Mukherjee (1997: 15).

14. This account has been condensed from Mukherjee (1997: 20–21).

15. In his *Prison Diary*, Tojo wrote the following while in jail awaiting his trial and execution (in 1946) for his World War II war crimes: "... in dealing with the China problem, the British and American side ... should have based its judgements about the origins of the problem in direct observation of the actual circumstances at the time. Moreover, both sides should have considered the point of view and survival of the billion people of East Asia, who were awakening to world development. Rather than be trapped in the narrow-minded maintenance of old power structures, it was necessary that both sides deliberate together, and work harmoniously, and take a broader view of mutual prosperity, cooperation, and the establishment of stability in East Asia." This was a less focused but comparable manifestation of the viewpoint which Taraknath Das expressed in his book.

16. Singh and Singh (1966: Appendix xxxiii, p. 92) compiled the names of all 15 Indians who were tried and convicted: "1. Gopal Singh (1 yr and a day); 2. Bhai Singh (18 mos); 3. Taraknath Das (22 mos); 4. Gobind Bihari Lal (10 mos); 5. Bishan Behari Hindi, *sic*. (9 mos); 6. Bhai Santokh Singh (21 mos); 7. Godha Ram (11 mos); 8. Niranjan Dass (6 mos); 9. Mahadeo Abaji Nadekar; 10. Munshi Ram (60 days); 11. Nidhan Singh (4 mos); 12. Iman Din (4 mos); 13. Dharmindra Sarkar (4 mos); 14. Chandra Kant Chakravarty (30 days/ $300 fine); 15. Sunder Singh (3 mos)."

17. I have taken much from Brown's account of these happenings because her research on the subject is the most exhaustive and authoritative.

# From Taraknath Das to Lajpat Rai

A major catalyst for the Indian cause on the East Coast was the fortuitous arrival of Lala Lajpat Rai (1865–1928) in New York in December of 1914. By then, he was already a noted, senior Indian nationalist who had more than paid his dues in the Indian freedom struggle. After reaching New York, Lajpat Rai was able to employ his reputation and his talents to gradually establish a host of relationships with what today would be called the "media," and to fashion an institutional base on the eastern side of the continent which was a counterpart to what Ghadr and other organizations had accomplished on the western side. His main organizational achievement was founding the Indian Home Rule League (at 1,400 Broadway), which, in the words of Joginder Singh Dhanki, "provided [in New York] his propaganda an institutional form, and made it possible for the Americans sympathetic to the Indian cause to work in collaboration with Indian Nationalists." In concert with this organization, he also established, by 1918, a monthly organ called *Young India*. N.S. Hardikar was appointed its editor and D.S.V. Rao its Managing Editor. Another important facility established by the League was the Indian Information Bureau whose purpose was "to furnish facts and reliable information about Indian affairs to editors of periodicals, writers, students and others, and to serve as a medium through which books on India might be ordered" (Dhanki 1978: 9). These accomplishments can be said to have moved Indian political activism in the United States from the soapbox onto the podium.

This was, for all practical purposes, the beginning of the "India Lobby." It was the point in time when the South Asian presence in the United States took the critical next step in institution building. It began reaching out in *systematic* terms to potentially sympathetic agencies, groups and individuals in the country who could enable South Asians to increase their social visibility, and open channels to the mainstream political establishment. Through this process, South Asian activists and their American cohorts would have at their disposal resources to influence public discourse and the flow of legislation pertaining to the Indian freedom struggle and the civil rights of South Asians living in the United States. There follows thenceforth a lineal progression from Lala Lajpat Rai and his compatriots in the New York area during World War I and its aftermath to the pubic relations and lobbying undertakings of Jagjit Singh("J.J. Singh") and his circle who had by the end of World War II achieved the ultimate political breakthroughs which finally persuaded significant sections of the American public, a majority of the US Congress, and indeed the president of the United States himself to decisively support independence for India and equal rights for Indian immigrants.

Lala Lajpat Rai was almost 40 years old when he came to America. By then, he had built an extensive career as a committed nationalist with considerable organizational and leadership capabilities. His decision to come to America from England was motivated by a determination to elicit greater overseas support for the freedom movement. He had been "officially" invited to come to the United States by N.S. Hardikar in his capacity as president of the Indian Students Association of America. After his arrival, he asked Hardikar, then a medical student at the University of Michigan, and 20 years his junior, to become his "full-time secretary." This request was not made until 1916, apparently because Lajpat had needed time to get his bearings in New York. Hardikar says he "felt a bit perturbed" by this request since it meant "disturbing the entire course of my life." But he ultimately "decided to give up the desire for the university degree and to jump into the ocean of patriotic work under Lalaji's guidance ..." (Hardikar 1966: 7).

Essentially, Rai had been "marooned" in England by the onset of World War I. In the summer of 1914, he had come to England along with Bhupendra Nath Basu, one of the initiators of the 1905 Swadeshi movement which undid the partition of Bengal. They had been invited by Sydney and Beatrice Webb, founders of the democratic socialist movement known as the Fabians, to attend a "Summer School" which was "held in the English lake district on a beautiful spot," where they "enjoyed a delightful communion

**Illustration 7.1**
**Lala Lajpat Rai**

*Source:* Kamath 1998.

with the best socialist workers and thinkers in England." Along with the Webbs, the gathering included George Bernard Shaw and G.D.H. Cole. Prior to the summer session, Rai undertook a tour of the Continent. "Several friends, including the Webbs, had given me letters of introduction for prominent people in these countries who could help me in the study of conditions there." When he returned to London, however, he "found the air full of war fears." As a committed Arya Samajist, Rai was bothered by the moral condition of the Indians he encountered in England. "The attitude of the Indians then in England showed me for the first time in my life, practically and concretely, how foreign rule leads to a complete deterioration of the manly virtues even among amongst the best men of the subject race." The reason for this denunciation of his fellow countrymen abroad was the manner in which "each tried to outbid the others in expressions of loyalty and devotion to the Empire ..." (Rai 1978: 50).

When war broke out, the British were unwilling to allow Lajpat Rai to return to India due to suspicions that he had been implicated in the Kanpur Conspiracy. He decided to go to America rather than remain indefinitely exiled in England. According to Hardikar, "Lalaji could not sit quiet." To satisfy his "need of doing some field work," he turned toward the United States, believing "that America provided such a field ..." (Hardikar 1966: 3). What was important was that he brought considerable political expertise, maturity and intellectual power to this task. His declared goal was to build durable institutions and not just engage in rhetorical *tours de force*.

Gradually, between 1914 and 1919 Lajpat Rai was indeed able to build a political base in New York City, which enabled him to distance himself from the more radical political elements which he found occupying centerstage when he arrived. As already suggested, this turned out to be a crucial element in the process of South Asian political evolution in the United States. Essentially, for a time, it involved a rather complex interplay between the three principal rival political groups that were in play. Confronting Rai's faction were the Ghadrites, consisting predominantly of Sikhs committed to a military showdown with the Raj on the 1857 model. Their ties with the Germans, as we saw, ultimately brought conspiracy litigation down upon their heads. Then there were the Bengalis, consisting of activists like Sailendranath Ghose and Taraknath Das, who overlapped the Ghadrites, to be sure, but were by no means coterminous with them either in personnel or in organizational and programmatic terms. They had by 1919 established an organization called the Friends of Freedom for India (FFI) which commingled old fashioned Bengali-style radical activism with more subtle efforts to garner support for their cause in the country's political mainstream. For a time, M.N. Roy (1887–1954), the consummate Bengali revolutionary-turned-Communist, was also in the mix, until he fled to Mexico after he and his then wife, Evelyn, faced arrest for their alleged involvement in the German Conspiracy Case.[1] Lajpat Rai himself was gravitating toward the Gandhian-style political morality and democratic constitutionalism being espoused by the Indian National Congress.

A unique source of insight into this evolving tactical and ideological differentiation taking place in the New York political milieu at this time is the tussle which developed between Lajpat Rai and the Bengali-dominated FFI leadership for the political soul of a young American radical named Agnes Smedley who arrived from the West Coast at the end of 1916.

In many ways her career exemplified the political turmoil of the times, i.e., the inter-war years that witnessed a rising tide of anti-colonial nationalism, the triumph of communism in Russia, the Spanish Civil War, and the eventual ascendancy of Nazism and fascism in Germany, Italy and Spain, ultimately leading to World War II. She was born in Osgood, Missouri, on February 23, 1892, the second of five children in a poor farming family. Her father, like so many turn-of-the-century men, was a restless creature who moved about the American West seeking the proverbial pot of gold while subjecting his wife and five children to a life of emotional turmoil and marginal living standards. Apart from the psychological impact of spending her early years in this unstable domestic environment, perhaps her most formative experiences in terms of laying the foundation for her political personality were those that occurred when the family settled in the town of Trinidad, Colorado, from 1901 until not long after her mother's death in 1910. Trinidad was the third largest town in the state, whose principal industry was coal mining. "Within the last ten years, the most extensive deposits of coking coal in the West had been discovered under the lush hills of pine, pinon and cedar that ringed the metropolis," declares Ruth Price (2005: 19). "The Colorado Fuel and Iron Company," she continues, "part of John D. Rockefeller's Standard Oil Trust and the area's largest employer, used the town as hub of operations for its scattered enterprises...." It was here, as a witness to labor strife between the mining companies and the exploited miners who struggled to form unions and fight for decent working conditions and a living wage, that she acquired her working-class orientation. It was during this period that she also became conscious not only of her proletarian roots but also of her ethnic roots. Technically she was a "mixed blood." Her maternal great-grandmother had Cherokee blood in her veins. During her Trinidad girlhood, she would write, her awareness that she was different from the "perfect" little white children who had made her so acutely self-conscious that she developed psychosomatic throat constrictions in response (ibid.: 37). This, she acknowledged, sharpened her subsequent perception of and identification with South Asians, and later East Asians as well, whose fight, like the native Americans from whom she was in part descended, was as much against White racism as economic exploitation and colonialism per se.

Despite the hardships, she was an excellent student, and doggedly pursued her quest for formal education. She successfully passed the New Mexico teacher's examination and commenced working as a teacher at the age of 16. When her mother died from a ruptured appendix, she was, due to her father's absences, compelled to remain in Osgood for a while to care for her younger siblings. By then, however, Agnes was determined to change her life. "She was too needy herself," Price declares, "to give herself over altogether to caring for others." The household drudgery and the managerial burdens of caring for her four siblings "oppressed her" and, "As she grew restless, angry and resentful, a desire to flee took hold" (Price 2005: 33). She dispatched her 16-year-old sister, Myrtle, to a ranch in Gunnison, Colorado, consigned the others to her father's "uncertain care," and embarked on her quest to find a place in the sun. The details of the early stages of this quest are described in Ruth Price's (ibid.) remarkably detailed biography.

In 1911, Smedley was back in the Southwest after successfully gaining admission to Tempe Normal School as a "special student," a status necessitated by the her lack of a high school diploma. Working part-time as a waitress to pay her way, it was there that she became involved in student politics, becoming editor of the student newspaper. Her stay there was "a time of intellectual and creative growth" (ibid.: 36). In 1912, she married an engineer named Ernest George Brundin, with whom she went to live in San Diego, California. "By the time she left Arizona, it was the darker skinned races who would always be *us* to her," while "Caucasians had become the other" (ibid.:37). In San Diego she joined the teacher-training program of San Diego State College, where she became increasingly involved in leftist politics. In her capacity as a leading light among her fellow politically active students, she invited prominent radicals of the era like Emma Goldman, Upton Sinclair, and Eugene V. Debs to speak on campus. This commenced a friendship with Goldman which lasted a lifetime. Finally she was dismissed from the university for her "socialistic" beliefs.

Her marriage to George Brundin formally ended in 1917, but only after years of ups and downs, much living apart, and bouncing back and forth between San Diego and San Francisco. During this trying period, her sister Myrtle also having migrated to the West Coast, and being more in touch with their rustic origins, was apparently able to divert Agnes from time to time into a little light-headed socializing, beach parties, motorcycle jaunts to Tijuana, etc. But Agnes had also begun establishing contacts with the Indian activists, including the Ghadrites, as well as other leftist intellectuals in the San Francisco area. This drew her farther away from her husband and any idea of having children (she had two abortions) and settling for conventional married life.

A seminal influence during this transition was her 26-year-old sister-in-law, Thorberg Brundin. Thor, as she was called, was a graduate of Barnard College, "who had abandoned her life in Greenwich Village to see a bit of the world before entering graduate school" (Price 2005: 37). Essentially, she became Agnes's mentor and role model. "Thorberg was part of a rising generation of women who thumbed their noses at the tradition of self-sacrifice and submergence in the family, and had become a proponent of self-expression, equality of the sexes, and the extension in every direction of the power and freedom of women ..." (ibid.). Her importance to Smedley's social and political maturation lay in the fact that she "was the first intellectual, the first bohemian, and the first socialist Agnes had ever met; she was also the most educated, cultured and sophisticated" (ibid.: 38). It was through her that Agnes met and eventually married her brother George.

Her first meaningful encounter with an Indian nationalist was apparently with Har Dayal in the summer of 1912, not long after his arrival in this country. Price says that Agnes became acquainted with him at the home of Gertrude Baldwin Woods, "renegade wife of a noted Harvard Sanskritist," where "she began to hear about the situation in India from a radical nationalist perspective, a fact that did not go unnoticed by British agents in the United States who opened a file on her" (ibid.: 44). This is where Agnes's class anxieties, radical political inclinations and ethnic sensibilities achieved some measure of reconciliation and opened the pathway to what would become her lasting sisterhood with Indian nationalism and attraction to South Asian civilization. "Having made greater peace with her racial identity than with the working-class background she still battled to escape, Agnes found it easier to identify with California's beleaguered Asian community than with Bay Area Socialists who wore buttons urging workers of the world to unite while simultaneously advocating Asian exclusion" (Price 2005: 45). Her commitment to the Ghadrite cause became so strong that "by August 29, when the first batch of ghadarites departed from San Francisco, she had abandoned her studies [at Berkeley] and became an active worker in the Ghadr movement" (ibid.: 51).

These new associations were crucial to her decision to move to New York. By the time Har Dayal's career in the United States had run its course, Agnes was a committed supporter of the Ghadr Party. She had become acquainted with the party's post-Har Dayal president, Ram Chandra, and close friends with his principal factional rival, Balwant Singh—so much so, in fact, that, "the new Ghadr leader visited Agnes at the ranch in Dulzura where Agnes spent weekends with her sister, scandalizing the conservative owners, who supported the taboo on interracial relationships." They pressured Myrtle to sever contact with her sister; but, as Price concludes, "Agnes appeared less interested in a romantic partner than in a continuing role in the Indian struggle for freedom" (ibid.: 55–56). On December 31, 1916 she departed for New York carrying documents which Balwant Singh had asked her to deliver to the branch of the Berlin-India Committee (BIC) for whom the German government had provided funds to establish on the East Coast of the United States. In this way, Agnes obtained immediate access to the Indian revolutionaries based in New York.

Once there, she landed a job at a magazine and began taking courses at New York University. Through the connections supplied by Balwant Singh, plus Indians she met at the university, Agnes got to know Lala Lajpat Rai. The Indian to whom she related the most strongly was probably Sailendranath Ghose, who persuaded her to join the ranks of the Bengali radicals. As this relationship deepened, and undoubtedly because of her already established identifications with Ghadr which she had acquired on the West Coast, Smedley gravitated away from her apparent initial attraction to the more moderate and venerable Lajpat Rai towards the more radical Bengali set who were already intertwined with Ghadr and the Berlin Committee. "Prodded by Ghose and [M.N.] Roy," says Hardikar (1966, emphasis added), "Smedley converted to the ways of the Bengali revolutionaries, *to the utter dismay of her teacher and mentor, Lajpat Rai.*"[2] This proved to be a great disappointment to Lajpat Rai, who seems to have developed a genuinely fatherly attachment to Agnes. Rai, says Price (2005: 65), repeatedly "tried to discourage her from further involvement [with the radicals] and threatened to have nothing to do with Agnes if she persisted in her relationships with them." But his "entreaties left her unmoved."

As his tenure in America wore on, Lajpat Rai had steadily parted company with the most strident of the Indian radicals. "I found all of them inspired by a high standard of patriotism," he wrote. But he could not abide their involvement with the Germans. "Most of them were extremists, only a few were moderates." Among the former were "some frank and open advocates of violence ...." What bothered him particularly was that these radicals "were in alliance with Germany and were being supplied with money by German government agents." To their dismay, the "Lion of the Punjab" refused to go along with the Bengali radicals for this reason and also, I believe, because by then the Gandhian movement and his identification with the Indian National Congress was beginning to deeply affect Rai's political orientation. "They told me only a little of their plans but what they did tell me was enough to convince me that they were contemplating and planning an armed insurrection in India, so timed as to be useful to Germany in her European campaign *even if it failed as far as India was concerned.*" For this reason, he declared, "They failed to convince me and I failed to convince them." As a result, as mutual enmity mounted, "They followed and shadowed me and used all their arts of persecution, but I was adamant" (Rai 1978: 69–70).

While Lajpat Rai turned toward making the Indian cause palatable to the American mainstream by emphasizing his country's quest for political freedom through democracy and social justice (and increasingly through non-violent methods), the Bengali set remained enmeshed in revolutionary extremism including the condoning of violence. For the next several years Agnes Smedley cast her lot with the latter.

Smedley's absorption into the more radical wing of Indian nationalism proceeded apace once she made her initial commitment. Smedley was clearly an extremely vulnerable young woman at this nascent stage of her entry into radical politics. She arrived from the West Coast saturated with a host of ideological ambivalences and emotional conflicts. She might well have been better off in the long run in sticking with the more mature, level-headed, fatherly Lajpat Rai. "Her view of the sex act as animalistic added to her emotional problems," notes Barooah (2004: 227). Among other things, it resulted in her succumbing "to a forced sexual adventure on the part of Indian nationalist Herambalal Gupta." In the light of the much deeper insight into Smedley's persona and exploits provided by Ruth Price, Barooah's characterization seems highly superficial, indeed sexist. However, this is a matter which cannot be resolved here. Nevertheless, it does appear to be plausible that Agnes's Bengali cohorts viewed her less as an equal and more as a useful tool in their conspiratorial arsenal. She "allowed herself to be used by Das and Ghose in a naive project in the name of their so-called Indian National party" (Price 2005: 69). But these young Indian revolutionary expatriates were certainly no less riven with emotional problems and identity crises than she! It was they, after all, who induced her to "hide the organization's codes, foreign addresses and correspondence in her room so that if any of the East Indians were arrested, this material would not be compromised," while lacking the integrity to make her aware that the group had for some time been monitored by the US authorities. To add to her predicament, by distributing birth control literature she had herself attracted official scrutiny through her activities in California and after coming to New York. This arose from the fact that since her arrival she had come under the spell of Margaret Sanger (1880–1966), one of the founders of the women's rights movement. In March 1918, she was arrested with Sailendranath Ghose: "Agnes was arrested and charged with violating the Espionage Act for conspiring to falsely represent herself as an official of the Indian National Party" (ibid.).

M.N. Roy and Evelyn were arrested along with Herambalal Gupta while attending a lecture by Lala Lajpat Rai at Columbia University. "Pending further investigations, Roy and Evelyn were released with a warning not to leave the city, but they fled to Mexico with Ghose" (Mukherjee 1997: 134). Smedley did not accompany them. Price (2005: 64) says that "before he left, Ghose had asked her, as a favor, to act as a 'kind of communication center' for the Indian revolutionaries abroad." She said his request "frightened" her, but she did it anyway, presumably because their relationship had become more than platonic. Agnes, therefore, remained in New York to face charges arising out of the documents which a search of her room had revealed, and from her connection with Margaret Sanger.

Roy, meanwhile, upon reaching Mexico, convinced the German agents there that he was "the most significant Indian conspirator in Mexico and therefore the best suited to maintain contact with his American-based counterparts and manage German funds." Roy had successfully and opportunistically seized the moment, obtained his German imprimatur, and received $50,000 "to dispense as he saw fit." By the time Sailendranath Ghose joined him in Mexico City, "Roy (using the *nom de guerre* Manuel Mendez)" had "established himself in a sumptuous house on the wealthy Colonia Roma," and "was passing himself off as an Indian prince ... mingling in the upper echelons of local society" (Price 2005: 64).

Ghose did not remain very long in Mexico with the Roys. All the while he was there, Agnes was in correspondence with him, filling him in on developments in the United States. During this period, the grand jury in San Francisco indicted all of them in the Berlin Conspiracy Case. At this point Ghose and the Roys testily parted company. Price's research indicates that the personal bond between Agnes and Sailendranath was the rub, perhaps primarily because Roy, who had once come on to Agnes sexually, with unsatisfying consequences, harbored a strong antipathy to her. He tried to induce Ghose to break off relations with her. "Convinced that their bond was sexual (*sic*), Roy would later write, he tried to discourage Ghose from becoming further involved with Agnes, warning that the infatuation of a young man with a woman 'much older' than himself (Agnes was two years Ghose's senior) was dangerous." He wanted Ghose to remain in Mexico, "doing something that would give him revolutionary experience instead of returning to the United States *as Agnes proposed*" (ibid.: 66, emphasis added).

Tapan Mukherjee (1997: 134, emphasis added) provides a somewhat different take on the parting of the ways between Ghose and Roy. "In November," says he, "tired of inactivity, and *Roy's ill treatment*, Ghose slipped back to San Francisco where Taraknath [Das] took him under his wing." Ghose, of course, was by this time technically a fugitive from justice. However, his return afforded him an opportunity to develop his own network connections on the West Coast. "Posing as H.P. Mitra, Ghose rented a room in the house of Lemuel Parton, associate editor of the *San Francisco Tribune*, and Taraknath introduced him to his long-time friends, William and Mary Wotherspoon." From this vantage point, says Mukherjee (1997: 134), Ghose developed further political relationships on his own, such as with socialists like Bluma Zalzanek. All this activity once again attests to how cosmopolitan the Indian revolutionary movement in the United States was becoming by World War I. These young nationalists were by now able to range quite freely around the United States and throughout Europe and Asia, with links to a host of kindred groups and individuals from a variety of revolutionary backgrounds in London, Paris, Berlin, Geneva, Stockholm, Shanghai, Hong Kong, and Tokyo. In political terms, the South Asians had moved appreciably beyond their tremulous beginnings no more than a decade earlier. Undoubtedly, the lubricant of German money had played a significant role in this scalar increase.

The Indian Nationalist Party, which Ghose and Taraknath teamed up to establish, was, it appears, conceived as an offshoot of the Government of Free India in Berlin. The latter was promoted as an Indian government-in-exile, for which its members unsuccessfully endeavored to be accorded official recognition by Germany and, of course, by any other state inclined to do so. In America, Rash Behari Bose was named Provisional President of the Supreme Council of the Indian National Party and Jadugopal Mukherjee Chairman of the Foreign Relations Committee. Essentially, this was a resolutions-generating, articles-producing, letter-writing front employing a glitzy letterhead which implied that it had some kind of official standing as a "foreign government." Attempting to act as a provisional government, "the first official manifestation of the Indian Nationalist Party in the United States was a letter written by Taraknath Das to [President Wilson] regarding the incarceration of two Indians in Jacksonville, Florida" (ibid.: 135). They brazenly directed letters to the Secretary of State and President Wilson, "introducing Bhagwan Singh, Taraknath, and Sailendranath Ghose 'as the personnel of a Special Commission of the Indian National Party working for the Independence of India and for the establishment of a democratic, federated republic of three hundred and fifteen million people'" (ibid.).

The US government, of course, bought none of this. It was on this basis, in fact, that a New York grand jury indicted Sailendranath Ghose, Agnes Smedley, Taraknath Das, Bhagwan Singh, Pulin Behari Bose, and Jadugopal Mukherjee as violators of Sec. 3, Title 8 of the Espionage Act and Sec. 37 of the US Conspiracy Code. Das, Ghose, and Singh were charged with misrepresenting themselves as "diplomatic officers acting 'as agents of a foreign government, without prior notification to the Secretary of State.'" Smedley was named as an accessory "for carrying out the correspondence with foreign legations" (Mukherjee 1997: 138). Mukherjee says that "no one could find Pulin Behari Bose"; he suspects that this is because Agnes invented him as a fictional character to throw the police off track. Bail was set at $25,000 for Ghose and the other men, and $10,000 for Smedley.

Agnes Smedley became a cause célèbre in her own right as this drama unfolded. It worked to her personal advantage because Margaret Sanger came to her rescue. She raised money to cover Smedley's bail from her own progressive constituencies around New York. She persuaded Gilbert Roe, a "prominent liberal defense lawyer" to defend Agnes. The upshot of all these maneuverings is that Smedley first got her bail reduced to $1,000. Ultimately, "In San Francisco, to the dismay of [District Attorney] Preston, the district court commissioner dismissed all charges against the Wotherspoons." On the other hand, "The indictments against Taraknath, Ghose, Smedley and Bhagwan Singh ... were not dropped until the summer of 1919." Their defense attorney, Gilbert Roe, was compelled to take the case all the way to the Supreme Court in order to get the New York indictments dismissed. "It was not until June 13, 1923, that the New York indictments were finally dropped" (ibid.: 139).

From June 5, 1918, to October 25, 1919, Taraknath Das was incarcerated in Leavenworth Prison. Two of the German conspirators, Franz Bopp and von Sheck, were also imprisoned with him, but it is not clear whether or how much contact Taraknath had with them while there. Almost all his contacts while in prison were with fellow Indian revolutionaries, American allies and persons in the legal profession. For the most part he was given jobs in the prison which enabled him to sustain his intellectual life, such as the library where he cataloged 8,000 volumes using the Dewey Decimal System before being transferred to other work. He did his share of menial work as well. His correspondence with Sailendranath Ghose and Agnes Smedley was extensive and revealed growing tensions between them. During this period, the latter two also spent time (though far less than Taraknath) in the Tombs, the prison maintained by the city of New York. Their main concern, of course, was to try and keep the pulse of their cause alive under such difficult circumstances. Mukherjee provides an exhaustive account of the Leavenworth phase which need not be repeated here, except for a few points.

Agnes Smedley worked hard to free her Indian compatriots once she was out of jail. The correspondence between her and Taraknath make it clear that her main preoccupation was with Sailendranath Ghose. There was undoubtedly some degree of romantic involvement there. In fact, during their arraignment, Ghose "proclaimed his love for Agnes" (Price 2005: 70). This also came out in letters in which she excoriated both Das and Ghose over their inclination to join the Socialist Party. Although a member herself, Smedley believed that the two were undertaking it for tactical reasons alone and not because they sincerely believed in its principles. She believed they were inveterate nationalists for whom Indian freedom was the only genuine passion. Her objections arose from her belief that getting involved with the socialists at a time when anti-Red hysteria was sweeping the country would simply reduce their chances of winning the legal cases pending against them. She saw it as quixotic behavior and made no bones about saying so. Her anger showed, for example, when she commenced using, as Mukherjee notes, "Dear Dr. Das" in her letters instead of, "My Dear Brother." Pointing out that Sailendranath "is still in jail," she says, "I think his correspondence with you, and yours with him, may be detrimental to him at this time ..." (Mukherjee 1997: 154).

When Sailendranath came out of prison, Smedley took pains to look after him. "He was a physical wreck; he could not even walk a few steps" (ibid.: 160). She had a friend put him up for a few days in her cottage in the country, and they then both plunged back into political work. They set up a Hindu Defense Fund to try and prevent the Government from deporting Indian patriots. Then, in March 1919, they established FFI. Smedley herself was the driving force in establishing FFI. This organization was a direct response to the efforts of the Berlin Committee to "establish a propaganda organization in the United States that would build on the Ghadr Party's achievement in fostering American support for India's independence" (Price 2005: 77). Declares Mukherjee (1997: 160), "Although Taraknath was not directly involved in the creation of FFI, Ghose and Smedley regularly sought his advice and intellectual guidance." One of the most important aspects of this undertaking was that it opened links between Smedley and Virendranath Chattopadhyaya that would pave the way for her eventual departure to Germany and her romantic involvement with "Chatto."

In its initial phase, this organization was able to draw extensively on the pool of liberals and radicals concentrated in the New York area. In this sense, it was a step removed from orthodox Ghadr and Bengali radical extremism and inclining toward an increased willingness to work within the mainstream American political system. Without acknowledging it, FFI was in fact borrowing a page from Lala Lajpat Rai's playbook.

Its original roster of office holders and executive committee members reflects this fact; it reads like a who's who of the progressive-liberal establishment of the day. Robert Morse Lovett (1870–1956), a University of Chicago professor of English, the editor of *Dial* and a resident of Hull House Settlement, was made its president; Frank P. Walsh, a noted anti-imperialist activist and writer, was vice-president; Louis P. Lochner, then editor of the *International Labor News Service* and subsequently a Pulitzer Prize-winning journalist for his inter-war-years and World-War-II reporting, became treasurer; and two prominent New York lawyers, Gilbert R. Rose and Dudley F. Malone, became the organization's legal counselors. On the executive board were Roger N. Baldwin, founder of the ACLU; Margaret Sanger; Socialist Party leader Norman Thomas (1884–1968); Henrietta Rodman, a prominent feminist activist of that era; and Rose Strunsky, a daughter of Russian radicals who migrated to California where she was active in the labor movement (she became an intimate friend of Jack London, and eventually one of his biographers). "Many office bearers and executive board members," declares Mukherjee (1997: 161), "were listed in *Who's Who in America.*"

At this point in time, FFI had the right mix to mount a comprehensive campaign against government attempts to deport Hindu radicals. "We believe," wrote Agnes Smedley, "that Hindus have a right to asylum in this country .... Right now, we believe that our job is to work for the right of asylum, and our president Lovett emphasizes that point. *He is a typical American, one who believes in fundamental justice"* (Smedley to Das, April 22, 1919, reproduced in Mukherjee 1997: 160–61, emphasis added). This indicates, of course, how far the South Asian activists had progressed in terms of broadening their political base and interfacing with intellectually and ideologically compatible individuals and groups in the wider community. In essence, there now were three formations with a national/international reach promoting the South Asian cause by various means: Ghadr, the India League, and FFI.

With Sailendranath Ghose as "national organizer," public meetings were conducted and an India News Service created whose purpose was to counter British propaganda, educate public figures on the plight of Indian émigrés, and highlight the evils of colonialism in India.

Along with Lajpat Rai's *Indian Information Service*, I believe this denotes the real beginning of systematic lobbying by South Asian activists in the United States. The *Service's* releases were distributed to 500 newspapers and magazines in the US and India. They published several pamphlets. "Every senator and congressman was provided with facts concerning the Hindu deportation cases, together with descriptions of the miserable conditions of Indians under British tyranny." In addition, says Mukherjee, "Six different delegations were sent to Washington to meet with government officials and legislators" (Mukherjee 1997: 161). This latter was certainly indicative of a growing recognition of the importance of systematic lobbying. The most important spin-off was the opening of a FFI office in Washington that was called The American Committee to Promote Self-Government (Swaraj) in India. "Two senators, one congressman, one ex-governor, two retired circuit judges, three religious leaders, and the mayors of six cities were on the roster as vice-chairmen .... Although the Commission's propaganda gave lip service to Gandhi's non-violent creed and promised coordination with the Indian National Congress, its message of armed revolt remained the central theme" (ibid.: 176). The fact, however, that Gandhi's and the Indian National Congress's doctrines had to be acknowledged (regardless of how much this may have been for tactical reasons) was of course an important development. Old-fashioned Bengali and Punjabi radicalism was on the threshold of being trumped by the "kinder and gentler" political strategy pioneered by Lajpat Rai. This Washington branch did not survive very long in any event; it was wound up by 1923 for lack of resources and public support. The same happened to branches in Chicago, Boston, and Detroit. Its importance, however, was that its programmatic orientation displayed a dawning realization among South Asians in the United States that coalition and consensus (viz., admixing the democratic secularism of Indian National Congress vintage and Gandhian means-ends morality) must share the stage with old-fashioned Hindu radicalism as necessary ingredients for a successful representation of Indian interests in the mainstream of American politics. Although these specific organizations waned, the methodology they cultivated lived on in other contexts to become the weapon of choice for the more sophisticated players who followed.

The FFI efforts were actually successful in awakening some segments of the labor unions, Socialists, and many human rights groups to the immigration rights of the Hindus. Perhaps the most striking achievement, says Mukherjee, was the success which Ghose, Baldwin, and Surendranath Kar, who had shifted to FFI from Ghadr at Taraknath's behest to manage the *India News Service*, had in persuading the AFL to modify its anti-Asian bias.[3]

Once out of prison, Taraknath became increasingly involved with FFI activities. As 1920 wore on, however, the wheels began to fall off FFI. Factional conflict, stubborn ideological adherence to violent revolutionary rhetoric by hard-line members, and a generally litigious atmosphere gradually undermined the organization's viability and legitimacy. Before the end came, however, Taraknath, Ghose, Smedley, and Kar attempted to play an active role in the major events of the day. The most important of these, of course, was the Paris Peace Conference which convened on January 18, 1919, would last for six months, and which, as it turned out, would be, as one scholar put it in a somewhat narrower frame, the "peace to end all peace" (Frumkin 1989).[4] "For six months in 1919," declares Macmillan, "Paris became the capital of the world .... The world had never seen anything quite like it and never will again." New challenges and new agendas had emerged after the four-year maelstrom of death and destruction had run its course. It was not anymore simply a matter of "drawing new lines on the map of Europe ... they also had to think of Asia, Africa and the Middle East." The watchword, says Macmillan, had become "self-determination" and heretofore politically mute and invisible social groups from around the globe emerged from the woodwork and lined up for their day in court (Macmillan 2001: xxv–xxviii).

It was in this context that FFI felt impelled to take its place in line. Taraknath Das, as the "expert" in foreign affairs, took a leading role in trying to gain admission to the dance. FFI, of course, did not succeed in having any significant effect on the outcome. Following the conference, President Warren G. Harding convened a gathering of nine nations in Washington for the ostensible purpose of trying to halt a naval arms race in Asia. The main purpose was to devise a mechanism whereby Japan could be deterred from creating naval forces of sufficient magnitude to rival the power of the British and American navies. "Japan, upset at the snub she received at Paris, was well aware of the Anglo-American motive behind the conference" (Mukherjee 1997: 178). It is well known that her reason for taking part was to preserve her conquests on the mainland. Prior to the convening of the conference, Taraknath attempted to formally dissociate "Republican India" from what the FFI claimed was a blatant attempt to preserve British naval superiority in Asia. Through this, Das asserted in an article in the *New York American* dated November 1, 1921, the British motive was to maintain their colonial empire. "Republican India is opposed to Britain's plan of world domination and refuses to be associated with Britain." He said that the FFI and the American Commission to Promote Self-Government in India would "endeavor to present India's case before the coming conference separately from that of the British delegation." Obviously the purpose was to try and establish a *national identity* for India that was distinct from the British.

An interesting new dimension to the group's propaganda campaign was the invoking of Gandhi. The manner in which it was done both symbolized the rising international influence of the Congress movement and the ambivalence which many of the old style radicals harbored about less than violent political approaches to the attainment of Indian freedom. Rather sanctimoniously, the doubters declared that they had given a "reprieve" to the Mahatma, during which time it was up to him to prove that his non-violence strategy will work. They claimed that a "million patriots have already been enrolled in the army of independence and have taken the oath to strike when the hour arrives." Gandhi was given a year to demonstrate that freedom could be attained through *Satyagraha*; if he failed, the clarion call would be issued for the multitudes of freedom fighters to rise up and drive the British out of India by force. Taraknath delivered this pledge at Fanuel Hall in Boston as the principal speaker at an Irish-Indian rally on November 2, 1921. In a sense, this quixotic declaration was the last hurrah of FFI. Most of the organization's moderate American supporters had been turned off by this kind of unrealistic ideological intractability. Mukherjee sums up the situation very poignantly:

> The loss of FFI's American supporters, the feud with Gadar revolutionaries, his own financial difficulties, failure of the Moscow mission to obtain Russian support, and the report of Smedley's miserable married life with Chatto, all contributed to Taraknath's search for a new direction in life (Mukherjee 1997: 182).

Taraknath, Ghose and the others seem largely to have retreated into their own personal bailiwicks. Taraknath continued to publish articles and pursue contacts which could provide opportunities for political expression. The time which he and Ghose spent in Washington in connection with the American Commission to Promote Self-Government (Swaraj) in India seems to have had the effect of sensitizing them both to the art of lobbying. In February 1923, Taraknath testified before the House Committee on Foreign Relations on the narcotics trade. At the same time, Taraknath had enrolled in the Georgetown University Foreign Service School and was awarded its first Ph.D. in 1924. Senator Robert LaFollette provided him space in his office on the Hill where he could study. In 1925, he and Mary Keatinge Morse fled the United States for Germany when Mary was denied a passport and Taraknath was avoiding being served a notification that his citizenship was to be revoked under the terms of the *Thind* decision of February 19, 1923.

A good indication that a mellowing process was underway is that he and Mary got married. "On May 5, 1924, Taraknath and Mary Keatinge Morse quietly registered their marriage in the New York City Court clerk's office" (ibid.: 186). She was a

Quaker, 20 years older than Das, a fact which would inevitably arouse all sorts of psychoanalytic speculations. Mary had two previous marriages, one to a noted inventor who "was known as the father of electric traction" and who had "electrified New York City's elevated train system" (Mukherjee 1997: 186). This marriage lasted 15 years and was followed by a brief one to a New York stockbroker. She herself had been a founder of the NAACP. As for her reasons for marrying "a penniless, dark Hindu man with a jail record whom the government was so desperate to throw out of the country," the explanation she gave to Ruth Cranston of the *Christian Science Monitor* was: "My father was Irish, my mother was a Quaker, and I was always a champion of lost causes" (ibid.).

Once Taraknath and Mary reached Europe, they nearly got marooned there when the government used the *Thind* ruling to void their American passports. They were able to return to the United States in 1926, probably as a result of intervention by one of Mary's high-level connections in Washington. While in Europe, Taraknath had a difficult time dealing with the post-war Berlin *baradari*. Mukherjee presents a long excerpt from an account given of this period for the Oral History Project at Nehru University by Ms Prabhabati Mirza. She says the American wing of FFI "was practically confined to Bengalis only." She came to New York from the University of Michigan to study at Columbia after she lost her scholarship at the former. After she finished at Columbia, she went to Germany and earned a doctorate at Frankfurt. She continues:

> I met Viren Chatto. M.N. Roy and his wife Evelyn wanted to convert me. Taraknath was President of the India Association in Berlin. When Sompath Nath Pillai died there was a huge funeral meeting at which Taraknath and Chatto presided. Viren Chatto and Roy used to fight. Roy called Chatto a British spy, and Chatto called Roy a Russian agent. Agnes Smedley and Evelyn used to intervene .... They were both communists. Bupendranath Datta used to say they both wanted to be Emperors ... (ibid.: 189).

All this turned out to be prelude for the next great battles which South Asians in the United States were compelled to wage now that World War I and the Peace Conference were history. For the next two decades, the focus would be on Indian civil rights and rallying support for the freedom struggle in India as it was unfolding under the leadership of Gandhi, Nehru, and the Indian National Congress. Lajpat Rai's four-year sojourn in the United States as a consensus builder can be said to have prepared the way for this political transition. Ghadr and FFI radicalism were gradually running out of gas and being superceded as the dominant theme in the expression of South Asian political interests in the United States by a new, more pragmatic political style.

As this was taking place, the center of gravity of overseas Indian radical revolutionism was shifting its venue to Europe and Asia. This change of focus was accelerating as the 1920s dawned. The triumph of Bolshevism in Russia and the rise of the Comintern had much to do with this, of course, as did the poisoning of the American political environment by the "Red Scare." With the FFI losing steam, Smedley and many of the Indian activists began turning elsewhere for a base of operations from whence their version of the nationalist movement could be sustained and revitalized. Along with the stresses in her personal life, Smedley received the news that her friend Emma Goldman (1869–1940) had been imprisoned in America for her political beliefs and then deported to Russia.[5] This seems to have been a prime motivation behind Smedley's impulse to pursue new horizons. But there were also substantive reasons which pertained to differences between M.N. Roy and Virendranath Chattopadhyaya over the role that Indian nationalists should play in the Communist strategy for achieving world revolution. While in Mexico, under the tutelege of Michael Borodin, Roy had converted to Communism and actually founded the Communist Party of Mexico. With these credentials in hand, he rapidly rose to a position of importance in the Communist movement.

Roy had become an orthodox Communist ideologue who advocated a policy of creating "Communist parties, revolution and the establishment of new soviet republics" in what would later be called Third World countries. Lenin, on the other hand, wisely saw that in countries like India where no Communist Party, or anything approaching it, existed, it would be best to support what he called "bourgeois nationalist movements" which fought for independence from their imperialist masters. By supporting such movements which attacked and weakened the imperialist infrastructure, Lenin believed, ground would be laid for the subsequent creation of communist parties in the colonial countries. This was the position held by Chattopadhyaya's and his Berlin circle, on the one hand, and by Taraknath Das and the FFI in the United States on the other. The two positions would have to be thrashed out at the next meeting of the Comintern. Taraknath asked Smedley to represent the FFI in the Moscow delegation that would be led by Chatto for this purpose. After much agonizing, since "she would have to do so in a clandestine manner, without a passport, forcing her into an underground existence and making it impossible for her to reenter the United States legally," Agnes agreed to go (Price 2005: 86).

Her trip was arranged through "correspondence with Maxsim Litvinoff," a Soviet diplomat who was one of Chatto's strongest allies. Thus the fateful relationship with Chattopadhyaya commenced! Her transit to Europe was facilitated by getting her a position as a stewardess on a Polish-American freighter. She was seen off on December 17, 1920, by her friend Thorberg Brundin and Taraknath Das. "Das asked her to deliver a briefcase filled with documents to Chatto in Berlin, and he carried the precious cargo himself until the last moment. Agnes did not know it at the time, but it would be thirteen years before she saw the United States again" (ibid.: 87).

After her freighter arrived in Danzig harbor, "Smedley received a telegram from Berlin welcoming her to the country." Agnes jumped ship and made her way to Berlin. This was accomplished by wiring one of Chattopadhyaya's colleagues, "as she had been instructed, requesting that the German Foreign Office have her stewardess papers visaed and authorize her to proceed to Berlin." Once in Berlin, she joined forces with Chatto and the Berlin Committee. As Price (ibid.) declares, "American authorities were only a few steps behind." She continues:

On January 10, 1921, a young J. Edgar Hoover ordered the post office to forward copies of all Agnes's mail to his Bureau of Investigation. The State Department also opened a file on her, and a military intelligence agent disguised as a reporter stopped by the FFI office in the hope of learning Agnes's whereabouts (he was told she was out). By the time the Justice Department confirmed that Agnes had indeed violated U.S. passport regulations in her flight, she had established herself in Berlin illegally.

It seems to have been love at first sight between Agnes and Chatto. She was "irresistibly" drawn to him; "love and mutual admiration developed between the two almost spontaneously" (Barooah 2004: 230). It was not long before they were living together. They did so for eight years in a common-law "husband and wife" relationship. Together they set up Berlin's first birth-control clinic. However, Smedley's life with Chatto was tempestuous. It can only be characterized as utterly neurotic and doomed to eventual failure. Barooah (ibid.: 229) calls it, "Love and innate incompatibility."

It all started on an idealistic note, however. There was a kind of "honeymoon" period when in early 1921 they went off to Russia together to attend the fateful Comintern gathering. They did a lot of sightseeing and commiserated with people like Emma Goldman, who had been exiled to Russia, and her close companion, Alexander Berkman (1870–1936).[6] When the Comintern decided to support M.N. Roy, Chatto and his supporters returned to Germany, tails between their legs.

There are some ambiguities concerning both the details of the couple's sojourn in the Soviet Union and the manner of their departure. Barooah's account states that the couple returned to Germany in September and encountered difficulties with German officials concerning Chatto's residency status in the country. He states that "under pressure from the British government, Chatto was refused a stay permit .... Consequently after the expiry of his temporary permit, the couple had to live under false names for many months, frequently changing their lodgings" (ibid.: 231).

Dennis Casey authored an article which paints a somewhat different, although not necessarily completely disparate, picture. He declares:

Agnes soon tired from lack of freedom in the Soviet Union and returned in October to Geneva ... with 5,000 marks from the Soviet legation in hand for travel expenses. Speculation has it that at this time she was probably a member of the Comintern .... She traveled under the alias of Mrs Petroikas, and occasionally used the name of Alice Bird (Casey 2004).

Casey's account obviously makes it appear that Smedley left Russia without Chatto, with a not inconsiderable amount of money in her pocket, and as a Comintern agent. Whether true or not, the fact is that in the end the couple did resume a life together in Berlin, amongst their Indian cohorts, but under more or less hand-to-mouth economic circumstances. The assumed names that Smedley allegedly used, however, may reflect nothing more than the fact that she and Chatto were for a while compelled to avoid apprehension by the German authorities in connection with their residence problems.

Whatever the precise details of their immediate post-Moscow activities, the wheels began to come off their relationship following their return to Germany. Smedley and Chatto were clearly in a psychopathological interlock that nearly destroyed them both. Much of the problem lay with Chatto who, despite his *avant-garde* social outlook, was never able to overcome in practice his middle-class Hindu sexism and paternalism. Despite having had numerous sexual affairs and at least one marriage prior to Smedley, he was bitterly condemnatory of her previous affairs and insanely jealous of every man whom she encountered in the ordinary course of their work: "Suspicious as hell of every man near me, and all men or women from America" (Barooah 2004: 233). He was equally jealous and denigrative of her intellectual capabilities and systematically attempted to reduce her to servile status. To use a Hindusthani word, Chatto wanted her to be his *gharwali*, his chattel wife. She resisted this, of course, while out of guilt and other self-deprecatory motivations still trying to cling on to the relationship. She finally began to suffer emotional breakdowns and sought help through psychoanalysis. As self-insight dawned, Agnes wrote to her friend, Frances Lennon: "... finding a man who will continue to use his intellect after marriage—that I doubt! Intellect and sex aren't on speaking terms in a man." Finally, she concluded, "I prefer death to returning to my husband." After she left him for good, she declared: "And now I am very, very calm, and we look at each other across an impassable gulf ... he knows at last that he has lost the power to hurt me" (ibid.: 239).

Her disillusionment with the India crowd was not total but it was sufficient to be instrumental in her life taking another dramatic turn, this time toward East Asia and an identification with the Communist movement in China and with leftist radicalism in

Japan. This came about through complex processes which are not germane to our narrative but which Ruth Price elaborates in great detail. Agnes's commitment to the Chinese people and the Chinese revolution became all-consuming, both because of the depth of her involvement and because along with it she found a new comrade and lover, who far transcended what she had known with Chatto. His name was Richard Sorge, a fellow Comintern agent, of mixed German and Russian parentage, whom she had met in Shanghai.[7] Sorge was an intelligence agent in the service of the Russian Communist Party and the Soviet state, who along with Agnes traveled the length and breadth of China during its interwar years' ordeal. Eventually, Sorge was executed as a spy in Japan, but he acknowledged in his memoirs (which he wrote while awaiting execution) that he could never have been as successful in his espionage operations without the help from Smedley (Casey 2004). Her China phase was also facilitated because through her German communist connections she was able to enjoy the cover of being a foreign correspondent for the prestigious *Frankfurter Zeitung* newspaper. What this says is that Smedley remained a dedicated anti-imperialist revolutionary while drifting in new directions, and not entirely severing her relationship with the Indian nationalists. Despite the failure of her "marriage" with Chatto, for example, she continued to be in touch with him on political matters. Her most dramatic turn was toward the Maoist revolution that was gathering momentum deep inside north central China. She made her way to Yenan and traveled as a journalist with the Eighth Route Army in the years leading up to the Sino-Japanese War. She wrote extensively and brilliantly on the subject for the *Frankfurter Zeitung* and many other publications. Along with Edgar Snow, Smedley was one of the earliest writers to realize that the Maoists, by concentrating on mobilizing the peasantry, were challenging the orthodox Communist thesis that the Chinese Revolution would have to begin among the urban proletariat (Price 2005: Chapter 8, esp. 184–93).[8]

By now, Smedley had become deeply enmeshed in the Comintern nexus as an undercover agent. Clearly her antipathy toward the Bolsheviks over their Russification of socialism and their treatment of Emma Goldman and other non-conforming radicals had waned enough for her to make peace with the Soviets. In part this was because she seems to have concluded that the Soviets and the

Comintern was the most formidable anti-imperialist, anti-capitalist game in town. In part, however, it was also because that was where the money was; that could keep food on the table of a talented, intensely ambitious writer and activist whose feminism and radicalism had little chance of finding any other outlet or rewards.

In her new incarnation, Agnes Smedley ceased being a significant player in the American context of South Asian political activity. As Smedley was settling into the East Asian political morass, and as the FFI and Ghadr were running their course, Lala Lajpat Rai had been consolidating his own political base among moderates and liberals in New York and around the country. Rai, as we saw, had started slow after his arrival in New York. It took him some time to get his bearings and acquire resources. He accepted help from Indians who were already on the scene, including many of the radicals with whom he would later part company. We saw earlier that he reached out to N.S. Hardikar to join him in New York and help him with his organizational and propaganda undertakings. Raising money was a particularly daunting task. The Indian community had limited means upon which he could draw. He knew he had to widen his net. This meant getting the attention of potentially sympathetic Americans, which, in turn, meant crafting his ideology to accommodate the more moderate political predilections which characterized even the mainstream American Left. Lajpat Rai, the mature professional political operative, was willing and able to make the necessary adjustments. While this alienated extremist elements in the Indian community, it opened the way for the pursuit of less strident means of fighting for South Asian rights which had a better chance of resonating with the American public at large.

The key to Lajpat Rai's rise as a credible spokesman for Indian freedom and South Asian human rights had been his ability to acquire a voice in the New York media and academia. At first, says Hardikar, local newspapers were reluctant to publish his articles and statements. It was also difficult to find hosts for his public talks. Lala's first breakthrough was the publication of his book *Young India*, which came out in 1916; it "relieved him of [his] difficult situation to some extent ... Lalaji's name slowly captured the minds of Americans through this book and its reviews published in the American press." The first edition ran out of stock in only eight months and a second edition came out in 1918. "Lalaji got slowly acquainted with Americans, and the local newspapers started giving good publicity to his articles." He began to get speaking engagements and "they were followed by educational institutions, Chancellors of Universities and students" (Hardikar 1966: 11). Despite British censorship, the Home Rule League of England managed to get his book into print in that country, thanks largely to the efforts of Col. Josiah Wedgewood (1872–1943), a Labor MP and strong critic of Ramsay Macdonald's introduction of separate electorates in India. He had written to Lajpat Rai describing the official policy as "deadly and stupid."

Lajpat's financial circumstances improved with time. Money became available from his publications and speaking engagements; his friendship with Lokamanya Tilak (1856–1920) paid dividends when the founder of the Home Rule League of India sent him $5,000 via Annie Besant.[9]

The book he published in 1916, titled *Young India: An Interpretation and a History of the Nationalist Movement from Within*, got the ball rolling for him. The publisher Huebsch had become his friend. It was widely praised among journalists, scholars and educated laymen. The Home Rule League of America, *Young India* (the monthly magazine), and the *Indian Information Service* soon followed. These afforded entrée into liberal and mainstream circles. Also helpful was the fact that by this time he had fully cast his lot with the more moderate politics of the Indian National Congress, and Gandhi's non-violent credo. While, as we saw, it put him at odds with the radicals, this enabled him to come across as politically safe to middle-class Americans whose support was essential to the success of Indian nationalism in the US. From his New York base at the Home Rule League, Lajpat Rai, with the help of his numerous American allies in the liberal establishment, was able to establish a lecture-circuit which spanned the United States. This would become an increasingly crucial resource as time passed, because it would afford opportunities for a host of Indian freedom fighters ranging from Rabindranath Tagore to Sarojini Naidu and Vijayalakshmi Pandit to impact on American audiences. In some ways, it was a further stage in opening up American society to Indian ideals which the old Yankee traders, the Transcendalists and the Unitarians had originally pioneered.

When Lala Lajpat Rai left America on December 24, 1919 for London, Oswald Garrison Villard, the editor of the *Nation*, bid him farewell: "He is a wise, brave, sound ambassador, a generous and moderate interpreter of great races to our American Democracies" (Dhanki 1978: 10). He left behind him an infrastructure through which the next generation of South Asian activists could move to the next level.

## Notes

1. Her full name was Evelyn Trent. She was a Stanford University student, whom he met while on the West Coast in 1916, and subsequently married in New York the following year, despite bitter opposition from her family. Roy's birth name was Narendranath Bhattacharya. He changed it to Manavendra Nath Roy at the suggestion of Dhan Gopal Mukerji (1890–1936), then a student at Stanford, who became the first successful Indian novelist and essayist writing in English in the United States. The alleged purpose of the name change was to disguise his identity from British agents who were stalking him because of his revolutionary activities in India.

2. "In the years to come," declares Price (2005: 65), "Agnes would exploit her brief attachment to the esteemed Indian moderate to disguise her more radical associations and activities, but her insistence on maintaining these connections at this time essentially killed her friendship with Rai."

3. Surendranath Kar (1892–1970) was a stormy petrel who caused much disruption in the ranks. He eventually achieved considerable fame as an artist in Bengal.

4. The events described by Frumkin in his classic work were, of course, among the outgrowths of the post-war power juxtapositions that emerged from the deliberations and political maneuvering which characterized the Paris Peace Conference.

5. Emma Goldman was perhaps America's most noted female anarchist and revolutionary (see Chapter 6). An article by Lance Selfa (2004) says of her:

   > Emma Goldman's life as an anarchist can be divided into three parts: Her earliest incarnation as "Red Emma," the firebrand whom the press labeled as a crazed bomb thrower, which lasts until about 1906; Emma the Bohemian anarchist in progressive America which roughly coincided with her editing of the magazine *Mother Earth* and lasted until the U.S. government deported her in the Palmer Raids in 1919; and finally, Emma in exile, whose main highlights are her experiences in revolutionary Russia in 1920 and 1921, and her role as English-Language spokeswoman for the Spanish anarchists in the Spanish Revolution of 1936–39.

6. Alexander Berkman, known as "Sasha," came to America from Russia when he was 15 years of age. "He modeled himself after his uncle, the Russian revolutionary, Mark Andreyevich Nateson." In 1889, he was running a café ("Sasha's Café")

on Suffolk Street in New York City, "the unofficial headquarters of young Yiddish-speaking anarchists in New York City's Lower East Side." It was there that he met Emma Goldman. "Their love and attraction would become the emotional center of both their lives," wrote historian Candace Falk. "Though their romantic episodes were fleeting, they would remain lifelong comrades." Berkman spent 14 years in prison for his involvement in the Homestead Steel Strike in Pittsburgh. He returned to Russia in 1920 along with Goldman after being expelled from the US along with Goldman during the "Red Scare." He lived the life of a revolutionary. In 1929, he published *Now and After: The ABC of Communist Anarchism.* "Written in a conversational style, the book became a classic of anarchist thought." He shot himself on June 28, 1929, "a result of the pain he could no longer endure" following two operations, "and because he was unable to support himself financially and refused to live off the support of others" (*People and Events, PBS*: American Experience, "Alexander Berkman," March 11, 2004).

7. Agnes Smedley met Richard Sorge in China in 1930. She wrote about their relationship in a letter to Florence Lennon in May 1930:

> I'm married, child, so to speak—just sort of married, you know; but he's a he man also, and it's 50–50 all along the line, with he helping me and I him and we working together or bust, and so on; it's a big, broad, all sided friendship and comradeship. I do not know how long it will last; that does not depend on us. I fear not long. But these days will be the best in my life. Never have I known such good days, never have I known such a healthy life, mentally, physically, psychically.

8. Smedley continued to publish pieces on India as well, including contributions to the *Voice of India* and *Modern Review*. In her *Voice of India* piece (November 1944), titled "Nehru and Jefferson," she declared, "It may sound sissified in this corrupt and cruel era to state, as I do, that wherever Nehru has appeared in any part of the world in the past quarter century, something new and pure has entered." In her *Modern Review* piece (Vol. 42, 1927, pp. 296–97), titled "Mother India," she took on Katherine Mayo, with Smedley accusing her of producing "a propaganda piece on behalf of British rule in India." "She quotes Gandhi, Tagore, Lajpat Rai, or other Indians, only when she can find something in their speeches to justify her thesis and to help her paint a picture against India. Then she stops." Her books *China Fights Back: An American Woman with the Eighth Route Army, China's Red Army Marches, China Correspondent,* and *Daughter of Earth: A Novel* grew primarily out of her China experience.

9. Annie Besant was a legendary figure in the Indian freedom movement. Born in 1847, the daughter of William Wood and Emily Morris, her father, a doctor, died when she was only five. When her mother found work looking after boarders at Harrow School, and Annie came under the care of a friend, Ellen Marryat. She married Rev. Frank Besant in 1866, a young clergyman with whom she had two children. However, they didn't get along. She was averse to traditionalism and refused to attend communion. As a result, her husband compelled her to leave the house. There was a legal separation. Her son Digby remained with his father, but the daughter Mabel went to London with her

mother. After leaving her husband, Annie Besant completely rejected Christianity and in 1874 joined the Secular Society. She fell in with Charles Bradlaugh, editor of the *National Reformer* and the leader of the secular movement in England. They fought for birth control and other liberal causes over the ensuing years. She published books and pamphlets on many subjects. In 1889, she was elected to the London School Board and spearheaded a host of reforms, including free lunches for school children. In the 1890s, Besant joined the Theosophy movement founded by Madam Blavatsky. Theosophy being based upon the Hindu doctrines of *karma* and reincarnation (*samsara*), Mrs Besant went to live in India. There she joined the Home Rule League and became an avid supporter of the Indian freedom movement. She was then interned.

# 8 Let the Lobbying Begin!

It must be conceded that in one respect both the Home Rule League and the FFI had got onto the right track: each had in its own way come to recognize the importance of lobbying the political establishment. We noted that Taraknath Das testified before a congressional committee in 1923 on the narcotics trade. Probably "the first student to testify before a Congressional Committee," Senator Cooper of Wisconsin said that Taraknath "gave the most illuminating statement they had yet heard" (Mukherjee 1997: 184).

But even here, Taraknath was probably benefiting from the ground which had already been prepared for congressional liaison years earlier by Lajpat Rai and his cohorts. Their first opportunity for legislative input came in the summer and fall of 1919, shortly before Lajpat returned to India. His supporters arranged for him to provide documentation to be used in hearings conducted by the Senate Foreign Relations Committee (66th Congress) on the state of the world with specific reference to poverty and human rights in the aftermath of the World War, and on the repercussions of the Paris Peace Conference. Robert LaFollette, the Progressive Party senator from Wisconsin, was a major force in convening these deliberations. Hardikar, who had already built up a modest network of congressional contacts, pushed hard to get his mentor on the witness list. He succeeded to the extent that at the last minute the Committee Secretary gave Lajpat 24 hours to prepare a statement. "In haste, Lalaji collected all facts and prepared the case and after sending it for printing, he met our lawyer in America, Mr. Dudley Field Malone, to whom he explained the case and requested him to accompany him to the Committee" (Hardikar 1966: 20).

LaFollette's long speech before the Committee was permeated with classic anti-imperialist rhetoric. Condemning the establishment of Mandates by the Paris Treaty, LaFollette declared, "Great Britain, France, and now Japan, under the leadership of their present reactionary rulers, desire this imperialistic peace and this coalition, which they will dominate, for the protection of their vast dominions." Speaking of the British Empire writ large, he said:

> I have heard it stated in this Chamber that Great Britain is the one great colonizing nation in the world. In justification of her wide dominion, it has been argued that she is peculiarly fitted to administer the government of distant territories. Senators who advance that doctrine ignore the fact that the day of colonization is past .... Britain holds these immense territories and administers the affairs of the native populations, not for purposes of colonization, but for the sole object of exploitation. Under the pretense of altruism, with much talk of bestowing the blessings of Christianity and civilization upon the "backward peoples," the imperial nations of Europe have ruthlessly exploited the rich resources and vast populations of Africa and Asia (Congressional Record, Senate Foreign Relations Committee, 66th Congress, 1919, p. 8727).

When he turned to India, the effects of the 12-page memorandum which Lajpat Rai prepared permeated the Senator's rhetoric. Obviously having been made aware of Gandhi, LaFollette stated: "Asia has produced the great moral teachers of history: Confucius, Buddha, Mohammed, Christ. To these great teachers may be traced the *nonresistance and pacifism* of the Asiatic peoples" (ibid., emphasis added).

LaFollette incorporated extensive passages, which address the economic consequences of British rule in India, verbatim from Rai's memorandum into the record.

> A Native Hindu [i.e., Lajpat Rai] ... has aptly described the conditions the treaty of peace will perpetuate:

> There are four main incentives for the subjection of Asia: (1) Rich material resources; (2) unlimited amounts of human material; (3) raw material for feeding the looms and factories

of Manchester and Lancashire; (4) markets—a place on which to dump the cheap manufactured trash of Europe.

And finally:

> In return for the possession and exploitation of natural resources and human beings, the exploiting nation establishes and forces on their unwilling, unarmed, and defenseless people, a political despotism the chief aim of which is to render economic exploitation more efficient .... Their industries have been destroyed that they might not compete with Manchester and Lancashire, and that they might remain producers of raw materials.

The Senator concluded: "Wherever the British flag flies over a subject people today, revolution is brewing." The "ugly truth" is that wherever British rule has been imposed, "it has brought famine, misery and rebellion." Prophetic words indeed, courtesy of Lala Lajpat Rai!

"After all this experience," Hardikar says, "Lalaji felt that we should have one of our workers in Washington during Congress Session who could carry on 'lobbying work'. *He repeatedly instructed me to go there and I started going there*" (Hardikar 1966: 20, emphasis added).

By the mid-1920s there was much for South Asians to do. On February 19, 1923, the US Supreme Court rendered the unanimous decision which struck at the heart of Indian efforts to become American citizens.

This, of course was the *Thind* decision which ruled that Indians are not "White" and therefore, like all other Asians (i.e., Japanese and Chinese) not entitled to American citizenship. We will address the details of this case presently. This had far-reaching implications because in essence it countermanded all of the prior rulings which ordained that Indians are "White," in the sense of being of the Caucasian race, and therefore eligible on racial grounds to become citizens. Under this prior interpretation, a number of Indians had obtained US citizenship. Now, that status and its attendant rights and privileges had been nullified. We noted that this decision affected the ability of Taraknath Das and his wife to be allowed back into the country, compelling them to sneak back in through the back door.

In the early phases of immigration, when there was some receptivity toward the import of Indian labor: a considerable number were able to acquire permanent residency rights, even citizenship, in the United States. Although there are no definitive statistics to bulwark this conclusion, it is not unreasonable to believe that a strong relationship existed between the acquisition of agricultural land or the equivalent in tangible assets (like shop-ownership, or a profession, etc.) and how successfully individuals could pursue citizenship. Even then, by no means all who acquired material substance could parlay it into citizenship status, but it is reasonable to conclude that almost no one who was not in this category succeeded in doing so. Within these parameters, however, as noted, one of the main devices employed was marrying an American. Even here, the racial factor was frequently in play since, as already noted, most of the spouses were Americans of *Mexican* descent. There were anti-miscegenation statutes on the books in California, but it seems that these could be easily circumvented by couples traveling to Arizona and New Mexico where there appeared to be a kind of "don't-ask-don't-tell" attitude about mixed marriages, even at times between Indian men and White women.

The limited number who by whatever means managed to achieve unfettered citizenship did so under the provisions of the Immigration Act of 1917. Together, these laws established a "minimum quota for any nationality" of 100 per year. There was, however, an intriguing qualification which led to great confusion and controversy down the road. Originally these laws benefited South Asian Indians because, surprisingly, natives of India were deemed to be racially "correct." This came about when the Supreme Court in the *Ozawa* case on November 3, 1922, ruled that the 1917 Act applied to members of the "Caucasian" and "Negroid" races but not to the "Mongoloid" race.

Takeo Ozawa had commenced his American life as a Japanese-born resident of Hawaii. Quoting from the Prior History section of the statement of the Supreme Court by the Ninth Circuit Court of Appeals: "He was a graduate of the Berkeley, California, High School, had been nearly a three year student of the University of California, had educated his children in American schools, his family had attended American churches and he had maintained the use of the English language in his home." Furthermore, that "he was well qualified by character and education for citizenship is conceded." However, "The District Court of Hawaii ... held that, having been born in Japan and being of the Japanese race, he was not eligible to naturalization under 2169 of the Revised Statutes, and denied the petition." He appealed their decision to the Court of Appeals for the Ninth Circuit, and the case finally reached the Supreme Court on October 3, 1922. His appeal failed on the ground that Section 2169 of the Naturalization Act of 1906 ordained that the granting of American citizenship is limited to "free white persons." This qualification reflected the strong prejudices against Chinese and Japanese immigration to the West Coast that had risen to hysterical proportions around the turn of the century. But ironically, for the time being, it benefited Indians who, even though "Asiatics," were adjudged to be "Caucasian" and not "Mongoloid" under the terms of this act. Anthropological testimony at the time asserted that South Asians were members of the "Aryan" race, and, therefore, unlike "Mongoloids," legitimate claimants to American citizenship. Scores of Indians were able to qualify under this categorical technicality, including a number of students, professors, traders, and clergymen who had trickled into the US over the years on temporary visas. This latter is an important datum in terms of securing the existence of a category of South Asians who were able to consolidate their presence in the United States and absorb the culture in a detailed manner. Some of these "veteran Indo-Americans" would prove to be assets later on in the battles for equal rights and Indian freedom waged by the India Lobby.

An example of this is Professor Sudhindra Bose. He came to America in 1904 at age 20, and in 1914 he was testifying before the House Committee on Immigration which was considering the "Restriction of Immigration of Hindu Laborers." His statement is revealing. Asked if he came as an "unskilled laborer," Bose replied, "I knew no trade, if that is what you mean by unskilled laborer ... I worked in a store ... and then I worked on a farm as common farm hand, [then] in an orchard, and gradually I worked [my way] into college." He said he first entered a college in Parksville, Missouri, and then attended the University of Illinois. He next attended the University of Chicago and afterwards returned to Illinois "where I took my masters degree and my bachelor's degree." Now, "at the present time I am lecturer on oriental politics and civilization in the State University of Iowa." He stated that he was born "near Calcutta" and that he attended the University of

Calcutta "for a short time." Pointedly asked about his class background, he said his family "came from the middle-class." Anticipating their prejudices, he added, "I did not come here as a pauper ... I had some money and I could pass the usual [literacy] test they applied."

The questions concerning Bose's class and literacy were, of course, not innocent or incidental. This, in fact, was what the hearings were all about. The leading figures on the Committee were racists whose purpose was to try and establish that "Hindus" seeking to gain entry to the United States were an ignorant rabble who should, in fact, be excluded, even deported. Goading them on the illiteracy issue, Professor Bose fought fire with fire. He cited a speech given on the floor by Representative Kemp on January 13 of that year (1914): "[Kemp] pointed out that, taking the number of migrants in the fiscal year 1899 and 1900 as a basis, we find that the percentage of illiteracy among Lithuanians is 48.9; among Syrians, 53.3; South Italians, 53.9; Mexicans, 57.2; Turks, 59.5, while percentage of illiteracy among the Hindus is only 47.2." His interrogator (Representative Moore) felt compelled to ask, "Then they stand fairly well with all other nationalities?"

"I am quoting from the Congressional Record," Bose replied.

The point is that here was this highly educated and intellectually sophisticated Indian who, like many others in his situation, would see his citizenship placed in jeopardy by soon-to-be-unfolding litigation. For "within three years, 1922–25, a series of test cases were taken before the Supreme Court challenging the eligibility of Indians, Japanese, and even Filipinos, for American citizenship. The result was for a time to render their citizenship invalid on the ground that they were not 'free white persons'" (Chandrasekhar 1944: 142).

The focal case for Indians turned out to be that of *US v. Bhagat Singh Thind* (261 US 204). Bhagat Singh Thind was a Sikh, of course, who had migrated to the United States from the Punjab in 1913. By working in an Oregon lumber mill, he managed, not unlike Sudhindra Bose, to pay his way through the university: in this case, the University of California. He then enlisted in the US Army in 1917 when America entered World War I and was honorably discharged in 1918. The tragedy was that Bhagat Singh had served with honor in the American military in World War I and now faced such indignity. He had actually been drafted. "Some Indians volunteered, and one Indian died on active duty in Pearl Harbor." The trouble is that the "number of Indians in the United States Army was not large, and there are few traces of their experiences" (Singh n.d.). Thind, says Jensen (1988: 256), wore his turban during his six months of service and received an honorable discharge. The fact that he had served only six months in the American military rendered moot his service as a basis for being admitted to citizenship, since the statutes ordained that aliens must serve for at least three years before this factor could be taken into consideration. In those days service in the military obviously did not result in automatic entitlement to citizenship. Therefore, in 1920, Bhagat Singh was compelled to apply for citizenship to the US District Court.

Thind was allegedly a graduate of Punjab University. He was a card-carrying member of the Loyal Legion of Loggers and Lumbermen, which must be a reflection of his early occupational history, since he appears to have subsequently acquired a doctoral degree of some kind and published several books on moral and religious themes. One, published in 1929, was titled *Divine Wisdom*.[1] When he was a student at Berkeley, he was on friendly terms with Ram Chandra, at the time when he was the leader of Ghadr; but Thind denied any involvement with the organization or sympathy with its advocacy of violence. He did admit, however, that he supported the ideal of Indian freedom. Judge Wolverton was sympathetic to his case and ordered that his petition be granted.

Given the fact that in the *Ozawa* case, Indians had already been classified as Caucasians, his attorney, G.S. Pandit, persistently believed that his client's litigation would be successful, especially in the light of the fact that, apart from the *Ozawa* decision itself, several subsequent cases employing the White Caucasian thesis had been favorably adjudicated. Thind himself had applied for citizenship three times before 1923 (in 1917, 1918, and 1919) and had already twice "won" his citizenship on appeal in lower court, after having been turned down by Immigration and Naturalization. Pandit foresaw a "slam-dunk." However, it was not to be. The Supreme Court, as we shall see, reversed itself and ruled unanimously that being Caucasian did not automatically qualify South Asian Indians as "White."

In the interim, however, the naturalization of Indians continued, employing the White Caucasian thesis. On January 17, 1922, "the western division of Pennsylvania, ignoring the previous decision of the court of the eastern division of the court (i.e., Judge Dickinson), admitted an Indian to citizenship." Up to this point in time, in other words, the situation remained highly fluid (Jensen 1988: 257).

The upshot is that the federal authorities did not succeed overnight in uniformly depriving Indians of the "White" designation which had become their ticket to naturalization. "Between 1908 and 1922, at least sixty-nine Indians were admitted to citizenship, the peak coming in 1917–1918, when thirteen gained citizenship in California alone" (ibid.: 255). But at the national level, the judiciary and the federal government were slowly chipping away at the broader definitions of "White" which equated whiteness with anthropologically defined categorizations like "Caucasian" or "Aryan." It was this latter "scientific" formulation which had successfully gotten many Indian petitioners through the lower courts. But as racist pressures mounted, judges at all levels were increasingly wavering on the issue, undoubtedly paving the way for the Supreme Court's eventual denouement on the issue.

Jensen provides a comprehensive picture of one such case that came before a federal district court in South Carolina, presided over by judge Henry A. Smith, himself a Southerner and clearly racist in orientation. Ironically, it did not actually concern an Indian but a 59-year-old Syrian Christian named Faras Shahid. Shahid spoke broken English and could read only Arabic script, which made him "illiterate" by American cultural standards. It came down to the judge having to "decide whether this man, the color of walnut, was white." Through the prolonged legal process that ensued, Shahid was ultimately denied citizenship on the ground that "the term *white* could only be interpreted as applying to people of European habitancy or descent." Therefore, Judge Smith contended, "All the inhabitants of Asia, Australia, the South Seas, the Malaysian peninsula and archipelago, and African descent could not be admitted." Smith had shifted the definition of *white* from an anthropological to a geographical frame of reference (ibid.: 253–54).

Despite this narrowing margin for the definition of who is "White" in courts like Judge Smith's, the tendency by defense lawyers to employ the anthropological definition of race persisted. It happened in the case of Sardar Bhagwan Singh in 1917. When the naturalization service denied Singh's application on the now standard geographical grounds, Singh employed the anthropological argument. This occurred in the court of a federal judge in Pennsylvania named Oliver B. Dickinson. He rejected Sardar Singh's "ethnological" claim to be a member of the White (i.e., Caucasian) race and explicitly reverted to Judge Smith's rationale. He carried the argument even further, notes Jensen, and rejected the geographical argument as well. While Congress had indeed envisioned America as a "melting pot" and had indeed over the years expanded the scope of who was eligible to become part of the melting pot, he declared, the intent was nevertheless to limit "diversity" only to the Caucasian race. Caucasian did not automatically mean the same thing as White, according to Dickinson; it's up to Congress to decide who is "in" and who is "out." And, "since Indians had not yet been accepted by Congress [as white], the court could not extend the word white to him without usurping the lawmaking powers of Congress." Disingenuous reasoning of this kind came spontaneously in the type of racist atmosphere prevailing in early twentieth-century America, where the idea of racial inferiority based upon differences in color was autonomically embedded in the public psyche.

At times, however, the ethnological argument did nevertheless succeed. It happened where individual judges did not feel comfortable with the prevailing prejudices, as in the case of Mohan Singh. After the naturalization service in California had rejected his application for citizenship, his lawyer, Sakharam Ganesh Pandit, himself a naturalized Indian, filed an appeal with the Los Angeles District Court (257Fed.209) (1919). (This same lawyer would represent Bhagat Singh Thind when the appeal went up to the Supreme Court.) Pandit based his case on three arguments: "legal opinion, anthropological authority, and the fact that other Indians had become citizens" (Jensen 1988: 255). To Pandit, it came down to a matter of a "preponderance of legal opinion" that Hindus were includable in the Caucasian (i.e, "White") race.

Pandit presented himself to the judge as a type-case of the legal standing he sought for his client. S.G. Pandit had arrived in California in 1909, gained his citizenship in 1914 on the basis of being White, and was admitted to the bar on November 20, 1917 without any hassle. "Convinced by the force of these arguments, the federal judge decided on 24 March 1919 that Mohan Singh was entitled to citizenship. The naturalization examiners did not appeal the case" (Jensen 1988: 255).

Ironically, Justice George Sutherland (1862–1942) was the designated spokesman for the unanimous *Thind* decision that decisively changed everything. He was born of British parents in Buckinghamshire, England, on March 25, 1862. His parents migrated to Utah when he was a boy, although he was not raised as in Mormon faith. He attended the University of Michigan law school, entered politics, served in the US Congress for 12 years and after this was appointed a Justice to the Supreme Court. It was in this capacity that Sutherland established himself as the Supreme Court's racist poster boy when, on February 19, 1923, he delivered the unanimous Supreme Court decision that Bhagat Singh Thind's appeal was rejected. *United States v. Thind, 261 US 204 (1923)* addressed two issues:

A1. Is a high-caste Hindu (*sic*), of full Indian blood, born at Amritsar, Punjab, India, a white person within the meaning of section 2169, Revised Statutes?

A2. Does the Act of February 5, 1917 (39 Stat. OL. 875, section 3), disqualify from Naturalization as citizens those Hindus now barred by that act, who had lawfully Entered the United States prior to passage of said act?

The answer to Question One was "No" and to Question Two was "Yes." What this meant was not only that Bhagat Singh Thind could not be certified as a "White man," who on that account is eligible to become an American citizen; it meant further that all Indians who had already been granted American citizenship were now susceptible to having their citizenship revoked. Correcting the implication that Caucasian automatically means "White," Sutherland declared,

What we now hold is that the words "free white person" are words of common speech, to be interpreted in accordance with the understanding of the common man, synonymous with the word "Caucasian" only as that word is popularly understood.

As so understood and used, whatever may be the speculations of the ethnologist, it does not include the body of people to whom the appellee belongs.

As one lawyer, quoted by Jensen (1988: 20, emphasis added), declared, *"Now ignorance would be bliss* ... for the most ignorant man would believe that he could infallibly say who belonged to the white race."

Sutherland's formal statement is a monumental exemplification of how the prevailing racial ignorance and bigotry of the day was pandered to:

It is a matter of familiar observation and knowledge that the physical group characteristics of the Hindus render them readily distinguishable from the various groups of persons in this country commonly recognized as white. The children of English, French, German, Italian, Scandinavian, and other parentage, quickly merge into the mass of our population and lose the distinctive hallmarks of their European origin. On the other hand, it cannot be doubted that the children born in this country of Hindu parents would retain indefinitely the clear evidence of their ancestry. It is very far from our thought to suggest the slightest question of racial superiority or inferiority. What we suggest is merely racial difference, and it is of such character and extent that the great body of our people instinctively recognize it and reject the thought of assimilation (United States Supreme Court, *United States v. Thind*, 261 US 204 [1923]).

"He ruled," declares Chandrasekhar (1944: 138), "that Indians are not 'white' to the man in the street," and furthermore, "that Indians were not a free people." He rationalized this latter stricture by pointing out that Canada does not admit Indians on this ground despite the fact the both Canada and India are members of the British Commonwealth. What made this decision especially loathsome is that the US government then commenced applying it *retroactively* to *de-naturalize* all Indians who had already received their citizenship under the 1917 and 1924 Acts! This, of course, put men like Professor Sudhindra Bose in immediate peril.

Sutherland had justified the Court's decision by engaging in what political conservatives today call "strict constructionism," by claiming that the Court's only purpose is to ascertain and affirm the intent of the US Congress, not to render judgments about alleged moral and scientific truths such as racial characteristics. Judge Sutherland declared: "The language of the naturalization laws from 1790 to 1870 had been uniformly such as to deny the privilege of naturalization to an alien unless he came within the description of 'free white person'." He saw no fundamental change in this in subsequent legislation or judicial decisions. Consequently, he rejected latter-day anthropological, or "ethnological," racial theories on the ground that these had not been addressed by the US Congress. Whatever else various racial or ethnic groups were or were not, the only criterion that mattered to the Court was "the class of persons whom the [founding] fathers knew as white ...." Citizenship must be denied "to all who could not be so classified." Only Negroes and American Indians were excepted due to the special status accorded to them *by Congress*. But Sutherland himself introduced an unintended note of ambiguity into the Court's judgment when he declared that "the words 'white person' are synonymous with the words 'a person of the Caucasian race' ...." He was referring to the fact that Mr Ozawa "is clearly of a race which is not Caucasian." His use of the word "Caucasian" in this phraseology was the rub, of course, because it could be legally construed that anyone who is "Caucasian" is definable as "White." This continuing ambiguity would be a foot in the door for subsequent litigants.

For the present, however, this pernicious decision implicitly voided all of the grants of citizenship which had followed upon the *Ozawa* decision. It also implicitly voided all the property rights which Indians had acquired conterminously with their citizenship. Indians in this position were compelled to develop all sorts of subterfuges to hang on to land and other tangible properties which they had acquired. The most common ways this was done were to put their property in the name of lawyers, White friends, non-Indian spouses, etc., or others whom they believed could be trusted. This was obviously a tenuous way to live!

The pattern of racial discrimination driving the pursuit of Indian civil rights through litigation against immigration laws was understandably instrumental in generating broader processes of politicization and resistance in the South Asian community. This is the important point: the two went hand in hand. Harish Puri (1983: 38) accurately refers to this as a "political awakening among Indians in Canada and the United States." He attributes it to three main factors: "Hostility and resentment against the white community for its prejudice and oppression, development of an ethnic identity, and nationalism directed against British colonialism in India."

The history behind this racist mentality goes all the way back to the Dred Scott case of 1856, which addressed the issue of whether African Blacks were entitled to citizenship. Dred Scott was a black slave who had moved to St. Louis with his owners in 1830 and the following year was sold to Dr John Emerson, an Army doctor, who was compelled to move from one military post to another. During those travels, Scott resided with his owner for a total of seven years in areas that were closed to slavery. On this basis, he went to court and sued for his freedom and right to American citizenship. His case trickled all the way up to the Supreme Court where in March 1857, Chief Justice Roger B. Taney, not unlike Justice George Sutherland 65 years later, played the racial card. He was "intent on protecting Southerners from Northern aggression," and ruled that because Scott was black, "he was not a citizen and had no right to sue" (US Supreme Court, *Dred Scott v. Sanford*, March 1857).

This set the stage for a struggle between racists and enlightened progressives over the relevance of skin color as an entitlement to citizenship and full civil rights that would endure in various permutations for the next century. Congressional debate and rulings in the 1880s had led to the conclusion that the "tawny races of Asia" would not qualify for citizenship under the term "White."

"Such commentary was academic," declared Jensen (1988: 247–48), "until the Chinese began to arrive in California in large numbers in the 1860s." Once the Chinese influx began, however, Congress added a clause to the treaty signed with China in 1868 that the agreement was not to be construed as giving the Chinese the right of naturalization. This inspired Californians to push Congress in 1882 to vote explicitly to deprive the Chinese of the right to naturalization. Decisions were pretty much left to local initiatives, however. "In 1893, one court excluded a Japanese from citizenship on the theory that he was 'Mongolian', but the supreme court made no decision on non-Chinese aliens." Beyond this, however, the Supreme Court issued no other rulings. It made no decisions concerning "a whole range of people who did not neatly fit into the then commonly accepted racial categories of Caucasian, Mongolian, and Negroid. The result was that, "Courts in Florida, Indiana, New York and Washington continued to naturalize 'tawny races' from Asia."

A storm of litigation ensued that culminated in the case of the *US v. Pandit* which reversed the Sutherland decision. No less a figure than Chief Justice (and former President of the US) William Howard Taft applied the principle of *res adjudicata* which ordained that the United States government had no right to cancel the citizenship of Indians (or indeed anyone else) who had acquired this status by due process of law. However, since Justice Taft did not rule on the legality of Justice Sutherland's formulations regarding the racial issue per se raised in the *Thind* case, the future prospects for Indian naturalization remained up in the air, i.e., whether subsequent Indian migrants could be admitted to citizenship, given the contention that they were "not a free people." For the time being, racism as it pertained to the condition of South Asian Indians remained alive and well! On the naturalization question, nothing had really been resolved.

Jensen says that the executive branch eventually moved in to try and fill this policy vacuum as the political saliency of race increased. Essentially, this meant greater direct involvement by the Bureau of Naturalization. "During the first decade of the twentieth century, the bureau of naturalization began to warn clerks of the court that they should inform persons who appeared to be 'non-white' that their applications for naturalization might be turned down by the courts." In this manner, the Japanese became the next targets of discrimination. The qualification in their case, however, was that Japan was achieving recognition as an emerging world power following her victory in the Russo-Japanese War. President Theodore Roosevelt was endeavoring to curry the favor of Imperial Japan, and urged Congress to pass a law permitting Japanese naturalization. It was never passed and, "Generally ... the clerks did not allow Japanese to become citizens," particularly on the West Coast. But Roosevelt's attempt to influence immigration policy in relation to political clout showed the South Asians that power and prestige counts.

The result of all this was that the local-level judiciary continued treating Indians in a very erratic fashion. Ironically, another early test case turned out to be Taraknath Das himself. As a result of his employment as a translator for the Canadian immigration service at Vancouver, and then a similar position in San Francisco after he moved there, he had acquired a considerable amount of expertise in immigration matters. With this in his background, Das applied for American citizenship in 1907. He ran into the usual roadblocks because so many officials, in the bureaucracies and the judiciary, including Charles J. Bonaparte (1851–1921), who served as US Attorney General from 1906 to 1909, were tinged with racism. Appointed by Theodore Roosevelt, Bonaparte, himself the descendant of immigrants (he was the grand-nephew of Napoleon Bonaparte), had no sympathy for immigrants of "color." He believed that the federal courts alone should have the power to naturalize and that only persons who were adjudged to be "White" should be accorded this status. When the US attorney in San Francisco, Robert T. Devlin, wrote to Bonaparte in 1907 that, "There is considerable uncertainty as to what nationalities come within the term white person," Bonaparte replied, *"It seems to me clear that under no construction of the law can natives of British India be regarded as white persons"* (Jensen 1988: 248, emphasis added). Bonaparte's decision generated considerable publicity, first in an *American Press* dispatch from San Francisco, then by the Toronto *Globe*, and finally in an editorial in the *New York Outlook* (September 7, 1907) with the headline "British Indians and citizenship in white men's countries" (ibid.: 248–49).

However, Taraknath, as we saw, kept up the fight. He had an exchange of correspondence with Bonaparte which got nowhere in the immediate circumstances, but did amplify the debate on who is "White," which would have repercussions later. "May I ask you if the Hindus who belong to the Caucasian stock of the Human Race have no legal right to become citizens of the United States, under what special law the Japanese who belong to a different stock according to the statements of various scholars of all parts of the world, are allowed to declare their intention to become citizens of the United States." The Attorney General's reply was predictable: "It is contrary to the practice of the Department of Justice to give advice as to questions of law, except in cases prescribed by the statutes" (ibid.: 249).[2]

In February 1908, Taraknath was able to persuade a Seattle court to accept his application for citizenship. This date is interesting in the light of the fact that it was ostensibly toward the end of his

period at Norwich University and before he made a more permanent switch back to the West Coast in 1909. It indicates either
that he had found ways to travel back and forth between the coasts
or that some of the dates pertaining to this period are inaccurate.
The 1908 date is Jensen's. It is largely incidental to the central point
anyway, because it is known that through 1909 and 1910 his attempts to get naturalized while the Bandon, Oregon, project was
being undertaken failed, partly due to the maneuverings of British
intelligence. What is significant for our purposes is that in addition
to Taraknath's "near-miss" in Seattle, two Indians in New Orleans,
Abdullah Dolla in Savanna, Georgia, a Parsi named Balsara in New
York, and an Armenian named Halladjian in Massachusetts
actually succeeded by pursuing the "local option" route. It was
instances like these, of course, that spurred the Justice Department
and the Immigration Service to intensify their efforts to implement
a national standard on immigration applications. In all of them
it was being claimed that the petitioners, while being Indian, were
nevertheless "White." This ran against the grain of the prevailing
racial prejudice that permeated the halls of the US Congress, the
federal judiciary and government agencies. Given this stubborn
fact, the federal authorities redoubled their efforts to close the
grassroots loopholes that were enabling a few South Asians to
wriggle through the cracks.

Denaturalization proceedings followed apace after the *Thind*
ruling. Technically, this of course included Taraknath Das. It also
enmeshed Sakharam Ganesh Pandit, the Indian attorney whose
defense of Mohan Singh in 1919 and Bhagat Singh Thind had been
a milestone in the Caucasians-are-White argument.

In Das's case, the justice department filed a petition on May 1,
1923, to denaturalize him. In Pandit's case, he was faced with denaturalization when towards the end of November 1923 he represented Akhay Kumar Mozumdar, the first Indian to contest his
denaturalization following the *Thind* decision. When in the course
of defending Mozumdar, Pandit openly criticized the *Thind* decision, the judge rebuked him and stated that "an alien when he
lands on the shores of this country, comes with no right at all of
any natural kind to have extended to him the privilege of citizenship." He then upheld the cancellation, and soon after this the
Justice Department filed to have Pandit denaturalized as well
(Jensen 1988: 261). Pandit defended himself. He fought his case

for the next several years. "Pandit argued ... that he had conducted himself as a responsible member of society, had practiced law for over ten years in the courts of California, owned a fifteen thousand dollar home in Los Angeles, and that cancellation of his citizenship would deprive him of his livelihood and his property, call into question the legality of his marriage, and, under current laws, cause his wife to lose her citizenship" (Jensen 1988: 262). His case finally reached the Supreme Court in 1927 where on March 14 of that year, "the government finally lost its case when the court refused a writ of certiorari" (ibid.: 264).

By 1927, however, 65 Indians had already been denaturalized and 45 more cases were pending. Equally pernicious was the application of the Cable Act, which ordained that "any woman marrying an alien ineligible for citizenship shall cease to be an American citizen." This meant, of course, that American women, like Taraknath's wife, Mary, lost their citizenship. Finally, the California Alien Land Law of 1913, revised in 1920, which prevented immigrants from owning and leasing their own land, was mobilized against the Indians. By 1920, Indians in the Imperial and Sacramento Valleys owned about 123,000 acres of land. By various subterfuges they controlled much more than that, using American friends, attorneys, etc., as "fronts." This in itself is a measure of how far the Sikhs and other South Asians had economically progressed in the last decade-and-a-half. The *Thind* decision, as Justice Sutherland and his ilk devoutly wished, had opened a Pandora's Box of racist machinations against the Indian community in America. The Justice Department now pursued Indians with a vengeance, although they publicly denied doing so, attempting to enforce what it believed to be its mandate to drive as many of them as possible into legal limbo and, indeed, hopefully out of the country.

Taraknath was, of course, a prime target of the witch hunters. He and Mary found themselves dodging paper-servers. The chief of the Naturalization Division went so far, when they could not lay hands on Taraknath to serve him with citizenship cancellation papers, as to actually publish them in the newspapers! As Jensen says, "Das had somehow eluded the government long enough to receive his doctorate at Georgetown University in June 1924 and to marry an American woman" (ibid.: 262).

Taraknath, however, played an active role in his own defense as well on behalf of his fellow Indians. By this time, he had learned the ropes, so to speak, when it came to employing political networks and resources in pursuit of his ideological goals. In this respect he was emblematic of what was taking place generally within the South Asian community in the United States as the 1920s wore on. Although Indians were still a pitiably small segment of the US population, they were learning how to fight back with increased effectiveness. They were still too scattered, doctrinally diversified, and devoid of material resources to form anything that could be construed as a "movement" or "party"; but they had reached a point where some measure of coordinated mobilization and lobbying could be generated on specific issues.

## Transitions

The manner chosen to combat the consequences of the *Thind* decision was an important transition from the rather crude and somewhat quixotic revolutionism that characterized Ghadr and even the FFI. Taraknath Das, Mary, Sailendranath Ghose and their Indian and American cohorts sought allies in the US Congress, in the judiciary and in the government agencies. The strategies of old-fashioned intrigue, violence and bomb-throwing were being replaced by more subtle, less violent methods of persuasion.

The particular issue of persons being retroactively deprived of their citizenship did not sit well even in some quarters of a deeply racist America, because it pertained to a widely held public conviction that citizenship rights, once attained, are virtually sacrosanct. After Pandit succeeded in getting the Supreme Court to vacate the government's order denaturalizing him on March 14, 1927, no more than a month passed before all the remaining cases were grudgingly dropped by the government. In the process, Taraknath, focused as he now was on the Washington political scene, had successfully elicited support for the cause of the denaturalized Indians from Republican Senator David Reed of Pennsylvania. He convinced Reed that stripping 69 Indians of their citizenship was a wrong which must be rectified. Consequently, on December 9, 1926, the Senator was able to persuade the Senate Committee on Immigration to conduct hearings that were entitled "Ratification and Confirmation of Certain Persons of the Hindu Race." The Committee declared that inasmuch as great inconsistency has been evident pertaining to naturalization procedures, resulting in cancellations in some instances and not in others, that "there is need of a uniform rule relating to" such cases. The resolution which came out of these hearings read as follows:

> Resolved by the Senate and House of Representatives of the United States of America in Congress assembled, That the naturalizations aforesaid are declared to be citizens of the United States, and no woman citizen of the United States shall be deemed to have lost her citizenship by reason of her marriage to any of said persons.

The hearings featured an array of witnesses, both Indian and American, on both sides of the issue. The Committee chairman was Senator Hiram Johnson of California (1866–1945), a towering figure in the Senate of that day. He was a founder of the Progressive Party in 1912; nominee for vice-president of that party with Theodore Roosevelt in 1912 (in an election won by Democrat Woodrow Wilson); and governor of California from 1911–1917, until he resigned to take up a seat in the US Senate to which he had been elected as a Republican in 1916. He remained in the Senate until his death in 1945. Johnson was a dedicated isolationist, opposing US membership both in the League of Nations and the United Nations, and was determinedly opposed to Asian immigration. Yet, on the specific issue of the denaturalization of Hindus, Johnson parted company with the racists. His belief in constitutionally guaranteed citizenship rights took precedence over his anti-Asian phobias. Besides the chairman, the committee was composed of the following senators: Henry W. Keyes (New Hampshire), Frank B. Willis (Ohio), David A. Reed (Pennsylvania), Rice W. Means (Colorado), Gerald P. Nye (North Dakota), William H. King (Utah), William J. Harris (Georgia), Pat Harrison (Mississippi), Royal S. Copeland (New York), and Cole L. Blease (South Carolina).

The fate of 69 denaturalized Indians was to be decided by the Committee's deliberations. As we have already seen, the Committee did indeed decide to restore the constitutional rights of these 69 complainants. They were divided into three categories. The first category was a list of 45 persons who were "naturalized Hindus"; the second was a group of 13 whose "cancellations are pending"; the third consisted of eleven who were "Soldier cases in which cancellation proceedings have not been initiated."

The demographics of these 69 cases are revealing (Tables 8.1 and 8.2). They show a considerable range of ethno-religious differentiation and they also show how widely dispersed South Asians had become. While the largest concentration was along the Pacific coast, Indians possessing American citizenship were living in 18 different states by the 1920s. They were to be found in most major urban centers. And it is implicit in these cases that all had become well enough established in their communities to possess the means to fight for their civil rights. They had come far since the first impoverished, bewild-ered "rag heads" walked down the gangplanks at Vancouver, San Francisco, and Seattle. In this sense they were part of a subcultural infrastructure of continental dimensions that would pave the way for the many who would follow.

Most of the major cities in the country were represented: Chicago, Detroit, Galveston, Houston, Miami, Los Angeles, New Orleans, New York, Philadelphia, Pittsburgh, Portland, San Francisco, Savanna, Seattle, Tampa, etc., plus a few smaller cities and towns.

These hearings provided an important forum for the advocates of South Asian rights. Several Indians testified at greater or lesser length. They received sympathetic encouragement, especially from Senator Reed and Chairman Johnson. Taraknath Das was pretty much the star of the show, although he was not the first to testify. Instead, the Committee began with L.S. Gokhale of Schenectady, New York, a very "safe" natural scientist who characterized himself as a "Magnetic Engineer, in charge of magnetic research for The General Electric Company." The fact that persons like this, who were not overtly activist, could be enlisted to engage in lobbying is in itself an indication of how far political awareness among South Asians was proceeding by the 1920s, and how far activists like Taraknath and Sailendranath Ghose had come in adopting the art of lobbying.

Each witness was asked to give a brief biographical sketch of himself and then to answer questions ranging from his

**Table 8.1**
**Ethno-religious characteristics of naturalized South Asians**

| Ethno-religious category | Number | Percentage |
|---|---|---|
| Hindu | 25 | 7 |
| Bengali | 7 | 11 |
| Other Hindu | 18 | 26 |
| Sikh | 19 | 28 |
| Muslim | 16 | 24 |
| Christian | 9 | 13 |
| Total | 69 | 102 |

**Table 8.2**
**Spatial distribution of naturalized South Asians**

| Regions | Number | Percentage |
|---|---|---|
| Pacific Coast | 22 | 32 |
| California | 17 | 25 |
| Oregon | 4 | 6 |
| Washington | 1 | 0.2 |
| Far West/Montane | 13 | 19 |
| Idaho | 2 | 0.3 |
| Montana | 1 | 0.2 |
| Texas | 4 | 0.6 |
| Utah | 6 | 0.9 |
| Middle West | 9 | 13 |
| Indiana | 1 | 0.2 |
| Illinois | 3 | 0.3 |
| Iowa | 1 | 0.2 |
| Michigan | 4 | 0.6 |
| Northeast | 19 | 28 |
| Connecticut | 1 | 0.2 |
| New York | 8 | 12 |
| New Jersey | 3 | 0.3 |
| Pennsylvania | 7 | 11 |
| South | 6 | 0.9 |
| Florida | 1 | 0.2 |
| Georgia | 1 | 0.2 |
| Louisiana | 4 | 0.6 |
| Total | 69 | 101 |

occupational skills to the extent of his involvement with Indian nationalism. On the domestic side, Gokhale said he was married to an Indian woman with whom he lived in the United States, and had five children, three born in America and two in India. He brought with him a photostat copy of his citizenship certificate, which Senator Reed told him it was not necessary for him to produce.

Gokhale also brought with him letters and testaments which showed that he had earned the respect and confidence of his American employers. Nevertheless, Senator Reed asked, "Were you ever charged with any political offense before you left India?" His reply was candid, "I was never charged, but I have reason to believe that I was strongly suspected." The Senator followed up by asking Gokhale, "Have you been guilty of any anti-British activities since you reached this country?" To which Gokhale could truthfully reply that he had not. He was asked if he knew any of the other persons whose cases were being addressed by the committee, including and especially Taraknath Das. Gokhale almost plaintively replied, "I am a man of retired habits. I happen not to be generally acquainted with any, except as I become acquainted with them in the course of my business." He acknowledged that he knew there were charges against "Dr. Das," but said he knew only one other person mentioned by the joint-commission: Doctor (Vanama Ramachandra) Kokatnur of Pittsburgh, Pennsylvania, because he was a fellow natural scientist, a chemical engineer.

Doctor Kokatnur also testified. His academic credentials were impressive, and so was his career as a "consulting chemical engineer." He said he had graduated from Bombay University with a Bachelor of Science degree and then Master of Science and doctoral degrees from the University of Minnesota. "I notice you are an honor man, from the key you wear," said Senator Copeland. "Yes, sir," Kokutnur replied, "the Phi Beta Kappa key." This clearly did not hurt his image!

World War I came to America in 1917 while he was working as a research assistant for one of his chemistry professors at Minnesota. He applied "to various departments after the declaration of war: to Chemical Warfare Service, Ordnance Department, Bureau of Mines and Civil Service ... I was rejected as a volunteer in any of these departments because I was not a citizen at the time." He then journeyed to Niagara Falls where he was employed by the Mathieson Alkali Works, and Niagara Alkali Company, "in the production of collodion gas," which was used for making weaponized poison gas. He claimed that while he was at Mathieson Alkali he "developed entirely new poisonous mustard gases ... and also ... a new chloropicrin or tear gas." These experiences motivated him to apply for American citizenship. "At the end of the war," Kokatnur declared, "the conviction was growing on me that the country which gave me an education was worth fighting for, and so I applied for naturalization." He was naturalized in 1921. He certainly fit the "American dream" to a "T"!

Senator Reed made one comment that revealed how successfully the Indians had lobbied for their cause. After hearing Gokhale and Kokatnur expound further on their scientific and technical accomplishments, he said to Kokatnur, "I think we may concede your technical qualifications, and I do not believe it necessary to go into them. All I am desirous of bringing out is that *these 69 men include a larger number of talented people than [any] 69 people taken at random through the country*" (emphasis added).

Taraknath Das's testimony was the pièce de resistance of the hearing. It was he who had inspired them, and it was he who was the most controversial witness. He was asked to describe his own background and credentials, and also those of his wife, Mary. Her family pedigree and social standing were stressed, clearly in order to enhance Taraknath's legitimacy as a bonafide, upstanding American citizen.

He told the committee that Mary was born in South Carolina but lived in New York. "Was she of American parentage?" Reed asked. "Her people came in 1700 to this country ... from England." Das said they had no children and characterized himself occupationally as a "publicist and educator." He stressed his academic qualifications, which culminated in his doctoral degree from Georgetown. Admitting that there were questions about his being awarded a degree because of his prison record, he declared that such an academic degree given by an American university "is not merely dependent upon educational efficiency, but moral character" as well. It was all "thrashed out" and "president Coolidge handed me the degree when I got it in 1924, and I was the first one to have that honor from that institution." They also asked him if he was a Christian. He said that both he and his wife attended the United Christian church in New York City whose minister is "Doctor Holmes." He declared, "I was the first person to organize what they call 'adult education' ... in that church in the last 40 years."

They asked him what he thought his fate would be like if he was deprived of his American citizenship. "Not knowing what is in the mind of the British Government," he replied, "and ... knowing that they will stoop down to such a dirty deal [as] to make a report that I was going to India at the time of the coronation of King George, when [in fact] I was a candidate for my masters degree in the University of Washington, I feel my fate will be very doubtful." What Das was implying is that the British were feeding US officials phony reports that Taraknath and others were plotting to go to India to commit terrorist acts while King George was making his famed state visit to India in 1911.

He was also asked about his role as an immigration official, mostly in Vancouver. He believed the British as well as the anti-Asian-Americans had it in for him because of his sympathetic treatment of the immigrants, and because he even helped them initiate legal action against the Canadian authorities who were contriving means to prevent them from entering the country.

> A boatload of Hindus came in, and they were examined at the rate of six a minute, and they were regarded thus, that they were physically disqualified, [allegedly] suffering from contagious disease; and these Hindus' cases were taken up by a local attorney for $10 apiece to defend them, and they wanted to find a Hindu interpreter and they did not find a competent one. So they asked the United States authorities if they would lend me to the court interpreter, and I interpreted [for] them, and it resulted in the reversing of the decision of the British Columbia immigration authorities, and these people were allowed to land; and that incensed them.

They grilled him intensely over the reasons why he left the Immigration Service in less than a year. The intent obviously was to try and get him to admit that it had something to do with his revolutionary activities. Taraknath dodged them. They brought up his role in publishing *Free Hindustan*, but oddly nothing explicitly about Ghadr. "I assume that the British Government was uncomfortable because of your writings about 'Free Hindustan'?" "Yes," Das replied. "And that brought it to the attention of our authorities and there was some communication either in writing or language to you, stating that you what? ..." asked Senator Copeland. Taraknath basically insisted that the only thing he was "guilty" of was wanting to see India become a free and independent "Republic." Otherwise, "I have no activities except my studies

since I came out of the penitentiary, and this question of my deportation was decided by the Labor Department. I have no activities
politically whatsoever. I am a student. I devote my time to study
... if I have any activities it is mostly in the form which is helpful to
the United States Government."

The other dimension of these hearings was the by-play that
occurred between the senators and the numerous American officials who were involved in trying to craft policies pertaining to
the plight of South Asians in the United States. The fundamental
issues, were, of course, in the immediate term, what disposition
would be made of the 69 who faced denaturalization, and, in the
broader sense, where Indians fitted into the racial scheme of things.
In a fundamentally racist society, are brown-skinned "Hindus"
Caucasians, and therefore technically White, or are they Asians
who are neither Caucasian nor White? Those were the questions
that were explored. The dialog itself revealed how deeply racism
pervaded American society, and how much anguish it had engendered in the minds of even the most well-meaning citizens.

One of the most surprising and pivotal developments that affected the political atmosphere pervading the Committee hearings
was the impact which Chief Justice, and former President of the
United States, William Howard Taft had upon its deliberations.
Taft had been part of the unanimous decision in the *Thind* case,
and so it was not anticipated that he would have anything positive
to say about the cases of the 69 denaturalized Indians whose
citizenship had been peremptorily jeopardized by that decision.
In fact, however, the Chief Justice publicly criticized this outcome
and in a letter to the Chairman of the Committee on Immigration
called for the restitution of their citizenship rights. This had spurred
the Immigration Committee hearings, and was attributable in large
degree to the lobbying efforts of Taraknath and Sarangadhar Das.
First, Taraknath, who was now studying for his doctorate at
Georgetown, successfully made contact with both Senators Reed
and Copeland, with whom he lobbied "for special legislation to
ratify and confirm the citizenship of Indians." Either through them
or despite them, it is not clear, he met Alfred Martin, of the Society
for Ethical Culture, who in turn introduced him to William
Howard Taft. Although Taft had not dissented in the *Thind* case,
"Taraknath's argument convinced him that an injustice was done.
Particularly by the fact that the denaturalized Hindus in America

had been rendered stateless because they ceased to be British citizens when they became American citizens." The Chief Justice wrote to Secretary of Labor, James J. Dean, about this matter, mentioning Taraknath Das in its text. Taraknath took the letter around to the State, Justice and Labor departments, but "only got a polite runaround. But he obviously hit pay-dirt with Senators Reed and Copeland" (Mukherjee 1997: 190).

Ghose, in the meantime, went to work on promoting broader legislation that would recognize all Indians as White, the argument which *Thind* had rejected. In this undertaking, in addition to Reed and Copeland, he garnered support and encouragement from Representative Emanuel Celler (1888–1981) from Brooklyn, New York. From the outset of Celler's career he had been a dauntless exponent of immigration and immigrants' rights. He was a natural ally for the South Asian community, and it is a sign of the growing sophistication of Indian lobbying efforts that they began identifying potential supporters in the mainstream political establishment. From this point on, Celler was constantly supportive of Indian immigration rights—he was a key player, as we shall see, in the 1946 legislation which granted full citizenship rights and provided the first official quota for South Asians. This initial effort did not succeed, however; it foundered on the rocks of racism when the bill that Copeland wrote was tabled by a Southern committee chairman.

What it all came down to is that this inaugural attempt at systematic lobbying achieved limited but not insignificant success. Chief Justice Taft's letter turned out to be the key, because the government agencies responsible for implementing these retrograde racist policies adamantly defended them throughout the immigration committee hearings.

Taft's letter is worth reproducing in its entirety. Addressed to the Secretary of Labor, on November 18, 1926, it said:

MY DEAR MR. SECRETARY: Mr. Alfred Martine, a gentleman of the highest standing, whom I have known for a great many years, and a member of the Society for Ethical Culture, has talked to me with reference to *the injustice that he conceives to have been done to Dr. Taraknath Das*, a Hindu who took out his papers of naturalization in this country in 1908, and when in 1914 he applied for his naturalization certificate, the examiner contested his right to become an American citizen. The matter was carried into court, and United States Judge Dooling, of the United States District Court in San Francisco, held that the applicant was entitled to a certificate, which was issued to him. Since that time he has traveled and received passports and has married an American-born woman. Now, by our decision, at the instance of the Government, it is held that such certificates are void, because under the law there was no authority to grant a certificate to anyone but a white person and that Hindus do not come within that description. There are about 40 Hindus who received certificates, and who, acting on the assurance that they had become American citizens, have lost the citizenship of Great Britain and are really without a country and without allegiance to any government. It would seem to me that such a situation calls upon Congress to right the matter and that the admission of a few Hindus would not at all break down our rule of rigid exclusion. There might well be special legislation on the subject to meet a real injustice. *Dr. Das has called on me* and has asked me to give him an opportunity to be heard by the heads of departments whose advice and wishes in the matter Congress would be certain to consult. *I have therefore given to Doctor Das a letter of introduction to you*, with the hope that some time, at his instance, you may be able to receive him for a few minutes and talk the matter over with him (Ratification and Confirmation of Naturalization of Certain Persons of the Hindu Race, United States Senate, Committee of Immigration, December 9, 1926, p. 4, emphasis added).

Taraknath had written Chief Justice Taft a three-paragraph letter, dated October 19, 1926, the day before Taft's letter was addressed to him. This letter makes a lot of the fact that he is married to an American woman who, should he lose his citizenship, would also lose hers. Judging from the tenor of Taft's reply, this may well have been an effective ploy. He says that since his naturalization in 1914, he had three times been granted passports without objection. Now because of the *Thind* decision, "I am rendered a stateless person. This means that my American-born wife has, according to United States authorities, lost her American citizenship and she is also rendered stateless." He concluded, "While I speak of our present unfortunate position, let me say that ... I am not pleading for my individual case, but for all those who are rendered stateless by the application of the decision of Justice Sutherland ...."

Statements and documents of various kinds came from W.W. Husband, Second Assistant Secretary of the Department of Labor; from Raymond F. Crist, Commissioner of Naturalization; James K. Fisk and V.S. McClatchey, Secretary and Chairman respectively of the California Joint Immigration Committee; from William C. Kronmeyer, a New Jersey lawyer representing Swami Yogananda; plus copies of the decisions in the Sakharam Ganesh Pandit and Akhay Kumar Mozumdar naturalization cases that were heard before the Ninth District US Court of Appeals in San Francisco. This list alone demonstrates how far the nascent Indian lobbyists had gone in drawing public officials into the political nexus they were attempting to create. They were evolving beyond mere agitational politics.

The common thread among all the government witnesses was that as far as Asian immigration was concerned they were unabashed racists. The hearings became a mechanism through which this fact was rendered explicit. They euphemized their bigotry by larding it over with legalistic clichés about the necessity to correctly interpret the will of Congress, and the fine-points of the US Constitution. The *Thind* decision itself was a racist edict which dismissed scientific veracity in favor of the prejudices of the uneducated mob. Judge Sutherland's decision even asserted that common prejudices took precedence over the indisputable determination by modern anthropology that Indians are Caucasians and therefore White. In some ways, of course, this finding itself had regrettable implications for the wider cause of racial justice, because it still pointedly left out the Negroid, Mongoloid and Austro-Asiatic races who were just as worthy of being accorded social justice as were Caucasoids. The result was, ironically, that the price of winning their case would be to place themselves in the same camp as the white racists. However, in the 1920s subtleties like these had very little saliency.

Crist's memorandum (October 26) went out of its way to describe Taraknath's political activities; it did so in a tone that was obviously intended to convey the impression that Das was what was called in the days of the 1950s McCarthy witch-hunts a "security risk." He raked up the Berlin conspiracy trial, pointing out the fact that "Mr. Das was one of 31 persons charged with plotting to violate the neutrality of the United States." He even repeated the intimation that Taraknath had maintained a safety-deposit box containing a bomb-making manual. He also mentioned the "shooting in the courtroom" on the last day of the conspiracy trial, when Ram Chandra was assassinated by a factional rival and his assailant was killed in a hail of bullets by the police. And, of course, he mentioned Das's 22-month imprisonment in Leavenworth.

One of the most outspoken opponents of renaturalizing the Indians was Secretary V.S. McClatchey of the California Joint Immigration Committee. On December 2, McClatchey, in a letter to Committee Chairman Hiram Johnson, reminded him that the *Thind* decision "held that all Hindus belong to the brown race and are ineligible for American citizenship under our naturalization statutes." For this reason, "The joint immigration committee respectfully urges that favorable action on the proposed bill be not taken without careful and deliberate consideration of the facts and possible consequences ...." And what about the fate of the denaturalized Indians? McClatchey was an insensitive man. Almost patronizingly, he declared, "It would doubtless be a hardship to be deprived now of these privileges, but they suffer no wrong in the matter anymore than wrong would be suffered by him who had enjoyed for some years the possession and revenues from a property erroneously awarded to him by one court but who was forced to relinquish it on final decision." His cold-blooded legalism could not distinguish between an inanimate piece of real estate and sentient human feelings. In fact, he concluded that the real "victim" was not the denaturalized and stateless Indians but the United States. "If there be wrong in this matter it has been suffered by the citizenry of the United States in the conferring of citizenship on those not entitled thereto."

Fortunately, in this instance, neither the Committee nor the Chief Justice of the United States agreed with this heartless conclusion, and the citizenship rights, including Taraknath Das's, were restored. However, the larger matters of rights of entry into the US and the rights of citizenship for those already here remained unresolved. The restoration of the citizenship of the 69 was, in fact, accompanied by the 1924 Immigration Act which was a veritable declaration that there would be no more "exceptions." "The immigration law of 1924," declares Jensen, "openly and officially committed the government of the United States to the ideology developed by the labor department years ago" (Jensen 1988: 267).

Asians in general reacted intensely to this legislation. Pearl Buck, who became a powerful voice against Asian racism, called it "a great white wall." Madam Sun Yat-sen "told reporters that she was the wife of a 'coolie' (Gen. Chiang Kai Shek) and that she would not return to the United States to visit her husband unless America repealed the exclusion law" (Jensen 1988: 267–68).

Taraknath himself would not be a major player in the next phase of the post-*Thind* era that was about to dawn. Others would move into the breach. After the hearings and the restoration of his and Mary's citizenship rights, they sailed for Germany and remained there until 1934, witnessing the early stages of the rise of National Socialism. The next few years were a period of consolidation and reconfiguration for the South Asian community in America. One could even say that it was a period of resource amplification, both material and ideological, thanks mainly to the Sikhs and other Indians along the Pacific Coast. In Jensen's words, "After 1925, immigrants settled down to make the best of their restricted life in America." Among the Sikhs:

> The majority continued to farm or perform manual labor, and a small minority, most former students, entered the professions or became merchants. Large numbers of Indians continued to organize for the independence of India and for the rights of Indians in North America, and to recruit allies for their cause. Some men married, others chose to remain in all-male living groups. Most attempted to maintain their old networks with other Indian immigrants. Together they faced the difficult task of living on the margins of United States and Canadian society (Jensen 1988: 270).

Jensen continues, saying that "the men achieved a surprising degree of economic success in California," so much so that it would seem to have affected domestic tranquility. Being peasants to their core, the Sikhs were obsessed with acquiring land, obviously because, not unlike in the Punjab from whence they came, it provided them with an economic base that protected them not only from poverty but from the depredations of predators who perpetually sought ways to deprive them of their human rights. One result was that disposable income was often sacrificed for land-ownership, which in turn limited the consumerism which brought contentment to wives and children. Despite formal restrictions on land owner-ship by Indians, and even prosecutions under the conspiracy laws against California Sikh farmers who had illegally acquired land, they continued to increase their holdings by a variety of subterfuges. When in 1933 the Supreme Court voided the right of California to convict Indians under its conspiracy laws for acquir-ing land, "Indians had little difficulty in controlling land." By then, the 123,000 acres allegedly controlled by South Asian farmers in 1920 had multiplied many times. What this meant in political terms was that the community resources upon which activists could draw, and the impunity with which they could draw on them, had also increased many times.

The world was now in the "inter-war" years where the rise of fascism and Japanese Bushido, culminating in the Spanish Civil War and World War II, would increasingly dominate the world stage. In America, the unresolved aspects of the civil rights issue, and the international ramifications of the freedom struggle being waged in India by the revitalized Indian National Congress under Gandhi and Nehru and the Muslim League under Jinnah, became the focal concerns of a new breed of South Asian political activists. Indian voices increased in volume, especially as they emanated from the large bloc of South Asians in the Western states and as networking proceeded. The Ghadr Party continued to energize and reinforce Sikh political awareness, though it no longer ex-tended its reach beyond the Sikh community, and no longer seri-ously contemplated an armed invasion of India. Its identification with the Indian freedom movement enabled it to intensify aware-ness among American Sikhs of the vital relationship between freedom in India and freedom in America. Most importantly, says Jensen (1988: 272), the party "Using a religious base for their polit-ical organizing ... continued to collect money and to search for international allies."

Although in the beginning there was doubt and ambivalence about Gandhi's doctrine of non-violence, especially before Nehru's more comprehensible secular nationalism emerged as a counter-part to the Mahatma's populist religiosity, the Congress party increasingly became the visible manifestation of a politically resur-gent India. This was particularly the case after the Salt Satyagraha of 1930 and the First Round Table Conference in London in 1930–1931.[3] From that point on, the Congress movement in India got the world's attention, and energized overseas Indians everywhere, but particularly in England and the United States. Jensen rightly points out that there was a progressive evolution of awareness and sympathy for Indian nationalism which enriched the political infrastructure that was gradually forming in the US. "American religious periodicals, once hostile to Indian independence, gradually moved toward support of the nationalist movement because of Gandhi's nonviolent crusade." A similar shift took place in secular publications. The liberal establishment especially began to come around in a more comprehensive manner. Jensen notes, as we shall soon see, "that middle-class Indians continued to build organizations *with which American supporters could work.*" What followed was a new genre of more sophisticated publicists and organizers, "led by a group of Indians who were successful businessmen or

Illustration 8.1
Mahatma Gandhi picking up salt

*Source:* Kamath 1998.

professionals," crucial to carrying the cause of Indian human rights and Indian freedom to fruition (Jensen 1988: 276–77).

As the 1920s lapsed into the 1930s, there were many enclaves of Indians residing in all parts of the United States, not only on the West Coast, especially in the major urban centers like Boston, Chicago, Detroit, New York, Philadelphia, St. Louis, and Washington, but even in more out of the way places like New Orleans, Atlanta, Savannah, and Houston, and also on university campuses along the East Coast (Harvard, Yale, Columbia, Pennsylvania), but perhaps especially in the Midwest at major Big Ten schools like Chicago, Illinois, Michigan, Minnesota, and Wisconsin. Racial prejudice in itself contributed to the crystallization of ethnic cohesion: "Restrictions probably encouraged some Indians who would have left [the US and returned to India] to remain and join permanent Indian enclaves" (ibid.: 270). Not only were activists able to build contacts with groups and individuals in their local bailiwicks, they were also able to offer hospitality to journalists, publicists and politicians from India who increasingly journeyed to America to promote the nationalist cause and counter British propaganda designed to discredit it. The British Embassy in Washington and its consular branches throughout the country had in fact become major engines of anti-nationalist propaganda.

With Har Dayal and Taraknath Das now more or less in the background, and with the changes that were taking place throughout the world as the inter-war years unfolded (including the Great Depression of 1929), a lot of new faces were appearing on the South Asian political scene. One has to say that in some ways a less strident, more subtle, but no less dedicated breed of activists came into play. Then too, the freedom movement in India was playing a much greater role both in the way resident Indians were perceiving and articulating their social grievances in the court of public opinion, and in the nature and magnitude of contacts between Indian activists in the US and persons in India who were players in the Indian National Congress, the Muslim League, and even in the Government of India itself. Understandably, most of them were younger: if not born in the twentieth century then much later in the nineteenth than their predecessors. Their awareness and emphases were primarily being molded by the political currents and events which characterized the interregnum between World War I and World War II: the rise of fascism, Soviet Communism, Japanese militarism, the struggle to keep the League of Nations alive and relevant; the Great Depression, and flickering anti-colonialism, not only in India but throughout what ultimately would come to be called the "Third World." Old-fashioned Bengali, Punjabi, and Maharashtrian radical revolutionism was, while not dead, yielding the stage to more sophisticated modes of popular resistance to tyranny and social injustice that were capable of building wider, more cosmopolitan constituencies.

There were five individuals who played especially important roles in ushering in the next generation of activists. They were Syud Hossain, Haridas Mazumdar, Krishanlal Shridharani, Anup Singh, and "Sirdar" Jagjit Singh ("J.J. Singh"). Taranknath and Mary Das and Sarangadhar Das remained in the game as well, but in more senior, one might even say more circumspect, capacities. Taraknath and Mary were out of the country until 1934, and when they returned Taraknath's career turned in a more academic-intellectual, shall we say more genteel, direction. He was now 50 years old and Mary was in her 70s. He was appointed a special lecturer in History at Catholic University in Washington for the winter term of 1935; then, after a six-months sojourn in Los Angeles pertaining to private family matters, the College of the City of New York, what today is New York University, offered him an opportunity to teach two courses. One was called "Modern India" and the other "The Near East in World Politics." He combined this with a wide-ranging pattern of lectureships at universities all over the United States. "His reputation as a strongly opinionated scholar of controversial issues spread among the academic community," declares Mukherjee (1997: 204). From this point on, he and Mary "took a long lease on a fifteenth-floor suite of the historical Ansonia Hotel on Broadway, which was their home for the rest of their life" (ibid.: 206).[4]

Many new faces were added to the roster of American allies during this phase, and played major roles in the crafting of lobbying resources. They included many individuals from academia, journalists like I.F. Stone, Walter Lippmann, and Drew Pearson; and luminaries like Pearl Buck, Will Durant, and Clare Booth Luce. They also included numerous figures in the US Congress, like Representative Emanuel Celler of New York, whom we have

**Illustration 8.2**
**Clare Booth Luce during her**
**congressional campaign in 1944**

*Source:* Library of Congress.

already encountered, as well as Clare Booth Luce in her incarnation as a member of the House of Representatives.

The Indian press was also coming of age at this time, especially English-language newspapers like the *Times of India* and the *Hindustan Times* in Delhi, the *Independent* and *Leader* in Allahabad, the *Pioneer* and the *National Herald* in Lucknow, the *Telegraph* in Calcutta, the *Hindu* in Madras, the *Chronicle* in Bombay, etc. With a vigorous sense of independence and a dedication to comprehensive reportage, in the face of determined efforts by the colonial administration to curb freedom of the press, they spawned a number of excellent journalists who stimulated public awareness of the nationalist movement on both sides of the globe. Their fluency in English, perhaps the most positive benefit of colonial rule, immensely helped them to internationalize their influence.

Somewhat ironically, a Muslim, Syud Hossain, would play a seminal role in the process of reinforcing the links between the Indian National Congress's political style in India and this emerging group of America-based Indian nationalists. Not unlike Lala Lajpat Rai, his route to the United States had been determined more by chance than design. Rai had in effect been marooned in the US as a result of World War I. Had it not been for this unforeseen eventuality, he would most probably have returned to India from England in 1914. Yet, when he reached America instead, Lajpat, as we noted, forged a more mature, politically palatable alternative to the romantic revolutionism propounded by the Ghadrites and the Bengali-Punjabi radicals.

Syud Hossain's arrival on the scene had in its background the stuff of a Bollywood romantic melodrama. Hossain came from a very elitist Muslim family of Delhi Muslims who had adopted a cosmopolitan lifestyle and a secular political orientation. When still very young, he had been attracted both by the Indian National Congress's democratic consensualism and Mahatma Gandhi's quasi-religious doctrine of non-violent action. Hossain joined the Congress party when he was very young, and soon won the admiration and approval of the Nehrus, so much so, in fact, that Motilal Nehru persuaded him to come to Allahabad as a journalist on the staff of his newspaper, the *Independent*. This in turn led to a love affair between him and Vijayalakshmi, the eldest of Jawaharlal's sisters!

The details of this affair are sketchy, but it seems they "eloped" to Bombay and were allegedly in some sense "married." Vijayalakshmi, born in 1900, could have been no more than 19 or 20 at the time. Haridas Mazumdar, whose memoir (1960) is an important document on the inter-war years, says that when he personally met Hossain in Bombay he was the sub-editor of the *Bombay Chronicle*, which means that he had changed jobs. Be that as it may, the Nehru family was supposedly deeply upset at this turn of events, perhaps for communal reasons, but certainly because it had occurred outside the bounds of the arranged marriage system that was traditional at that time (and indeed remains common today for orthodox Indian families). But even more poignantly, Mahatma Gandhi was opposed to it. His will prevailed and the couple were "uncoupled," as it were. An anonymous friend of mine who had some knowledge of this matter quipped that once the Nehrus and Gandhi caught up with the young lovers, "Mr. Hossain wisely caught the next ship departing for America!" This was no doubt an over-dramatic characterization, since Syud Hossain states, "I first came to Washington, DC, in 1921 to attend the Washington Arms Conference as Press Representative for India (*Voice of India*, September 1944, p. 4).[5] At any rate, Mazumdar, who had known him in Bombay, says, "So it was renewing an old acquaintance when I met him in New York city soon after his arrival."

Hossain, however, was by no means your average destitute student. He was already an established journalist and publicist. Nor, which is the important point, was he alienated from the Congress party as a result of this domestic misadventure. He tarried in England for a time, and somewhere along the way studied law. "He attended the Lincoln's Inn to study his favorite subject: constitutional law." However, "He did not take the law degree as he found his niche in journalism," declares Mustafa Zaman. (2003).

Hossain reached America in 1921 and plunged into both scholarly and political work. He published a short-lived magazine called *Ars Islamica* (Islamic Arts), whose purpose was to document the ways in which the Islamic world contributed to the West's knowledge of mathematics, science, art, etc., during the Renaissance. Hossain also founded a magazine called *The New Orient*. Both failed for lack of sufficient funds and circulation. He eventually became a co-founder with Anup Singh of the National Committee for Indian independence, headquartered in Washington, concerning which more presently. He also performed legal services for California Sikhs and other Indians with immigration problems, which shows that he quickly adapted to the South Asian grassroots subculture in the US. No doubt it became quickly apparent that the large Sikh community on the West Coast was a lucrative source of financial support for political activists. However, to establish his bonafides as a Gandhian/Congress-style democrat, he publicly opposed the Ghadrites and other radical extremist groups, which may have constricted the range of support he could generate from this quarter for his enterprises.

Apropos of this point, he had a reputation for living well. Declares Mazumdar, "Austerity and Hossain never went together. He enjoyed living in style ... 'saints and I do not get along together,' he said jokingly." In Mazumdar's (1960: 12; see Chapter 6, note 3) words, "Immaculately dressed, polished in manners, brilliant in oratory, Dr. Hossain immediately captivated his audiences from coast to coast." Gobind Behari Lal, who had by now had become a professional journalist writing on Indian matters, reinforces Mazumdar's assessment of Syud Hossain's significance. "It was Hossain," he declares, "who first brought the message of Gandhi to America ... *in an authentic Indian manner*." He adds that "He was

Illustration 8.3
Syud Hossain in America

*Source:* Mazumdar 1960.

generously supported by Indian residents of California, Michigan, New York, Chicago, all imbued with the national spirit generated by the earlier struggle I have depicted" (*Modern Review*, Vol. 92, July 1952, p. 33, emphasis added).[6]

This, of course, testifies to how widely the networks of interaction were ramifying. Hossain typified this new breed of Indian nationalist who were the legatees of the type of responsible advocacy for which Lajpat Rai had stood. They created a nexus of advocates for Indian independence, and correlatively equal rights for resident Indians, who traveled the country giving public lectures to civic and church groups, on college and university campuses, and informal aggregations of concerned private citizens. Most important, however, they advanced the arts of political lobbying by many degrees. Organizations like the India League of America and the National Committee on Indian independence were highly instrumental in developing access to the political establishment, as well as employing professional "lecture managers" to arrange speaking tours both for resident South Asians and a steady stream of visiting politicians, journalists, scholars, writers, artists, and religious figures who came over from India to champion the cause and challenge the pro-colonialist line of the British.

A particularly important aspect of Syud Hossain's role was his opposition to communalism. While a dedicated proponent of Islamic culture and religion, he followed Maulana Azad and other secular, pro-Congress Muslims in opposing separatists like Muhammad Ali Jinnah for their advocacy of Pakistan. This made him an especially valuable asset to the Congress movement and to secularists in the United States.

Dr Haridas Mazumdar was a fascinating transitional figure between the earlier hard-line revolutionaries and their Gandhian/ Congress-oriented successors. He came to America much in the same way as did the former, as a student in search of an education and a political identity. He obtained a Masters Degree at North-western (1926) and a Ph.D. at the University of Wisconsin in Socio-logy (1929), just in time for the Great Depression! He concluded his academic career in 1960 as a Professor of Sociology and Social Work at Cornell College in Mt. Vernon, Iowa. As well as being an extremely active participant in South Asian immigrant politics, Mazumdar also became perhaps its most articulate chronicler. His memoir (1960) very nicely captures the flavor of those inter-war years in down-to-earth language: the touching idealism that motivated them, at times the political naiveté that afflicted them, their efforts to run a revolution on a shoe-string, their triumphs and tragedies.

Mazumdar reached America in 1920, half a generation later than the old guard who had started it all around the turn of the century. He says he came as a "self-supporting student ... with $350 in his pocket," a not inconsiderable sum for a student in those days, which bespeaks his middle-class roots back in Bengal. "By a curious irony of fate, in 1920, the ship carrying Lajpat Rai to India crossed on the high seas the ship carrying a twenty year-old Elphinstonian (the present writer) to America." To him, this meant being "denied the privilege of meeting the great man, but his example served as a model to me in my work in America." He says he was moved by Lajpat's statement that "the lot of a patriot even in a hospitable country such as America is a hard one," even to the point of having to live on coffee and doughnuts! You may be "eulogized by poets, praised to the skies by civic leaders, dined and feted by women's clubs, and yet you may not know where the money is going to come from for the next day's breakfast." It's the price you have to pay, he laments, "for espousing the cause of one's choice" (Mazumdar 1960: 12).

He hung around New York, getting familiar with the city, until the beginning of the next academic year, before enrolling in Columbia University. For the first couple of years, Haridas says he took menial jobs to make ends meet: at night as a switchboard operator, as an elevator operator, sweeping the floor in a tailor shop, working as a gardener's assistant, posing as an artist's model, collating newspapers in the New York Public Library. Through the latter job, he discovered the wonders of the New York Public Library, which opened up "whole new worlds: the world of American literature and history, the world of European literature, and above all the world of India's cultural heritage" (ibid.: 14). He also became aware of the street-corner speakers who addressed crowds on every subject, from Irish freedom, socialism and atheism to evangelism. It gave him the idea of himself addressing street-corner audiences on the freedom struggle in India under Mahatma Gandhi's leadership. He mentions meeting Americans while at Columbia whom he befriended and who became important influences in his American incarnation. This included people like Norman Thomas (1884–1968), Unitarian Minister John Haynes Holmes (1880–1964), and Robert Morse Lovett (1870–1956), who encouraged him to write his first book, entitled *Gandhi the Apostle*.

After he moved on to Chicago to become a student at Northwestern University in 1922, he demonstrated entrepreneurial as well as intellectual talent by founding his own publishing company (Universal Publishing Company) and through it publishing his book in 1923. He published another work the following year, which was an edited version of Gandhi's *Hind Swaraj* under the title *Sermon on the Sea*. Thus, by 1924, as his post-graduate education proceeded, he managed to establish himself as a publicizer of Gandhi's political doctrine. Mazumdar says he subsisted on a mixture of odd jobs, income from his publications and fees from public lectures. "At this time, Mazumdar was the only competent public lecturer in the Midwest on India, and his biography of Gandhi ... was the only available source book ... on Gandhi and India's nonviolent revolution" (Mazumdar 1960: 18).

Interestingly, during his Wisconsin period, he speaks of encountering Sarojini Naidu, Virendranath Chattopadhyaya's sister, who was visiting at Hull House in Chicago and had come up to Madison as part of a 1928 national lecture tour. By then she had become the Congress party's female poster-child. It was the time when the US Congress was considering whether the United States should sign the Kellogg–Briand Treaty, an international agreement whose purpose was to foster worldwide arms control and eliminate war as an instrument of national policy. Senator John James Blaine (1875–1934) of Wisconsin introduced Ms Naidu's statement into the Congressional Record (US Senate, 70th Congress, Session 2, January 9, 1929) in the following words: "The people of India have sent to America their representatives, as the colonies went from port to port in Europe through their representatives in aid of the war that made our nation possible." In like fashion, he continued, "... the people of India are speaking their hope through a woman of India. Sarojini Naidu, a cultured, refined and intelligent representative of the people of India, trained in the great universities of Great Britain, speaks at least the spirit of India and the voice of India, so far as an unofficial representative of an original people can speak it." Because the treaty pertained to the exercise of national sovereignty, an issue concerning which the United States Congress itself expressed so many reservations that it passed by only a single vote, Naidu's statement made much of the fact that under British rule the Indian people had no rights of national sovereignty.

> ... Though India has always upheld the higher gospel of peace toward the recognition of which principle this pact in its original intention constituted an admirable gesture, she cannot be held bound in all circumstances to honor any vicarious pledges made in her behalf and without her consent which deprives her of a single national or international right, but still she must reserve to herself complete independence of action in all its implications

to establish and maintain her undeniable and inalienable birth-right of political liberty.

This was, of course, a golden opportunity for a nationalist polit-ician of major stature (she was ex-president of the Indian National Congress) to forcefully assert her country's cause to the American people.

While working on his doctorate at Wisconsin, Mazumdar says he wrote a letter to the Mahatma expressing his views on the free-dom struggle and India's reconstruction once she became free. Gandhi replied and invited him to come and stay at his *ashram* when he next came to India. Gandhi might well have been sur-prised at how quickly Haridas took him up on the invitation. Armed with his Ph.D. in sociology, he left for India during the Christmas week of 1929. His memoir speaks not at all of the Great Depression which had struck in that year and what effect this had on his own condition or his perceptions of the political situation.

He attended the Lahore session of the Indian National Congress at which the party adopted *Purna Swaraj* (Complete Independence) as its political goal. He lingered at Satyagraha Ashram "as Gandhi's guest" from January to March, 1930, and studied the "Hindese scene from that vantage point under Bapuji's loving guidance." He participated in part of the Salt March, but broke away "with Bapuji's blessings" and went to Ahmedabad where he undertook to write an account of the Great March. From there, after Gandhi's arrest, he journeyed to Bombay to meet his "idol," Jawaharlal Nehru. Haridas sought permission to be arrested as a *satyagrahi*. Both Jawaharlal and his father, Motilal Nehru, encouraged him to return to the United States and spread the Congress message there. Motilal told him, "We have already enough people behind prison bars; there is no need to add more to the nose count." Instead, "I suggest you go back to America and interpret to the American people the story of India's fight for freedom as you have seen it from the inside." Motilal arranged for the Bombay Provincial Con-gress Committee to pay his passage back to the United States. He was, he says, designated as "The Unofficial Ambassador of Goodwill from India in America."

Back in America, he embarked on a program of nationwide speaking tours arranged by the Open Forum Speakers Bureau of Boston, the Foreign Policy Association of New York, and the Adult

Education Council of Chicago. Through Oswald Garrison Villard
(1871–1949), editor and publisher of the *Nation*, who was an admirer of Gandhi and friend to a host of Indian nationalists,
Mazumdar was able, "at nominal rent," to acquire office space in
their building from which between 1930 and 1932 he turned out
four volumes in a series called *India Today and Tomorrow*. For a
while, he had a small staff of secretaries, "all paid from ... lecture
fees," and through his office worked with several local Indian and
American writers and scholars on this project.

Krishnalal Shridharani (1911–1960) is another exemplification
of the Gandhian/Congress breed of activists who were gradually
replacing the Har Dayal/Taraknath Das generation. He arrived
in New York in 1934 and studied at New York University where
he earned an M.A. in Sociology, and then at Columbia University
where he obtained a Ph.D. in social science and journalism.
He was already a veteran of Gandhi's Salt March and a product
of Gandhi's "university," Gujarat Vidyapith, and Tagore's
Vishwabharati University. His doctoral dissertation at Columbia
was on *satyagraha*, entitled *War Without Violence*, which he published
in book form in1939. It was followed by another book in 1941
entitled *My India, My America*, which is a well-written, informative
socio-political disquisition on contemporary Indian politics and
society, the country's historical roots, and India's place in the world.
It enjoyed a reasonably wide distribution, and established him as
a serious spokesman for the nationalist cause. The author Louis
Bromfield, upon whose novel the famous movie, *The Rains Came*,
was based, wrote a very appreciative introduction to this book.
He declared:

> I suspect more rubbish has been thought, spoken and written
> about India than about any country in the world. There are a
> good many reasons for this. India has been exploited for nearly
> two hundred years by all sorts of individuals and organizations,
> from the East India Company to Madam Blavatsky and
> Katherine Mayo (Shridharani 1941: vii).

By contrast, he said, "For me, Shridharani has presented India
through the eyes of an Indian but in the idiom of an American,
and so the people in the book, their backgrounds, their customs,
their traditions, become human and real" (ibid.: xi).

What made Shridharani especially provocative was his belief that Gandhianism was not merely some kind of mystical cult, as many devotees both in the East and West treated it. He claimed that non-violent resistance was basically a technique for secular political action which did not require the accompanying "spiritualism" associated with it. The religious trappings, he said, were mainly there to satisfy Gandhi. He contrasted *satyagraha* with American pacifism. He claimed that, ironically, American pacifism is essentially religious and mystical, and consequently "passive," which indicated to him that the West can be as "unworldly" as the East. It was not pacifism which explained the Indian freedom movement but bloodless revolution, i.e., *collective action* of a particular kind *in this world*. It was political, not reclusive and effete. Shridharani based his politics on pushing this activist viewpoint both among his fellow South Asian revolutionaries and the American groups with whom he interacted. One of the most significant contacts he made was with James Farmer and the Congress of Racial Equality (CORE), where Shridharani's non-violent activism, shorn of mysticism and asceticism, rang a bell. "Unlike the asceticism and the piousness of the white pacifists, Shridharani's more human lifestyle (with drink, smoke and sexuality) appealed to the young Americans" (Prashad n.d.).

As for the British, Shridharani depicted them as White racists who feed on stereotypes of both themselves and their Indian subjects. They live in their posh ghettos on the outskirts of Indian towns ("civil lines") and on army posts ("cantonments") where the only Indians they deal with are servants and boot-lickers. They are the "White *Sahibs*." Most *Sahibs*, paraphrasing him, have a similar view of Indians: the Indians in their eyes are just stereotypes, such as the Indian servant and the dancing girl, the Hindu *swami*, the Pathan, the moneylender, the nationalist, the boot-licker—never human beings with distinctive personalities. To such *Sahibs*, the whole of India is a canvas on which can be depicted the exploits of the ruling race.

The point is that Shridharani's political orientation was by no means equivocal on issues of colonialism, yet at the level of action it remained within pragmatic parameters. The aim of this new breed of activists was to generate support from a broader spectrum of the American public than had proved to be possible with the more blatantly radical, at times quixotic, tactics employed by their

Illustration 8.4
Krishnalal Shridharani

*Source:* Mazumdar 1960.

predecessors. While they remained unequivocally anti-British and anti-colonialist, they modulated their political rhetoric to conform to what they believed would resonate with freedom-loving, middle-of-the road Americans. Their styles were not by any means identical. In Mazumdar's (1960: 28) words, "Hossain, Anup and I looked upon ourselves as crusaders for India's freedom first and as professional lecturers or writers second; Krishnalal looked upon himself as a professional writer or lecturer first and as a crusader for India's freedom second." What they all shared was a pragmatic, politically circumspect bent which Lala Lajpat Rai had imparted and which, in fact, even Taraknath Das and Sarangadhar Das, perhaps somewhat grudgingly, had come round to by the 1930s. What this comes down to is that the Gandhian impact on the freedom movement had become a pervasive force which gave greater coherence and legitimacy to the movement, which was lacking when it was dominated by strident, turn-of-the century Punjabi,

Maharashtrian and Bengali revolutionism. *Ghadr, Swaraj,* and *Swadeshi* had been superseded by *Ahimsa, Satyagraha,* and secularism. The latter were politically more palatable and comprehensible to middle-class Americans and the political establishment generally.

Anup Singh (1903–1969) was born a Sikh in Jhapal village, Lyallpur district, in the Punjab on March 5, 1903. He is said to have fled India as a political fugitive during the early days of the freedom movement and in the 1920s found his way to the United States. Following his arrival, he was able to enroll in the University of California. It is said that during this early phase of his career Anup was compelled for a time to live in a tent near the Berkeley campus in order to make ends meet. Eventually, however, Anup made his way across the country to New York and Washington with stops en route at the University of Kansas and Harvard University, where eventually he obtained his Ph.D. in political science.

He briefly returned to India, did not like the conditions he found there, and returned to America in the early 1930s. He developed a relationship with Haridas Mazumdar in New York. Mazumdar says, "At our first meeting ... he showed me his article on Gandhi and Nehru and asked me to advise him about the magazines that might publish it." After reading it and deciding it was well-written, Mazumdar put him in touch with *Asia Magazine,* which "immediately accepted the article; this was the beginning of a very fruitful relationship between Anup and Mr. Richard J. Walsh, editor of *Asia* and head of the John Day Publishing Company" (Mazumdar 1960: 27). In essence this was the real beginning of his career as a "Hindese" activist. Walsh induced Anup to write a monograph on Nehru which he saw as a prelude and companion piece to Jawaharlal's autobiography, which he was getting ready to publish. Singh's book came out in 1939 under the title *Nehru: The Rising Star of India,* and Nehru's autobiography followed in 1941 under the title *Toward Freedom.* Along with articles in *The Nation* and other publications, this established Anup Singh's bonafides as a recognized player in nationalist circles and simultaneously helped to make Nehru a household word in America. With these credentials, Anup Singh, "soon began to reinforce, on the public platform, the work that Hossain and I had been engaged in" (ibid.).

**Illustration 8.5**
**Anup Singh in America**

*Source:* Mazumdar 1960.

As we shall see, Anup became a very active participant in the affairs of the New York-based India League of America, especially after it had been transformed under J.J. Singh's leadership into a major publicity and lobbying force. He shifted to Washington, DC after J.J. diluted the League's leadership positions with prominent Americans. There, he resided in a facility called the Cairo Hotel, located at 16th Street and New Hampshire Avenue, from whence he conducted his publicist and lobbying activities. It was there that he founded The National Committee for India's Freedom, whose leadership positions pointedly consisted exclusively of Indians. Although an independent organization, and despite the personal differences between Anup and J.J., the National Committee nevertheless coordinated its activities in the nation's capital with the India League. Anup also founded the Research Bureau of the India League and served as its Director from 1937 to 1941.

The purpose of the latter was obviously to produce and make available information on the Indian nationalist movement to people in high places. One of its productions was entitled *India Facts in Brief*, which succinctly provided a wide range of data and information on India's economy, politics, and social conditions, along with a selected bibliography. He also published a monthly magazine called the *Voice of India*, which became an organ through which a wide range of Indian and American authors could express themselves on South Asian affairs.

Each of these four men became prime movers in the nationalist movement from the 1930s through to the end of World War II. They led peripatetic lives, moving about the United States and Canada as well as overseas, expounding the causes of Indian freedom and South Asian civil rights as their predecessors had done, as indeed in fact these predecessors, like Taraknath, Sarangadhar, Har Dayal, and Gobind Behari Lal, had paved the way for them for them to do. They produced a torrent of political literature which got widely distributed through the relationships they built with sections of the American media. They built institutions through which they could mobilize and coordinate the energy and talents of fellow Indians who were by now widely distributed throughout the country. Perhaps most important of all, they amplified the process of developing contacts in the political establishment, with members of Congress and other government officials, because in the last analysis it was access to the halls of power that mattered most. Clearly they profited from the accomplishments of those who had gone before them, but it was they who carried the process to its eventual, necessary culmination—viz., America's unequivocal acceptance of Indian independence, quotas for Indian immigrants and civil rights for Indian residents.

Three or four times a year, J.J. Singh, Syud Hossain (who also increasingly came to center his activities in Washington) and Anup, under the auspices of the India League of America and/or the National Committee for Indian Independence, would hold "public debates" in prominent places in the city, announcing them in half-page newspaper advertisements. These debates featured journalists like I.F. Stone, members of the US Congress, and other notables opposing Great Britain's alleged political repression of the Indian people. This medium gave them a setting where they could refute

British claims that the Indian nationalists were mindlessly imped-ing the Allied struggle against fascism. Syud Hossein, for example, would arm himself with factual details on the Cripps Mission, obtained from moles on the Indian High Commissioner's staff, which purportedly showed that Churchillian duplicity had sabo-taged the attempt by the Indian National Congress to reconcile their differences with the Raj and establish an honorable basis upon which the Indian people could participate in the war.

Events such as these reinforced the nationalists' overall modus operandi, viz., to generate as much publicity, particularly press coverage, as possible for the causes of Indian freedom and human rights. Through journalistic contacts, they would generate headline stories stating, for example, that Sirdar J.J. Singh, President of the India League of America, had journeyed to Capitol Hill to confer with members of the US Congress on matters pertaining to Indian immigration rights and India's political plight under the British Raj. Accompanying such stories would be an announcement of a press conference for, say, 4 pm at the Mayflower Hotel, which invariably featured at least one member of the US Congress or some other notable, along with a full buffet of food and drink in order to attract as wide a spectrum of journalists and politicians as possible, who would then hopefully go forth and further public-ize the nationalist cause and the plight of Indian immigrants.

As an illustration of how fragile public understanding of India was in those days, there is the story of one senator from a Western state, probably Pat McCarren (1876–1954) of Nevada, whose pre-sence at these events was avidly sought because "he always had something very courtly and very vague to say about India" (Anonymous informant). The problem, however, was that at times this senator would use the phrase "American Indians" instead of "Indian-Americans," indicating that he was probably not clear in his own mind whether he was referring to native Americans (who were abundant in his state) or South Asian Indians (most of whom lived in California)!

This brings us to Sirdar Jagjit Singh, known publicly as J.J. Singh, who emerged to become the maestro of the final phase of the India Lobby's trek through American history. He was born on October 5, 1897 in Rawalpindi, now in Pakistan. His father, Sardar Roop Singh, served all his life as a civil servant in the Northwest Frontier Province and retired as Extra-Assistant Commissioner, "the highest executive post attainable by an Indian in those days in the NWFP" (Singh 1997).[7]

In 1917, J.J. left school and joined the Congress movement. He organized the first Congress Committee in Hazara district and went on to get elected to the Punjab Provincial Congress Committee in 1918. However, he quit the Congress in 1923 after Gandhi suspended his *Satyagraha* (specifically the no-tax campaign in Bardoli) due to the mob-indiscipline which resulted in 22 policemen being killed at Chowri Chaura in the United Provinces. In 1924, Singh emigrated from India to study law in London. At that time the British Empire Exposition at Wembley was taking place, which King George V opened on St. George's Day (April 23). The Empire Stadium, subsequently known as Wembley Stadium, the home of British football, was a by-product of this event. In July and August, "it was the setting for the British Empire Exhibition's Pageant of Empire ... a spectacular illustration of the history of the British Empire with a cast of 15,000." J.J. Singh was induced to participate in a business venture in connection with the exposition and this diverted him for the rest of his life into the business world. This first venture into entrepreneurship proved to be successful and he never looked back. However, although he strayed for a few years, he never forsook his identification with the cause of Indian independence. You might say that, ultimately, J.J. mixed business with patriotism!

Success in London led to migration to America in 1926. Singh and his London associates were invited to come to the Philadelphia Sesquicentennial and exhibit Indian silks, handlooms, artifacts, and art objects. The undertaking was a financial disaster and the entrepreneurs lost their shirts. J.J. briefly recouped some of his losses but suffered another setback when the Great Depression hit in 1929. He returned to India to discuss his situation with "some of his earlier associates who were now influential people." They advised him to return to the US and establish an organization that would promote bilateral trade between the two countries. He seems to have sat on this idea for the next decade and in the meantime spent his time building up his own business in New York City. Then, late in the 1930s his life changed again.

Jagjit's existence in the hurly-burly commercial environment of New York City yielded a very different persona from that which was characteristic of virtually all of the other Indians who were active in the political arena. One has to say that, whatever their not inconsiderable talents, they were fairly conventional people, conventional products of the their Indian socio-political environment. J.J. Singh was a departure from the norm. His immersion in the economic life of America's most commercially dynamic city and in its cosmopolitan lifestyle transformed him into a suave, highly Westernized Indian, an "unshorn Sikh," who mastered the art of fitting into the social and political mainstream.

The renowned journalist, Robert Shaplen, did a definitive profile of J.J. in 1951 for *New Yorker Magazine*, entitled, "One-Man Lobby." He later wrote a compelling book on the emerging conflict in Southeast Asia which culminated in the Vietnam War (Shaplen 1969). He characterized Singh: "As a living refutation of Kipling's never-the-twain shall meet thesis; he eclectically embraces India and the United States with equal and unflagging devotion." Years ago, J.J. "discarded his sectarian turban, beard and long hair held up by a comb for the Occidental conceits of a black Homburg, a daily shave, and periodic visits to his barber." His shop at 14 East 56th Street, called India Arts and Crafts dealt in "luxurious Indian silks and cottons, and ... numbers among its steady customers some of the more or less well-known individuals Singh encountered in his earlier, self-described 'play-boy days', before he renounced dancing, bridge, and fancy-dress parties for the relatively sedate life of an evangel of Freedom for India." For the first 10 years that he lived in America, Singh admitted, he lived the life of what in India is called an *ayyashi* (hedonist). Shaplen (ibid.) says, "During the first ten years ... his main interest in life, aside from his business, was having a good time, with many of what he considered the best people as possible. It included some of New York's better-publicized hostesses ... whose debutante daughters he took dancing."

The year before J.J. really got politically involved, the India League of America, originally created by Lajpat Rai, had, after languishing for several years, been resuscitated. Its meetings were held in the Ceylon-India Inn, at 148 West 49th Street, then the only Indian restaurant in New York, and were presided over by the conventional run of Indian patriots and intellectuals. According to Malti Singh, J.J.'s widow, "the evenings would be reverently devoted to reading from the works of Rabindranath Tagore, or some other poet, author or philosopher." What is more, "The intellectuals who ran these rather somber gatherings looked down on the businessmen in their midst" (Singh 1997).

In his later incarnation as a political activist, J.J. placed his business side somewhat on hold, leaving it in the capable hands of Ms Suzanne Goutel, who was once a buyer for Best's. By the 1940s, Shaplen could say of him, "He rarely goes out to greet a customer himself unless it is some old friend who has traded with him for years, such as Leopold Stokowski, Greer Garson, Mrs. Wendell Willkie, Mrs. John Hay Whitney, Charles Laughton, or Laughton's wife, Elsa Lanchester." By arranging his affairs in this fashion, it became possible for him "to assume a fairly cavalier attitude toward commerce." In his own words, "I am not avaricious where money is concerned ... I gave up the idea of becoming rich when I decided to devote myself to public life."[8] The upshot, of course, is that all this provides an insight into the scope of the social skills he developed and the networks he established, which would stand him in good stead in his new role as a publicist and lobbyist.

Basically, J.J. Singh gained control of the India League of America and made it, along with the Indian Chamber of Commerce, the focal point of a lobbying machine which took the lead in projecting the South Asian message in Washington, New York and indeed throughout the country. It impacted heavily on the actions of Syud Hossain, Anup Singh, Haridas Mazumdar, Krishnalal Shridharani and many of the other, lesser-known nationalists, even though they were not at all times of like mind. Even older players like Har Dayal, Taraknath, and Sarangadhar felt his effect to the extent that they remained in the game.

The turning point for J.J. Singh came between 1935 and 1937. Shaplen (1951)[9] says two events produced an "Augustinian change" in him. The first were the free elections that were held under the new Constitution which had been adopted in 1935, known as the Government of India Act. In those elections, held in 1937, the Congress party emerged triumphant in 11 provinces and took control of the legislative assemblies in them. The second event was the publication of Nehru's autobiography, *Toward Freedom*. Shaplen says that J.J. was so moved by the book that "he wrote to Nehru about having it published in America." He sent a copy to President Roosevelt through "my good friend Jimmy Roosevelt" (FDR's son). How much credit for getting the autobiography published should go to J.J. or to Anup Singh remains an open question. But the point is that Richard Walsh, the owner of John Day Publishers, did indeed produce an American edition.

When Singh returned to India for a home visit, he met with many old friends and prominent Congress leaders, including, of course, Jawaharlal Nehru. Now committed to actively serving the cause, J.J. asked for guidance. He was urged by Nehru, as had happened with Haridas Mazumdar before him, to return to America and employ his considerable means and skills to promote bilateral trade between India and the United States. He was told to establish an India Chamber of Commerce, which he did. One suspects that this might have been a bit of a put-down, because it suggests that the highly intellectual Nehru did not see J.J., a mere businessman, as being in the same league with the movement's *corps d'élite*. But J.J. wanted to do more. Singh found that "the dull commercial dickering involved failed to satisfy his newly resurgent revolutionary spirit." So he returned to India once more for further discussions about his political role. This time he got Nehru's "unofficial blessing as the man to stir up support in this country for India's fight for independence."

When he returned to New York, J.J. Singh struck! One night in 1939, he showed up at the Ceylon-India Inn, "at one of those sleepy, sporadic meetings in New York of the India League ... whose active membership had dwindled to twelve." The following passage from Shaplen's narrative nicely captures the flavor of the moment.

> Singh listened to the expression of lofty thoughts for a while and then *proposed that the League pay less attention to culture and philosophy and more to politics and propaganda.* He also proposed that the League abandon its policy of restricting its membership to Indians and that it set about corralling some prominent American members. The intellectuals, regarding Singh as a shallow fellow who had never known his Bhagavad-Gita and who was at best a sparkling social phenomenon, looked upon his proposal to sell Indian nationalism by methods similar to those he employed to sell saris as fantastically gross (Shaplen 1951, emphasis added).

A donnybrook of sorts ensued and J.J. ultimately won the day. Those who could not accept the new dispensation distanced themselves from the League in its new incarnation and found alternative places to hang their political hats. As already noted, Anup Singh and Syud Hossain, while they did not dissociate themselves completely from the League, acted out their ambivalence by moving their act to Washington, DC. This was the context in which they established the National Committee for Indian Independence. While allied with the League, this organization was more congenial to their intellectual and cultural style. They all held doctoral degrees and were immersed in the intellectual life to a far greater degree than was J.J. They thought of themselves as more "Indian" than he. However, as is attested by Haridas Mazumdar, there was by no means a complete rupture between the factions. After all, they needed each other despite their differences. Haridas says that Anup Singh actually continued to work with J.J. in the League, providing "editorial direction" for their monthly publication, *India Abroad*, "with the aid of Madam [Hilda Wierum] Boulter." A close relationship had developed between Madam Boulter and Anup, which would have some unpleasant repercussions a few years down the road (Mazumdar 1960: 44–45).[10]

Now that he had committed himself to becoming its shepherd, J.J. Singh was elected president of the India League in 1939. Before we discuss further the transformation that took place in the League and the activities of the National Committee in Washington, however, we should look at two other organizations that were established at this time which also were factors in the political process that was developing as World War II loomed on the horizon. In part they reflected some of the factional differentiation that was taking place; while in part they reflected the escalating demographic scale of political mobilization. There was even an ethnic tinge to some of the organizational spin-offs. It stemmed from the fact that so many Indians did not approve of opening up membership of the India League to Americans. The fact Americans were accepted not only as members but even as office-holders in the organization particularly rubbed some Indians the wrong way. One could call this a manifestation of old-fashioned Indian "caste-ism," or just plain "reverse white-ism." The redeeming aspect is that this never became serious enough to detract from the overall mission of the lobbying coalitions that formed. Consensual politics had come to stay.

The positive side, in fact, is that these spin-offs reflected the degree to which it identified persons who wanted to make sure that a sharp focus would remain on immigration issues—i.e., that there be no forgetting that the racist ramifications of the *Thind* decision had never really been resolved; and that public attention not be allowed to fixate exclusively on the freedom struggle in India. Even J.J. Singh was cognizant of this matter. He was, after all, a Sikh himself, albeit a highly secularized one, and relied on the moral and material support of the West Coast Sikh community. He never ceased employing the resources of the League as well as his interpersonal capabilities to actively lobby for immigrant rights along with Indian independence.

There were three groups who entered the picture in this regard. One was the India Welfare League founded by Mubarak Ali Khan. Another was the Indian Association for American Citizenship, founded in Chicago by N.R. Checher, a businessman who had once been president of the India League before J.J. Singh took it over. Finally, there was the Indian National Congress Association on the West Coast, created by Dalip Singh Saund (1899–1973), who would one day become the first Indian to serve in the US Congress.[11] These organizations acted as a reminder that there was a grassroots constituency out there whose interests lay in achieving the hard currency of citizenship rights and immigration quotas, and not merely in philosophical abstractions about non-violence, the glories of Indian civilization and the evils of colonialism.

With the outbreak of World War II in 1939, followed by the Japanese attack on Pearl Harbor on December 7, 1941, the India League and its extensions faced a host of new challenges. This is the point where the Congress Movement embarked on a collision course with Great Britain's determination to have a free hand in using India's strategic resources to prosecute the war against the Axis powers. The progress achieved toward representative government under the 1935 Act and the 1937 elections was wiped out when negotiations between the Government of India and the nationalists over what role the latter would be allowed to play in the war's decision-making process could not be resolved. Gandhi then initiated the Quit India *satyagraha* after the 1942 Cripps Mission failed (despite American prodding), and Gandhi, Nehru and other Indian leaders were arrested and incarcerated without due process for the remainder of World War II. It was from this point on—with America's own strategic situation directly affected by political conditions in India, and with the resulting new political atmosphere which this evoked in Washington—that the South Asian activists significantly escalated their lobbying and propaganda effort. J.J. and his cohorts rightly perceived that here lay a golden opportunity to get the United States government more directly committed to Indian independence following the war, getting the American public more conscious of the plight of the Indian people under colonialism, and eliminating the racist immigration policies which left resident Indians in America unprotected by the constitutional guarantees that should be theirs, and which prevented Indians from legally migrating to this country.

These were the issues which J.J. Singh and his cohorts felt compelled to place at the center of their political agenda from Pearl Harbor on. They followed the permutations of the Cripps Mission and the circumstances leading up to it, particularly the American role in events; and they organized rallies and public meetings to publicize the nationalist version of why it failed. They denounced the puppet diplomacy which underlay Sir Girja Shankar Bajpai's role as India's first quasi-ambassador (i.e., Agent-General), in response, as we saw, to American urgings that the Indian people be accorded direct diplomatic representation in Washington. They employed the various publications which the India League and the National Committee for Indian Independence created to widely disseminate their message. They strongly endorsed Roosevelt's decision to send William Phillips as his personal emissary to India with de facto ambassadorial status as well as other actions which enhanced the visibility and relevance of India to the American public. And, of course, in 1943, they exulted in Drew Pearson's revelation of William Phillips's sensational final memo to President Roosevelt. They solicited and publicized support for Indian independence and human rights from noted journalists, religious figures, academics, and politicians across the country. Most of all, however, with J.J. Singh's personal flair for cultivating members of the power elite, the major emphasis was placed on directly and indirectly lobbying the US Congress.

Robert Shaplen provides the most detailed and vivid picture of how J.J. operated. Shaplen depicted him as "always elegantly set off by neatly tailored two hundred dollar suits [which] has frequently helped him gain access to cloistered places and to command an audience with their occupants once he gets there." He describes an incident with the *New York Times* in 1942, when J.J. strode into the office of its managing editor, Edwin L. James, and denounced the paper for not covering a League meeting held the previous evening which the *Herald Tribune* had covered. "James called a reporter, and the next morning the *Times* printed a long interview with the president of the India League that more than made up for the oversight."

In another instance, J.J. succeeded in enlisting media support from the famous, or should we say infamous, William Randolph Hearst. This occurred as a by-product of Singh's injunction to the India League that speeding the course toward Indian freedom would require "influencing the influencers." To accomplish this, he declared, the League's "principal objective should be to convince Americans that the Indians would put up a real fight for the Allies only in return for Britain's promise of freedom." This would require getting after the columnists, the radio commentators, and the rest of the "blah blah people who make public opinion ...."

When Hearst stated in one of his columns that the British should grant independence to the Indians, Singh wrote him a letter of thanks, "which so impressed the publisher that he used it as the basis for a second column on the subject and asked Singh for more." With his instinctive media savvy, Singh "quickly adapted himself to the peculiar chest-thumping, boldface-caps San Simeon style." He spoke of "the blood-stained claws of the Japanese," and sounded dire warnings about America's "duty to herself and the cause of democracy to make the British yield."

"Singh invaded Washington," said Shaplen. The wife of a Washington-based journalist, whom "Singh had met personally," convinced him that the way to make mass press conferences successful, i.e., newsworthy, was to spice them up with "spot news." He describes one of those press conferences which was held at the venerable Willard Hotel on Pennsylvania Avenue which was completely renovated just a few years ago and once again functions as a showplace for the politically *chic*.

He declared that he had "received 'secret information' that the British were ready to quit India and that the Japanese were about to invade that country with Burmese and dissident Indian troops." Image was everything in this performance: "His dashing appearance, the passionate note of sincerity in his voice, and, above all, the fact that he was something new under the Washington sun were effective." Soon, declares Shaplen, "people were asking each other over cocktails, 'Have you seen this Indian yet, J.J. Singh?'"

Lobbying on the Hill was his forte. He was reinforced in this respect by Anup Singh, Syud Hossain, Haridas Mazumdar, Krishnalal Shridharani and even Taraknath Das, who also worked hard and coordinated with him on developing congressional contacts. J.J.'s ability to be in the right place at the right time and to take advantage of opportunities when they presented themselves is illustrated by Shaplen's account of how he corralled Henry and Clare Booth Luce into his network of influence. Henry Luce was, of course, the publisher of *Time* and *Life* magazines; his wife, Clair Booth, was a glamorous woman, a socialite, and a highly successful playwright, who in 1942 won election to the House of Representatives from the Fourth Congressional District in Connecticut and was re-elected in 1944. She and J.J. Singh had become acquainted in the course of their public and social lives in New York and Washington. Singh related to Shaplen how he had been a weekend guest at their Greenwich, Connecticut, estate shortly after Mrs Luce had returned from a trip to India which J.J. had arranged for her. In the course of that weekend, Singh had predicted that the British were about to imprison Nehru. When his March 1942 prediction came true in August 1942, the Luces were deeply impressed. J.J. wired Henry Luce, saying "I won't say told you so," and, striking while the iron was hot, followed this with, "But now I need your help." He asked Luce for *Time's* support, and got it. *Time* came out with a cover story on Nehru!

Informants have said that the relationship between J.J. and Clair Booth Luce became extremely close, implying some measure of intimacy. The setting may have been a mansion called "Castle Rock," situated in the Maryland suburbs of Washington. It had been engaged by a very well-heeled Indian businessman named K.C. Mahendra, of the Bombay import–export firm of Mahendra and Mahendra, who had come to Washington as a member of the India Supply Mission, an organization whose purpose was to expedite the flow of strategic supplies to India. Mahendra was a very determined and outspoken Indian patriot who gladly did all in his power to help the lobbyists by feeding them classified information from the Agent-General's office—behind Sir Girja's back, of course.

Castle Rock became a social headquarters for the India Lobby throughout the war years. With J.J. Singh as the principal attraction, weekend soirees of various kinds were held there, to which the elite of Washington political, government, journalist, and academic society were invited. There was good food and plenty of drink, dancing and even a little gambling on the weekends. It was here that some of the better-known heterosexual liaisons, including J.J.'s with Mrs Luce, often took place. As one of my informants put it, "at the beautiful mansion across the river, she and J.J. were often seen as being closer together than was purely social." Singh himself commented that "Clare could provide access on many issues ...." It was also valuable, he said, because she could persuade her husband, Henry, who inclined toward Anglophilia, to go easier on Gandhi and the other Indian nationalists in *Time* than he might otherwise have been inclined to do.

Another example of J.J. Singh's lobbying proclivities pertains to the role he played in getting an amendment passed to the 1924 Immigration Act which ended total exclusion and established a quota of 100 Indians per year. It was a two-year effort which paid immense dividends. Singh acquired staunch allies in this quest. One was Clair Booth Luce; the other was Congressman Emanuel Celler (1888–1981) from Brooklyn who served for almost 50 years in the House. Because he was Jewish and acutely aware of the fate of European Jewry, Celler manifested strong sympathy for minority rights. "Celler acted as Singh's mentor," says Shaplen. Celler said, "He never made a nuisance of himself." Yet, J.J. "covered miles in Congressional hallways."

This in itself shows how successfully he had mastered the lobbying arts! Because this is what successful lobbyists had to do then, and must still do. "As time went on, Singh grew to enjoy winning over a senator or a representative as much as dancing attendance on a debutante, and to be equally adept at it." Singh himself told Shaplen the story of how he won the respect and a modicum of support from a "salty-tongued" southern senator on a piece of legislation he championed. It is not made clear whether the specific piece of legislation was the Immigration Amendment or something else. This was a legislator whom the president himself had been unsuccessful in persuading. "I set up the usual pressure tactics," J.J. declared. He got church groups in his native state to write letters. The senator had several times refused to see him:

Along about the sixth time I called ... the pressure [had] started to show, and, sure enough, he said he'd see me. So I walked in. He gets up and shakes hands with me. "Sit down Mr. Singh," he says. He looks me in the eye and says, "I'm against your bill." Now, I say to myself, he's a straightforward guy. I look him in the eye and say, "Senator, you're the kind of guy I like. I like a man who shoots straight from the shoulder." Within ten minutes, we're getting along famously. He says to me, "You know I'm going to do my damnedest to beat this bill," and I say, "And I am going to do my damnedest, Senator, to get it through." So I tell him, "Senator, you're a fair man and a strong man. At least give me a chance. Unless you, as chairman, call up your committee, how can I have a chance to beat you?" He looks back at me and says, "Damn it, Singh, I'll bring the bill before the committee." I didn't waste any time after that, because I knew I had the committee with me, three to two.

Although characterized by the press and many members of Congress as a "one-man lobby," J.J. was in reality just the leading figure among what had become a mobilized group of lobbyists, publicists and propagandists who had acquired considerable savvy about representing various South Asian interests both in the United States and in India. The India League of America had drawn a wide range of Indians and Americans from all walks of political life into the fray, as had the National Committee for Indian Freedom. As the war years wore on, both organizations were able to raise sufficient funds to stage public events, pay the expenses of their operatives, enable Indian political figures visiting from India to go on lecture tours, etc. Particularly effective as far as the intellectual and journalistic communities were concerned were their connections with publishers like pacifist Oswald Garrison Villard (editor of the *New York Post*) and Richard J. Walsh (John Day Publishing Company), B.W. Huebsch (Viking Press), and the liberal monthly magazines like the *New Republic* and the *Nation*, which provided outlets for books and articles presenting the nationalist perspective and, especially crucial after America entered the war, countering a massive propaganda campaign waged by the British government and the Government of India, both from London and New Delhi as well as from the British Embassy and the Agent-General's office in Washington.

Particularly important were the monthly magazines, *India Today*, published out of New York from 1940 by the Indian League, and *The Voice of India*, published out of Washington by the National Committee for Indian Independence from 1943 to 1947 by Anup Singh (in collaboration with Syud Hossain).[12] In the context of the times, these were remarkable publications which covered an enormous range of cultural and political subject matter. At one time or another almost anybody connected with the Indian freedom movement had their say in their pages. In addition to regular articles and news items about the comings and goings of just about anyone who ever had anything to do with India, they also published book reviews which kept readers abreast of the good, the bad and the ugly among works dealing with South Asian subject matter. Most reviews were written, as noted, by Madam Hilda Wierum Boulter, the enigmatic New York widow who had grown particularly close to Anup Singh. An example of her critical style is to be found in a review she did of a book by Beverley Nichols entitled *Verdict on India*. Nichols was a well-known apologist and propagandist for the British Raj, one who was widely employed to go about America disparaging Gandhi, Nehru and the Indian National Congress. Boulter likened his "manner" to that of Kathleen Mayo, author of the notorious book *Mother India*. She accused him of trotting out "the customary list of the faults of Indian society and the Indian people which alone, according to him, prevent India's freedom." She tartly concluded that "In attempting to pass a verdict on India, Mr. Nichols has unconsciously passed a hardly complementary verdict on himself" (*Voice of India*, January 1945, p. 70).

Boulter herself wrote an extensive article for *Modern Review* (July 1943) describing the activities and the accomplishments of the various organizations, groups and individuals who by the 1940s were at work throughout the country. Speaking of the India League, she emphasized its cosmopolitan character; its mixture of Indian and American members; and the many "prominent Americans" on its advisory board. She asserted that its monthly magazine, *India Today*, had grown from "small beginnings ... until it is now recognized by Universities, Public Libraries, and such sections of the Press and Radio as are at all open-minded, as the best source of authoritative news from India." She noted the existence of a Bureau of Research, directed by Dr Anup Singh, which, of course, indicates that there was collaboration occurring between the League and the National Committee despite the intellectual and tactical differences between their leaders. "Every day," said Ms Boulter, "this Bureau receives inquiries of all sorts, from all possible sources, for every conceivable variety of information on India—her culture, her customs, her geography, her natural resources, her industrial development, her history and, above all, her politics."

Boulter makes it clear that the League was from its inception a more broadly structured organization than was the National Committee. This is an interesting observation in the light of the fact that many of the cultural and political purists in the Indian community opted out of the League after J.J. Singh assumed control of it, and joined the National Committee or other groups because they regarded him as some sort of Philistine. J.J., in fact, did nothing to sully the Indian image. Since its earliest days, Boulter declared, the League "has sponsored exhibitions of the works of Indian artists, and recitals of Indian music and dance." Moreover, "It holds annual meetings on the occasion of the birthdays of Gandhi and Tagore and on the Indian Independence Day." With New York being a far more culturally and ethnically diversified, and indeed more cosmopolitan city than Washington, especially in those days, this made perfect sense. Boulter conceded that at first such gatherings attracted small audiences, but in time they took off, as public consciousness of India grew. This came about especially after Pearl Harbor, with the US Government's now having a strategic, and not merely a sentimental, interest in wanting to see a political solution between the British and the incarcerated Indian nationalists. India had become a vital staging zone for what was called the China-Burma-India (CBI) theater of war, which was simultaneously fighting the Japanese in Southeast Asia and funneling supplies to Chiang Kai Shek by air "over the Hump" and by land up the Ledo Road. Americans were therefore more conscious of India than ever before, and the India Lobby had more infrastructural resources available than ever before to take advantage of this fact.

An illustration of how far the movement had proceeded was attested by the turnout for an Indian Independence Day Dinner on January 26, 1943, held at New York's Biltmore Hotel. Over 700 persons came! The speakers included Pearl Buck, William L. Shirer, and John Gunther, as well as the usual array of Indian notables. Boulter speaks of meetings held in conjunction with the East-West Association (founded by Pearl Buck) at Town Hall, New York, a famous forum for public debates. At this event Norman Thomas and Anup Singh took the positive side while Bertrand Russell and H.L. Pollard took the negative side. She mentions a full-page ad taken out in the *New York Times* sponsored by the India League, containing the signatures of forty prominent Americans urging the British to grant India her independence. Perhaps most important of all, Boulter speaks of "great meetings" being held in Washington, Detroit, Chicago, Boston, and other cities "at which speakers from the India League have appeared. "One could cover pages merely by listing these meetings, great and small, and the speakers' names." The networks were rapidly expanding!

## Notes

1. Others included: *Spiritual; Science Marriage Ceremonial; Radiant Road to Reality: Tested Science of Religion; Jesus, The Christ, in the Light of Spiritual Science*, or *Sant-Mat, The Most Precious Patrimony and Most Glorious Heritage of the Sikhs of India for Mankind; Science of Union with God, Here and Now; House of Happiness; The Pearl of Greatest Price*, or *Nam-Rattan*.
2. The specific references to this and related correspondence may be found in footnotes 7 and 8 of Chapter 11 of Jensen's excellent work (1988: 322).
3. The late 1920s to the early 1930s were especially tumultuous years in Indian politics. It was a time when the Congress party was in the process of becoming a mass-based movement that was reaching into almost every corner of Indian society. Gandhi's impact was a decisive factor in this transformation, because it was he who had crafted the symbols and strategies which were making it possible. It was he who had crafted what Morris-Jones called the "saintly politics" which had given Congress its mass bass by conjoining the urban middle-class with the agrarian peasantry. In Morris-Jones's words, "When Gandhi emerged into prominence ... he did so by an act of political invention which at once amply met the needs of a new and insistently Indian generation and was later to present itself as a universally valid challenge of 'orthodox' politics" (1964: 28). The party's non-violent tactics on a national scope presented a major challenge to British suzerainty which clearly threw the Raj off guard and compelled it to grope for some mixture of violence and conciliation in its efforts to remain in power. The viceroy responsible for coping with the new politics was Lord Irwin, who as British Ambassador to the US under the title of Lord Halifax, was during World War II destined to face the India Lobby, which

ironically was in many respects an overseas extension of the turmoil which had confronted him a decade earlier in India.

Trouble began in India when Mahatma Gandhi, who had become temporarily estranged from the Congress leadership over tactical issues, returned to the fold at an All-Parties Conference convened in 1928 in the wake of great discontent over the fact that the Simon Commission, which the British had created to determine India's political future, included not a single Indian. This, as Smith et al. (1958: 794) assert, "cast a slur on the ability of Indians in political matters, to flout the idea of a round table conference, and by emphasizing parliamentary control of Indian affairs, to challenge the right of Indians to work out their own destiny."

This was the opening Gandhi had been hoping for. It enabled him to "re-radicalize" the Congress movement, first by inducing the party to demand immediate dominion status for India, and a round table conference to ratify the commitment and work out the details. In 1929, when this was refused, he launched his famous "Salt March" from Sabarmati to Dandi. The effect was to consolidate Indian resistance to British rule as never before and impelled them to convene two sessions of the Round Table Conference that took place on and off between January and March 1931. Although dominion status was not achieved, the conference which included face-to-face dialogs between Lord Irwin and Mahatma Gandhi, led to the so-called Gandhi–Irwin truce. The outcome was the abandonment of civil disobedience, the release of all political prisoners, and Congress attendance at the Second Round Table Conference in London. Another civil disobedience movement followed when Gandhi was arrested upon his return from London in 1932. This renewal of direct action proved less effective than its predecessor, but it is agreed that in its entirety this period of confrontation between the Raj and the nationalists paved the way for the Government of India Act of 1935.

4. One of the few living mainstream academics who has recollections of Taraknath Das based upon personal contact with him is Professor (Ret.) Ainslie Embree, who was in those days on the History faculty of Columbia University. He actually attended a few of Taraknath's lectures on *Modern Asia*, and found him to still be a very strident critic of British colonialism. I am indebted to Professor Embree for this personal insight, and for many other ways in which he has provided help and guidance with this study.

5. The *Voice of India* was the monthly magazine established by Anup Singh as the propaganda organ of the National Committee for Indian Independence, which he established in Washington, DC, following his parting of the ways with J.J. Singh and the India League of America.

6. Gobind Behari Lal's career carried him a long way. He outlived most of his contemporaries: born in 1890, he passed away in 1982 at the age of 92. He was associated with the Hearst newspaper empire as science writer and editor from 1925 until his death. He shared a 1937 Pulitzer Prize for distinguished reporting with Howard W. Blakeslee of the *Associated Press*, William L. Lawrence of the *New York Times*, John J. O'Neil of the *New York Herald Tribune*, and David Dietze of the *Scripps–Howard* newspapers. In the words of his *New York Times* obituary, "Mr. Lal interviewed some of the most distinguished scientific, literary and political figures of the twentieth century, including

Albert Einstein, Mohandas K. Gandhi, Sherwood Anderson, Sinclair Lewis, H. L. Mencken, Edna St. Vincent Millay and Enrico Fermi" (*New York Times*, Saturday, April 3, 1982).

7. Malti Singh is the latter-day wife and widow of J.J. Singh, who remained a bachelor throughout his American years.

8. I can personally attest to the fact that J.J. did not allow his idealism to plunge him into abject poverty. By an embarrassing mischance, I once found myself in his palatial residence in South Delhi in the mid-1970s, not long before he passed away. In those days, I knew almost nothing about his American period. I was attempting to make contact with the veteran Congress socialist, Jayprakash Narayan who, I was told, was staying at J.J.'s as a house guest. Impulsively, without making prior arrangements, I engaged a taxi and was driven to his residence, believing that as a research scholar I might be allowed to meet and interview him. A servant, assuming I must a person of substance, let me in, and ushered me to the sitting room. A very embarrassing encounter ensued with a person whom I believe, in retrospect, was his young wife, Malti, whom he had married following his return to India. I was served tea and politely questioned about my purpose in coming unannounced to their place. My explanation proved to be an unsatisfactory basis for being allowed to meet either J.J. or Jayprakash, and so a taxi was summoned to return me, tail between my legs, from whence I had come.

9. Page numbers are illegible due to the condition of the manuscript. With regard to the grassroots electoral process in India in those and subsequent times, see Gould (1994).

10. Madam Hilda Wierum Boulter was another of those American women who, like Agnes Smedley, became enamored of the Indian way of life through her association with South Asian political activists. She was a widow, whose closest personal tie seems to have been with Anup Singh. This apparently included some measure of romantic involvement, even though, like Har Dayal before him, Anup had a wife in India (Shrimati Iqbal Kaur) to whom he had been married since July 1921. Madam Boulter was allegedly not aware of this and expected to accompany him back to India once his American sojourn ended. Madam Boulter acquired quite a lot of familiarity with India and identified with its culture and civilization as well as with the freedom movement. She wrote book reviews for both *India Today* and the *Voice of India*, and occasional brief articles for these and other publications. In the April–May 1947 edition of *Voice of India*, there was an announcement that Madam Boulter was leaving for India on June 12, 1947, "to collect material for another book." There was also a headline story, "MRS BOULTER TO INDIA," which read:

> We take this opportunity of expressing our profound appreciation of the work that Mrs. Hilda Wierum Boulter has been doing for the cause of India, first through the India League of America, and after through the National Committee for India's Freedom. She has been of immense help to the *Voice of India*.

Private informants say that this was her swansong with the India Lobby and that she believed she would join Anup Singh in India on a permanent basis.

When she reached India, it is alleged, she then discovered that Anup had a wife and family and was not in a position to be with her. Boulter's daughter (from her prior marriage) told an informant that her mother returned to America a deeply saddened woman.

11. Dalip Singh Saund was born in Amritsar on September 20, 1899, educated in boarding schools and at Punjab University. He came to the United States in 1922 to attend the University of California, and obtained M.A. and Ph.D. degrees. He became a lettuce farmer in the Imperial Valley (1930–1953) and a citizen of the US in 1949. He was a delegate to Democratic National Conventions in 1952, 1956, and 1960; and was elected as a Democrat to the US House of Representatives in the 85th, 86th, and 87th Congresses (January 3, 1957 to January 3, 1963)

12. Hossain shifted to Los Angeles and took up a chair at Southern California University. After this he "commuted" to Washington and New York.

# 9 | The Propaganda Wars

The networks were indeed sorely needed, not only to cope with the customary range of South Asian human rights issues and the Indian freedom movement in general, but also to parry and refute a mounting torrent of propaganda which the British and Indian governments targeted directly at the American people and whose purpose was to confuse issues by discrediting and denigrating the Indian National Congress and its leaders. Their alleged sin, of course, was their demand for political autonomy in exchange for cooperation in the war effort. Otherwise, Gandhi declared, there could be no cooperation, and the British must quit India at once. His edict was pronounced on August 9, 1942, after the failure of the Cripps Mission. Gandhi had rendered his judgment on the moral qualifications of the British to wage war in the name of democracy three months before his "Quit India" pronouncement: "They [the British] have no right to talk about protecting Democracy and protecting civilization and human freedom unless the canker of white superiority is destroyed in its entirety" (*Harijan*, May 24, 1942, p. 168). The British answer had been to outlaw the Congress Party and indefinitely confine its leaders, from Gandhi and Nehru on down, in jail. At one point, after the failure of the Cripps Mission, according to Venkatraman and Srivastava (1979: 289), the Assistant Secretary of State Adolph Berle concluded that "it was evident ... that the British did not want to solve the Indian problem and, as the tide of war turned in their favor, they might become even more stubborn."

It was especially from this point onwards that the Imperial propaganda machine shifted into high gear. In his *Confidential Dispatches, 1935–1945*, Lord Halifax, previously an Indian viceroy himself from 1926 to 1931 (as Lord Irwin) and now British Ambassador to the United States, laid out the British rationale for dealing with the nationalists: "The aim of British publicity in the United States has been to maintain before the public a clear picture (*sic*) of the British, both in their war effort and in their domestic affairs, as an advanced society of democratic peoples and an ally whose strength will be no less vital in the peace to come than it is in the partnership of war." He went on to point out that the present modus operandi was gradually taking shape from 1942, "with the policy-making center at the Embassy in Washington, the main center of operations in New York, and branch offices in Washington, Chicago and San Francisco." He added that their consular offices throughout the United States "were progressively organized for publicity purposes, and as their number increased, a growing network of information centers was established throughout the country" (Halifax 1974: 66).

Implying that the foregoing institutions were expected to engage in "discrete", low-key manipulations, the British Information Service was designated to make its approach

> *openly* by offering material to the newspapers, the news services, the radio networks, the press and radio commentators; by *placing articles in magazines*; by *sponsoring the publication of books*; by the production of information papers, pamphlets and a weekly bulletin for which a monthly magazine was later substituted; by the loan of books and the sale of official papers; by answering individual inquiries orally, by telephone, telegram and letter; by *providing specialist speakers* in response to American invitations and by means of films and exhibitions (ibid.: 66–67, emphasis added).

Gary Hess (1971: 113) confirms Lord Halifax's concern for shoring up the British image in America through comprehensive measures. "In the six months following Pearl Harbor," Hess declares, "the British were comparatively inactive. By the summer and fall of 1942, however, the pro-nationalist sentiment in America had begin to arouse British concern." Hess fails to give a direct explanation for this downturn, but Venkatraman and Srivastava (1979) do. A precipitating factor seems to have been the reaction

in influential circles to Winston Churchill's vituperative denunciation of Gandhi and the Indian National Congress in statements
he made before Parliament on September 10, 1942, not long after
the failure of the Cripps Mission. It was a "slashing attack" in
which the Prime Minister presented what he called the "fundamental facts" about the Indian problem. To cheers from the Tory
benches, he declared, "The Congress does not represent all India.
It does not represent the majority of the people. It does not represent the Hindu masses. It is a political organization, part of a political machine, sustained by certain manufacturing and financial
interests ...." Churchill claimed that Muslims, untouchables and
the people of the Princely States, who comprised 230 million of
India's 390 million people, along with Christians and Sikhs, were
"bitterly opposed" to Congress. He accused Congress of being an
organization "committed to criminal courses," which was probably
being aided by a Japanese Fifth Column. "Amidst derisive laughter
and cheers," Venkatraman and Srivastava (1979: 282) say, the
Prime Minister derisively stated, "Mr. Gandhi and other principal
leaders have been interned under conditions of the highest comfort
and consideration and will be kept out of harm's way until the
trouble has subsided."

The counter-productive impact in America of this intemperate
statement, then, was what alarmed Halifax and Bajpai, and fueled
Halifax's determination to engage in damage control. When
Dennis W. Brogan, "a perceptive observer of the American scene
... toured the United States in early 1942, and found that British
stock was lower than at any time since the beginning of the
European war, he noted that British imperial policy was the
principal cause" (Hess 1971: 113). Brogan argued, "British
imperialism is defensible in American terms, but the defense
requires skill, candour, and a knowledge of what Americans dislike
in our imperial attitude." The Churchill outburst later that year
certainly failed to move things in the direction which Brogan
believed appropriate.

In response to this image problem, there occurred the aforementioned mobilization of information and propaganda both
by the British Embassy and the Agency General. "In late 1942,"
asserts Hess (ibid.: 114), "the British began an extensive effort to
influence American opinion." "The objective of British policy was

to ensure that the American Government continued to adhere to its policy of non-interference in the Indian question." One aspect of their campaign "centered on the assumption of British expertise on India" (Hess 1971: 115). That had become a considerably more challenging task once Churchill had shot his mouth off! It was seen as a matter of touting the alleged "long-experience, maturity and benevolence" of British rule in India by contrast with the "immaturity, mendacity and naivete" of the nationalists. Another aspect was "Their immediate fear ... that his Majesty's critics, both inside and outside Government ... would arouse widespread hopes of American intervention in India." That fear had increased not only due to the activities of the India lobby following the failure of the Cripps Mission, but also due to the convergence of this factor with the "arrival of numerous American war correspondents in India as a result of the approach of the war to that continent" (ibid.: 114). It might be added, as we shall see, that there was a corresponding fear of the effects that increased numbers of Indian journalists accredited to Washington by major English language Indian newspapers like the *Hindu*, the *Times of India*, the *Hindustan Times*, and the *Indian Express* were having on the political dialogue in both directions. And finally, of course, the stakes were further increased by the physical presence of American troops in India, who would be eyewitnesses to the depredations of colonialism.

Thus began a war of images and words waged in Washington, and around the United States, between these two bitter adversaries—the "India Lobby," embodied by the India League and the National Committee for Indian Freedom, led by Sirdar J.J. Singh, Dr Anup Singh, Dr Syud Hossain, Dr Haridas Mazumdar, Dr Krishnalal Shridharani, Dr Taraknath and Mary Das, and their many followers, supported by sections of what Halifax termed "doctrinaire left-wing circles" and the increasingly vocal Indian press; versus the "Imperial Lobby" led by Ambassador Lord Halifax, the British Establishment, the Agent General Bajpai, and their intellectual hirelings. The latter's path was being smoothed as well, in the name of "Allied unity," by a passive, officially "neutral" Roosevelt administration.

The Indian publicists were consequently up against a formidable adversary who was determined to checkmate them at every turn. To this end, the British Embassy wheeled out numerous "authorities" on India, ranging from former civil servants, including ex-viceroys, to scholars and journalists who would cast aspersions especially on the leadership qualities and allegedly "impractical" political aims of the Indian National Congress. Many of these propagandists depicted leaders like Nehru either as naive politicians and thinkers, out of contact with the hard realities of world war and international politics, or as potentially "reasonable" young men who were held in thrall and misled by the mystical machinations of Mahatma Gandhi. They definitely saved their most vitriolic denunciations for Gandhi, whose charismatic powers they clearly feared the most. In the early going, some of their spokesmen even claimed that the Mahatma was secretly in league with the Japanese, and a Nazi sympathizer as well. Even when they did not go this far, they still persistently depicted him as a political buffoon who quixotically claimed that he could repel a Japanese invasion of India with his non-violent tactics.

In the forefront of this campaign, of course, was the British ambassador, a highly skilled publicist, who, because he had once been viceroy, passed himself off as a balanced, reasonable, fair-minded authority on things Indian. Lined up behind him stood an army of "authorities" prepared to authenticate his and the British Information Service's carefully crafted biases. Some were touted as "old India hands" by virtue of their service in India, extensive study, or travel on the subcontinent (Hess 1971: 115). They included men like Lord Hailey, who had spent 40 years in India and been governor of both the Punjab and the United Provinces (now Uttar Pradesh); Henry Hodson, who had been reform commissioner of the Government of India in 1941–1942; Sir Frederick Whyte, who had been president of the Indian Legislative Assembly from 1920 to 1925; Sir Robert Holland, who had served in the Indian civil service from 1895 to 1931; and Sir Frederick Puckle, whose long career in the ICS included service as secretary of the Department of Information and Broadcasting from 1941 to 1943, prior to being deputed to America as an advisor on Indian affairs at the British Embassy.[1]

Opinion surveys were virtually non-existent in those days, and so it was never possible to be absolutely sure about what impact either side was having on American public opinion. All one could rely on for impressions and insight were editorials, commentaries and news stories emanating from the press, the statements and actions of politicians and public officials, and viewpoints expressed by informed citizens. J.J. Singh was especially energetic in his efforts to elicit support from what is today called "the media" and, of course, from members of the US Congress. He, along with the other members of the India Lobby, had worked hard, within the limitations confronting them, at becoming "media savvy" and constructing political networks. By today's standards, of course, their efforts and their accomplishments would appear to be modest in the extreme. But in the context of their time, and given the limited manpower and material resources available to them, their effort was remarkable; their accomplishments impressive. It required a lot of leg-work, a lot of resourcefulness, and a lot of face-to-face contact with people in medium to high places in Washington and New York, and indeed many other parts of the country as well. Did the effort pay dividends?

Judgements inevitably differ on this. Venkatraman and Srivastava (1979: 291) conclude that, in the last analysis, appearances tended to triumph over substance. "Singh," they say, "began to make several pilgrimages to Washington to meet important politicians, officials and journalists. They were ready and willing to listen to the earnest and impressive-looking Indian. But conversions to the cause of an immediate American initiative relating to India were few." Had that been the sole criterion of success or failure then Venkatraman's conclusion was undoubtedly accurate. J.J. characteristically called on many members of Congress, pleading with them to "urge Roosevelt to use his good offices to bring about a settlement in India." They included, he says, Senators Elmer Cooper (Oklahoma), Claude Pepper (Florida), Tom Connally (Texas) and Robert M. La Follette (Wisconsin). Pepper wrote Singh saying, "I shall certainly do my best to be helpful in this most vital problem (ibid.: 191). The letter sounds like one that had been perfunctorily written by a legislative assistant!

Singh also approached persons like Owen Lattimore (1900–1989) and Lauchlin Currie (1902–1993), both noted Far East experts who at the time had a lot of influence in Washington because of the strategic importance of China, but who later became victims of McCarthyism during the1950s witch-hunts, and Manuel Quezon, the refugee president of the Philippines. He had better luck with the journalists, and succeeded in enlisting the support of Raymond Clapper, an extremely popular journalist of that period, and also I.F. Stone and Louis Fischer. At J.J.'s behest, Pearl Buck, along with Clare Booth Luce, drafted an advertisement for the *New York Times* entitled, "THE TIME FOR MEDIATION IS NOW." Published on May 19, 1943, the advertisement asked rhetorically, "Is India America's business?" The answer was: "We need India's millions on our side against Japan. The people of India do not want Japan .... They want freedom. The Indian readiness to negotiate is unchanged." It went on to "urge upon President Roosevelt and Generalissimo Chiang Kai-shek that they recognize the interest of the United Nations in the Indian dilemma," and take the initiative in bringing about a fair and equitable settlement between the nationalists and the British Government (Venkatraman and Srivastava 1979: 292). There were 57 signatories to the advertisement: the list read like a who's-who of the progressive and liberal segments of informed America. Venkatraman and Srivastava (ibid.) concede that a "very high proportion of them were journalists, writers and college teachers from the Eastern seaboard." Not many of them "had access to America's 'corridors of power.'"

However, Venkatraman and Srivastava's skepticism notwithstanding, the publicity being generated by the India League was having the effect of widening public awareness of the India problem, especially because it could now be directly linked to the strategic requirements of the American share of the war effort. The next day, the rally organized by the India League at New York's Town Hall attracted over 2,000 people, while hundreds more were turned away by the police. Similar events took place at Old South Meeting House in Boston and the National Press Club in Washington. Even the Town Meeting of the Air, in those days a very important public forum, featured a debate in which J.J. Singh and other notables participated.

In this intensified political environment, J.J. Singh demonstrated that he could more than hold his own with the various notables with whom he was rubbing shoulders. He equipped himself well in the Town Hall discussion, which also included H.S.L. Polak, a former friend and biographer of Mahatma Gandhi from his South African days, and Professor Frederick L. Schuman, a Chicago political scientist who had become well known not only for his Asian scholarship but also as an ideological whipping boy of William

**Illustration 9.1**
**Full page advertisement in the *Washington Post*, sponsored by the India League of America, May 19, 1943**

# INDIA

## "The Time For Mediation Is NOW"

**On September 28, 1942, fifty-seven famous Americans said:**

"Is India America's business? Yes, because we need India's millions on our side against Japan . . .

"Our Chinese Allies are greatly disturbed and are anxious for the allied cause in Asia . . .

"We urge upon President Roosevelt and upon Generalissimo Chiang Kai-shek that they recognize the interest of the United Nations in the Indian dilemma and that they use their good offices to ask the British Government and the National Congress of India and other leaders to open new conferences, with mutual determination to find that way of action which will [illegible]

[illegible]

These excerpts are from a full-page advertisement in [illegible] September 28, 1942, signed by:

**LOUIS ADAMIC**
*Trustee, Common Council for American Unity, N. Y.*
**ROGER N. BALDWIN**
*Director, American Civil Liberties Union, N. Y.*
**BRUCE BLIVEN**
*Editor, "The New Republic," N. Y.*
**CLARE BOOTHE**
*Author, War Correspondent, Conn.*
**MRS. GEORGES BRIDGES**
*Civic Leader, Ala.*
**LOUIS BROMFIELD**
*Author, Pulitzer Prize Winner, Ohio*
**VAN WYCK BROOKS**
*Author, Literary Critic, Conn.*
**PEARL S. BUCK**
*Nobel Prize Winner, Pa.*
**JOHN CHAMBERLAIN**
*Author and Literary Critic, Conn.*
**WM. HENRY CHAMBERLIN**
*Journalist, Mass.*
**STUART CHASE**
*Author, Economist, Conn.*
**CHRIS L. CHRISTENSEN**
*Dean, College of Agriculture, University of Wisconsin, Wis.*
**GEORGE S. COUNTS**
*Former President, American Federation of Teachers, N. Y.*
**DR. TYLER DENNETT**
*Former President, Williams College, N. Y.*
**C. HALLIWELL DUELL**
*Publisher, N. Y.*
**DR. SHERWOOD EDDY**
*Former Y. M. C. A. National Secretary in India, N. Y.*
**DR. CHARLES K. EDMUNDS**
*President Emeritus, Pomona College, Calif.*
**JOHN ERSKINE**
*Author, Educator, N. Y.*
**DOROTHY CANFIELD FISHER**
*Author, Vt.*
**PROF. CARL J. FRIEDRICH**
*Harvard University, Mass.*
**CLINTON S. GOLDEN**
*Asst. to President, United Steel Workers of America, Pa.*
**SAMUEL GRAFTON**
*Columnist, N. Y.*
**DR. FRANK P. GRAHAM**
*President, University of North Carolina, N. C.*
**JOHN GUNTHER**
*Author, N. Y.*
**HENRY I. HARRIMAN**
*Former President, U. S. Chamber of Commerce, Mass.*
**SHELBY M. HARRISON**
*General Director, Russell Sage Foundation, N. Y.*
**ARTHUR GARFIELD HAYS**
*Attorney, N. Y.*
**LILLIAN HELLMAN**
*Playwright, N. Y.*
**PROF. WILLIAM E. HOCKING**
*Harvard University, Mass.*
**JOHN B. HUGHES**
*Radio Commentator, Calif.*
**FANNIE HURST**
*Author, N. Y.*
**PAUL KELLOGG**
*Editor, "Survey Graphic," N. Y.*
**DR. FRANK KINGDON**
*President, Union of Democratic Action, N. Y.*
**FREDA KIRCHWEY**
*Editor and Publisher, "The Nation," N. Y.*
**ALFRED M. LANDON**
*Former Governor of Kansas, Kan.*
**PROF. MAX LERNER**
*Williams College, Mass.*
**PROF. ROBERT S. LYND**
*Columbia University, N. Y.*
**PROF. ROBERT M. MacIVER**
*Columbia University, N. Y.*
**Bishop FRANCIS J. McCONNELL**
*Former President, Federal Council of Churches of Christ in America, N. Y.*
**ADA P. McCORMICK**
*Civic Leader, Ariz.*
**Esther Morgan McCULLOUGH**
*Civic Leader, Vt.*
**DR. FELIX MORLEY**
*President, Haverford College, Pa.*
**CLARENCE POE**
*President, Progressive Farmer & Southern Ruralist, N. C.*
**PROF. JAMES B. PRATT**
*Williams College, Mass.*
**JOSEPHINE ROCHE**
*Former Assistant Secretary, U. S. Treasury, Colo.*
**PROF. FRED. L. SCHUMAN**
*Williams College, Mass.*
**PROF. ROBERT L. SCHUYLER**
*Columbia University, N. Y.*
**WILLIAM L. SHIRER**
*Author, N. Y.*
**RABBI ABBA HILLEL SILVER**
*The Temple, Cleveland, Ohio*
**UPTON SINCLAIR**
*Author, Calif.*
**HERBERT BAYARD SWOPE**
*Publicist and Journalist, N. Y.*
**NORMAN THOMAS**
*Chairman, Post War World Council, N. Y.*
**RICHARD J. WALSH**
*Editor, "Asia," N. Y.*
**PROF. FRED J. WAMPLER**
*Virginia College of Medicine, Va.*
**DR. JAMES P. WARBASSE**
*President Emeritus, Cooperative League of U.S.A.*
**WALTER WHITE**
*Executive Secretary, National Association for Advancement of Colored People, N. Y.*
**DR. MARY E. WOOLLEY**
*Former President, Mt. Holyoke College, [illegible]*

## The Time For Mediation Is Again NOW

**Today, May 19, 1943, this appeal is more urgent than ever:**

**NOW** the United Nations are celebrating their victory in Africa, and can foresee their certain victory in Europe.

**NOW** President Roosevelt and Prime Minister Churchill are meeting to discuss further strategy for victory in Asia without which the war cannot be finally won.

**NOW** Allied military leaders of the Far Eastern theater are conferring in Wa[illegible] further steps.

**NOW** Ambassador William Phillips, President Roosevelt's personal envoy to India, is in Washington reporting to his chief.

**NOW** the eyes of the world are on India because India is the key to victory over Japan.

To defeat Japan we need China—a China that is not simply resisting heroically but is fighting offensively.

To sustain China we need Burma.

To regain Burma we need India.

To mobilize India fully we need to free the imprisoned democratic leaders of the Indian people who alone can arouse them to action for victory.

India's millions want the opportunity to fight for freedom. If only a fraction of India's vast manpower and resources are in action today, it is because Indians—like other men—can fight for freedom only if they are themselves free.

WE—the United Nations—must break the political deadlock in India which is a repudiation of all we are fighting for.

**NOW** —while President and Prime Minister are talking face to face—is the time to set in motion the machinery that will mediate the problem, translate freedom from a word to an act, and give all Asiatic peoples the essential motivation they lack today: faith in our profession of the Four Freedoms for *all* people.

INDIA LEAGUE OF AMERICA
40 East 49th Street
New York, N. Y.

PERSONS in sympathy with these statements are urged to contribute to help pay the cost of this advertisement. Make checks payable to India League of America, 40 East 49th Street, New York, N. Y.

NAME ..............................................

ADDRESS ..............................................

..............................................

*Source: Washington Post.*

Randolph Hearst's Yellow-Dog Press. A *Herald-Examiner* editorial
in 1935 had described him as one of "these American panderers
and trap-baiters for the Moscow mafia," who should be investi-
gated by Congress and "gotten rid of as a 'Red.'" In that Town
Hall meeting, Schumann proposed that a United Nations tribunal
be established, which would be chaired either by Vice-President
Henry A. Wallace or Wendell Wilkie, the 1940 Republican presid-
ential candidate. Polak's position is unknown, but may not have
been particularly favorable toward Gandhi.[2] Singh weighed in with
a proposal of his own that was given wide publicity by a Scripps–
Howard columnist named William Howard Simms. J.J. advocated
a high-powered United Nations commission composed of Wendell
Wilkie (the United States), Lord Halifax (Great Britain), T.V. Soong
(China), Manuel Quezon (the Philippines), and Maxim Litvinov
(the Soviet Union), which he claimed might be able to achieve an
"interim solution" to the dispute. This did not happen, of course,
but these events and this kind of publicity clearly increased the
visibility and the credibility of the India Lobby. The White House,
the State Department and the Congress were increasingly feeling
pressure from all this activity, even though it never reached a level
that would force a major reversal of public policy. Its culmination
over the following two years, however, would, as we shall soon
see, reveal that the lobbyists' efforts had by no means been in vain.

Among the Americans who came on board at this time, few
were more gratifying to the Lobbyists than the liberal journalist
I.F. Stone, and the political essayist and future biographer of
Mahatma Gandhi, Louis Fischer.

Fischer traveled to India in May 1942, stayed for two months,
spent a week with Gandhi in his *Ashram*, became enthralled with
him and wrote a small book on that immediate experience called,
*A Week With Gandhi* (Fischer 1942). He later wrote a definitive
biography of Gandhi (Fischer 1950), which would many years later
become the basis for Sir Richard Attenborough's academy award-
winning movie, *Gandhi*. Fischer summed up his estimate of Gandhi
this way: "In his pursuit of independence there is a musical harmony between Gandhi and millions of Indians." This conclusion
was diametrically opposite to the manner in which Churchill and
the British propagandists at work in America were depicting him.
"You follow a leader who is you in a better edition," said Fischer.

"Gandhi is father and brother to millions of semi-naked, half-starved, not-too-intellectual peasants and workingmen who want to attain dignity and prosperity through national effort" (Fischer 1950: 122). Through this "conversion," Fischer had become a valuable member of the circle of American intellectuals upon whose support the India Lobby would depend.

Isidor Feinstein Stone (1907–1989), known professionally as "I.F. Stone," became a steadfast and articulate supporter of the Indian freedom movement throughout the war years. Like Fisher, he was available whenever the India League and the National Committee called upon him. As editor of *The Nation* from 1940 to 1946, he was in a position to heavily influence the India debate by making the pages of this influential magazine available to pro-nationalist writers. The denunciation of colonialism was a consistent theme in his own writings and public statements. The way to resolve the political impasse between the two countries, he repeatedly declared, "would be to give India a responsible government and make its people feel that this is their war" (*The Nation*, December 11, 1943, pp. 686–87).

Typical of the intellectual struggle that was being waged for the hearts and minds of educated Americans between the apologists for British rule and the supporters of Indian independence was that which occurred between Professor Lennox A. Mills and the economist Kate Mitchell in the magazine *Amerasia*. As with many of the pro-British types, Mills was not virulently anti-nationalist; he could give a learned disquisition on why not rocking the boat, at least until war was over, would be best for the Indian people themselves. He had a dim view of Gandhi and the Indian National Congress, however, implying that he did not think them capable of running India. Mills had good credentials: he was an Associate Professor of Political Science at the University of Minnesota, one of the premier Big Ten universities and had authored several books on South and Southeast Asia, including *British Rule in Eastern Asia* (Mills 1970, see also Mills 1945). All this, of course, made him appear to be highly "authoritative" on the subject.

Kate L. Mitchell was, however, no slouch herself. She was a noted scholar in her own right, and a member of the editorial board of *Amerasia* at this time. Her books included *India Without Fable: A 1942 Survey, Japan's Industrial Strength,* and *The Industrialization of the Western Pacific.*

Professor Mills recited what had become a litany for the proponents of continued British rule. In erudite, scholarly language, he claimed that India's socio-political divisions were so great that no indigenous party could successfully govern the country, especially in wartime. As with all other such critics, the Congress party and Mahatma Gandhi were his principal targets. The Congress allegedly had a very limited following; Gandhi was allegedly a Hindu mystic who turned off all other groups in society. The Muslims, mobilized by the Muslim League, he asserted, would never accept being ruled by a Hindu majority, which would allegedly be the case if there were a Congress-dominated government. He ignored the ideological differences between the two parties—the fact that Congress was a declared secular party while the League was an explicitly "communal" party. He inferred that the princely states and the untouchables were major segments of the population which had rejected political dominance by the Congress. In other words, Mills lumped the highly multiplex Indian population into four simplistically defined cultural-demographic categories and pronounced them politically irreconcilable, thereby making the all-encompassing British colonial regime a "regrettable" necessity if "order" were to be maintained throughout the war. This was, of course, precisely the position taken by Lord Halifax and the entire British establishment, and the one they were determined to convey to the American public.

Kate Mitchell's rejoinder endeavored to refute these arguments point for point. She had conducted a lot of serious research on India for many years, including in India itself, and was able to marshal extensive data on behalf of her position. Her principal purpose, as with the pro-nationalist intellectuals in general, was to refute the British claim that India's ethno-cultural diversity was an insurmountable obstacle to the ability of the Congress movement to create a viable government acceptable to the majority of the Indian people. She challenged the contention that Hindu–Muslim differences were insurmountable. She particularly stressed the fact that Congress was a secular party that was pledged to build a political system in which all groups and interests would be accommodated under the rubric of a democratic constitution on the model of the British parliament itself. The Indian National Congress, Mitchell declared, "is not a communal organization." On the contrary:

It has a large Moslem membership, and includes representatives of all the minor religious groups, although the majority of its members are Hindus. The Congress has always insisted on the indivisibility of India; its declared aim being a united, self-governing India led by men who are Indian rather than Hindus or Moslems. It is programmatically opposed to communal separatism, and its leaders have consistently maintained that the Moslems as well as the other communities could secure their legitimate interests in a Constituent Assembly based on universal adult suffrage (Mitchell 1942a: 31).

However, other authors who hewed to a similar anti-nationalist, pro-British line included Reginald Coupland (*The Cripps Mission*, 1943), Peter Muir (*This is India*, 1944), Beverley Nichols (*Verdict on India*, 1944), and Katherine Mayo (*Mother India*, 1928). Certainly the most notorious of these was Mayo's *Mother India*. Mahatma Gandhi had labeled the author a "drain inspector" because she emphasized only the most repugnant features of Indian society in an obvious attempt to demonstrate that British rule was essential if India had any chance to overcome its "backwardness." Because Mayo was a professional journalist, she enjoyed considerable credibility and for a while had a major impact on public perceptions of India. The journalist, Chaman Lal, declared that the Information Office, despite denials, "distributed copies of Miss Mayo's notorious book, while thousands of politicians, professors, libraries, schools and radio stations receive free copies. Some persons received two copies each." When he was in Washington, Lal says the book was being distributed by two agencies in the city. Moreover, he continues, "Who does not know that the late Miss Mayo was a guest of the Viceroy, Governors and Princes and was given fullest assistance by the Government of India" (Lal 1945: xiv).

One of the most distressing sources of anti-nationalist propaganda in America was the Indians who sided in whole or in part with the British. Among them was the Agent-General, Sir Girja Shankar Bajpai; two members of the viceroy's executive council, Sir Firoz Khan Noon and Sir Ramaswami Mudaliar; and a member of the Legislative Assembly and former president of the Muslim League, Sir Muhammad Zafarullah Khan (note that all had been knighted and that many were Muslims). "Begum Shah Nawaz, who had been a leader among Muslim women, was seen as a member of that group's identity with the Government of India." Also, "Serving as an adviser to Amery, Sir Samuel Ebenezer Raghunandan spoke on behalf of the Indian Christian community" (Hess 1971: 116). Because ostensibly "Indian," they provided an aura of added legitimacy to the claims made by the British and their American mouthpieces that the Congress party and Gandhi could not reliably replace the Raj as India's governing body. The most notorious of these indigenous detractors was T.N. (Thirulingam Ramanujan) Raman. Headquartered in London, Raman's books,[3] singled out Gandhi and the Indian National Congress for special vilification. He favored independence but not under their tutelage. In his book, Raman declared, "... Indians who want their country to be free and, therefore, are determined that the war shall be won, must reconcile themselves to a final break with Gandhian perversions of their country's policies during the war."

Chaman Lal probed deeply into Raman's career background and sarcastically referred to him as "Bajpai's understudy":

> Raman, while a student in England, is said to have failed to have received financial support from his parents and had to live occasionally on doles from fellow students. He took up a job to report the activities of Indian students in Britain. He was sent to France, but had to flee from the wrath of some Indian students in Paris who knew all about him. He was then sent to the United States of America in behalf of the B.I.S., but under the garb of a "staunch Indian nationalist journalist whose journalism is unimpeachable for its accuracy and fair-mindedness." (This appears on the cover of his notorious book, *What Does Gandhi Want?*) ... He always traveled first-class and stayed at the costliest hotels. Raman gave out that he had come to India on behalf of an American newspaper alliance. No such newspaper alliance has been heard of (Lal 1945: 41–42).

Lal claimed that Raman's two books (*What Does Gandhi Want?* and *A Report on India*), were published under the auspices of the British Information Service, a fact which he nowhere acknowledged. "They were said to have been written in the India Office in London and revised by Miss Harrington of B.I.S. in New York and by Mr. [J.] Hennessy [Information Officer of the Agent General]" (Lal 1945: 42).

Chaman Lal, who wrote for the *Hindustan Times* and other publications, was a particularly tart manifestation of the Indian journalists who came to America as correspondents for their home newspapers. They were a far less compliant breed. They tended to tell things as they saw them. As the foregoing excerpt demonstrates, Chaman Lal's book, *British Propaganda in America* (1945) is a no-holds-barred denunciation of British propaganda tactics, very much in the investigative reporter tradition. He referred to Legislative Council member, Sir Sultan Ahmed, as "A gramophone of his British masters ... [who] denies that any Anti-Indian books have been published, subsidized or circulated by the Indian Information Office in Washington" (ibid.: x). In fact, declared Lal (ibid.: xii), "[Agent-General] Sir Girja Shankar Bajpai personally admitted having circulated these books ... I secured free copies of about two dozen books from his office." He charged that the authors of many of these books, "were generously subsidized and enjoyed the hospitality of the Government of India and through them the Princes. Some of them were whole-time paid agents and their tours were arranged by Sir Sultan's department" (ibid.). He said that 30,000 copies of Peter Muir's book were purchased and distributed free by the "B.I.S and its Indian appendage." He claimed that Sir Girja Shankar Bajpai himself "costs $52,000 a year, which is more than the salary of the President of the United States of America" (ibid.: xiii). The *Voice of India* in its May 1946 issue published excerpts from an editorial in the *Amrita Bazar Patrika* giving figures on what the Government of India's Information Department was spending for propaganda in America. It claimed that its head, Sir Akbar Hydar, admitted spending Rs 462,000 in 1942–1943, Rs 708,000 in 1943–1944, and Rs 859,000 in 1944–1945. "In other words, over Rs 20 lakhs have been spent for misrepresenting the Indian national movement and confusing the American public with tendentious propaganda." The editorial added that it would like some "vigilant member of the Legislative Assembly to try and find out what is being spent through the External Affairs Department, under which Sir Girja Shankar Bajpai's India Agency General functions .... This is, of course, all apart from what the British Embassy and British Information Service themselves spend on anti-Indian propaganda" (*Voice of India*, May 1946, p. 294).

Even the manner in which Chaman Lal came to the United States brimmed with controversy. He was already in hot water with the British authorities in India for his blunt rhetoric, so when they issued him a passport it was only on the condition that he promise not to deliver any public lectures while in America. "I tried to keep my word and devoted most of my time to historical research on the ancient relations between Hindu, Astic (*sic*), Maya and Inca cultures of America. " He broke that promise, he declared, when the British authorities "depicted me as an agent of Japan and tried to prove that my book, *Vanishing Empire*, was almost certainly published by the Japanese Government." He said he was quoting from a memorandum written by Bajpai, a copy of which he was able to obtain, but which was confiscated on his return to India via Karachi where "I was thrown in the Military lock-up" (Lal 1945: viii–ix).

Lal lashed out in every direction against British propaganda. While he was in the United States, he castigated establishment members of the American press like Walter Lippman, Dorothy Thompson, and Major George Fielding Elliot for "openly championing the cause of British Imperialism." He contrasted them, however, with "the vast majority of American newspapers [that] are openly for India's freedom ..." (ibid.: 12). Chaman Lal's tour de force certainly reflected the deepest feelings of the Indian nationalists in both countries, and he helped bring prominence to the fact that the Indian-owned English language newspapers had become a vital force in Indian political life.

Certainly men like Chaman Lal were an asset to the India Lobby. They needed all the help they could get in the face of the massive propaganda apparatus that was arrayed against them. Among their own publications, *India Today* (the India League's monthly magazine published out of New York) and Anup Singh's *Voice of India* (published out of Washington from 1944 to 1947), were the best. Anup had made the Cairo Hotel in Washington his headquarters. With the help of Syud Hossain, Haridas Mazumdar, Krishnalal Shridharani, J.J. Singh, and a network of contacts reaching into the US Congress, the State Department, the Library of Congress, and other public and private agencies around the city, he compiled and published information about all aspects of the movement and attracted a wide variety of persons to contribute articles of varying length to his magazine. In the September 1944 issue of *Voice of India* were listed what were called "Regional

Representatives" of the National Committee, which demonstrated the scope of the organizational network which had been created:

- Atlantic City: Mirza T.K. Alexander, D.M. Sulaiman
- Boston: Rama Chattopadhyaya, Thomas Yakhub
- Chicago: M. Kitchlew-Mumtaz, Tarini Prasad Sinha
- Cleveland: Shanti Bahadur
- Detroit: Balwant Singh Grewal, Saed Ullah Khan, Jack Munir, Nirmla C. Mukerji, Sher M. Quraishi
- El Paso: Pala Singh, Ram Singh
- Los Angeles: Mohammad Shahzad, J.N. Sharma, G.J. Watumull
- Marysville: Karam Chand, Ram Partap, Bishan Singh
- New York: S.R. Bomanji, N.R. Checher, A. Choudry, N.M. Heeramaneck, K.Y. Kira, S.K. Marathe, R.S. Modak
- Philadelphia: S. Chandrasekhar, Mirza Jaffer
- Phoenix: Rustam Khan, Rahmat Ullah
- Pittsburgh: P.C. Mukerjee
- Sacramento: Mohammad Ali, Munshi A. Box, Rahmat Ali Khan, Nana Lal Patel
- San Francisco: Godha Ram Channon, Mrs Ram Chandra, S.S. Shadi, Bhagat S. Thiara
- Washington: George M. Baksh, Mrs Ram Mohan Rai
- Wellesley: Miss Chandralekha Pandit, Miss Nayantara Pandit (Madam Pandit's daughters)
- Yellow Springs: N.M. Chatterjee

This list reveals how extensive the organization had become in spatial terms and how widely dispersed Indians had become throughout the United States. Their "ethnic" characteristics were interesting as well. There were 23 Hindus, six Muslims, four Sikhs, four Christians, four women, and four whose precise ethnicity could not be determined. Among the Hindus, six were Bengalis, two were Kashmiris (Madam Pandit's daughters at Wellesley), three were Maharashtrians, and 12 were not differentiable by caste or regional ethnicity. Given the fact that communal antipathy between Hindus and Muslims had intensified in India and that the Muslim League was claiming exclusive suzerainty over Muslims, it seems striking that this many Muslims showed up on the Committee's list, no doubt helping to confirm its secular bona fides. One would have expected Sikhs to have been better represented, given their concentration on the West Coast. The omission may be because the Sikh community, with its roots in the agrarian economy, was more focused on domestic issues like property rights and citizenship and less on the struggle between the British and the Congress party over the governance of India and the timetable for Indian independence. Also, the Ghadr Party, albeit much transformed, still commanded varying degrees of allegiance from most Sikhs.

The content of the *Voice of India* over the approximately four years of its existence provides a good picture of the India Lobby's intellectual reach. In a content analysis of 22 issues (from September 1944 to May 1947), there were 46 articles of varying length. There were two book reviews written by Madam Boulter, one by Sudhindra Bose, and one by Chandralekha Pandit (Madam Vijayalakshmi Pandit's daughter), who was studying at Wellesley. The Indian contributors ran the gamut of the India Lobby: Gobind Behari Lal, Chaman Lal, Taraknath Das, Syud Hossain, Haridas Mazumdar, Krishnalal Shridharani, Anup Singh. There were articles by some of the long-standing American supporters: Congressman Emanuel Celler, Professor Albert Guerard, E. Stanley Jones, Oswald Garrison Villard, and Richard J. Walsh. There was a brief contribution by Jawaharlal Nehru, and a "Letter to American Friends" from Mahatma Gandhi. Mirabehn and Ananda Coomaraswamy wrote letters, as did Roger Baldwin, Louis Bromfield, Congressman John M. Coffee, novelist Dorothy Canfield Fisher, Senator Guy Gillette, Norman Thomas, Agnes Smedley, Abdul Kalam Azad, Bennett L. Williams, and a host of lesser-known persons.

In its September 1944 issue, *Voice of India* addressed the charges emanating from British sources that Gandhi was somehow in league with the Japanese. They published the full text of a letter which Mirabehn (the Indian name of Madeline Slade, the well-known English follower of Mahtama Gandhi) addressed to Lord Linlithgow posted from "Detention Camp, Aga Khan's Palace, Poona, Christmas Eve, 1942." In this letter, Mirabehn alludes to stories in the *Bombay Chronicle Weekly*, the *London Daily Sketch*, and the *London Daily Herald* which contained "the assertion that Gandhi and the Congress are pro-Japanese," while employing such lurid headlines as "Gandhi's Indo-Jap Peace Plan Exposed" and "English Woman Gandhi's Jap Peace Envoy." She refers to *Punch* cartoons that are "if possible even more disgraceful." After presenting documentary evidence refuting these assertions about Gandhi and the Congress, she urges the Viceroy to publicly repudiate them which, of course, Linlithgow did not do. Mirabehn states, "I can say with confidence the feelings of [the Working Committee of the Indian National Congress] have been *unequivocally anti-Japanese and anti-fascist throughout*." Appealing to Linlithgow's sense of honor, she declares: "Seeing that no God-fearing Ruler could, with any peace of mind, allow [such] slanderous propaganda on the part of his own people against those whom he had rendered unable to reply, to continue unchecked once he had unchallengeable proof of its falsehood, I put trust in the belief that you will publish the enclosed correspondence [refuting the slander] together with this covering letter, and refute the assertions of the British journalists"(*Voice of India*, September 1944, p. 13, emphasis added).

Despite the wartime preoccupation with the political repression taking place in India, citizenship rights were not ignored in the *Voice of India*. Anup Singh wrote an article in that same September 1944 issue, in which he linked the plight of "three thousand nationals of India now living in the United States" to the depredations caused by the *Thind* decision of 1923 and the Immigration Act of 1924. He called it "a simple and a sad story." He reiterated the numerous cases that were fought in vain efforts to rectify the wrongs inflicted on South Asians due to the racist mentality of immigration officials, the courts, and Justice Sutherland, "which brought the present hardships to the Indians." Acknowledging the plight of the West Coast Sikhs, he declared, "Those who suffer most from ineligibility for American citizenship are the Indian farmers of California, who by their labor have contributed so much to the prosperity of the state, but may not own nor lease land in their own names" (*Voice of India*, September 1944, pp. 11–12).

What was important was that Anup Singh was able to discuss this issue not merely in the abstract, but in the light of some tangible hope for amelioration which the India Lobby was instrumental in bringing about. He mentions legislation pending in the US Congress which he, J.J. Singh, Syud Hossain and others had been able help develop through their lobbying activities. "In the House there are the Luce Bill: H.R. 4479, sponsored by Mrs. Luce of Connecticut, and H.R. 4425, sponsored by Emanuel Celler of New York, and in the Senate, S. 1595, sponsored by William Langer of North Dakota. The House bills call for the naturalization of qualified Indians and a quota for Indians .... The Langer bill calls for the naturalization of only those Indians already here" (*Voice of India*, September 1944, p. 12).

Chaman Lal characterized India as a "Vast Concentration Camp" in a short piece he wrote for the October 1944 issue. "Where else in the allied world," he asked, "has a government arrested a hundred thousand people and thrown them behind prison bars?" That's what happened in September 1942, he said, referring to the Quit India movement. He called the C.I.D. (Criminal Investigation Division), "popularly known as the 'Cruel Indian Dogs'", an Indian version of the Nazi Gestapo. They "rule the land," he declared, and are shepherded by a British officer in every district," and "Innocent and respectable citizens can be, and are, arrested and locked up ... without trial." He cites an example of a merchant from his hometown whom he met in the Multan (Punjab) prison to which he was transferred following his arrest after returning from America. "I asked him, 'What brings you here. You never participated in the Congress all your life, nor even used handloom cloth ....' The merchant touchingly replied that, 'I pay for the sin of my ten year old son who happened to shout "Long live Gandhi".' While the police did nothing to the boy, 'They came to my house and arrested me, and here I have been for months.'" It was common practice for the Punjabi police to punish parents for the political views of their children! (*Voice of India*, October 1944, p. 27).

The magazine took a scholarly turn in December 1944 when it published an article by the demographer, S. Chandrasekhar, titled, "Is India's Population Increasing too Rapidly?" He attacked the prevailing and widely disseminated stereotype promulgated by the British that India's "teeming millions" and not colonialism was the principal cause of her poverty; and that the benevolence and enlightenment of British rule in fact shield India's people from demographic catastrophe. Chandrashekhar refers to a speech which Churchill made in the House of Commons on October 19, 1944. The prime minister claimed that the recent famine that killed millions of Bengalis was an aberration, solely the result of "Military conditions affecting transport," when, in fact, "under British rule in the last eighty years incomparably fewer people have perished by steel or firearms than any similar area or community throughout the world." Churchill asserted that "behind the imperial shield ... India met an increase of population exceeding in speed that of any increase throughout the whole world."

Chandrasekhar retorted, "This is neither an accurate nor an honest description of India's population growth." He accused Churchill and his advisors of distorting the demographic facts by employing absolute numbers (i.e., India's numerical base) and other distortions instead of data on units of proportionate size and rates of population growth. "What are the facts?" he asks. In the first place, in the Bengal famine in 1942, "More people died ... than all the allied casualties." Something deeper was involved than a mere breakdown in transportation! Even on population size per se, however, India's then population of 403 million was almost the same as Europe's. Europe's area, minus Russia, is about 1.5 million square miles, the same as India. Therefore, the comparable units— Europe and India—are about the same size in both numbers and area. "What is so peculiar about that?" asks Chandrasekhar. It was certainly not indicative of a radical difference between India's alleged "teeming millions" and Europe's allegedly more "manageable" numbers! With regard to growth rates, Chandrasekhar showed that India's population between 1872 and 1941 grew by 54 percent, whereas England's grew by 56 percent! "So India's rate of increase has not exceeded that of any other increase throughout the world." As for population density, the figure of 246 per square mile is admittedly "nearly five and a half times the density of the United States ... but *considerably lower than that of England*" (*Voice of India*, December 1944, p. 57, emphasis in original). So much for British demographic propaganda!

There was a flurry of congratulatory messages in the *Voice's* pages in response to Independence Day celebrations on January 26, 1945. As a means of drawing attention to the freedom struggle, the India Lobby had in recent years organized public events to commemorate it. On three pages (pp. 84–86) of the February 1945 issue, there were brief messages from a number of people including Roger Baldwin, Louis Bromfield, Congressman John Coffee, Upton Close, Norman Thomas, Senator Guy Gillette, and Dorothy Canfield Fisher. Even Agnes Smedley returned to the fold for this tribute. Baldwin declared in his letter, "Let no Indian be deceived by the silence of our government that the vast majority of thinking Americans fail to have the liveliest sympathy with India's cause as inseparable from our own in the future peace and security of the world." Louis Bromfield concluded his message with, "Good luck and God speed to the awakening of this giant nation." Congressman Coffee said, "I believe in India's freedom because due to the exigencies of the war situation we must have a politically satisfied India on our side to expedite our victory over Japan." Upton Close said he looked forward to the end of the "empire racket in our day or there will be an end of civilization." Dorothy Canfield Fisher said that "the hearts of all forward-looking Americans are full of anxious solicitude for India, and of unshakable hope that the door may soon be opened for Indian [freedom] ...." Senator Guy Gillett declared, "It is the hope of friends of the people of India that the time is not far distant when Independence Day for India will be as much of a reality as our own Independence Day." Norman Thomas said, "The cause is one which I want to aid in the interest of world justice and world peace." He added, "I have read your new magazine the *Voice of India* with interest. Its articles are very intelligent contributions to a subject of the deepest importance." Earl Stanley Jones in an accompanying article paid high tribute to Nehru. With India unfree, he wrote, Nehru is in jail: "That one single fact is the greatest condemnation of the present dominant powers of the world. All talk of democracy and freedom with a man like Jawaharlal Nehru in jail grates on sensitive souls."

## Notes

1. The list of these and other such notables were compiled by Hess (1971: 115 passim).

2. H.S. Polak was a Transvaal representative of *Indian Opinion* and associated with the Christian Socialist movement. He and his wife lived in Gandhi's South African domiciles for many years and shared both his lifestyle and his political values, until Gandhi's departure from South Africa in 1914. In Gandhi's words, "Just as I had Indians living with members of my family, so I had English friends living with me as members of my family."

3. Quoted by Chaman Lal (1945: 45). Chaman Lal, however, gave no citations of the authors he cited, nor page numbers. Regarding the two books which Chaman Lal cited, *What Does Gandhi Want?* and *Report on India*, the latter was published by the *Infantry Journal* (Washington, 1944); the former has disappeared from the bibliographical lists and it has proved impossible to locate the name of the publisher or date of publication. The Library of Congress does not list it among the 14 bibliographical citations it provides for Raman's writings.

# 10 "Deep Throat" and the "Washington Merry-Go-Round"

It can be said that the India Lobby jelled and reached its climax during the war years. In part this is because the principal players themselves represented a kind of maturation process, a consummation of all the lessons which they and their predecessors had garnered from years of fighting for Indian freedom abroad and South Asian civil rights in America. What it all came down to is that they had learned how to work the system more effectively. The wartime political atmosphere in the United States had changed everything. Massive military spending was at last lifting the American economy out of the doldrums of the Depression. Workers, both men and women, were flooding into the country's work places, producing "guns and butter," as the popular slogan intoned. Young Americans were being drafted into the military by the millions. People in uniform were omnipresent. Washington was awash with new government agencies created to cope with the complexities of waging global war. Social ferment was in the air. This meant all sorts of opportunities for Indian activists to meet and interact on an unprecedented scale with persons from all walks of political, governmental, and intellectual life. This now included many new faces that were less set in their ways, more prone to give a sympathetic ear to forms of political dissent that in an earlier time might be deemed to be "subversive." At the same time, particularly as the war was moving toward an Allied victory, a whole range of major initiatives were now in the wings aimed at dealing with the war's impending conclusion and the post-war world to follow. This would give added scope to the lobbyists' activities. The most important of these initiatives, as far as the India Lobby was concerned, were UNRRA, Breton Woods, and the San Francisco Conference (convened for establishing the

United Nations) at the international level; and, at the domestic level, the impending legis-lation to accord unrestricted citizenship rights to resident Indians, and an immigration quota for future South Asian migrants.

Between August and October 1944, an international conference was convened at Dumbarton Oaks in Georgetown with the pur- pose of preparing the ground for establishing an international organization to replace the old League of Nations after the war. This gathering of world statesmen was followed by the United Nations Conference on International Organization held in San Francisco from April 25 to June 26, 1945, which created the UN Charter. Following this achievement, the United Nations Organ- ization was born on October 24, 1945.

A big tragedy occurred in 1943 when, due to the economic and transportation dislocations brought on by the war, hundreds of thousands of Indians in the province of Bengal died of starvation. The causes of this catastrophe were complex, as much a result of moral lassitude as of technical failure and global war. From the latter standpoint, the Japanese conquest of Burma, whose rice surpluses had always acted as a buffer against crop failures in India, played a major role in what took place. At the time when this had occurred, and indeed as a direct consequence of it, the concentration of British and American armed forces in north- eastern India, whose logistical requirements were enormous, placed extra strains on an already frail Bengali economy. The *coup de grace* had then been delivered by Mother Nature in 1943 when an unprecedentedly violent typhoon swept up the Bay of Bengal and wiped out a huge proportion of the province's grain crop.

Estimates of the number of persons who perished in the 1943 famine range from an official figure of 1.5 million supplied by the government of India to unofficial claims that the death toll ex- ceeded 3 million. Whatever the true figure, Venkatraman (1983: 9) rightly observed that "Hundreds of thousands of Indians in the province starved to death in 1943 while the 'United Nations were engaged in a war to make the world safe for democracy.'" In his view, these thousands of human beings "were as truly victims of the Second World War as were the casualties on battle-fields and in bombed cities" (ibid.: 10).

Friends of India in the United States tried desperately to get the government to take some kind of decisive action to save lives once the proportions of the tragedy in Bengal became known.

What they envisioned, of course, was for the Roosevelt administration to either use its influence to prod the British government into finding more effective ways to combat the famine *in situ* or, failing that, take measures to ship food from its own stockpiles directly into India. It was pointed out that coordinated action was always possible under the aegis of the Combined Food Board, a British-American apparatus that had been created to prevent the development of food shortages in Allied countries which might impede the war effort. Responding to this suggestion, the American members of the Board recommended to their British counterparts that a special allocation of rice be authorized for dispatch to India as soon as possible. But even in this context, the British proved to be so touchy about American meddling in imperial policy toward India that they turned the proposal down. In Cordell Hull's words, "the British representatives on the Combined Food Board in Washington insisted that the responsibility for Indian food requirements be left to Britain, *and we perforce had to agree*" (Hull 1948: 1496, emphasis added). This was a response which could be interpreted (and was indeed so interpreted in many quarters) as an assertion that saving the imperial face took pre-cedence in the eyes of the British government over saving Indian lives!

With the failure of this effort to generate Anglo-American action, attention turned to UNRRA (United Nations Relief and Rehabilitation Agency), a humanitarian organization which had been established on November 9, 1943, consisting of 44 nations, including India. It was an outgrowth of a prior organization called the Inter-Allied Committee on Post-War Requirements, which had been brought into being through British initiative in September of 1941. In spirit and structure it was a precursor of the United Nations Organization itself inasmuch as it looked toward post-war rehabilitation under a new and more humane world order. The proposals for this new organization had been drafted in the US State Department by the then assistant secretary in charge of economic affairs, Dean Acheson. Observes Venkatraman (1983: 10):

It was quite clear from the start that American funds, personnel and influence would be dominant factors in the operations of UNRRA. Since the new organization was an international body believed to be specially intended to provide relief to the Hungry and the Needy, American friends of India entertained the hope that their government might find it possible to channel some aid to India through it without provoking open opposition from the British. Unfortunately, however, they had reckoned without the "fine print" in the draft agreement that Dean Acheson had so laboriously wrought for the first organization to be launched by the United Nations.

The catch to which Venkatraman alludes was a phrase in the preamble which stated that UNRRA assistance was designated for populations *liberated* from the enemy. And since the starvation which afflicted the people of Bengal had been caused by acts of commission and omission committed by America's principal ally, it was decided that UNRRA's mandate did not apply to India.

J.J. Singh and others in the India Lobby jumped feet first into this emerging crisis. J.J. himself, with his public relations flair and network connections, took the lead. He insisted that the UNRRA mandate did (or must) apply to India, in that the famine was both directly and indirectly a result of the war. The Japanese conquest of Southeast Asia, which brought their forces to India's eastern border, had resulted in the stoppage of almost 2 million tons of rice a year from Burma, the diversion of large quantities of India's wheat crop to the Middle East, massively increased food requirements for the military establishment in India itself, and major disruptions in an already fragile Indian transport system. Acheson responded to these exigencies with a bureaucratic coldness bordering on indifference. Not only did he reject J.J. Singh's argument as to the war-relatedness of the Bengal tragedy, but he even opposed its being discussed by a meeting of the UNRRA Council that was occurring in Atlantic City at the very time that the India League was appealing for action.

Singh went to Atlantic City anyway to try and persuade the Council to reject Acheson's interpretation of UNRRA's mandate. He won over Dr T.E. Tsiang, the head of the Chinese delegation, who assured Singh that if the question of famine relief for Bengal was raised by the council he would support the proposition. J.J. Singh told a press conference that he had also elicited the support of Chile, Mexico, South Africa and Australia, provided that the Indian delegate, Sir Girja Shankar Bajpai, took the initiative in the matter. *Sir Girja Shankar, however, did not do so.* In Venkatraman's words:

> In Atlantic City *he was a mere echo of the chief British delegate,* Colonel J.J. Llewellyn. India's delegate conducted himself "with a propriety becoming in a servant of the British Raj," sarcastically observed I.F. Stone, columnist for the *Nation.* Bajpai failed to raise the question of the Indian famine before the conference *because the British Government was opposed to any such course* (1983: 23, emphasis added).

I.F. Stone was, in fact, incensed by the conduct of the British delegation on this occasion and by what he seems to have regarded as at the least some measure of tacit complicity on the part of Dean Acheson. "Colonel Llewellyn and Assistant Secretary of State Dean Acheson," he wrote, "dominated the proceedings, and it behooved the other delegates to behave" (*Nation*, December 11, 1943, p. 686). Alluding to the British delegate's insinuations that the food crisis in Bengal was more the result of hoarding and market manipulations by unscrupulous native profiteers than by the consequences of broader structural and policy failures, Stone asserted that "*the basic cause is imperialism*" (ibid.: 687). He concluded with the statement that a just political settlement of the Indian question was the real key:

> The real point, it seems to me, is that only a national government of Indians could hope at a time like this to squeeze from the peasantry the necessary driblets of food by which urban India is normally fed. Conversely, the present government of India could hardly expect to antagonize the large landowners, who are among its few supporters, by instituting really vigorous controls (ibid.).

The creation of a government genuinely able to deal with the internal dimensions of the country's economic crisis would be possible, Stone continued, if, "Gandhi and Nehru were in office instead of in jail."

In the end, of course, nothing was done. Colonel Llewellyn, says Venkatraman, "spared no efforts to ensure that his fellow crusaders kept their attention firmly away from India." Having refused to concede that "the starving Indians were 'victims of war,'" Llewellyn found that "as far as Acheson was concerned that assertion was apparently tantamount to proof" (*Nation*, December 11, 1943, p. 686).

The arrogance and insensitivity of Dean Acheson at Atlantic City aroused the ire of Representative Carl Mundt, the conservative, ex-missionary (to China) Congressman from South Dakota. Appraised of what had transpired at the UNRRA meeting by a letter from J.J. Singh, one which he had sent to every member of the House Foreign Affairs Committee but which only Mundt had responded to, the Congressman was highly critical of what had transpired and of Acheson's role in it. When Acheson and the State Department proved unresponsive to his criticisms, Mundt took the issue to the floor of the House where he was successful in putting enough pressure on UNRRA to get it to amend its charter in such a manner that its food relief activities could be conducted anywhere in the world where the government "exercising administrative authority" agrees to it.

Ultimately, however, the Joint Resolution of the US Congress engineered by Representative Mundt, and Resolution 54 adopted by the UNRRA Council in response to it, failed to alter the situation in India. Stipulating that the responsible government of a country or region must request UNRRA assistance before such assistance could be forthcoming simply gave the Churchill Government a way out of experiencing the loss of political prestige which they believed an UNRRA relief undertaking for Bengal would comprise. To avoid implicitly conceding that their own malfeasance had had anything to do with Bengal's plight, they simply did not request any assistance from the body.

Countless thousands of Bengalis perished in 1943, the innocent victims of the political stalemate between British imperialism and Indian nationalism, as well as of the short-sighted determination of the Roosevelt Administration to at all costs avoid making political waves.

It is surprising, really, that Indian bitterness over the role played by the US government at Atlantic City was not greater and did not last longer than it did. The fact that the damage to future relations was not as severe as it might have been can be attributed in some measure to the diversionary influence of global war and also in some measure to the incarceration of the nationalist leaders who would otherwise have certainly been determined, and in a better position, to draw more world attention to the calamity that was taking place and identify the responsible culprits. The burden instead fell on a small band of dedicated Indian expatriates with meager resources, fortunately supported by numerous public figures both in and out of government who did what they could to expose and criticize official American conduct at Atlantic City and the disastrous consequences it was having in India. Their efforts clearly made a difference, but fell far short of what was needed. The main effect was to further heighten public awareness of the evils of colonialism, which in turn made the job of the India Lobby that much easier.

Ultimately, however, the Joint Resolution of the US Congress engineered by Representative Mundt, and Resolution 54 adopted by the UNRRA Council in response to it, failed to alter the situation in India. But it did help the India Lobby's overall image. This was apparent in the light of Representative Mundt's success in persuading the US Congress to pass the joint resolution urging a change in UNRRA policy. This received wide publicity in India, as had public statements by Pearl Buck, William Phillips, and other noted Americans. These gestures served at least to remind Indians that the heart of the American people was in the right place even at times when it seemed that their official representatives had no heart at all. More tangible gestures were forthcoming, such as a $100,000 donation for famine relief in India from the War Relief Committee of the AFL-CIO and modest amounts from other sources. However, these efforts were always to some extent undercut in the end by government actions which tarnished the idealistic image they were intended to create. For example, it took prompting from the Quakers, who said relief efforts in India would require $100,000 a month for at least one year, to get the President's War Relief Control Board to finally allocate $900,000 toward this goal. The money was to be provided through the British War Relief Society (obviously out of deference to British imperial sensibilities) which was affiliated with the National War Fund. Unaccountably, however, on July 1, 1944 the Fund suddenly cut this already inadequate sum by almost $356,000 and announced that aside from $200,000 that had been donated by the AFL-CIO, no further funds would be forthcoming for Indian famine relief! Clearly the atmosphere of pique which pervaded the Atlantic City proceedings of UNRRA, and which lurked in the corridors of the State Department and the British Foreign Office, had seeped into the councils of the National War Fund as well.

Not long after the famine relief turmoil was running its course, two events occurred in Washington which would strongly influence the subsequent course and effectiveness of the India Lobby's activities. One was the convening of the Dumbarton Oaks Conference from August to October 1944, whose purpose was to prepare the ground for the San Francisco Conference scheduled to convene on June 26, 1945, which would give birth to the United Nations. Dumbarton Oaks was actually a series of meetings that were held in this historic site in Georgetown, attended by representatives from the Soviet Union, Great Britain, China and the United States. The general purpose was to consider the structure and form of a new international organization that would eventually take the place of the still extant but virtually moribund League of Nations. Technically it addressed the potential make-up of the proposed Security Council that would be the governing body of the new organization and, in the meantime, interface with what remained of the old League. But basically these deliberations were really concerned with how much sovereignty member nations would be prepared to surrender to a world body. The principal result was the adoption of the veto power by members of the Security Council.

It is not clear how much direct contact members of the India Lobby had with the Dumbarton Oaks participants or their deliberations; one suspects that it was minimal. Its importance for the South Asians lay in the fact that this was a seminal conclave being held in Washington amidst a lot of publicity, which was contributing to the atmosphere of ferment and expectation pervading the city as the lineaments of the post-war world were increasingly occupying the minds of all parties whose fate would be affected by what was to come.

## "Deep Throat": The Drew Pearson Bombshell

It was just as the Dumbarton Oaks Conference was winding down, however, that the Drew Pearson story broke on July 23, 1944. This pertained, it will be remembered, to Pearson's revelation in his *Washington Post* column, the "Washington Merry-Go-Round," of the William Phillips letter to President Roosevelt which harshly criticized British policies toward India, and most particularly their failure to achieve political reconciliation with Gandhi, Nehru, and the Indian National Congress.

Pearson opened his article by calling attention to the political stalemate in India. "As the war moves faster in Asia," he declared, "Administration advisors are convinced that the ticklish problem of India, *which Roosevelt repeatedly has postponed*, must be tackled soon" (emphasis added). He noted Prime Minister Churchill's intransigence on this issue. At FDR's request, said Pearson, United States Ambassador William Phillips, following his return from India, went to see Churchill at the behest of Roosevelt at the British Embassy, during Churchill's visit to the US, to try and reason with him. Churchill, of course, was by then fully aware of Phillips's opinions about the Raj. Pearson reported that the prime minister "banged the table" and declared, "I have always been right about Hitler and everyone else in Europe, and I am right about Indian policy." He claimed that any relaxation of the political suppression in India at this point in the war "will mean a blood bath."

Pearson then went on to present long passages in his column from Ambassador Phillips's letter to the president. Since detailed reference to what Phillips said has already been made, it is unnecessary to repeat them now; we will only reiterate here the points made by Phillips which particularly irritated the British and set off the political furor. Phillips had especially challenged the British proposition that Indian policy was none of America's business. On the contrary, he insisted, the US indeed had every right to play a role in resolving the problem. "I feel strongly, Mr. President, that in view of our military position in India, we should have a voice in these matters." He said it was not right for the US government to be shut out of the deliberative process "when we alone will have the major part to play in the struggle with Japan." Pearson also called attention to Phillips's belief that the British should, as a gesture to the nationalists, unequivocally declare their intention to grant independence to India once the war ended. Finally, Pearson justified his decision to publish such long excerpts from the Phillips letter on the ground of the Ambassador's senior status. "Ambassador Phillips's report is considered so important inside the State Department, and the whole India picture is so vital to Allied success in Asia, that a large part of his report follows ...."

At least as great was the impact of Pearson's second column (August 28, 1944) on the Phillips imbroglio, in which he revealed that the British had demanded a formal apology from the US government over the content of the Phillips letter; that the External Affairs Minister of the Government of India, Sir Olaf Caroe, had declared Ambassador Phillips *persona non grata*, even though Phillips had no intention of returning to India in any event; and that the British government had retaliated even further against Phillips by denying him the right to serve on General Eisenhower's staff as a military advisor at Supreme Headquarters Allied Expeditionary Force (SHAEF) in London, where he had been deputed following the Indian mission.

Actually, Pearson followed all this up with still a third column revealing the content of a later "report" which Ambassador Phillips prepared for President Roosevelt where he provided a more measured, historically detailed analysis of the Indian situation. Like its predecessors, this one too fell into the hands of the lobbyists and was shunted to Drew Pearson approximately a year after it had been written. The *Voice of India* (December 1944), in addition to reporting on Pearson's use of the document, published its entire text and accompanied it with a commentary by Syud Hossain. What was distinctive about this Phillips memo was its recommendation that the "way out of the deadlock" was for the United States, "with the approval and blessing of the British Government," to invite all parties to the dispute "to meet together to discuss plans for the future." He suggested that an American be designated to preside over the conclave "who could exercise influence in harmonizing the endless divisions of caste, religion, race and political views." Such a conference, Phillips declared, "might well be under the patronage of the King-Emperor, the President of the United States, the President of the Soviet Union and Chiang Kai-shek, in order to bring pressure to bear on Indian politicians."

Phillips himself foresaw that Churchillian intransigence and pique constituted the greatest impediment to bringing about such a conclave. "Behind the door," Phillips declared, "is Mr Churchill, who gives the impression that personally he would prefer not to transfer any power to an Indian government either before or after the war and that the status quo should be maintained" (*Voice of India*, December 1944, p. 54).

Syud Hossain, in his accompanying article, seconded Phillips's skepticism about British and American sincerity. "We have no means of knowing," he lamented, "whether this suggestion was put to Mr Churchill. All we can say is that had it been carried out, the embittered impasse in India would in all probability have been ended." His conclusion: "What precisely are 'British promises' worth in India, or elsewhere in the Orient? ... The British have made promises galore, but does anyone in the East *trust* them? From Palestine to China it is the same" (ibid.: 55, emphasis in original).

The Drew Pearson revelations were a political windfall for J.J. Singh, Anup Singh, Syud Hossain and their India Lobby co-horts. Clearly, the India Lobby had, as we shall soon see, acquired a "mole" in the State Department who was feeding them documents. This was allowing them for the first time to expose the pique which behind the facade of "Allied unity" was simmering between the British and American governments over the India question. In particular, the maladroit manner in which the British had handled things proved to be grist for the lobbyists' mill.

Particularly satisfying was the brief furor it generated in the halls of the US Congress. British arrogance and imperiousness had always rubbed many American legislators the wrong way; this was a legacy dating back to the American Revolution and its aftermath, which was much more alive 60 years ago than it is today. The more populist among them never tired of twisting the British Lion's tail when the opportunity presented itself. The disclosure of Ambassador Phillips's strong criticism of imperial policy toward India and the apparent attempt to have him declared *persona non grata* and consequently barred from England, and furthermore to cover up the deed, provided a golden opportunity for empire bashing. Some of their rhetoric was delightfully scathing and clearly redounded to the advantage of Britain's critics both within and outside government circles.

The Pearson revelations were the last straw for loquacious Senator A.B. "Happy" Chandler (1898–1991) of Kentucky and for tart-tongued Representative Leon Harry Gavin (1893–1963) from the Pittsburgh area. Both fired heavy rhetorical salvos at the British for their imperiousness—and, by implication, at the Roosevelt

Administration as well, for allegedly knuckling under to British pressure.

In keeping with the Senate's carefully cultivated image of dignity and restraint in public discourse, Mr Chandler's remarks were somewhat more circumspect than were Mr Gavin's, but nevertheless unmistakably to the point. The Senator said that he had learned "with dismay and shock" that William Phillips had been declared *persona non grata* in India (and pressured to leave England as well) simply because "this emissary of our Commander-in-Chief has made a report on conditions in India which the British do not like." It turned out that Chandler had obtained through a "disgruntled British embassy official" (probably someone on Sir Girja Shankar Bajpai's staff) a copy of a letter from Sir Olaf Caroe, addressed to Sir Ronald Campbell, stating as much. This disclosure considerably compromised British credibility when at first they attempted to deny these charges. Reviewing the circumstances of Phillips's original assignment to India, Senator Chandler asserted that the conditions which the ambassador found and reported on ("the miserable condition of the Indian people" and the "mismanagement of the Indian [political] situation"), and "which the British want to cover up," cannot be ignored by the United States Government, given India's strategic relevance to the war effort in Asia. "India may well become a country dogged by civil war," he declared, "civil war which may even be a stab in the back for our brave young men in the China-Burma-India theater of operations" (*Congressional Record*, Senate, August 29, 1944, p. 7336).

Gavin was far more blunt. "I do feel," he declared, "that the arrogance of British statesmanship has reached a new high when they ask for and evidently, I understand, have secured the removal of William Phillips ... from the staff of General Eisenhower." Such high-handed behavior evoked in Gavin's mind reminiscences of the circumstances which led to the parting of the ways between America and Great Britain almost 170 years earlier. "Evidently," the Congressman intoned, "there are a great many in the British Empire who fail to recognize the fact, and it is properly recorded in a document known as the Declaration of Independence, that we declared our Independence on July 4, 1776, and *certainly we cannot but sympathize with India who, like ourselves, seeks its independence*" (ibid.: 7584–86, emphasis added).

Taking note of the publicity campaign which the British mounted in reaction to the public disclosure of the Phillips letter, Gavin inserted into the Congressional Record news stories and editorials from the Pittsburgh area which bitterly denounced British attempts to get that document suppressed wherever possible, in addition to their attempts to get Phillips's views officially repudiated. One of these articles (*Pittsburgh Sun-Telegraph*, September 1, 1944) refers to a demand by Calvin D. Johnson, a Republican House member from Illinois, that both the British Ambassador (Lord Halifax) and the British Minister for India (Bajpai) be declared *persona non grata* in retaliation unless the British ceased their efforts to "mold public opinion" to their advantage in the Phillips case.

Regarding the matter of their propagandizing in the United States, Gavin accused the British of directly meddling in domestic American affairs. He noted Pearson's claim that "the British consuls throughout the United States had been instructed to ask local newspapers to counteract the Phillips letter to the President." Gavin found this to be hypocritical in the extreme. "Now it appears," he declared, "that it is all right for British executives to potshot at Uncle Sam and get away with it, but when William Phillips... courageously presents his views, he finds himself on the way out." He also revealed considerable sensitivity to the longer-range implications of what was taking place in India. "The four freedoms is a great instrumentality for the nations of the world when it does not affect the British Empire; but when it comes to India for the Indians, Ireland for the Irish, Hong Kong for the Chinese, and Palestine for the Jews—well, that is just another story!"

There can be no question that the Pearson columns and the official British reaction to their disclosure (along with the congressional fireworks this ignited) increased American consciousness of India's plight under British colonial rule. It clearly brought out the fact that America, both officially and in the public mind, was by no means an uncritical supporter of British policies toward India or indeed any of her colonies. While it may be true, as Hess avers, that "Chandler's role resulted mostly from personal political considerations, rather than from any convictions about India,"[1] it nevertheless helped the nationalist cause in organizational and public relations terms, and enhanced feelings of goodwill toward America among many Indian nationalists and educated segments of the Indian public. In sum, it was a public relations windfall for

J.J. Singh, Anup Singh, Syud Hossain, Haridas Mazumdar, Taraknath Das, and Krishnalal Shridharani. Among other things, it enabled them to speak in more authoritative tones about things Indian. The editorials and other writings both in the *Voice of India* and *India Today* reflect this newfound self-assurance. Syud Hossain, for example, in the March 1945 issue of *Voice of India* (p. 102) published a full-page "Report" to President Roosevelt, which urged that India's plight not be forgotten "On the eve of your departure abroad for momentous deliberation on the issues of war and peace." He reminded Mr Roosevelt of the many "distinguished Americans in various responsible capacities [who] have gone to India under your authority," such as Colonel Louis Johnson and Ambassador William Phillips, who returned from their missions to voice sympathy and support for the cause of Indian freedom. "We earnestly trust and pray that in your forthcoming conferences you will not forget the cause of 400 millions of the Indian people." Finally, he reminded the President that, "An imperial and alien autocracy deriving its authority and power from London, and ruling by fiat and force, can be no substitute for national self-government, morally or psychologically, whatever clams it may make for its own benevolence or efficiency." The old hard-line radicals like Har Dayal, Taraknath Das, Sarangadhar Das, Khankhoje, and Bhagwan Singh had given way to a more socially sophisticated and, it must be said, more educated breed, personified by J.J. Singh, Anup Singh, Syud Hossain, and Krishnalal Shridharani. The former believed the answer lay in shattering the existing system in a stroke of revolutionary fury; the latter believed that more could be accomplished by working within the existing system and reforming it.

More satisfactory results would obviously have ensued, of course, had it proved possible to induce the Roosevelt administration to be more politically aggressive. Its reticence was especially bothersome when in nationalist eyes the Pearson flap appeared to have offered a golden opportunity to give a sharper pro-democracy edge to America's South Asia Policy, at a time when the Atlantic Charter was on everybody's lips and the India question was more prominent in the public's mind than ever before. The Roosevelt administration's reticence was one more manifestation of an ambivalence which had persisted since the Cripps Mission, would unfortunately remain in place throughout World War II, and not entirely disappear until India finally gained her independence from the British in 1947.

## "Deep Throat"

A compelling question, of course, is the identity of the "mole" who was feeding confidential State Department documents to members of the India Lobby, which they in turn were feeding to Drew Pearson. One can say that this mysterious individual turned out to be for Anup Singh, Syud Hossain and the India Lobby what "Deep Throat" was for the Watergate investigators, Woodward and Bernstein, a few decades later! Before we identify him, however, let us examine the impact which his actions had on the contest that was taking place between the South Asian activists and their British adversaries.

The Pearson leaks created great consternation in the British camp. This indomitable investigative reporter had truly stirred up a hornet's nest that was proving to be a public relations windfall for the India Lobby. The theatrical attempts that were made by Halifax to contain the political fallout at times assumed comic opera proportions. Not only were the British alarmed about the effects that the Phillips letter was having on their ability to manage the media in the United States, they were if anything even more concerned about preventing its ramifications from infecting India.

The negative publicity which Happy Chandler's perorations on the Senate floor generated particularly stuck in their craw. While Lord Halifax had assured Foreign Secretary Anthony Eden that Chandler's outburst could be dismissed as a political aberration, Eden was not so sure. "I have now seen press reports of Senator Chandler's iteration in the Senate of Drew Pearson's allegations," he telegrammed. "I realize that in Washington this may do him more harm than good (*sic*), but *we also have to consider [the] credence that both are likely to have in other parts of the United States*, and I regret that in view of [the] strength (*sic*) of our case and of President Roosevelt's having recently stigmatized Pearson (*sic*), you do not feel able to make [a] general comment that his article was inaccurate in almost every statement" (Mr Eden to the Earl of Halifax, quoted in Manserge and Moon 1944: 1234, emphasis added). In fact, the implication that Roosevelt had successfully "stigmatized" Pearson was pure wish fulfillment. So was the smug belief that Senator Chandler was some kind of political buffoon who could be readily manipulated and dismissed. They soon discovered that the Senator had the goods on them. Unknown to them, he had obtained documentary proof that the British had lied when they claimed that Ambassador Phillips had not been declared *persona non grata* by the Government of India, and that he had not been prevented from remaining in Britain on the SHAEF staff.

This came out in conversations which Assistant Secretary of State Breckinridge Long had with Lord Halifax and Senator Chandler in September 1944. The Senator's principal bone of contention with the British government was that Halifax had implicitly accused him of lying when he stated that William Phillips was *persona non grata*. Chandler had acquired a copy of a telegram sent by the External Affairs Department of the Government of India to the Secretary of State for India in London, which confirmed his contention that it was the British who were actually doing the lying. Signed by Olaf Caroe, the message declared that the Government of India "are doing our best to prevent entry of letters or newspapers carrying [the] text of Drew Pearson's article," into India, while lamenting that whatever may be done, "it is possible that copies will slip through and obtain publicity in India." He went on to say that, "Publication of Phillips' views *which seem to be authentic* would have a deplorable effect," especially what Caroe termed "unworthy sneers at the Indian Army."

It was then that Caroe essentially confirmed Chandler's assertion about Phillips's diplomatic status: "A further point arises [from the fact that] we understand [that the] designation of Phillips is still [the] President's personal representative in India." This being the case, "Whether or not he was in any way concerned in the leakage, [the] *views he has stated would make it impossible for us to do other than regard him as persona non grata, and we could not again receive him*. His views are not what we are entitled to expect from a professedly friendly envoy" (Government of India, External Affairs Department to Secretary of State [for India], quoted in Manserge and Moon 1944: 1203–4, emphasis added).

Breckinridge Long asked Chandler if he would be willing to divulge the source of his information. He, of course, refused and perhaps indulged in a bit of disinformation by claiming that his copy of the Caroe telegram had been obtained "directly from a high United States official," who had himself obtained it "either directly or indirectly ... from some source in the British Embassy itself." The next day, Chandler released the text of Caroe's cable to the press. This was his "reply to charges by the British Ambassador, the Earl of Halifax," that "persons in responsible quarters" had made assertions which are quite untrue" (*Foreign Relations of the United States* [*FRUS*] 1994: 246). The Senator had obtained his revenge! On September 4, Merrell, the American *Charge d'affaires*, was reporting to the Secretary of State that the Indian press "gave renewed prominence to Mr Phillips's letter to the President ... and published for the first time the substance of the telegram sent by Sir Olaf Caroe, the Foreign Secretary, in which he referred to Mr Phillips as *persona non grata*." Merrell said he called Caroe on the phone and that Caroe confirmed the authenticity of the telegram. "Caroe appeared shattered that his telegram had been made public and said he had no idea how the leak had occurred" (ibid.: 247).

Evidence that the Phillips letter and the Drew Pearson article about it was being capitalized upon by the India Lobby, and for that reason had greatly heightened anxieties at the British Embassy, is contained in a note which Sir Ronald Campbell addressed on August 8 to Edward R. Stettinius who at the time was Acting Secretary of State. It stated that "J.J. Singh's India League was about to publish an appeal to His Majesty's Government for immediate grant of Indian independence." He said that Singh intended the next day to *publish "a photostatic copy of the Drew Pearson article."* Campbell wanted Stettinius to immediately authorize "a statement clearly dissociating the United States Government from the opinions expressed by Phillips on three matters ... (*a*) morale of the Indian Army, (*b*) the British role in the war against Japan, and (*c*) Mr Churchill's statement on the application of the Atlantic Charter to India" (*FRUS* Vol. V, 1944: 209–10, emphasis added). Regarding these points, Churchill had stated that as a British possession, the Atlantic Charter did not apply to India! He had also indicated in a speech before Parliament that Britain might begin demobilizing its armed forces once the European war was ended but before the war with Japan was concluded, thus leaving the US to carry the burden in Asia!

It was at this point that the United States decided to put some distance between itself and the British on the India question and, to the extent that they did so, handed a significant tactical victory to the India Lobby. This took the form of a discreet refusal by the State Department to officially and publicly repudiate the William Phillips letter, as the British had requested. Stettinius put the issue directly to President Roosevelt:

> It is the Department's feeling that it would be impossible to issue a statement satisfactory to the British *inasmuch as we share in general the views expressed in the Ambassador's letter.* Unless you feel that we should comply with the British request, I would appreciate having your permission to tell the British that we consider it preferable to make no public statement on the subject." (*FRUS* 1944: 242, emphasis added).

Roosevelt agreed, and no public statement was made. Privately, Halifax, Eden and Churchill were livid. In a sense, it had been Caroe who had really opened the Pandora's Box with his intercepted message to the Secretary of State for India, revealing the depths of the Imperial government's pique they harbored over Ambassador Phillips. Thanks to Drew Pearson and Happy Chandler, the India Lobby had enjoyed the last laugh!

Speculation in Washington, London, and New Delhi was rife concerning how the Phillips letter found its way into Drew Pearson's hands. But the culprit was never accurately identified. Sir Ronald Campbell and Lord Halifax believed that Assistant Secretary of State Sumner Welles was the guilty party. Reporting on a conversation with Cordell Hull, Campbell said: "Hull reminded me that the President had publicly described Pearson as a chronic liar ..." Welles was a different matter, said Campbell: "There was only one person in the State Department who could have given or shown such a text to Pearson and that was Welles, whose relations with Pearson had been particularly close. In fact, Welles used to show Pearson documents and with him concoct attacks of Mr Hull himself" (Sir R. Campbell to Mr Eden, in Manserge and Moon 1944: 1120).

Some believed that members of the Indian National Congress had found some way to feed the letter to Pearson, but no credible evidence for such a maneuver was ever forthcoming. Merrell speculated from New Delhi that one of the mission's Secretaries, James L. Berry, might possibly have handed the letter to the Indian industrialist G.D. Birla, "about June 24, for delivery to Gandhi" (*FRUS* 1944: 236). This was in response to an inquiry by Cordell Hull about the possibility that "Indian Congress circles" could have transmitted the letter to "sympathizers in the United States" (ibid.: 239). Hull was closer to the mark than he realized when he suggested that sympathizers in the US might have been responsible. Ultimately, however, even Hull had to admit that the source of the leak was unknown. To John Winant, the US Ambassador to Great Britain, Hull was compelled to say: "This publication was made without any prior knowledge of the Department and we do not know how Pearson came into possession of a copy of this letter addressed to the President."

## "The Robert Crane Factor"

It turned out that "Deep Throat" was not a major figure in the intense political games that were swirling over South Asian policy during World War II in Washington, London, and New Delhi. It was not Sumner Welles, James L. Berry, G.D. Birla or any other notable personality. It was actually an obscure junior officer on the India Desk in the Division of Cultural Relations in the State Department who was responsible for leaking the Phillips letter. By a complicated series of actions, he made it possible for members of the India Lobby in Washington to view the *original* text, not merely a copy. They did the rest. This person was Robert I. Crane (1920–1997), who had spent his early years in Bengal as the child of missionary parents and would, following the war, enroll in Yale and become a noted historian of South Asia. Crane joined the State Department in 1943.[2] His knowledge of and sympathy for India soon drew him to members of the India Lobby, as well as to a number of other Indians at work in other Washington venues like the Agency-General and the Indian Trade Commission. He was part of a small circle of Americans around the city who had like him been missionary brats in India or had come from academic environments where they had acquired an awareness of the Indian freedom movement. Many, like Crane, were employed by government agencies in various capacities in the wartime atmosphere of Washington. Being for the most part pro-Congress, they gladly participated in events, both formal and informal, staged by the India Lobby; and indeed energetically supported the Congress cause whenever and wherever possible.

Obviously, Crane's position in the State Department made him an especially attractive recruit. He was readily taken into the group. He attended their public events and wrote an occasional short article for Anup Singh's magazine. He was a regular guest at Castle Rock, the mansion across the Potomac in Falls Church, which K.C. Mahendra had acquired as a personal residence but which was also used for lobbying purposes. There, "they wined and dined people whom they wanted to impress." The high points of the social activities which occurred there were "weekend parties that would commence on Saturday evening and last into Sunday .... Sometimes we would play poker half the night ... Naoroji loved to play poker ...."

**Illustration 10.1**
**Robert I. Crane (1927–1997)**

*Source: Journal of Asian Studies, 1998, Vol. 57, No. 2, p. 633.*

The Mission was charged with acquiring and shipping military supplies to the sub-continent. The Deputy Director was K.A.D. Naoroji, the grandson of Dadabhai Naoroji, whom everyone called "Kish." Both Mahendra and Naoroji were very suave and sophisticated gentlemen who despite their wealth and lofty status were, in Crane's words, *"pukka* nationalists," utterly opposed politically to Agent-General Sir Girja Shankar Bajpai, whom they regarded as a British tool. They were compelled to conduct themselves with great circumspection, however, because technically speaking the Supply Mission was a British (Government of India) operation. Like J.J. Singh, and indeed in concert with him, they learned how to work the system with considerable aplomb. The Lobby avidly welcomed Kate Mitchell to the fold because of her very pro-Indian book, *India Without Favor*, in which she provided a detailed picture of how the British were exploiting India and pedaling myths in America about the "benevolence" of the Raj. It was through Mahendra and Naoroji that Crane was first introduced to Mitchell. She in turn introduced him to J.J. Singh, who introduced him to Clare Booth Luce. Crane had some less than flattering things to say about Singh's entrepreneurial proclivities, however: "He ran a very exploitative business in which he imported *khadi* cloth from India and had a sweat shop in New York where little old ladies worked ten hours a day turning out very attractive ladies garments."

Crane provided a grassroots perception of J.J. Singh's manipulative capabilities. "He had a genius for PR," Crane declared,

> One of his major sources of revenue and supply were the Sikh community out in California. These Sikhs had the equivalent of "Green Cards"—i.e., many were married to American women; they put their money in their wives' names to protect it from currency laws, etc. They were all willing to throw money around trying to buy influence that would enable them to get American citizenship. They were all patriots and wanted India to be free, *but they also wanted American citizenship.*

J.J. Singh willingly accommodated them. Thus, Crane characterized Singh as playing a dual role in the nationalist movement. "Luckily they were not incompatible." On the one hand, "He was a spokesman for India," while, on the other hand, he was "also a

**Illustration 10.2**
**J.J. Singh, President of the India League of America (second from right)**

*Source:* Kamath 1998.

spokesman for changes in the immigration laws that would make it easier for Indian immigrants to become American citizens."

As by Shaplen, Singh's lobbying style in Washington was colorfully described by Crane:

He lived in New York City, used to come down to DC two or three times a week, where he would rent a suite in one of the best hotels in town, put out a very nice bar, and then hold a press conference which was announced in advance. He would manage to get on the press wires and the ticker tapes (I never knew how). He'd get headlines saying that "J.J. Singh, President of the India League of America, has journeyed to Washington to speak with Congressmen on immigration matters. He will give a press conference at the Mayflower Hotel at 4 PM. All members of the press are cordially invited. Food and drinks will be available." He was a very colorful guy. Furthermore, he was so shrewd. He always brought a Congressman or a Senator with him which naturally drew a crowd .... He had one very prestigious Senator from a Western state who was his prize contact [Author's note: I think it was Pat McCarren (1876–1954) of Nevada]. J. J. had sold him completely on the idea of citizenship for Indians. *The joke is that [the Senator], who had a large American Indian constituency, thought J.J. meant American Indians!*

Crane said his closeness to the India Lobby perpetually kept him in a delicate position at the State Department. In that era, State was a very conservative place, dominated, according to Crane, by WASPs who were anti-Semitic, racist and disdainful of people with ethnic roots in what would today be called the Third World. Crane's immediate superior, C. Hawley Oats, exemplified this haughty establishmentarianism. In Crane's words, Oats "was the worst type of the old-image foreign service officer; he pretended to be a Bostonian with the phoney accent and all that; but he was actually from Texas." He played down his rustic roots to make himself acceptable to the East Coast establishment. He had actually served some time in India as a vice-consul, but maintained that Indians were incompetent and inept and that, anyway, "Britain was America's ally." Oats insisted that State Department officers must have no relationships with Indians that could be construed as "sympathetic," a dictum that especially applied to young officers like Crane, whom he regarded (because of his status in the cultural rather than the political division) as "adjuncts" who must never dabble in political matters.

Crane was undeterred, however, and continued socializing with the India crowd anyway. His value to the lobby was enhanced by a friendship he had developed with Horace Poleman who, at the time of the Drew Pearson incident, was head of the Southern Asia Section of the Library of Congress. It is not clear how the two met. Poleman was very close to the India lobbyists, so much so that on May 9, 1941, he delivered the main address at an India League-sponsored gathering in New York to celebrate Rabindranath Tagore's 80th birthday. He described how, "less than a year ago," in Keshab Chandra Sen Street in Calcutta, he had addressed an audience of several hundred "learned Pandits, lawyers and teachers trained in the West, yellow-robed religious men, Jains, Hindus, Mohammedans," to whom he had "the temerity to talk about the meaning of culture and to suggest ways and means of a better understanding between the East of India and the West of America" (*India Today*, May 1941, p. 20).

Poleman had acquired his India expertise as a graduate student at the University of Pennsylvania under the mentorship of

W. Norman Brown, about whom more presently. His doctoral dissertation was a commented "census" of Indian manuscripts in US and Canadian libraries. Like his mentor, W. Norman Brown, Poleman was learned in the sub-continent's literatures, history, cultures, and religions, fluent in Sanskrit and Hindi, and highly sympathetic toward the freedom struggle. It was both his scholarly ability and his *in situ* experience which had resulted in Poleman's appointment to the Library of Congress position. Toward the end of his New York speech, Poleman enunciated his mission as America's principal South Asian archivist. At the Library of Congress, "we are developing services to implement the study of India," he declared. "Other libraries will be expected to cooperate and to use these services as the demand for them increases." He spoke of how the Library of Congress and the American Council of Learned Societies had cooperated to establish a microfilm copying facility at the Royal Asiatic Society of Bengal in Calcutta for the benefit of American scholars. He also spoke of many other undertakings of a similar kind. Horace Poleman made himself a driving force in the establishment of South Asian studies in the United States.

But Poleman was far more than a mere bibliographer. Equally important, he had good contacts in key government agencies. In one instance, for example, Poleman fingered a British agent named Jocelyn Henessey who had been positioned in the Indian Agent-General's mission and whose principal responsibility as Girja Shankar's Information Officer was to systematically discredit Indians and their American supporters when they tried to present the Indian side of the nationalist cause in a favorable light. At some of the public conclaves which the British Embassy regularly staged, Henessey would trumpet the official British line on India and claim that people who criticized the Raj were undermining Allied unity. Crane recalled one such occasion when Poleman took matters into his own hands by standing up and bluntly asking Henessey during the question period following his talk how much money the British were paying him to propagandize against the Indians around Washington!

From his vantage in the State Department, Crane was able to scrutinize many official documents that came across his desk. One day, he noticed a file containing William Phillips's letter to President Roosevelt. By its "route markings" he could tell that it had transited Assistant Secretary of State Sumner Welles's desk to another Assistant Secretary of State whose name Crane could not recall, thence to C. Hawley Oats, and finally to the junior officer, Robert Crane, for deposit in whichever filing cabinet it belonged.

Since there had never been any public airing of the tensions existing between the United States and Great Britain over India policy, Crane immediately understood the import of the Phillips letter. He wanted his friends in the India Lobby to see it in the hope that they could make some use of it in formulating their strategies for aiding the nationalist cause. Crane sneaked the letter out of State and showed it first to his friend, "Kish" Naoroji. When Naoroji read it, he exclaimed, "Oh, this *is* interesting! I must show it to K.C. [Mahendra]!" Crane agreed to let him do this, but insisted, "I *must* have it back tomorrow!" Naoroji promised, and took it home with him. "Tuesday, the next day, we met for lunch and he returned it to me." Naoroji reiterated how fascinating it was and how grateful they were that I had allowed them to see it." He said "they hoped and prayed that it had been seen by FDR." Crane says he returned the letter to the filing cabinet and assumed that "this was the end of it."

However, "three or four weeks later, no more than that, to my amazement, it appeared in Pearson's column. When I read that," Crane declared, "I damn near fainted!" He contacted Naoroji and asked him, "What have you done?" Naoroji "rather shamefacedly" replied that, as a matter of fact, he and Mahendra agreed that this document was too important to be allowed to just get buried once again in the State Department's vaults, never to be seen again. So they summoned one of their "most safe" secretaries who (in the days before copying machines!) sat up half the night typing copies of it.

Crane asked Naoroji how the letter found its way to Pearson, but Naoroji was evasive. He obviously wished to cover himself and others who were involved in engineering the leak. It was only after the war ended and India had attained its independence that Naoroji revealed what the next steps had been. He said that he had shared the letter's contents with Obaidur Rahman who then also made a copy of it. Obaidur Rahman was a key figure in the India circle. He was Press Officer at the Indian High Commission. He had a degree from the London School of Economics. He had become press officer for the Government of India just prior to the Cripps Mission and was in charge of all press releases pertaining to it. He knew all its twists and turns inside out. Crane characterized Rahman as a "fiery patriot" and very pro-Congress despite his official position and despite being a Muslim. Yet, after independence, he opted to live in Pakistan. He, along with Colonel Altaf Qadir, the chief military attaché, also very pro-nationalist, had lots of inside information that he was willing to share with the lobbyists because he was responsible for carrying Sir Girja Shankar's briefcase for him. He used to quip that the aristocratic Agent-General "never ever carried anything himself!"

Rahman somehow knew Pearson personally and said that the investigative reporter published a column based on the letter "the day he got his hands on it." There is no evidence that Drew Pearson had any significant involvement with India and her problems prior to the journalistic windfall that befell him. However, since we know that Obaidur Rahman was the person who actually transmitted the document to him, one must assume that he had some awareness of the views and activities of the India Lobby, including at least occasional contacts with some of its members. Needless to say, his courage in publicizing the Phillips letter in one of his columns endeared him to the Indian nationalists. It is said that some years later, Pearson actually made a "sentimental journey" to independent India and received a very cordial reception.

Crane himself met Pearson after the war and at that time confirmed that Rahman was the person who actually gave him the letter. This too is interesting in the light of the disinformation in which Pearson himself engaged in one of his subsequent columns concerning his sources. He simply reinforced the Sumner Welles thesis. "Secretary Hull," he wrote, "informed Sir Ronald [Campbell] that the Phillips letter had undoubtedly leaked out through former Undersecretary Sumner Welles—which the British, of course, knew was not the case." To further muddy the issue, in the same article, he quoted Assistant Secretary Adolph Berle to the effect that "they had a suspicion regarding the news leak but were not prepared to reveal it at that time" (Pearson's column, August 28, 1944). Whether Berle meant by this remark that they suspected someone as far down in the pecking order as Robert Crane was never revealed.

There followed a furor at the State Department, as C. Harley Oats and other high ranking officials frantically searched for the responsible culprit. Crane was, of course, from the outset considered a prime suspect because of his known contacts with the pro-nationalist groups in the city. But nothing could be definitively proved. He said that he was closely grilled about the leak, directly accused of having given the Phillips letter to Drew Pearson and threatened with disciplinary action. Crane admitted to his inquisitors that he had shown the letter to an Indian acquaintance but could truthfully say that he did not know how it had found its way to Pearson. That is because initially, as already noted, he himself did not know the exact route which the letter had taken. Henceforth, however, Crane found himself isolated within the agency and eventually compelled to seek his fortune elsewhere.

The wartime environment of Washington provided a unique opportunity for Crane to avoid any immediate legal repercussions from his alleged misdeeds. His friend Horace Poleman and Professor W. Norman Brown, both of whom knew the truth, were able to come to his rescue by offering him a new assignment that on the one hand made use of his partisan involvement with the India Lobby, and on the other afforded a means of freeing him from the State Department's menacing clutches.

W. Norman Brown was a renowned Sanskritist who had spent his childhood and adolescence in India in a missionary family. There he had acquired fluency in Hindi and had developed, through his father's influence, a deep interest in classical Indian civilization. He returned to the United States when he was 17, enrolled in Johns Hopkins University, and received a Ph.D. in Sanskrit in 1916. By the early 1920s, Brown had moved to the University of Pennsylvania where he gradually laid the foundation for the first South Asian area studies program in the United States. Brown was more than a mere "Sanskritist." He was interested in the entire spectrum of Indian society and civilization, from the ancient Indus Valley Civilization to the country's contemporary politics and social systems. Strongly pro-Indian and anti-colonialist, he published numerous articles on this subject in the *Baltimore Sun*, the *Saturday Evening Post* and elsewhere. He was, of course, strongly sympathetic to the activities and goals of the India Lobby. The regional studies program he established at Pennsylvania transcended the antiquarian style which characterized "Indic studies" on the few other American campuses where in those days any-thing concerning India was taught. Instead, his program adopted a holistic approach which made its curriculum and its matriculates extremely attractive to an American government that was groping for a strategic perspective on a part of the world that was virtually unknown to them. This problem was further compounded by the fact that what little was actually known had been filtered primarily through British eyes and interests, and was for this reason, as the Cripps Mission machinations and the Louis Johnson and William Phillips episodes demonstrated, of dubious value to an American government which now had compelling reasons for wanting to develop independent perspectives on the region.

At a time when the American military commitment to the region had become so substantial, and when it was becoming increasingly clear that America was destined to emerge from the war as a major world power that would have vital strategic interests in Southern Asia, Professor Brown's reputation for scholarly excellence and criticism of British rule made him the ideal person to help develop an independent source of intelligence on India. In 1944, therefore, Brown was recruited by the OSS (the progenitor of the CIA) to establish an India Section within its British Empire Division, and under this identify American operatives with the cultural and lin-guistic skills necessary to gather as much independent intelligence as possible on all aspects of India, including, indeed especially, the political situation and its possible implications for the present and future American roll in the sub-continent.

The OSS was established on June 13, 1942, by Major William O. Donovan and was by war's end employing over 21,000 people in the business of intelligence gathering and covert action It was not until August of 1943 that Donovan was able to work out an agree-ment with the British through which an OSS station could be estab-lished in New Delhi. This is because the British were well aware of its possible implications for their ability to manage American perceptions of their political wiles in India. When William Phillips was sent out in January 1943 as Roosevelt's personal represen-tative, one of his charges was to open the way for the OSS to operate in the Far East. With Linlithgow's paranoia and obstructionism, it took seven months to get the station up and running. The oper-ational details were handled by one of Phillips's assistants, Richard

P. Heppner, who had been in charge of OSS Special Operations in Europe and had served briefly with Phillips when he headed the OSS in London. Once Heppner had completed his work, a permanent station came into existence, headed by career diplomat George Merrill. Even after the station commenced operations, says Elizabeth McIntosh (1998: 246), "the British relied on bureaucratic maneuvering between London and Washington to stall further OSS buildup in India as long as possible." A "stormy interview" occurred between the head of Indian army military intelligence, an Australian Brigadier named W.J. Cawthorne, and General Donovan, who told him that "if he didn't let the OSS in the door, he would come through the transom."

Once the way had been cleared, a number of young Americans were recruited into the OSS for duty in India, where they were not only obliged to peruse the usual documents and contact the usual members of the official establishment, but also to do their utmost, "within the bounds of discretion," so to speak, to develop contacts with figures in the anti-colonialist nationalist movement. This included, where possible, even those who, like Gandhi, Nehru and many other top Congress leaders, were in jail or on the run from the British authorities. But it was not until well into 1944 before persons like Crane with special cultural and linguistic skills were able to arrive on the scene.

The US approach to India, as the Phillips letter had indicated, was driven in part by New Dealers in the Roosevelt administration who believed that Great Britain's intractable policies towards the nationalists were not only morally reprehensible but strategically counterproductive. That is a point which Ambassador Phillips energetically stressed throughout his diplomatic mission and to FDR in the messages whose content surfaced in the "infamous" Washington Merry-Go-Round Drew Pearson columns. The concerns became all the more compelling once America entered the war and the British had locked up the entire senior leadership of the Congress party. The situation grew increasingly dangerous once younger, more militant elements in the party (most notably the Congress Socialist and Communist factions) disavowed Gandhian non-violence, went underground in the countryside, and promulgated the so-called "1942 Movement" whose purpose was to wage guerilla warfare against the Raj.

The expertise required meant training recruits in Indian languages, and grounding them as much as possible in the details of Indian social, political and cultural life, so that they could move outside the prescribed and zealously maintained orbits of official India. Brown was uniquely qualified to undertake this assignment given his scholarly credentials as a classical scholar who had also spent a major portion of his life in India and thus melded his academic expertise with a profound understanding of contemporary Indian society and politics and great sympathy for the desire of its people to cast off the yoke of colonialism. Upon the recommendation of Horace Poleman, Robert Crane was recruited into OSS as a member of Brown's intelligence team. In 1944, he was commissioned as a second lieutenant, sent to the OSS training facility on Catalina Island (California), and then flown out to India for the remainder of the war. He returned to the United States in December 1945, to his old job at State, "to a very chilly reception," and was soon afterwards forced to resign.

Almost at once, his former boss in Cultural Affairs, Ralph Turner, with whom Crane had enjoyed good relations, contacted him. (Turner too had left the foreign service and had accepted a South Asian history professorship at Yale.) Crane's wartime experiences in the State Department, in the idealistic world of the India Lobby and the arcane world of the OSS's India operation had prepared him well for this new profession. He became one of America's premier South Asia historians, with professorships at Duke and Syracuse universities, and remained throughout the rest of his life a powerful advocate for policies and programs that would enhance American understanding of India. Evidence of the impact which those formative years had upon him is embodied in the doctoral dissertation he submitted at Yale in 1951, and in the dedication he wrote for it. Its subject was "The Indian National Congress and the Indian Agrarian Problem, 1919–1939." The dedication was inscribed to "Syed Hossain, Vyanktesh Ramchand Jog, Obaid Rahman, Anup Singh, who gave me insight." These were his principal cohorts during those heady days of World War II when a small band of Americans and Indians did what they could to achieve political justice for India and social justice for Indians in America. Robert I. Crane passed away in 1997, less than a year after he recounted his story to me.[3]

## The India Lobby and the San Francisco Conference

As the impact of the Pearson affair was waning, another critical opportunity for the India Lobby arose with the convening of the San Francisco Conference. The new Viceroy, Lord Wavell, designated three pillars of arch conservatism (Sir Feroze Khan Noon, Sir Ramaswamy Mudaliar, and V.L. Krshnamachari) as the Government of India's official representatives to the San Francisco Conference. These appointments produced an immediate uproar throughout nationalist circles both in India and the United States, and a vociferous demand by the Indian National Congress and other grassroots political groups that the Indian delegation to the UN Conference include what were called "popular representatives." This demand was introduced as a resolution in the Council of State in New Delhi but was defeated when the Raj rallied the body's nominated members to its side. To counter this move, Mahatma Gandhi and other Congress leaders, now released from jail, hit upon the idea of utilizing Madam Vijayalakshmi Pandit's impending unofficial journey to the United States via England as a means of publicizing their cause and pressing their demand that Indian representation in San Francisco reflect the popular will.

Madam Pandit, as she was called, had obtained permission to make this trip late in1944. It had been endorsed by Mahatma Gandhi. Prior to her departure, her trip pointedly commenced with a well-publicized audience with the Mahatma. Pandit was greeted very warmly by the American public as a symbol of India's struggle to enjoy, in her words, the political freedom which America had wrested from Great Britain 175 years earlier. However, official American attitudes left a bad taste in everybody's mouth. The problem for the official establishment was that Vijayalakshmi's sharp intellect, enormous charm and striking appearance enabled her to be a highly effective spokesperson for a viewpoint with which the mainstream American diplomatic establishment still felt far from comfortable. This, of course, made her a tremendous asset to the India Lobby, who proceeded to capitalize to the maximum on her celebrity.

Upon her arrival, Madam Pandit was greeted by J.J. Singh, Anup Singh, and Syud Hossain. This was, of course, a sentimental moment for Hossain and Madam Pandit because they had not met since their brief love affair back in the early 1920s. The India Lobby and India's approaching independence had brought them together once again! There are no reliable accounts of what transpired other than (according to witnesses) that it was filled with tender reminiscences. Each had traveled very different roads which led them to this fateful brief encounter. Vijayalakshmi had in the interim married a man named Ranjit Sitaram Pandit. The *Dictionary of National Biography* (pp. 297–300) characterizes him as a "cultured Barrister-at-Law from Kathiawar" and says the match was a "love marriage" consummated when Vijayalakshmi was only 21 years old. This confirms that she was a teenager when her elopement with Hossain occurred. Even though Vijayalakshmi's husband had passed away in 1940, and Syud had never married, there was no overt resumption of the relationship. Too much water had seemingly passed over the dam.

Eleanor Roosevelt, as might have been expected of this remarkable woman, hosted a luncheon for Madam Pandit at the White House, a gesture which provided her and the India Lobby with a windfall of valuable media attention. Ambassador Phillips, who had become an outspoken advocate of Indian independence after his unpleasant experiences with British umbrage, followed suit with a reception in Boston on February 12, 1945. These were obviously important gestures, of course, because they did indeed express, in an ex officio manner at least, the sympathy which many people in the Roosevelt Administration harbored for the establishment of genuinely representative political institutions in India. As Hess puts it: "Her charm, keen mind, first-hand experience, and sincerity made Mrs. Pandit the most effective voice of the nationalist cause heard in America during the war" (1971: 152).

While the public's attention was focused on her, the India League of America and the National Committee for India's Freedom took advantage of the opportunity presented by her presence in the United States to name Madam Pandit *their representative* to the United Nations Conference! In the June 1945 issue of *Voice of India*, it was announced that "The National Committee for India's Freedom and the India League of America jointly designated Mrs. Pandit to be the sole spokesman for the cause of India during the United Nations Conference in San Francisco." Claiming that "all other Indian organizations in the United States and Canada also accepted her as their spokesman," the magazine informed its readers that "Dr. Anup Singh, secretary of the National Committee, reached San Francisco two weeks before the Conference opened to make preparations for Mrs. Pandit's visit" (*Voice of India*, June 1945, p. 152).

In the course of his stay in San Francisco, Anup Singh was able to have a direct exchange with British Foreign Secretary Anthony Eden at the latter's press conference. Eden complained that the arrest of 16 Polish leaders was preventing a settlement of the critical Polish question. This was an opening too tempting to be ignored. Singh asked Eden, "If it is really true that the arrest of the Poles is obstructing the settlement of the Polish question, then isn't the arrest of thousands of Indian leaders by the British obstructing settlement of the India question?" Eden reportedly "joined in the laughter." Singh replied, "All very well but is the arrest of thousands of freedom-seeking Indians a laughing matter?" (ibid.: 149).

With endorsements by the India Lobby in hand, Madam Pandit set out for San Francisco where she was, as anticipated, denied any official standing in the conference. But just as predictably, she remained in town and used the occasion as a platform for promoting the nationalist cause. The *Voice of India* listed Madam Pandit's "program" in San Francisco:

**April 25.** Arrival in San Francisco; welcomed by a large number of countrymen at the station.
Garlanded and photographed.

**April 26.** Press conference, attended by more than 400 newspapermen.
(At one point in this conference, she declared: "Britain's excuses and alibis no longer carry conviction among well-informed and responsible persons in America and elsewhere. I desire to make it clear too, that the so-called Indian 'representatives' attending the San Francisco Conference have not the slightest representative capacity, no sanction or mandate from any responsible groups in India, and are merely the nominees of the British Government.") (ibid.: 154)

**April 27.** Addressed a public meeting held at Scottish Rite Auditorium. Syud Hossain presided.

Other speakers: Dr. Frederick W. Roman, Regent of University of California; Dr. Krishnalal Shridharani; Frank J. Burke, radio commentator; and Dr. Anup Singh.

**April 28.** Addressed a mass meeting of her countrymen in Sacramento.

**May 4.** Spoke before the Friday Morning Club in Los Angeles. Over 2,000 attended.

**May 5.** Addressed a meeting of the India National Congress of America (the Sikhs organization).

**May 11.** Sent a message of greeting to the people of China through the Office of War Information (OWI, later to become the *Voice of America*, VOA).

**May 13.** Addressed a meeting at the Sikh Gurdwara in Stockton.

**May 14.** Addressed the California State Legislature in Sacramento, followed by a tea party in her honor attended by 300 people.

"Mrs. Pandit's press conference," declared Shridharani, "rivaled that of Anthony Eden, and it also made good copy not only locally but throughout the nation .... Radio commentators again and again paid tribute to Mrs. Pandit's work and described in detail the campaign of the National Committee for India's Freedom" (*Voice of India*, June 1945, p. 156).

In contemporary basketball parlance, it can be said that the India Lobby put on a full-court press in San Francisco. Admittedly, said Shridharani, Free India's fight was not within the conference halls. By definition, it was a lobbying operation "carried on from outside the periphery ... in the corridors of the conference."

The California trip also provided opportunities for the Lobby's leaders to reinforce their ties with the the grassroots Indian communities scattered throughout the state whose citizenship rights were for them perhaps of higher priority than India's political independence. Shridharani noted that "California is the adopted home of the majority of Indian immigrants to this country, these sturdy patriots who have made repeated sacrifices for the cause of Indian freedom ...." The Lobby's leaders traveled with Madam Pandit to Stockton and other places where "they had an opportunity to visit them in their homes, to address their meetings, and to receive their homage and tributes for which some of us thought we were not qualified." Shridharani said that these migrants "have created a little India on American soil and have done India proud" (*Voice of India*, June 1945, pp. 156–57).

Mrs Pandit's exploits and those of others participating in the Conference got wide coverage in the Indian press as well, by a few Indian correspondents who managed to reach and report on San Francisco despite the fact that the Government of India refused to encourage or assist them in any way. This was another respect in which the India Lobby with its indigenous networks and resources was a valuable tool. J.J. Singh personally obtained accreditation from the *Hindustan Times* and the *Tribune of Lahore*. This afforded him access to the Conference's proceedings. Krishnalal Shridharani represented the *Amrit Bazar Patrika* of Calcutta. Shiva Rao, "one of the top-ranking journalists in India," represented the *Hindu* of Madras. Sabavala reported for the *Bombay Chronicle*; Shivaraman was accredited by the *Madras Express*. This assured reporting on the Conference from "the Indian point of view" (ibid.: 149).

"In press conferences, speeches and petitions," staged by the India Lobby, says Hess (1971: 153), "Mrs. Pandit presented her case effectively, attracting considerable public attention—much more than did Mudaliar, Noon and Krishnamachari." She upstaged the official Indian delegation to the Conference, then challenged their credentials, and demanded acknowledgment of her own. And while she failed to persuade the United States or any other major power to support this demand, Madam Pandit focused the attention of both her fellow countrymen and many thoughtful persons in the international community on the glaring disparity between the pronouncements and the deeds of those countries whose stated reason for establishing a new world body was to set right the wrongs of past generations.

She submitted a memorandum to the secretary-general of the United Nations Conference on International Organizations which powerfully expressed the position of the Indian people. In an especially poignant passage, she declared that while India comprises some 400 million people,

Yet, India is today a dependency of Great Britain, which is represented at this Conference by the grace and the agents of her imperial government. She is without a national government, a national flag, and without any national representation or diplomatic exchange in the councils of the nations except by the employees and appointees of her British masters. Such a state of affairs, I submit, is not only a grave moral and political wrong to India but a travesty of the claim that the United Nations Conference consists of representatives of sovereign nations (*Voice of India*, June 1945, p. 153).

The most substantive controversy in which Mrs Pandit was able to involve herself from her sidelines vantage on the UN Conference was that concerning the wording of Article 73 of the Charter. This was essentially an attempt by the major powers to have their cake and eat it too on the matter of imperialism. The article, in Hess's words, "obligated members controlling non-self governing regions to prepare their subject peoples for self-government, depending upon circumstances and varying stages of advancement" (ibid.: 154). However, there was no definitive denunciation of imperialism as such and no suggestion that the UN itself would be empowered with effective mechanisms for hastening its end.

Mrs Pandit, herself a personification of the nationalist ferment that was sweeping across the non-Western world, spoke out eloquently against devices such as this that were obviously designed to delay as long as possible the attainment of independence for colonial peoples. "What is the criterion of this preparedness," she asked, "and who is to determine it?" Speaking with the *déjà vu* of one whose family had long been in the forefront of freedom struggles, Madam Pandit declared that Great Britain "has created conditions in India which provide a convenient and plausible plea to go on denying the right of the Indian people to their freedom." Colonial overlords such as the British see to it that their subjects never manage "to achieve that hypothetic preparedness" (ibid.: 154). Only new initiatives can break this vicious cycle, she contended, and pointed out that unfortunately the UN Charter in its current form failed to create a real basis for any such initiative.

Her disappointment seemed to focus especially on the United States whose new Secretary of State, Edward R. Stettinius, had affirmed America's endorsement of Article 73. "Mr. Stettinius and other statesmen of the United Nations," declared Madam Pandit, "who are sincerely anxious to achieve a free and peaceful world would do well to address themselves realistically to the core of this [colonial] matter" (quoted in Hess 1971: 154).

Singling out the United States in this way, identifying by name only the American Secretary of State, was a manifestation of what would become the pattern of pique that would increasingly haunt relations between the two countries in decades to come (see Gould 2002). Indians always seemed to expect more of America than of other Western countries. This had been true since at least the days of the Cripps Mission and in a generalized way even before that. It was a by-product of the idealistic image which America had successfully projected of itself throughout the world. Like other people, Indians had come to think of America as a nation apart whose greatness lay not in empire building but in championing the rights of the downtrodden everywhere. Therefore, when policies of the United States government appeared to be at variance with the lofty ideals by which it purported to live, anger and disillusionment often followed.

Another harbinger of things to come was the manner in which the Soviet Union managed to exploit this flaw in the American image in ways that enhanced her own image in the emerging Third World. Basically, the Soviets were able to have their political cake and eat it too. While the Russians had also gone along with the proposition put forward by the conveners of the UN Conference that the grievances of colonial peoples were not germane to its current proceedings and had not shown any inclination to challenge the wording of Article 73, V.M. Molotov, the Soviet foreign minister, nevertheless did manage to make a public gesture at San Francisco which won plaudits in India and with the India Lobby at a time when American stock was looking a bit shaky. This happened at a press conference where Molotov declared that the official representatives of India did not really represent the Indian people. By according such implicit endorsement to Mrs Pandit's lonely struggle for recognition of the nationalist cause, the Soviet Union deftly escaped being lumped with the United States and other major powers as acquiescing to the procedural devices which had kept the colonial question off the table and outside the purview of Article 73. As Hess (1971: 155) states: "The Russian interest in India had developed slowly during the last stages of the war ... Molotov's gesture thus signaled the beginning of Russian efforts to support nationalist aspirations in Asia."

Roosevelt died shortly before the UN Conference met, a fact which in itself had probably rendered the US position on colonialism, and the kind of rhetoric employed by Molotov, more difficult to handle than it otherwise might have been. For despite Roosevelt's frustrating reluctance to be as publicly forthcoming on British colonialism as he privately felt about it, he was by and large a known quantity. At the time of Roosevelt's passing, a brief editorial in the *Voice of India* (May 1945) was titled "A Great Man Passes." It came as a "terrible blow" said the author. "To the peoples of Asia, as yet unliberated from a far longer subjugation [than Europe], it means the loss of the one leader among the great Powers whose words had given them real hope." There is ample evidence that the American president was indeed especially sympathetic to Asian nationalism and aware that America's interests were going to be profoundly affected by the way it was dealt with. It is known, for example, that FDR was opposed to a resumption of French colonialism in Indo-China. He was certainly opposed to its continuation in India. In addition, he enjoyed a universal reputation as an idealist and humanitarian. His charisma was enormous. Had he lived a little longer, and once the need to suppress such concerns in the name of inter-Allied unity had lost its salience, his sensitivity to the aspirations of the people of India, China, Indonesia, the Philippines, and the Middle East to be unequivocally free from colonial domination would almost certainly have become a more manifest part of US foreign policy.

Harry Truman, on the other hand, whatever may have been his political virtues, was not a known quantity either on the colonial question or indeed on any foreign policy question. His political career had neither afforded him any meaningful experience in this domain, nor had he in his private life gotten much exposure to things foreign. To his credit, Truman was an avid reader of history and had some sense of Europe through his service in World War I as an artillery officer. Asia was almost a total blank to him, however. Yet, despite these meager gifts, President Truman had become part of the "New Deal tradition," and had inherited the leadership of what had become the most powerful nation on earth, possessing the atomic bomb, and committed by stated principle as well as material circumstances to becoming a vital force in the affairs of the post-war world.

More than is true today, US foreign policy during and immediately following World War II was formulated almost exclusively by the president and a small band of advisors. The Department of State provided the bulk of what expertise was available, while Congress had virtually no say whatsoever in what the administration undertook abroad except to respond to it after the fact. Therefore, what the president *thought* and *knew* about foreign policy was far more central to what the US *did* in the world than is true today, when not only Congress but many other institutions, including the media, play such powerful roles in determining the thrust of American diplomacy. As one student of this era put it, "By the spring of 1945, President Harry S. Truman and a small number of advisers controlled foreign policy, allowing their final decisions to be determined neither by public opinion nor by Congress" (LaFeber 1977: 61). The more inherently conservative foreign policy orientation of the emergent Truman administration would therefore set the stage for the directions that the United States would take in South Asia during the impending Cold War. These would negatively impact relations between the United States and India. But consideration of this phase of America's involvement with South Asia exceeds the purview of the present essay.[4]

It was about this time that the Government of India, still under British suzerainty, but moving rapidly toward increased amounts of independence, decided that outside assistance was after all an urgent necessity if another round of starvation, possibly even more extensive than in 1943, was to be averted. An approach was made to the Combined Food Board, headquartered in Washington and run by the United States, Great Britain, and Canada. Although this was really the only game in town (because the US and Canada had most of the grain stocks available in the world) the Board was plagued with ideological and philosophical problems stemming, on the one hand, from having surplus food to dispense and, on the other, from massive demands upon what were, compared to the need, still finite resources. In the face of rising and conflicting demands for food relief from numerous countries and regions around the world, Truman received a report from Secretary Stettinius, which Secretary of War Henry L. Stimson and others in his entourage strongly reinforced from their respective doctrinal vantages, primarily linking this crisis to what they perceived to be the mounting "Communist threat." This meant that their focus was primarily upon using food as a strategic weapon—i.e., in Europe, and especially Eastern Europe, where American and other Western Allied troops were facing Soviet forces along a line running through the middle of the continent which had been established following the Axis surrender and where the lineaments of the Cold War were already becoming visible.

Truman responded to this viewpoint by sending his (and before him Roosevelt's) trusted advisor, Judge Sam Rosenman, to Europe to study the situation at first hand. Significantly, therefore, Judge Rosenman confined his inquiries to Europe and returned to recommend that 12 million tons of food grains would be needed to sustain its people through the impending winter. Following this trip, the president appointed Herbert Hoover to coordinate food relief for Europe as the ex-president had done after World War I. Then on June 2, 1945, Truman appealed to American farmers to increase their food production in order to provide the additional stocks that would be needed for this effort to succeed.

Alarmed by the Eurocentrism of the US food policy as so far enunciated, the India Lobby swung into action. Ironically, so did Clement Atlee, Churchill's successor as British Prime Minister. Atlee embodied the rise of the labor government in post-war Britain. He was both personally familiar with India from past experience, and in principle sympathetic to India's plight. For a time, therefore, the India Lobby and the British government became allies! Atlee called Truman's attention to the grave food situation in Asia in a communication dated January 4, 1946. He followed this up with a visit by Sir Ben Smith, Great Britain's Food Minister, who made a direct appeal for consignments of grain to India from the Combined Food Board. He was followed to Washington by Sir Robert Hutchings, the Food Secretary, whose task was to make the Americans understand why India needed food imports when its deficit was a comparatively small proportion of total food production. He had to explain how a peasant economy works and what the procurement problems for government are in such an economy. In Venkatraman's (1983: 48) words: "The American officials who listened to this presentation of the Indian problem were apparently not unsympathetic but somewhat baffled. They did not realize that India's food procurement officials had to go to the villages and collect grain literally by the basketful ...."

Neither Smith nor Hutchings got any firm assurances either from the US government or the Combined Food Board, but India was allowed to present its case in Washington before the Board. Sir Ramaswamy Mudaliar headed a delegation that was sent from India to ask for 1 million tons of rice and 3 million tons of wheat. But Eurocentrism and anti-Communism remained the dominant preoccupations of the US side. Mudaliar's impression was that the American representative on the Board was not very sympathetic. This representative, Mudaliar wrote, "began by assessing India's allocation so low as 80,000 tons, and went on to make India's claim a special target of attack, while resisting sug-gested cuts in the claims of other countries in which the United States was interested" (Venkatraman 1983: 57). The politics of strategic priorities was rearing its ugly head!

Mudaliar did get a brief meeting with President Truman which had been arranged by Loy Henderson who was very sympathetic toward India and later became America's first ambassador to that country following independence. But this encounter achieved no results. Neither did a second trip abroad by Herbert Hoover who this time was to inspect the situation in the Middle East and Asia. When Pearl Buck and others protested that his itinerary didn't even include India, a stop was added but in the end he never reached India because Truman called him home after he had gotten only to Cairo. The president wanted Hoover, ironically, to partici-pate in a national media campaign designed to call public attention to the world food crisis! From the standpoint of Indian public opinion, of course, this was perceived as a symbolic indication of how low on the totem pole of American post-war priorities India ranked.

While it cannot be gainsaid that American responsiveness to matters pertaining to India which had the greatest relevance for the nationalist leadership had been ambivalent at best and callous at worst, whether the issue was immigration policy, Madam Pandit's visit, or the food crises, the principal reason for such col- lective insensitivity cannot be said to ever have been merely out- right malice. The work done by the India Lobby over the years in raising American's consciousness of the India question had certainly not been in vain, especially during this later phase under J.J. Singh's leadership. Indians themselves showed a sympathetic understanding of where the problem lay. The underlying causes

Illustration 10.3
**Mahatma Gandhi with former US President Herbert Hoover**

*Source:* Kamath 1998.

were ethnocentrism and historical ignorance. The problem remained, for those with greater than average insight into what was
taking place in grassroots India (as in other places where political
and economic realities had so long been obscured behind the
facade of "normalcy" perpetuated by colonial regimes), was how
to get the message home to a novice American administration that
the United States must begin to think and act for herself with regard
to what was soon to be called the Third World.

A slight measure of success was achieved toward this goal after President Truman committed a *faux pas* during the course of a press conference he convened in part to push for greater American involvement in ameliorating food shortages around the world. Despite the fact that his relief emissary, Herbert Hoover, had failed to make it to India during his recent abruptly attenuated inspection trip, Truman blandly declared that India's crop prospects had improved and that consequently her requirements had lessened!

The reaction in India was, as might be expected, dismay tinged with outrage. This consternation was picked up by the India Lobby in America and strenuous efforts were made to disabuse Truman of this erroneous piece of information, which he had obviously received from someone in his official circle. Loy Henderson, who had become one of the most knowledgeable and sympathetic persons on India in the Truman Administration, attempted to persuade his boss that a mistake had been made and should be corrected, but to no avail. Even Lord Wavell wrote to Truman on April 15 appealing against any reduction in the 1.4 million tons of food grains being requested for India, which in India it was assumed that the Combined Food Board had awarded to her. This lack of responsiveness appears to have stemmed in some measure from feelings of pique that arose inside the Truman Administration over the intensity of the criticism to which the president's remarks at his press conference had been subjected, both at home and in India. Some had said that America's defeated enemies, Germany, Japan and Italy, were given more sympathetic consideration than India was receiving. Pearl Buck was outspokenly critical, as was Chester Bowles, then the Director of the Office of Price Administration, but already showing signs of the warm humanism that would one day carry him to India as America's most popular ambassador to that country.

It must be said, however, that there is much less information on the Lobby's activities respecting the 1946 food crisis. This is probably because in the long run it turned out to be not as serious as it was in 1943. There really was no mass starvation, because it proved possible to provide sufficient foodstuffs from a combination of indigenous and external sources to avert the worst case scenario.

# Notes

1. Hess (1971: 143–46) provides some useful observations on Senator Chandler's role in exposing the British cover-up of Caroe's insistence that Phillips be declared *persona non grata*.
2. The account that follows is derived from interviews and conversations I had with Robert Crane in the last years of his life. He was a close personal friend as well as a colleague in the South Asian Studies field, whom I knew and trusted for the better part of 30 years. However, even I did not know of the role he had played in the Drew Pearson matter until it emerged from a casual conversation we had at the Graylin Hotel in London on August 26, 1986. After several subsequent hours of interviews with him about the event and the times in which it took place, I secured his permission use his account in this book.
3. Still another footnote on this fascinating period concerns an experience which Robert Crane had at the conclusion of his tenure as an OSS operative in India. His last assignment had been to Rangoon, Burma, where he was able to retrieve a large assemblage of documents which had been accumulated by and concerning Subhas Chandra Bose. Recognizing their historical importance, Crane had them loaded in canvas mail bags and stowed them aboard the troop transport which would carry him home. The ship was returning to America via the Pacific, making stops at numerous American installations along the way. At one of these stops (Crane did not remember which), the mail bags were ordered to be offloaded from the transport in order to make room for what was termed "more vital" cargo. The Bose papers were left sitting on a South Pacific beach and were never retrieved!
4. See Gould and Ganguly (1992); Bowles (1954); Schaeffer (1993); Rudolph and Rudolph (1980); McMahon (1994); Kux (1993); and Kapur et al. (2002).

# 11  The Final Challenge

The final major challenge which the India Lobby faced was completion of the battle over Indian citizenship and immigration rights. In this, J.J. Singh perhaps played the major part. He never forgot his grassroots constituency, the "Little India in America," to which Shridharani had alluded during the San Francisco Conference. Also, his lobbying skills were especially crucial to the outcome.

The final push on the immigration battles had actually begun as early as 1943, after Singh had gained control of the India League of America. One aspect of J.J.'s strategy was to link the purely political aspects of immigration policy with its business and commercial aspects. This was an angle which came naturally to him, given his long experience in the business world. The goal was to broaden the coalition by pushing for the necessary changes in immigration law in the name of entrepreneurial common sense as well as social justice. His reasoning was that the American business community—which, after all, was, always had been and would always be the dominant interest group in the country—could exert decisive influence on any legislation with which they became identified in the name of economic self-interest. Therefore, he believed, if one could connect the immigration question and political freedom for India to the post-war potential for expanded trade with India, the American business community might be brought on board. This was the old "China Market" logic applied to India. If opening up China could mean free-market access to China's multitudes, then how about the "India Market": India's 400 million people? J.J. Singh stressed this potentiality in a statement he gave before Congress in early 1945. "The 400,000,000 East Indians represent a great untapped trade reservoir," he declared. "There exists over there a great demand for American goods, particularly as a result of lend-lease." It is in America's economic interest, Singh insisted, to speed Indian independence, thereby eliminating the trade restrictions and controls imposed by the British Raj which had always stood in the way of open commerce between the two countries. Achieving social justice for Indians resident in America as well as for subsequent migrants would also help develop an atmosphere of amity and mutual trust which would redound to the benefit of trade. Not only were restrictive US immigration laws morally reprehensible, declared Singh, they were also just plain bad for business because of the inhibitions they imposed on inter-course between the two countries (US House of Representatives, 79th Congress, Committee on Immigration and Naturalization, March 1945, pp. 83–94).

It was in this spirit that Singh formed the Indian Chamber of Commerce of America in 1938. He hoped to use this organization to help make his point that trade with India is good for American business. In the context of their respective times, Alexander Hamilton and J.J. Singh had things in common!

By 1944, the same basic coalition of Indians who had tried to awaken the American public to the tragedy in Bengal two years earlier had successfully convinced several members of Congress on both sides of the aisles to support changes in the immigration laws. Most important, they had persuaded Representatives Clare Booth Luce of Connecticut and Emanuel Cellar of New York to introduce bills in the House that would enable a maximum of 100 Indian nationals a year to gain naturalization privileges. Undoubtedly, the personal relationship which J.J. had built up between himself and Mrs Luce was a key factor in eliciting her sustained support for the legislation. It is equally true that Singh's charm and sophistication had been a major factor in winning over Emanuel Celler. The "New York City connection" certainly didn't hurt either. In sum, there is no question that without J.J.'s special talents, especially his American-style cosmopolitanism, the campaign to achieve Indian immigration rights might not have succeeded as quickly as ultimately it did.

His polyglot style, however, inevitably evoked ambivalence among some of his fellow Indians, even at the height of his success. Mainly, as we have seen, this was because Singh's willingness to work closely with American supporters, and especially to bring them into his organization, rubbed a lot of his fellow Indians the wrong way. We noted earlier that this issue was instrumental in the formation both the National Committee for India's Freedom under Anup Singh and Syud Hossain, and the India Welfare League under Imrat Khan. From the inception of J.J. Singh's ascent to the presidency of the India League in 1940 Anup Singh and Syud Hossain had worked closely with him within the ambit of the League. In Volume 1, Issue No. 1 (April 1940) of *India Today*, Anup Singh is listed as the Director of the Research Bureau of the India League of America. His staff consisted of eight individuals, all but one of whom was an Indian. This arrangement continued until June of 1944 when *India Today* carried an announcement that Anup Singh had tendered his resignation as editor. The announcement said that Anup had been a "constant guide and able editor in presenting the case for India's freedom to the American public." It was stated that Dr Singh had assumed new responsibilities as Secretary of the National Committee for India's Freedom, whose offices would be in Washington, DC. "We wish Dr. Anup Singh all success in his new position."

By this time, the officers and executive committee of the League had become overwhelmingly non-Indian. The honorary presidents were Pearl Buck and Dr Lin Yu Tang, the chairman of the executive committee was Richard J. Walsh, the president was J.J. Singh. Louis Fischer and Dr J. Holmes Smith were vice-presidents. The secretary was an Indian, Hemendra K. Rakshit, while Roger Baldwin was the treasurer. The remaining members were Herbert J. De Varco, Sidney Hertzber, Mirza Jaffer, Dorothy Norman, Josephine Rathbone, S.S. Sarma, Mai Mai Sze, and Rustom D. Wadia. In other words, of 14 executive committee members, only five were Indian.

By contrast, and indicative of the factional differentiation which had developed, the National Committee for India's Freedom announced that the formal connection which had existed between it and the India League "has by mutual consent been severed" as of May 1944. All its office-bearers were Indians. The honorary chairman was Dr Ananda K. Coomaraswamy and Syud Hossain was the chairman. Dr Haridas T. Mazumdar and Dr Krishnalal Shridharani were vice-chairmen, Dr Anup Singh was the secretary, and Dr Kamala Kosambi was treasurer. They listed their offices as the Portland Building, 1129 Vermont Avenue (Room 214), Washington, DC, Telephone: National 4796.

Apart from the obvious ethnic considerations, some rationale for this division undoubtedly arose from the process of increasing demographic complexity and consequent organizational differentiation that was taking place in the Indian-American community as a whole. This was undoubtedly as responsible as was J.J. Singh's partiality toward Americans for the formation in Chicago of the Indian Association for American Citizenship by N.R. Checher, formally a president of the India League, and the establishment by Dalip Singh Saund (who would one day become the first Indian to serve in the US Congress) of a Sikh-based organization on the West Coast called the Indian National Congress Association of America. The political environment was simply growing more complex.

While such factors undoubtedly did play a significant role, it was also a fact that J.J. Singh didn't quite "fit" the conventional image Indians had of themselves as embodiments of an ancient, non-Western traditional civilization. He just didn't seem to be "Indian" or "nationalist" enough in many eyes. Even Nehru had his reservations about J.J. He rarely displayed the customary accouterments of "Indianness"—he was a shorn Sikh; he wore Western business suits, not *khadi*; he rarely spouted the Gandhian mysticism and other Indic religio-philosophical mantras which had become standard fare in the Indian political lexicon. J.J. Singh was, in short, a consummate secular man, an Indian who fitted well into the Western socio-political lifestyle. In this sense he was ahead of his times: today he would not seem out of place among India's middle-class, and especially its corporate class. The positive side of this, of course, was that J.J. made American politicians feel much more comfortable with him than they did with the general run of Indian nationalist politicians. The drawback, on the other hand, was indeed that he made many of his fellow Indians feel uncomfortable around him.

Despite the strains, however, and largely because he was a consummate political pragmatist, Singh was able to build consensuses among the different groups sufficient to maintain a common front toward a political establishment that was becoming ever more favorably disposed toward Indian civil rights now that Indian freedom was seen to be an essential ingredient of the war effort. Even the split with the National Committee for India's Freedom did not produce any overt bitterness or recriminations. They continued to work together smoothly on Capitol Hill.

In the case of the naturalization hearings in the 1940s, the main complications concerned the degree to which these ethno-social differences between the groups affected their action styles and their viewpoints on priorities. All were agreed, however, on a common denominator: that the starting point of their effort must be the alteration of the Nationality Act (1940). The differences that arose, as we shall see, were over whether immigration and naturalization rights should be sought only for the original victims of the *Thind* decision, or whether they should be sought for all South Asians, past, present, and future. The latter implied, of course, applying the logic of the legislation which as of December 13, 1943 nullified the Chinese Exclusion Act and accorded naturalization rights to "all persons of Chinese descent" (Public Law 990, 78th Congress).

In a general sense, all groups were in agreement that this should in the long run be the end result. However, Imrat Khan's India Welfare League had on its own persuaded Congressman John Lesinski to introduce a bill initially confining legislation to granting citizenship only to Indians already resident in the United States. Senator William Langer of New York was persuaded to introduce a comparable bill in the Senate. However, both the India League and the National Committee for India's Freedom wished to see the more comprehensive approach that incorporated the logic of the Chinese legislation. J.J. Singh, therefore, played down the League's support for the Langer bill and, as we shall see, in effect used it as a ploy for pursuing higher stakes. Initially, before the lobbying drama fully unfolded, this evoked criticism from men like Khan and G.J. Watumull, a very successful businessman located in Hawaii and California. He wrote to Singh that "Citizenship may not help you or me but it is a question of life and death for the farmers of California." He believed that "the citizenship issue was more vital to the Indians in America than was independence for India" (Mukherjee 1997: 210).

The Senate hearings on the narrower Langer bill commenced on September 13, 1944 before the Subcommittee on Immigration, United States Senate, 75th Congress, Second Session. They pertained to "S. 1595: A Bill to Permit Approximately Three Thousand Natives of India Who Entered the United States Prior to July 1, 1924, to Become Naturalized." The chairman of this Sub-committee was Richard A. Russell of Georgia, already one the most powerful and conservative members of the US Senate. Among the 14 members, four were from Deep South states (Georgia, Florida, South Carolina, Mississippi), three were from border states (Tennessee, Maryland, Delaware), two were from Middle West states (Ohio, Michigan), two were from the Far West states (Oregon, California), and only two were from the more liberal Northeastern states (New Jersey, Connecticut). Four Indians were officially listed as witnesses: "Ramlal Bajpai, vice-president of the India Welfare League; Dr. Anup Singh, editor of *The Voice of India* and secretary of the National Committee for India's Freedom; Mubarak Ali Khan, president of the Indian Welfare League; and Dr. Krishnalal Shridharani, research associate in sociology, Columba University, and vice-president, National Committee for India's Freedom." There was one American official witness: Joseph Tenner, counsel of the India Association for American Citizenship. Despite not being formally listed, J.J. Singh actually did testify at some length, and in addition had a number of documents read into the record. Taraknath Das submitted a written statement in which he declared: "It has been my intention to attend the hearings .... Owing to unavoidable circumstances, it is impossible for me to appear ... and, therefore, I ask your committee's favor and consent to have the following statement incorporated as part of the hearing ...."

Despite the differences among them, the witness list indicates that the principal players at this time were nevertheless trying to coordinate their efforts. Also remarkable is what it showed about the India Lobby's persistence in fighting to nullify the *Thind* decision of 1924, which had been on the books for 20 years. Their determination had been sustained across the generational changes that had occurred in the South Asian leadership.

On the specific issue of the racist implications of the *Thind* decision, even the testimony of Edward J. Shaughnessy, Special Assistant to the Commissioner, Immigration and Naturalization Service, had a positive ring. Stating that the "original statute of 1790 limited the rights of naturalization to free white persons, and then in 1870, following the Civil War, persons of the black race," Shaughnessy noted that in 1940 some new language "crept into the statute" which first accorded citizenship rights to American

Indians and then in 1943 to "persons of the Chinese race ...." Clearly there had been progress: "... we have progressed to include the white, black, American Indians, and the Chinese" (*Hearings before a Subcommittee on Immigration, US Senate,* September 13 and 14, 1944, p. 6).

The question now remaining to be answered was whether the South Asians' turn had finally come, and, if it had, whether it would merely be a matter of settling for the restoration of the citizenship status of 3,000 resident Indians whose rights had been rescinded by *Thind,* or making citizenship available to all Indians—past, present, and future—who wished to become Americans? It was the latter that J.J. Singh wanted to hold out for, and which his political orchestration in the end brought about.

The underlying dilemma was clearly apparent in the dialogs that took place in the September 13–14 hearings on S. 1595. What became ever clearer as the hearings proceeded is that J.J. Singh's strategy for attaining citizenship rights was gaining momentum even within the proceedings themselves. It had begun as an attempt by lobbyists like Mubarak Ali Khan, who wanted to maintain some measure of distance from J.J. Singh and the India League by exploiting the relationship they had built with Senator Langer and Representative Lisinski. But this meant supporting Langer's bill, which would apply only to restoring the citizenship of Indians who had lost it before 1924 due to *Thind.*

Naturally, the hearings commenced with a recapitulation of the basic issues raised by the *Thind* decision. Shaughnessy recounted how the Supreme Court, in its determination of the racial status of the Indian plaintiffs, "said that they were not going into the matter from the ethnological standpoint at all, and held that a Hindu was not a white person within the meaning of the naturalization laws, and, therefore, that the term 'free white person' was to be interpreted in accordance with popular understanding and not on any technical scientific basis" (ibid.: 7). Senator Burton (1884–1964) of Ohio then wondered, "If the statute had read 'Caucasian' there would have been no question [about the Indians being white]." Shaughnessy's answer was that it was implicit that it would not have made any difference because then the Court "would have to determine whether the Hindu race are Caucasians." What soon began to emerge was the conclusion that the only way "Hindus" could escape from the legal clutches of

*Thind* would be for Congress to do what they had done in the case of previous categories of people who had been admitted into the citizenship fold, namely, *amend the law*. The 1943 statute would have to be amended once again to include Hindus. This, of course, played right into J.J. Singh's hands, and is no doubt the reason why at the last minute he showed up on (Tennessee) Senator Stewart's (1892–1972) doorstep. "You were in my office this morning, and you wanted to make a statement, and, then, also, in addition to that, would like to put into the record these exhibits you sent over" (ibid.: 20).

The "exhibits" that Singh brought with him were many and varied, but all reinforced his contention that the time had come to finally resolve the citizenship conundrum through the legislative process. His approach revealed a well thought out scenario by a man who had mastered the art of lobbying. In this respect he stood far above his peers and has to be credited with being the architect of the last phase of the South Asians' struggle to achieve untrammeled immigration rights and full American citizenship.

The first document he presented before the Committee was a letter dated September 12, 1944, to Arthur Stewart, Chairman, Senate Immigration Subcommittee, asserting that "Our organization (i.e., J.J. Singh!) has taken keen interest in Senator Langer's bill to the Senate and Representative Clare Booth Luce's and Representative Emanuel Celler's bills to the House" (ibid.: 21). This set the stage for elucidating Singh's basic thesis: that Langer must be subsumed by Luce-Celler. In retrospect, it was a brilliant maneuver, because it first brought the Senate into the game through the more limited Langer Bill, and then used the broader, more comprehensive legislation on the House side as a basis for expanding its provenance to match that of the latter. If this scenario succeeded, then the long battle which began at the turn of the century would at last be over!

J.J. next provided a long list of "Prominent People Who Support the Present Legislation." The 44 names included Albert Einstein, John Dewey, Ralph Milliken, Marshall Field, Pearl Buck, William E. Hocking, Louis Fischer, Upton Sinclair, Reinhold Niebuhr, Louis Adamic, Harry Emerson Fosdick, Rabbi Abba Silver, Norman Thomas, Arthur Garfield Hayes, A. Philip Randolph, Upton Sinclair, and G. Bromley Oxnam.

There was an announcement from the *Washington Star* concerning the May 4, 1944 "Public Meeting to Support Legislation Authorizing United States Immigration and Naturalization of Nationals of India," held at the National Press Club Auditorium. Chaired by J.J. Singh, the speakers were: Representatives Clare Booth Luce and Emanuel Celler, Senator William Langer, and author and war correspondent Leland Stowe.

Paving the way for the present hearings, the chairman moved the following resolutions:

> Whereas this war is professedly being fought to achieve democratic equality among all nations; and
>
> Whereas the nationals of India are objects of discrimination under our present immigration and naturalization laws; and
>
> Whereas the United States has recognized the Injustice to the Chinese people by lifting immigration and naturalization barriers against them, and
>
> Whereas India is allied with the United Nations in the conduct of the war; therefore be it
>
> *Resolved*, That this audience assembled in National Press Club Auditorium urges Congress to enact immediately pending legislation which would permit immigration under quota of nationals of India and make them eligible to United States citizenship.

There were excerpts from the speeches which Clare Booth Luce, Emanuel Celler, Senator Langer, and J.J. Singh gave on this occasion.

"I consider this bill of mine, and of Mr. Celler," declared Mrs Luce, "not so much an immigration bill as a diplomatic and political measure against our present and future enemies. It bears precisely the same relation to our war effort and the peace effort that must follow as the recent bill passed by Congress admitting a hundred-odd Chinese to our country" (*Hearings, House Committee on Immigration*, 1945, pp. 10–11). Representative Celler emphasized the hypocrisy of our exclusion laws: "Here we are fighting racial arrogance .... Is not such an exclusion an echo of the totalitarian ideology that we seek to crush? *Under our violently discriminatory laws, a guttersnipe from Prussia, a disguised fascist from Spain, can enter, but the late Rabindranath Tagore or Pandit Nehru could enjoy no such right*" (ibid.: 2–6, emphasis added). Noting that "The record made by the people from India who have came to this country has been outstanding," Langer focused on the agricultural achievements of Indians in California, producing "magnificent fields of wild rice, in hitherto barren areas." Yet, he said, "Practically all of these [lands] were lost to the Indians as a result of the decision of the Supreme Court in 1924 ... a decision which is a shameful page in the history of the Supreme Court of the United States" (ibid.: 888–89). J.J. Singh stressed the indignity of the existing immigration and naturalization laws: "The people of India," he declared, "have no desire to ask for any special privileges or treatment. They do not seek unrestricted immigration into the United States, but they do ask that the stigma of inferiority may be removed: *as it has been rightly done very recently in the case of the Chinese*" (*Hearings, Senate*, 1944, p. 39 passim). One can see how heavily the moral implications of the war and the recent inclusion of the Chinese into the ranks of American citizenship were influencing the India Lobby's tactical calculations.

Singh reinforced these public statements with excerpts from newspaper articles and editorials endorsing the cause. On the war service and China precedents, he reproduced a *New York Times* editorial (February 8, 1944) which stated: "The removal of a mark justly offensive to [Indian] pride and self-respect will be not merely testimony of our gratitude for their armed aid but a matter of justice and equality of treatment. *We have lifted the bars on the Chinese. We can afford to do the same for the Indians.* We can't afford to do otherwise."

A *Los Angeles Times* editorial of March 21, 1944, made the same points: "There is a bill pending in Congress which would extend to natives of India the same concession of quota immigration and of naturalization recently extended to China. It seems worthy of adoption, for much the same reason as in the case of the Chinese: it would remove a discrimination against a people who are fighting hard side by side with American soldiers." Other editorial endorsements were included from such newspapers as the *Baltimore Sun, The Washington [DC] News, The Kansas City Star*, and *The Columbia [South Carolina] Star*.

When his turn came, Singh's testimony was quite eloquent. He chose the occasion to clarify who the "Hindus" actually are. This arose from the long-standing tendency of Americans to refer to all Indians as "Hindus." He explained to the Committee members that out of 390 million "nationals of India," 260 million are indeed Hindus; but 130 million are not. There are 90 million Muslims, 7 million Christians, 6 million Sikhs (J.J.'s own faith), and 120,000 Parsees (Zoroastrians who originated in ancient Iran). "Thus it is incorrect to refer to all nationals of India as Hindus." J.J.'s explanation for this misconception was "that Americans did not want to call the people of India Indians because of possible confusion with the American Indians. It will be recalled that Singh had already personally experienced an example of this kind of confusion during one of the press conferences he staged in Washington in which he used Senator Pat McCarren of Nevada as media bait. He reminded everyone that even the discoverer of America had been confused: "Columbus thought that he had found India: his destination" (ibid.: 29).

On the substantive issue of the pending legislation, reference was repeatedly made to the Celler and Luce bills that were being initiated at the same time in the House after the texts of both bills were read into the hearings record. This arose after Senator Harold H. Burton (Ohio) observed that the Langer Bill, the one they were considering, would, if passed, leave things exactly where they presently were. That is, the Indians who had been de-naturalized by *Thind* would be eligible to be re-naturalized, while all Indians subsequent to 1924 would remain in limbo. "Because the act would then say," declared Burton, "that after July 1, 1924, the Congress was in agreement with the Supreme Court, and expressly prescribes that after that date East Indians cannot be naturalized" (ibid.: 9).

It was actually Shaughnessy (from the INS) himself who made the point that the House bills accomplished what the Langer Bill could not. The restrictive principle inherent in the July 21, 1924, ruling, he said, "is attempted to be overcome in the provisions of the Luce and Celler bills in the House." Anup Singh had stressed this point in his testimony, showing, of course, that he and J.J. Singh were essentially on the same wavelength. "I personally would like Senator Langer to amend his bill to make it all-inclusive, *to make it on the same basis as the House bills.*" When Senator Burnet R. Maybank (1899–1954) of South Carolina observed that neither of these bills had any restrictive date connected with them (i.e., that they had universal applicability), Shaughnessy replied that this was precisely the point: "These bills have no date at all .... They are patterned after the Chinese Exclusion Act." He identified in this connection two Celler bills (H.R. 4415 and H.R. 4636) and one Luce Bill (H.R. 4479), all of which followed the Chinese model. J.J. Singh admitted that he had a hand in the phrasing of all three. "*It was at our request,*" he stated, "*that Representative Clare Booth Luce and Representative Emanuel Celler introduced a bill*" (ibid.: 30, emphasis added). In each there was a provision which essentially amended the 1940 Act to include Indians:

(1) *H.R. 4414 (Celler)*: "The right to become a naturalized citizen under the provisions of this Act shall extend only to white persons, persons of African nativity or descent, descendants of races indigenous to the Western Hemisphere, Chinese persons or persons of Chinese descent, *and natives of India, and dependencies thereof or persons descended from natives of India and dependencies thereof.*"

(2) *H.R. 4479 (Luce)*: "The right to become a naturalized citizen under the provisions of this Act shall extend only to white persons, persons of African nativity or descent, descendants of races indigenous to the Western Hemisphere, Chinese persons or persons of Chinese descent, *and Eastern Hemisphere Indians or persons descended from Eastern Hemisphere Indians.*"

(3) *H.R. 4636 (Celler)*: "The right to become a naturalized citizen under the provisions of this Act shall extend only to white persons, persons of African nativity or descent, descendants of races indigenous to the Western Hemisphere, Chinese persons or persons of Chinese descent, *and Eastern Indians or persons descended from Eastern Hemisphere Indians of India* ... all Eastern Hemisphere Indians of India or persons descended from Eastern Hemisphere Indians of India entering the United States annually as immigrants *shall be allocated to quota for Eastern Hemisphere Indians of India and be given a preference of up to 75 per centum of the quota ....*"

The purpose of the quota provision in the second Celler bill was to deter resident, non-naturalized Indians from dashing to Canada or elsewhere to get on the immigration quota in order to speed up the naturalization process for them personally, thus occupying slots which would otherwise be available to overseas Indians wanting to migrate here directly from India.

Singh felt the need to address another source of anxiety which plagued the effort to open up migration opportunities for South Asians. This was a residue of the old "Yellow Peril" bugaboo which had obsessed Californians and other West Coast states, as well as Canadians, since before the turn of the century. As we have seen, it fueled the White hysteria which resulted in ugly confrontations like the *Komagata Maru* incident and the pervasive restrictive legislation promulgated by British Columbia and the State of California, including the machinations which led to *Thind*. Consequently, J.J. felt the need to alleviate such fears by pointing out that a quota would allow no more than 75 Indians a year to enter the United States. The figure of 75 reflected the idea that about 25 resident Indians per year would still find their way into the quota. "Obviously, the admission of 75 nationals of India, if the Cellar-Luce bill passes, per annum into the United States will create no economic or social problems" (ibid.: 14). No one, of course, especially the Indian side, was prepared at this point to consider the long-range, "foot-in-the-door" implications of this change in the immigration laws: namely, that a new precedent had been set which in the future could lead to further expansions of the quota. It was a point, however, that was not overlooked by the enemies of these bills in the floor debate that occurred when Luce-Celler–Langer reached the floor of Congress in 1945.

The remainder of the hearings on the Langer Bill were more or less perfunctory. With time running out on the first day, despite the committee chairman's reluctance, it became necessary to prolong the hearings long enough for L.R. Checher of the Indian Association for Indian Citizenship to offer his testimony. He told the committee that he had to leave Washington that evening and could not remain overnight. He was allowed to briefly present his views before adjournment. Checher said he had studied political economy at Columbia University but did not obtain a degree. His statement laid stress on the plight of Indian farmers in California due to the denial of their citizenship rights, and upon the future prospects for trade and commerce between India and America if the wrongs that have been committed are not rectified (ibid.: 32–33). The next day, Mubarak Ali Khan, president of the India Welfare

League, testified. His emphasis, like Checher's, was on rescinding the *Thind* decision, rather than on the broader issues raised by the India League and the Committee for India's Freedom. The Indian farmers in California were his principal beat: "These farmers have turned their backs to their old homes and have come to a new country, but have not been given the opportunity to enjoy freedom." They have brought many benefits to the state of California, to the Imperial Valley, and southern California, "where all was mud and sand and where the American farmers were not interested in taking this land for one nickel per acre, but these Indian farmers have taken it and cultivated it, and have made good rice fields there" (ibid.: 36–38). All this was true, of course!

Joseph Tenner, counsel for the Indian Association for American Citizenship, was the final witness. His appeal, like Khan's and Checher's, was principally for restoration of citizenship to "approximately 3,000 people of India who have been here prior to July 1, 1924." These are persons, he said, who have been rendered "truly stateless," and include "some very prominent scientists who have contributed a great deal toward the progress of this country." He mentioned Dr S.S. Chandrasekhar, professor of astronomy at Yerkes Observatory, University of Chicago; Dr Saklatwalla, consulting mineralogist and president of United States Rustless Steel Corporation; Dr V.R. Kokutnur, chemist and chemical engineer, and also a captain in the US Army; Dr Subbarao, biological chemist, and director of research, Lederle Laboratory, Perle River, NY; Dr Kathju, industrial chemist, technical director, Gray Company, "important for war work, especially camouflage operations..."; Dr A.B. Singh, chemist connected with the University of Illinois; Dr Shadu, chemical engineer, engaged in important war production work; Dr Gobind Behari Lal, scientist and journalist, winner of a Pulitzer Prize, science editor of Hearst Publications, and incidentally, the nephew of Har Dayal; Dr A.K. Coomaraswamy, curator, Boston Museum. These citations certainly demonstrated how far South Asians in America had progressed, despite the odds, since their tremulous beginnings half a century before. But the fact that persons of such eminence were still devoid of citizenship dramatized equally how far the South Asian community still had to go. This, of course, was the lobbyists' point (ibid.: 38–42).

Tenner injected a humanizing note into the hearings by relating an experience which he and Senator Langer recently had on a home visit:

> Senator Langer and myself had occasion to visit the home of an Indian in Jersey City, and that happened to be on the eve of the boy's departure after furlough. The usual scene took place where the mother cried and the father cried, and the boy went off. Here is a boy who has been in the service, he has been rewarded with citizenship, but his father, who has sacrificed all his life to bring that boy up a good, loyal American ... stands there absolutely helpless, without any fault of his own whatsoever. He has done everything as an American. He is too old to get into the service, he works, he pays income taxes, and he has done absolutely nothing to merit the inferiority, and I think situations of that kind should be removed (ibid.: 42).

When Senator Maybank noted that the Langer Bill actually does not cover this case, since the parents had been in the US for only ten years, Tenner responded saying, "I have to confine myself to the present bill." But it is clear that he too was thinking strategically; because he referred to the Celler Bill, thus himself implicitly recognizing that Langer's Bill was only a step toward the ultimate goal; that, in his words, "we are hoping [for] in the future under Celler ...."

On the second day (September 14) of the hearings, in addition to the testimony of Mubarak Ali Khan and Joseph Tanner, a statement was read into the record, at J.J. Singh's request, which listed the names of the officers and members of the National Advisory Board of the India League of America.

Also read into the record was the wording of a "redraft of the bill with amendments that were discussed here yesterday ...." It read: "A BILL, To permit Eastern Hemisphere Indians of India, of persons descended from Eastern Hemisphere Indians of India who entered the United States prior to July 1, 1924, to become naturalized." The remainder of the text elaborated the details of this proposed law if enacted both by the House and the Senate. To emphasize the law's acceptability to the government, a letter from Secretary of State Cordell Hull written several months earlier

(January 22, 1944) to Committee Chairman Richard Russell was incorporated into the record (ibid.: 36). It said:

> MY DEAR SENATOR RUSSELL: I have received your letter of December 16, 1943, requesting the views of this Department on S. 1597, a bill to permit approximately 3,000 natives of India who entered the United States prior to July 1, 1924, to become naturalized.
>
> No objection is seen to the passage of this bill.
>
> Sincerely yours,
> Cordell Hull

Virtually at the last minute, the simmering differences between the two factions which had come to Capitol Hill to promote immigration and naturalization reform in the context of the Langer Bill erupted. As we saw, the India League of America and the National Committee for India's Freedom had a broader agenda than did the India Welfare League and the American Association for Indian Citizenship. In effect, the latter faction came prepared to settle for the Langer Bill with its limited goal of rescinding *Thind*, whereas the former clearly viewed Langer as a stepping-stone, a foot in the door, as it were, for moving the Senate toward the more comprehensive resolution of the immigration and naturalization legislation encompassed both by Celler and Luce on the House side. Put bluntly, what was seen by J.J. Singh, Anup Singh and Krishnalal Shridharani as a tactical ploy was seen by Mubarek Ali Khan and Joseph Tenner as a final solution, at least in the short run.

This difference became evident when Krishnalal Shridharani made his statement on behalf of the National Committee for India's Freedom. Shridharani did not mince words. While conceding the importance of legislation designed to re-naturalize the 3,000 Indians deprived of their citizenship prior to July 1, 1924, he declared, "But I must confess a more vital issue is at stake." By confining this legislation to "those nationals of India who came to this country before July 1, 1924, as S. 1595 contemplates, the fundamental issue of human equality is not only sidetracked, but it is also negated." If the bill is passed as it now stands, he declared, "it would put the Senate on record for the first time that nationals of India as of July 1, 1924, and on, are not of Caucasian race and therefore not fit to be citizens of the United States ... I therefore urge that the bill S. 1595 be readjusted to resemble bills H.R. 4479 and H.R. 4415, now pending in the House of Representatives. This would place India in the same category as China" (ibid.: 49–50).

Senator Maybank interrupted at this point to say that amending the Langer Bill in this fashion would be tantamount to shelving it, and would necessitate holding new hearings. The Senator asked Shridharani if the viewpoint he had just expressed represented his personal position or that of the National Committee for India's Freedom. He claimed it was his personal opinion. But it obviously expressed what J.J. Singh, Anup Singh, Syud Hossain and other members of this faction felt in their hearts; indeed, it reflected what had undoubtedly been their underlying strategy all along.

Mubarak Khan reacted testily against this maneuver, so much so that it got a little personal. He broke into the dialog to say,

> I do not wish to enter into any discussion with this gentleman, but these people here (*sic*) they have no experience of their country brothers, and [are] only interested in themselves; *I wish these newcomers would not interfere in this bill* ... we have been fighting for this bill for the past 5 years, and it is no joke to travel throughout the country, from village to village, appealing to the American public, begging them for their support, and when the time comes to listen and consider this bill, some newcomer (*sic*) comes in and says, "well, your home is no good; forget your home and come into my home" (ibid.: 50).

This outburst vividly illuminated the differences in perspective and interests between the East Coast, predominantly middle-class, Hindu, urban-oriented Indians, and the predominantly Sikh, West Coast, agrarian-rooted segments of the American South Asian community. For the latter it was primarily a matter of acquiring the citizenship status that would enable them to own land out in the open without having to engage in myriad subterfuges. Yes, they were saying; Indian freedom is a worthy goal which we support in principal; but rescinding *Thind* and regaining our property rights is our bread and butter.

Senator Maybank restored order and allowed Shridharani to complete his statement. He reiterated his position and tried to minimize the differences between the two factions. "We are all for what the Senator's bill is, except we wish to go a little further, and if I may continue, the changes that I am suggesting would place India in the same category as China ..." (ibid. :50).

At this point, Tenner entered the fray to assert his agreement with Mubarak Ali Khan. On behalf of the Indian Association for American Citizenship, "we agree with Mr. Mubarek Ali Khan in the matter, to let he matter stop *at the present time* with Senator Langer's bill." In stating his organization's position, however, Tenner sought to be less strident. "I do not want you to get the impression that we are fighting among ourselves." He simply believed that the two issues—of citizenship for de-naturalized Indians, and the Indian Freedom Movement—were separable issues. While absolutely meritorious in its own right, "I agree with Mr. Ali Khan that is not the subject matter here." While the National Committee and the India League "have meritorious work," Tenner feared that dealing with its implications in this committee might "destroy our present opportunity of helping 3,000 people in the United States ... I think the 3,000 people in the United States are entitled to this relief immediately, and we can all go on with our work, if we desire, on the question of India." In other words, according to Tenner: "First things first" (ibid.: 50–53).

Either because of, or despite, the differences that arose between the two factions, neither the Langer Bill nor the Lesinski Bill, its House counterpart, were acted upon in the 78th Congress. Both were tabled, i.e., not voted out of committee.

The battle then shifted to the House of Representatives, where J.J. Singh and his cohorts were on much more solid political ground. The Celler-Luce Bill had first been introduced in the House in 1943. Over the span of almost three years, several attempts had been made to enact a bill which essentially modified the Immigration Act of 1940 to conform to the changes made in 1943 that had authorized the naturalization and quota-based immigration of the Chinese. The goal was to do the same for what were termed "Eastern Hemisphere Indians from India."

A number of attempts had been made over the ensuing almost three years, spurred by the efforts of the India Lobby, led by J.J. Singh, Anup Singh, Krishnalal Shridharani, and Haridas Mazumdar. Hearings had repeatedly taken place in the House. The last round of hearings occurred on March 7, 8, 13, and 14 of 1945. They featured all the customary witnesses in favor of the legislation. Despite these efforts, the initial outcome was that the Bill was once against tabled. The coalition of Southern Democrats and Conservative Republicans who dominated the Committee prevailed by a 10 to 6 vote. *India Today* reported, "The Committee tabled the Bill on March 20, 1945." However, by this time, the India Lobby had a lot of momentum going for it and did not take this setback lying down. They used their lobbying resources to persuade the Committee to reconsider their decision. They were able to enlist the support of the White House, the State Department, the Immigration and Naturalization Service, and even the British Ambassador, Lord Halifax. A critical moment came when Ambassador William Phillips weighed in on the side of the Indians. Shortly before he passed away, President Roosevelt addressed a letter to Committee Chairman Dickstein (1885–1954) (*Congressional Record, House*, March 4, 1945, pp. 9523–24), urging House action on the Bill. It read:

My Dear Mr. Chairman:

I understand that your Committee soon will hold hearings on legislation to authorize the admission into this country under a quota of persons of the East Indian race, and to permit persons of this race to become naturalized citizens.

I regard this legislation as important and desirable, and I believe that this enactment will help us to win the war and to establish a secure peace. I am sure that your Committee is aware of the great service that India has rendered to the United Nations in their war against the axis. The Indian army, raised entirely by voluntary enlistments, has fought with great courage and skill in Europe, Africa and Asia. India has furnished and will continue to furnish substantial amounts of raw materials and manufactured products of great assistance in the prosecution of the war.

The present statutory provisions that discriminate against persons of East Indian descent provoke ill-feeling, now serve no useful purpose, and are incongruous and inconsistent with the dignity of both our peoples.

The quota for East Indian persons would be approximately 100 immigrants a year. There can be no real danger that this small number of immigrants will cause unemployment or provide competition in the search for jobs.

It is my hope that the Congress will take steps to remove the present provisions of our Immigration and Naturalization laws that discriminate against persons of East Indian descent.

Very sincerely yours,

Franklin D. Roosevelt

With so much political pressure impinging on them, the Committee reversed itself and voted the Bill out by a 9 to 6 margin. A minority report was filed disagreeing with the decision, but this, of course, did not prevent action on the Bill by the full House.

Finally, on June 14, the Committee moved to consider the Luce bill (H.R. 1584) along with one introduced by then Representative (later to become Senator) Everett Dirksen of Illinois (H.R. 2256). This latter was important because Dirksen was a rising Republican star whose conversion to the side of Indian immigration and naturalization represented a crucial turning point. The floor debate and its outcome provided a fascinating glimpse into the moral and political atmosphere existing in America as the post-war era was about to dawn.

In the final March hearings, as on previous occasions, the Committee—certainly at the prodding of Representatives Celler and Luce—had invited an array of witnesses who stressed India's contributions to the war effort, her potential importance to American commerce and trade, and the entitlement of Indians to be treated as an independent people with the same rights and dignity as other free people. Indian witnesses did not participate at this stage; this was an all-American prelude to the final showdown. The witnesses were from such organizations as the India Committee of the Federal Council of Churches of Christ in America; the Foreign Missions Conference of North America; the American Asiatic Society; and, at the behest of the Federal Council of Churches, from V.A. Dodge, the president of a New York business firm called Dodge and Seymour, who had for years conducted extensive commercial relations with India.

The hearings commenced with a statement read by Representative Celler, and one by Representative Luce, which the Congressman had entered into the record on her behalf since she was not physically present for these hearings. In his opening statement, Celler reiterated the now well-worn point that the bill now up for consideration was inspired by the bill passed in the previous Congress "which provided for the removal of the so-called Chinese exclusion provisions from the Immigration and Naturalization Acts." What it essentially came down to, Celler declared, is that the Luce and Celler bills, "do for the natives of India what you heretofore have done for the natives of China." Being Jewish and, therefore, acutely aware of the Holocaust which Nazism was perpetrating in Europe, it was natural for him to point out that American racial policies undermined the very cause that America was supposed to be fighting for. "The Johnson Act of 1924 discriminated against people of eastern and southern Europe, and in its utter exclusion of nationals of Asiatic countries [it] anticipated Hitler's theory .... Is not such an exclusion an echo of the totalitarian ideas we seek to crush today?" (*Hearings, House*, 1945, pp. 2–3)

Adhering to what had obviously become a key strategy, Representative Celler made much of India's status as an ally in the war effort. "The Indian people have joined us on the battlefield," he asserted, "Two million Indians are fighting in the Army, Navy and merchant marine of Great Britain." Moreover, "They are among the dead, wounded and missing."

He tried to put to rest the South Asian version of the "Yellow Peril" bugaboo, by minimizing the potential demographic consequences of a proposed immigration quota of a mere 100 persons per year. "The hue and cry," he said, "that might be raised in opposition to the proposed establishment of an immigration quota for Indians, and their right to citizenship, making much of the competitive labor argument and evils of widening immigration legislation, have, therefore, no validity, no foundation in fact, when we consider that only 100 may come in each year. It would take 100 years to admit 10,000 ..." (ibid.: 4). This was a slap at the American trade unions, which, since the first Indians came to US shores, had opposed their assimilation into American society on the grounds that their willingness to work for lower wages weakened the bargaining position of White workers. In the present debate, the AFL was opposing a quota for Indians in the name of the usual stereotypes.

Reflecting the awareness which his association with J.J. Singh and other lobbyists, plus his own visits to India, had imparted to him, Celler dismissed the time-worn stereotypes about India as a land of *yogis* and snake-charmers. "India is no longer the India of

Marco Polo," nor of "Kipling's Barrack Room Ballads." She has emerged from her "ancient chrysalis ... and has become quite modern and up-to-date." Celler declared that contemporary Indians "are as modern-minded and up to date in mode and manner as any man in this room." As for Indians who have settled in America, he proffered, obviously with J.J. Singh in mind, that "they already ... have become thoroughly Americanized and steeped in our traditions" (ibid.: 5).

Emerging modern India, Celler contended, spelled good business prospects for American industry. "India is a huge untapped reservoir for American goods, capital goods and consumer goods. And we must take advantage of that reservoir. We must tap it." He warned that if we discriminate against India in this manner, "they are naturally not going to view with any degree of kindliness our attempts to sell goods in India." Celler declared that "with the proper infiltration of western ideas in India, you could set up tremendous demands for western goods." For example, he speculated, rather naively, that if Indians "could be persuaded to wear hats—just hats—there would not be enough machines in this country to supply the demand." This once again was a variation on the old "China Market" theme (ibid.: 6).

The discussion that followed Celler's disquisition revolved mostly around technical details that would have to be resolved before any bill reached the House floor. There was one exchange, however, which highlighted the factional differences existing between the groups representing resident aliens desirous of achieving only the amount of change needed to nullify the *Thind* decision—namely, the India Welfare League and the India Association for American Citizenship—and those groups—namely, the India League of America and the National Committee for Indian Independence—that wanted comprehensive immigration and naturalization legislation on the China model. Celler was asked by Representative Kearney, "it is true, is it not, that there is an organization composed of Indians in this country, who is interested solely in securing the right of naturalization for those Indians who are in this country now?" Celler replied that indeed there is such an organization, *rather a selfish one that "seeks to feather their own nest; and I think they do a woeful injury to their own people, and in my humble estimate they should bow in shame."* When Kearney asked him if they too were Indians, the representative said indeed they were, "But they are a pitifully microscopic few in comparison with the others who want the larger bill" (ibid.: 9–10).

Celler chose this moment to declare that both the State and Justice Departments favor the larger bill, and that the president of the United States also does. It was at this point that he introduced the statement prepared by Clare Booth Luce in lieu of her absence. "She speaks out of a wealth of knowledge."

Mrs Luce focused her attention heavily on India's contribution to the war effort. She pointed to the sad irony that "As it now stands, *Eastern Hemisphere Indians are legally classified by us as undesirable aliens, along with the Japanese.*" Despite this fact, she continued, "India has been, and is today, of immense value toward our joint victory over our enemies."

The Indian army, she declared, is the largest volunteer army in the world, indeed in all human history. All two million native troops are volunteers; more than half a million are serving on fronts outside India. The Indian Navy and Air force number about 300,000. "Also, there are 59,000 Indians in the British merchant marine, enough to man a quarter of Britain's merchant fleet." She spoke of the fact that Indian units were the "backbone" of General Montgomery's Eighth Army, which had routed Rommel in North Africa and then fought its way up the Italian peninsula. "In that campaign, the Fourth India Division suffered 100 percent casualties, and captured ten times its own number in enemy prisoners." With such a record of achievement and dedication to the cause of freedom, "Failure to extend to this people the same recognition as we give the Chinese is to work an injustice; a continued affront to the pride and self-respect of a valuable ally" (ibid.: 10–11).

The rest of these hearings were dominated by representatives of the Federal Council of the Churches of Christ in America, the American Asiatic Association, and the Dodge & Seymour Company. The spokesman for the Federal Council was its secretary, Walter W. Van Kirk. He presented the Committee a list of 36 religious bodies from around the country who endorsed the organization's stand against racism. "The Federal Council ... asks only that under such restrictions as may now be in force, and within the framework of a quota system, East Indians be not discriminated against for reasons of color." He then named the 36 religious bodies that had approved the Council's resolution. Van Kirk stated that in addition to these official bodies, he had received letters from several religious publications supporting the proposed legislation (ibid.: 13).

An interesting exchange occurred when Representative Asa Leonard Allen (1891–1969) of Louisiana raised questions concerning Dr Van Kirk's positions both on the generality of the legislation and the issue of quotas. It brought out the fact that Van Kirk and the Federal Council saw the proposed legislation as a matter of principle—namely, that Asians in general, not just Indians, were being discriminated against on racial grounds, and that this was deemed to be morally wrong. However, with World War II still going on, especially in the Asia-Pacific theatre, the Chairman and other members of the Committee wanted to know if any quota assigned to Asians would include the Japanese. Van Kirk wriggled out of this dilemma by stipulating that while all resident Asians should be admitted to American citizenship, quotas should be assigned only to those Asian countries with whom the United States is at peace. Representative Allen asked, "Now you would go the balance of the way and break down the barriers against all Asiatics?" When Van Kirk answered in the affirmative, Allen countered, "You include in that the Japanese?"

It was in this context that Van Kirk qualified his position. Allen, however, wouldn't let him easily off the hook: "Well ... but you just said you wanted to break down the barriers as to all Asiatics." Then it came out that Van Kirk thought that once the war ended, the Japanese, as Asiatics, might indeed be given the same quota as other Asiatics. Van Kirk wisely left this matter in limbo, saying, "I should want to cross that bridge when I came to it and consider the situation that existed at that time and the considerations under which the peace had been established between ourselves and Japan." This was certainly a reasonable way out; but the Chairman, Samuel Dickerson, would have none of it. Fueled by the bitterness and hatred which World War II had engendered, he declared, "So far as I am concerned, I would not want to see a quota for Japan for the next thousand years!" And "That goes for the Germans, too. I think something should be done about cutting the German quota." Dr Van Kirk's final response was a reiteration of his organization's position: "We are simply asking that under such restrictions as may be in force, and within the framework of the quota system, that this principle of discrimination be removed" (ibid.: 16).

The remaining testimony dealt with the commercial implications of ending discrimination and racial prejudice against India
and Indians. John B. Chevalier, Secretary of the American Asiatic
Association, commenced this phase of the hearings. The first thing
he did was to present the committee with a resolution by his organization endorsing the changes being sought in immigration and
naturalization laws, plus a compilation of 150 names from all walks
of the American business community, and supporting groups, who
endorsed the proposed changes. These consisted of high-ranking
persons representing several major corporations doing business
in whole or in part in Asia. Former President Herbert Hoover was
a signatory along with former ambassador William Phillips, State
Department diplomat Joseph C. Grew, *Asia Magazine* editor
Richard J. Walsh, PanAm president Juan Trippe, and a host of
others. This was obviously to draw the legislators' attention to
the commercial potential of post-war India. Accompanying
Chevalier was, as noted earlier, V.A. Dodge of the Dodge &
Seymour Company, whom he had met 30 years ago while traveling
in India. "Every American in the Far East knows about Mr. Dodge
and Dodge-Seymour" (ibid.: 21).

Chevalier's performance, however, failed to make much of an
impression on the committee members. He was obviously something of a romantic who chose to recite a parable about the great
Persian poet, Omar Khayyam; its purpose was to illustrate the
grandeur and subtlety of the "Oriental Mind," and thus the entitlement of Asians to "come here on the basis of full equality." To a
group of seasoned, hard-bitten, grassroots politicians, mostly from
the South and the Border States, Chevalier's exotic intellectual deli-
cacies were hardly appetizing fare! Celler seems to have grasped
the situation and quickly moved to bring on Mr Dodge, who had
a long, practical experience of doing business in South Asia. "I have
never lived permanently in India," Dodge declared, "My visits,
which were on business, have been for from 4 months to 6 months,
one of 18 months." His association with India dated back before
the war, he said. "Since the war I have been associating with Indian
businessmen and industrialists, not politicians." He spoke of
the impediments to profitable business enterprise stemming
from the immigration and visa restrictions, as well as the impediments to American commercial intercourse with India stemming
from British colonialism. The latter pertained especially to the

preferential tariffs which had to be coped with. "In our business, and in the business of many others, we tried to find things that were made in the United States which could not be made in England as well, made at a more favorable price that would sell against the inferior article." He said his Company had offices in Bombay, Karachi, Lahore, Delhi, Calcutta, and Madras. In a bow to his interlocutors, Dodge declared, "I think all of your States through us and others have been shipping goods to India." In a lighter vein, Representative Arnold of Missouri asked, "Did you find any Missouri mules out there?" Dodge replied, "I have known of them being shipped to Karachi" (ibid.: 25).

Dodge enthralled his listeners with an account of how in 1902 he and his brother took a four-horsepower car out to India, the first American car to be sent there. "There had been two or three French cars brought out by Indian princes." But it was they who brought "the Oldsmobile, developed by R.E. Olds ... and we started to sell it through the development of agents." There were then only bicycle and carriage dealers in India so, "We decided we had to find somebody that could sell motorcars." He said they established dealerships and repair facilities through which they dispensed not only Oldsmobiles but Fords as well. "I mention that particularly because the United States leads in the automotive trade of the world ...."

The representatives asked Dodge many questions about conditions in India. In a sense, he proved to be the type of down-to-earth informant who could impart common sense insights into India that resonated with practical politicians far more than the perorations of romantic dilettantes and political ideologues. Representative Allen wanted to know about the size of the family farm in India, and how fertile the agricultural lands which they cultivate. They were somewhat appalled to learn that the average size of a family plot was only 3–3.5 acres, supporting families numbering four to five individuals. Compared to American farms this was viewed as meager indeed. Dodge conceded that the soil is not overly fertile and must be irrigated. Moreover, it was estimated that around 80 percent of Indian farm families exist at this level. "Well," exclaimed Representative Allen, "it is no wonder that they do not make a very good living." On the other hand, Dodge pointed out, there are regional and other differences in Indian agriculture which had not been factored into his remarks. There are larger farms as well, "depending on the crops grown." India is a big country, he pointed out.

He was also asked about road conditions and was told that India at that time had abut 150,000 miles of roads, including "hard-surfaced roads developed over the past twenty-odd years." He cited the road between Bombay and Delhi, stretching over a thousand miles, "which you could call a fairly good road."

Because Dodge was familiar with conditions in India, the committee members wished to ask him questions about the "internal, not racial groups." What they were thinking about, of course, was caste and religious groups. "I have understood," said Representative Allen, "in India there are many groups that probably do not affiliate so very much with each other." Here, he meant Hindus and Muslims. Allen wanted to know whether "any Hindus become Mohammedans." Not to his knowledge, Dodge replied. "I never knew one." Then Allen wanted to know, "what is the basic religious faith of the Hindus as a race?" Dodge did not venture an explanation, probably because as a journeyman businessman he was very much akin to supercargoes and other merchants who had plied their trade in India during the era of the Yankee clippers. "It would take a long time to answer that question," he replied. "You are just a practical businessman," interjected Representative Noah Morgan Mason (1882–1965) of Illinois, "and know something about business conditions?" "That is all," said Dodge, "I have never felt that it was my privilege to discuss the religion of a Hindu or a Mohammedan, any more than I would discuss religion with you gentlemen." Dodge stated that the Indian business world was his exclusive beat. "I have developed a very intimate knowledge of the Indian businessman, because I have seen him rise." Somewhat in the spirit of the old Yankee traders, he declared, "I know his sons and nephews and his children." He held the Indian businessman in high regard. "I know he is a man of as fine honor as anyone I have ever done business with, and I have done business with people all over the world" (ibid.: 28).

Even with Dodge, the committee members kept reverting to what seemed to be their principal preoccupation: whether to extend immigration privileges to all Orientals and not only Eastern Hemisphere Indians. Essentially, Dodge said he believed the privilege should be so extended, although he was guarded in his comments about regions outside the sub-continent. His testimony concluded with a dialog over whether East Asians in general and Indians in particular would be inclined to migrate to America in large numbers if quotas were provided for them. Of course, there was an unreal quality to this discussion, inasmuch as the proposed legislation would limit immigration to a mere 100 persons per year. The underlying reason for raising the issue, of course, was the ever present "Yellow Peril" stereotype. This came out when Representative James Isaac Dolliver (1894–1978) of Louisiana predictably asked, "Do you consider, Mr. Dodge, that this quota of 100 is an entering wedge for a larger quota in later years?" Mr Dodge, you might say, "dodged" the question. "I cannot tell," he replied, "None of us can predict the future well, Mr. Dolliver." Of course, everyone knew down deep that immigration quotas were inevitably negotiable in the long run. But this was clearly not the moment to raise this touchy issue.

The final supportive testimony came from the missionary wing of Protestant Christianity. It was enunciated by Sue Waddell, executive secretary of the India Committee (New York) of the Foreign Missions Conference of New York. She submitted a document containing the names of 123 boards and organizations that conducted missionary activities of various kinds in India. She included a resolution passed on April 11, 1944, by the Executive Committee, which declared: "To record our deep concern that discrimination against citizenship of Eastern Hemisphere Indians of India be removed." In addition, it pledged "To collaborate with the Federal Council of Churches of Christ in America on plans for a joint effort to secure favorable consideration of bills designed to admit Indians to the United States on a quota basis and to citizenship privileges" (ibid.: 39).

With 285 members of the House present, the floor debate commenced on October 10, 1945. The formula followed was for the Bill to be first read and entered into the record, and then for its advocates to state the reasons why they believed it must be passed into law. This would be followed by the House constituting itself as a "Committee of the Whole" for two hours in order to facilitate debate on the Bill before a vote was taken. It was during this floor debate on H.R. 3517 that the opposition had its day. At this point, all J.J. Singh, Anup Singh, Syud Hossain, Taraknath Das, Krishnalal Shridharani, Haridas Mazumdar and all the other India lobbyists could do was to wait in the wings and see whether all their efforts were at last destined to pay dividends.

Democratic Representative Adolph Joachim Sabath (1866–1952) from the Chicago area began the advocates' presentation. Sabath was himself an immigrant from Czechoslovakia. He had been born there in 1866, came to America in 1881, graduated from the Chicago School of Law in 1891, was admitted to the Bar in 1892, got elected to the House of Representatives in 1900 (60th Congress), and served there until his death in 1952. Symbolically speaking, he was the right man to start the ball rolling.

After reiterating the Bill's purpose, he declared, "The enactment of this legislation will place the East Indians in the same status as the nationals of other Asiatic nations who are permitted to enter the United States in limited numbers and whose subjects residing in the Unites States are eligible for naturalization if able to meet the requirements for citizenship." He anticipated the main objections that would be raised by the opponents of the legislation. "I realize there are a few gentlemen in the House who will endeavor to create an issue and shout that the enactment of this bill will open the door for the admission of millions of immigrants." Sabath dismissed such assertions out of hand. Claims of this kind are, he said, "not unusual on the part of these gentlemen, who fail to realize that our country has not been injured by the admission of immigrants in the past but, to the contrary, has benefitted to a great extent by reason of the large immigration prior to the First World War." He declared that "The opposition is aware and familiar with these facts and their opposition to the pending measure is due to unwarranted and unjustifiable prejudice" (*Congressional Record, House*, 1945, p. 9520).

Others followed. Representative Earl Cory Michener (1876–1957), a Republican from Michigan, who had served in the Spanish-American War, studied law at the University of Michigan and obtained his law degree from George Washington University, swallowed his conservatism and came over to the pro-immigration side. "Personally, I have always supported strict immigration laws," but in this case, he declared, he did not believe "that this bill violates that policy," given the fact that "This bill has been throughly considered by the committee having jurisdiction" (ibid.). After him came Noah Morgan Mason (1882–1965), a Republican from Illinois who had come to America from Wales when he was a child. In his support of the Bill, Mason displayed early glimmerings of the emerging Cold War by invoking the specter of Communist expansionism as a reason to win favor in Asia. "Mr. Speaker, we all know that Stalin is seeking a controlling influence in both Europe and Asia; we all know the effort Stalin is making today, through his Communist agents all over the world, to undermine [General Douglas] MacArthur [in Japan] and to weaken Uncle Sam's position in Asia." At this point, Mason read from a statement he made at the time of the 1943 Act, explicating his reasons for ending Chinese exclusion. He urged his listeners to apply these to the present legislation: "to think India every time I say China" (ibid.: 9522).

Key moments came when two major Republican members, Joseph W. Martin (1884–1968) of Massachusetts, soon to become Speaker of the House, and Representative Everett Dirksen, destined to become a major force in the US Senate following his House career, both came out in support of H.R. 3517. This undoubtedly helped tip the balance in its favor. Dirksen gave an amazingly spirited endorsement. There were three reasons, he said, for his support. The first was moral. "It is difficult to develop good will with a country and still proscribe them and say, 'Well, obviously, we are only too glad to deal with you, but your people can't come to this country.'" The second reason was economic. India "will develop a tremendous outlet for the agricultural products of this country." The third reason was political: "India is going to have her freedom some day," and once she does it is going to be in America's interest to have good relations with her. "Today we enjoy a friendly diplomatic relationship with India. Why not promote it by devel-opment of further good will."

Dirksen then added a fourth reason for supporting the Bill. It was, he said, the fact that India is essentially an English-speaking nation, as far as her political culture is concerned. "It is amazing the number of people in India who speak the English language." It is the language they speak in their legislative bodies. The Indian is a Caucasian, he declared, a statement which implicitly refuted the contention of the *Thind* decision. And since they are Caucasians, "I see no reason why the limitations of the act of 1924 should be permitted to continue."

Dirksen concluded his remarks with a touching tribute which once again reflected the transcendentalist influences that

commenced permeating the cultural fabric of America from the
time of the Yankee traders: "Mr. Speaker, I *think some of the finest
things that have ever been written upon the parchment of ancient
literature come from India*" (ibid.: 9523, emphasis added).

After Representative Dirksen's pean, Chairman Dickstein used
one of the two hours allocated for general debate to review once
again the reasons why the committee's majority now favored the
bill's passage. It was at this point that letters and statements from
President Roosevelt, President Truman, the Acting Secretary of
State Joseph C. Grew, the Attorney General Madame Frances
Biddle, and British Ambassador Lord Halifax, endorsing H.R. 3715
were read into the Record. Then the opponents of the legislation
got their chance.

During this hour, a string of predominantly segregationist
Southern Democrat and conservative Republican House members
rose and delivered heated denunciations of the Celler Bill. Representative Edward Oscar McCowan (1877–1953) of Ohio fired the
first shots. He came from the Columbus area, had attended Ohio
Northern University, Ohio State University and the University of
Cincinnati, and had been a school teacher before being elected to
the House in 1943. Such a background might have been expected
to place him in the progressive camp; but alas it did not.

"I rise in opposition to the passage of this bill," he declared. He
viewed the effort to admit Indians to citizenship as being based
on what he called "dollar propaganda." That is, the belief that
opening up trade and liberalizing immigration laws with respect
to India would yield a panacea of profitable business and mutual
goodwill. This is the same delusion about Asia from that we suffered since before the turn of the century, he said. In 1854, "We
tried the same thing with Japan." And look what happened. "We
sold her everything with which to make war, from gas to scrap,
and got it shot back at us at the expense of many thousands of
lives of American boys." He asked, "Shall we start that with India,
that is said to have 400,000,000 people?" (ibid.: 9524).

In addition to these historically and culturally shallow perorations, Representative McCowen tried to make it appear that the
advocates of Indian immigration and naturalization were claiming
that their admission was a *right* when, in fact, it was only a *privilege*
which it was the prerogative of the United States to grant as it saw

fit. "If it be a privilege and not a right, no injustice and no discrimination can be correctly charged."

McCowan, like other opponents, also employed the "inundation thesis" concerning Asian exclusionism. He drew an analogy to the old "Peter-and-the-Dyke" fairy tale. "Do you remember the story of the break in the dyke?" he asked. "This attempted break in the immigration laws should be prevented and thereby stop the danger to the immigration system and secure perfect safety of American labor and the American form of government." The protection of White American labor argument was, of course, an echo of the racism that originated against Sikh—and before them, Chinese and Japanese—immigration on the West Coast. Unfortunately, almost 40 years later, McCowan could still justify this racism by citing the opposition of the American labor movement to South Asian immigration and citizenship. "The American Federation of Labor is against this bill," he declared. Turning to outright demagoguery, the Representative asked rhetorically, "Shall we let thousands, as will be requested later, take the place of dead Americans killed in battle or the place of others maimed for life?" Therefore, he concluded, "I object to repealing the immigration law now and I object to repealing it and breaking it down little by little" (ibid.: 9525).

Predictably, Representative Asa Leonard Allen (1891–1969) from Louisiana resorted to fundamentalist Christian rationalizations for keeping things as they were. In the proper Christian spirit, he was not against the Indian people at all, he reassured his colleagues; he was merely in favor of keeping Indians in India and exporting the Gospel to them. "I am affiliated with a church that believes in sending the Gospel to the Hindus," Allen declared. "I have been trying to contribute throughout the years out of my meager means to send the Gospel to them and expect to to keep it up. *There is your remedy.*" He also mentioned that he had "read in the paper" about Hindu–Muslim violence in India and asked, "Does anybody want to transport to America that internal quarrel that has been going on for ages over there?" (ibid.: 9526).

And so it went, until Clair Booth Luce rose to challenge the bill's detractors. She reviewed the outcome of all the hearings that had gone before. She mentioned the fact that the Bill was finally voted out of Committee "as a result of the administration's and the State Department's increased and increasing support of the bill from the time of its introduction ..." (ibid.: 9527). This was crucial to the track the bill was now on; without it there is doubt that it could have made it out of Committee at this time, given the number of conservative doubters and outright opponents. She chose to let stand the statements that had already been made in the hearings and on the floor concerning why, from the standpoint of military, economic and political expediency, the Bill made sense. Mrs Luce chose instead to emphasize the broader moral and ethical issues which she believed this legislation addressed. These concerned where the world was heading once hostilities ended, and the challenges that would confront American values, especially democracy and freedom, as non-Western peoples throw off the yoke of colonialism and make institutional choices among the alternatives that will be available to them.

"Many expert witnesses," she declared, "pointed out that in the years ahead it will matter greatly to us, in terms of our own national security, whether the Asiatic countries veer toward democracy as we know it, or toward the Soviet brand of democracy." She then went on to refer to the observations of Professor Owen Lattimore who, before being politically demonized by the McCarthyists in the 1950s, and virtually driven out of the country, was regarded "as one of the experts on the Far East, who is currently being widely read and listened to, not only by laymen but by people in the State Department ...." Mrs Luce noted Lattimore's belief that "after the war there is going to be a great deal of shopping around, so to speak, among the Asiatic peoples, particularly colonial peoples, for political ideologies." It was her belief, like Lattimore's, "that that nation whose system or ideology shows the greatest hope for their own economic and political advancement is the one which is bound to have the greatest appeal for the oriental peoples." America's racist immigration and naturalization policies toward India and other Asian societies would put the country at a distinct disadvantage as far as winning the hearts and minds of emerging nations is concerned. She contrasted this with the egalitarian, anti-racist doctrine propounded by the Soviet Union which "seems to make room for men of all colors and, therefore, nations of all colors. Whether one judges it as sincere or not, that is the image which Soviet Russia projects to the world which makes the appeal of Communism to the colored peoples of every colonial empire on earth" so great.

Finally there came a statement that clearly reflected the strength of her close relationship with J.J. Singh and the educative impact he had had on her. "I believe that every Member of this House is familiar with my stand on the subject of Indian independence." For many years, Luce intoned, "like many others in America and England, I have urged upon the British, for reasons of principle no less than for expediency, that India be given a near date for independence." She noted having made this point recently in a radio speech. "I said that if India did not get its independence freely from Great Britain she might in her despair turn to Communism for comfort, and toward the Kremlin for aid" (ibid.: 9527).

Despite Mrs Luce's spirited statement favoring the legislation, she was afterward confronted with a rather caustic refutation by one of the House's other female legislators, Republican Representative Jesse Sumner (1898–1994) from Illinois. Despite her cosmopolitan credentials—a graduate of Smith College, and the University of Chicago Law School, plus post-graduate work at Columbia University and Oxford—she obviously was no admirer of Clair Both Luce, and no friend of immigration and naturalization liberalization. She bluntly declared that "the gentlewoman is giving the Russians too much credit when she believes their talk about having no racial discrimination." After all, "They persecuted the Jews in Poland." Furthermore, "They are back of the Arab movement to prevent the immigration of Jews to Palestine." She insisted that any quotas granted to the South Asian Indians would be employed to infiltrate Communists into the United States (ibid.: 9528–29).

Mrs Luce's answer to this silly charge was appropriately dismissive: "It could be exceedingly difficult for the gentlewoman to prove that if 75 Indians came to this country, they are all bound to be Communists." Mrs Luce further countered Miss Sumner's doctrinaire anti-Communism by pointing out that sometimes in the domain of international politics, appearances matter as much as substance. "Whatever their secret practice is, their official propaganda is against racial discrimination." Sarcastically, she added, "I take it that the lady from Illinois is also against the principle of discrimination [inasmuch] as she indicts Stalin for practicing it, in which case she must unavoidably vote for this bill."

Interestingly and not surprisingly two particular members immediately came to Mrs Luce's defense. They were Walter Henry

Judd (1898–1994) of Minnesota and John Martin Vorys (1896–1968) of Ohio. I say not surprising because both, despite being very conservative Republicans, had been medical missionaries in China. Vorys, in fact, had taught medicine for 10 years at the College of Yale in Changsha, China. Despite their conservatism on domestic social policies and their strident nationalism, their long association with China and the Chinese people had molded them into staunch opponents of anti-Asian racism. In direct support of Mrs Luce, Representative Judd asked, "Does the gentlewoman agree with the statement of the gentleman from Louisiana [Representative Allen] that we are departing from our immigration laws and destroying the basic principle, or is it not rather the case that we are merely extending the principle and for the second time bringing in some of these peoples around the world under the [existing] formula?" Indeed, we are not abandoning an existing formula at all, Judd averred. "I believe the gentlewoman will agree with me that ... we are merely carrying on with other peoples the same principles and policies we have followed hitherto all through our history." Clearly relieved, Luce declared, "I am in complete accord with the gentleman" (ibid.: 9529).

Then Representative Vorys followed Mr Judd with a comparable endorsement. "It is at our peril that we, representing white folks, will continue to practice discrimination against various kinds of colored folks in a world where they outnumber us tremendously." He said, "I thoroughly agree with the high moral principle that the gentlewoman bases her plea on." Mrs Luce in turn thanked Vorys for his "fine speech," and said that while he spoke she was thinking of what were the moral implications of the "categorical question" raised by Representative Allen. He had asked, she said, what would become of our children and our children's children if we let 75 Indians a year into America. Her counter-question was, "*What would become of them, if we did not?*" (ibid.).

The debate among Congressmen and other House members ebbed and flowed until Emanuel Celler, the Bill's principal sponsor, finally entered the fray. While not ignoring the moral issue which Luce and other proponents had enunciated, Celler placed great emphasis on the contributions that India and Indians in America had made to the war effort. He gave this a personal twist by relating an encounter he had with a delegation of Indians from the Imperial Valley of California:

They were businessmen, they were farmers, they were professional men; they were all upstanding gentlemen, cultured, refined, educated, soft-spoken, *thoroughly Americanized*. Those men would be permitted to become American citizens under my bill. *Over 200—in fact, 215—of their sons served in our armed forces*. Many were born here, and thus could vote. All of the others will, under my bill, become eligible for citizenship. All who come in under the quota of 100 will be entitled under proper regulations, to become citizens (ibid.: 9531).

What is striking about this passage is what it tells us about how far the South Asian community in the United States had come in terms of their socio-economic development since the first immigrants arrived near the turn of the century. Congressman Celler could demonstrate in this manner what, against all odds, these pioneers had been able to accomplish and why, therefore, so-called "Eastern Hemisphere Indians from India" had earned the right to be treated as fully enfranchised citizens of the United States, and why, as well, their brethren in India are entitled to enjoy the same quota-determined immigration rights as the Chinese and Japanese.

Most of the rest of Celler's statement pertained to the strategic and commercial importance of India, not only to the war effort but to the peace that would follow. Addressing the performance of Indian troops in battle, Celler singled out Congressman Allen for special criticism: "May I say to the gentleman from Louisiana who did not speak too feelingly of the Indian effort in the war that he might read what Gen. Mark Clark [commander of the Italian front] said concerning the Indian troops under his command." General Clark said on February 27, 1945, the following: "No obstacle has succeeded in delaying these troops or lowering their high morale in fighting spirit. I salute the brave soldiers of these three great Indian divisions." He then quoted General Lucian Truscott to similar effect: "The Indian troops in this theater won the respect and admiration of all Allied soldiers with whom they have been associated. It is an honor for any commander to have such troops under him."

Celler reiterated points that he had made in earlier testimony: namely, that the Indians had the largest volunteer army (2.5 million) of any Allied country; that 60,000 Indians were serving in the British merchant marine; that over 300,000 Indians were serving in the Air Force, etc.

Regarding a proposed "treaty of commerce and navigation" between the United States and India, Celler invoked J.J. Singh's expertise. "I am informed," he stated, "by Mr. J.J. Singh, president of the India League of America, *a very distinguished gentleman*, that high Government officials of the Government of India are holding up the proposed treaty ... pending the outcome of this legislation." Negotiations had been going on for 42 years, said Celler, and both sides "are anxious to go forward with this treaty ... so that there may be increased international trade between the two countries." Should the bill be defeated, Celler claimed, the outcome of this treaty would be placed in jeopardy, because acquiring the necessary visas and residency requirements by both parties would be inhibited, in addition to the ill will that would be crated in India. He made a revealing statement about monetary balances. Celler claimed that the United States actually owed India $1.5 billion for the supplies of jute, manganese, bauxite, tin and other strategic purchases that were made during the course of the war, while there was little that India could buy from us. "That money is locked up in the Sterling area bloc pool on Threadneedle Street , England, but England cannot keep its hands on those dollars much longer." When finally they are set free, India will want to use this money to purchase capital goods and consumer goods from the United States (ibid.: 9531).

One of the bitterest denunciations of the Bill followed Celler's presentation. It came, not surprisingly, from a California House member, Bertrand Wesley Gearhart (1890–1955). "Everybody wants to come here," said Gearhart, "Everybody wants to stay here. Is our first obligation the uplifting of our own unfortunate? Personally, I think that is our first responsibility." And who specifically are the persons who want to come here, he asked:

> Those who want come here are the most unfortunate, the worst off in the other parts of the word, the peons and coolies, people who have been deprived of their inalienable rights to life, liberty and the pursuit of happiness for generations untold. The Hindus who would come have no appreciation of what liberty means. What can they contribute to the up-building of our country?

Why should we multiply our already many problems by augmenting our underprivileged groups? (ibid.: 9533)

Representative John Marshall Robsion (1873–1948) of Kentucky, however, introduced the bottom-line conclusion to be drawn from Celler's words. "The gentleman says that England will have to take her hands off those dollars in the bank that are supposed to belong to the business people of India." If so, then, "That would suggest that she would have to take her hands off the people of India, would it not?" All proponents of the bill heartily agreed (ibid.: 9531).

After much more back and forth discussion, the Clerk was asked to read the bill for amendment. The relevant amendment was contained in Clause 3, which read: "EXC. 303. (a) The right to become a naturalized citizen under the provisions of this act shall be extended only to: ... (3) Chinese persons and persons of Chinese decent *and persons or races indigenous to India* ...." (emphasis added).

The House version of the India Immigration and Naturalization Bill (H.R. 3517) was passed by the House of Representatives on October 10, 1945. It was, said *India Today*, passed by an overwhelming voice vote after a motion to recommit the bill to the Committee was defeated by a vote of 207 to 83. The bill was then sent to the Senate for consideration by the Senate Immigration Committee, chaired by Senator Richard Russell (1897–1971) of Georgia. The entire process on both sides of the aisle did not work itself out until June of the following year. There were some touch-and-go moments. As *India Today* (June 1946) reported, "Several last minute complications arose which for a few days endangered the passage of the Bill in this session of the Congress." This occurred, "when the Senate Immigration Committee, on June 5th, acted favorably upon both the Indian Immigration and Naturalization Bill (H.R. 3517) and the Filipino Naturalization Bill (H.R. 776) at the same time." When they then were passed by the full Senate on June 14, "it was realized that the language of both bills amended Section 303 of the Nationality Act of 1940, and that the language of both bills was such that if President Truman signed the Filipino Naturalization Bill first and the India Immigration and Naturalization Bill afterwards, it would nullify the Filipino Naturalization Bill." This would be the case because, "if the provisions of the last bill signed by the President are in conflict with the provisions of the previous bill, it automatically nullifies such previous bill." The solution was to work out the bugs in Conference. On June 25, the conferees agreed to incorporate the Filipino bill into the India bill, thus making it a single package which avoided legal incompatibilities between the two separate bills. The Senate, on June 26, and the House, on June 27, accepted this revision. The bill then became law, retaining its original designation, H.R. 3517, as introduced by Representative Celler, when the House passed it on June 27, 1946.

# 12    Aftermath

J.J. Singh and the India Lobby had triumphed at last! Indians residing in America could become citizens, and Indians wishing to come to America could do so legally under a formal quota. A headline in the June issue of *India Today* said it all. It read, "INDIA CITIZENSHIP BILL PASSES." The process which began at the turn of the century with what Har Dayal called "Sikhs, Swamis, Students and Spies," had by the end of World War II culminated in immigration rights and equality under the law for "East Asians of Indian descent."

There is a memorable photograph of the actual signing of the Celler-Luce Bill on July 2, 1946, which shows its principal beneficiaries standing behind President Harry S. Truman as he affixes his signature to the legislation. The witnesses present were representatives of the Philippines as well as members of the India Lobby (see cover photo).

The politicization process that led to this consummation had evolved over about half a century. The Sikhs and other South Asian immigrants along the Pacific Coast of Canada and the United States who started it all began arriving in significant numbers around 1904 and 1905. Their numbers increased gradually, but at no time did they amount to more than a few thousand, even when taking account of those who were illegal immigrants, and allowing for demographic expansion through intermarriage and natural increase. Let us recall that, as late as 1924, the battle to rescind the *Thind* decision addressed the plight of only 3,000 denaturalized South Asian Indians.

Yet, from the outset, their impact in the deeply racist social world in which they found themselves was not inconsiderable. Their image as brown-skinned "rag heads," and as perceived threats to the White labor market made them ready targets for discrimination. Also, the Indians themselves proved to be far from passive: imbued as they were with a cultural pride that had deep historical roots, they were well equipped with the moral resources needed to cope with the challenges they faced. Sikhs are a disciplined, proud, strong-willed people, the products of a monotheistic religious tradition which in many respects is a counterpart of the "protestant ethic" to which White Anglo-Saxons adhere. The Hindu and Muslim immigrants, far fewer in number, also had moral resources of their own upon which they could draw, stemming from ancient cultural and religious traditions that imbued them with the self-confidence and resiliency required to resist the mob mentality that confronted them at every turn.

The result was that beleaguered South Asians countered with leaders of their own who set about mobilizing and organizing their community to fight for their civil rights. It became clear, almost from the outset, that this goal could not be detached from the struggle to free India from colonial domination. The South Asians drew the correct conclusion from the example set by Japanese migrants: namely, that a strong, caring, politically independent government at home put its migrants abroad in a stronger bargaining position. The connection between nationalism and the condition of South Asian emigrants became clearer as politically conscious, middle-class students, professionals and activist exiles entered the mix. Men like Teja Singh, Har Dayal, and Taraknath Das exemplified this vital connection. Har Dayal's observation that the early South Asian pioneers consisted of "Sikhs, swamis, students and spies" was an apt short-hand characterization of the original categories of South Asians who, as Jensen put it, undertook "the passage from India."

The Sikhs were an agrarian peasantry who sank deep roots into the soil of their adopted land. Against all odds, applying technological and organizational models they brought with them from the Punjab, they gradually created the material and fiscal wherewithal needed to expand their patrimonies. To accomplish this they were compelled to challenge the legal and political obstacles that were hurled in their path by White society. With great tenacity, they built the institutions required to do so. *Gurdwaras* sprang up in many places on both sides of the border, and became not only foci for their cultural and religious life but also headquarters for the promulgation of political action. They found lawyers who would represent their interests in the American and Canadian courts and, as their fortunes improved, eventually produced their own lawyers. They created agro-businesses and mercantile enterprises which funded education and political action. The intellectuals and activists from middle-class Bengali, Maharashtrian and Hindi-belt families who filtered onto college and university campuses, or who found other niches around the country, provided mobilizational skills, including ideological articulation, as they joined hands with their rustic brethren. The intellectuals were especially crucial in developing the various organizations that promoted political awareness and provided frameworks for collective action. Ghadr was a classic manifestation of this fateful conjuncture, as were the organizations that followed, such as the Friends for Freedom of India, the India League of America, the Indian Chamber of Commerce of America, the National Committee for Indian Freedom, the India Welfare League, etc.

We have seen how political mobilization among South Asians in America passed through a series of phases. Underlyingly, these reflected the evolution of political processes in India, in the United States, indeed in the world writ large, over the first half of the twentieth century. Milestones along this political trek were the early radical revolutionaries (Har Dayal, Taraknath Das, Gobind Behari Lal, Sarangadhar Das, Sailendranath Ghose, Virendranath Chattopadhyaya, etc.), culminating in Ghadr; World War I, and the coming of Lala Lajpat Rai; the *Thind* decision and its aftermath; the emergence of the India Lobby under the tutelage of J.J. Singh and his compatriots (Anup Singh, Syud Hossain, Haridas Mazumdar, Krishnalal Shridharani), largely in the context of World War II; the achievement of Indian citizenship and immigration rights with the passage of Luce-Celler; and finally the attainment of Indian independence.

The days following the passage of Luce-Celler and President Truman's signing of the Act saw the gradual winding down of the India Lobby, as the chief participants dispersed to the postwar horizons that beckoned them. There were, however, two final events that took place that truly marked the end of this adventure which the South Asian community in the United States had experienced. They pertain to the period culminating in the achievement of India's independence on August 14, 1947.

The first was the naming of India's Ambassador to the United States, thus signifying her entrée into the community of free and independent nations. Interestingly, indeed pointedly, in order to emphasize India's commitment to democracy and secularism, the appointee was Asaf Ali, a Muslim. He was born in 1888, educated in Delhi and Lincoln's Inn, London, served in the Legislative Assembly from Delhi, "by the joint votes of Hindus and Muslims" (*Voice of India*, December 1946, p. 371). He was a member of the Congress Working Committee and Deputy Leader of the Congress party in the Central Assembly. On February 26, 1947, the National Committee for India's Freedom held a reception for him in Washington. It was said that around a thousand persons attended this event. In the words of the *Voice of India*: "As one paper put it, 'shoals of Senators and their wives,' more than forty members of the diplomatic corps, admirals and generals galore, State Department officials and leading figures of Washington's 'civilian' society, passed by the receiving line which was headed by Dr. Anup Singh, Secretary of the National Committee for India's Freedom." Many other notables were also mentioned, of course. Also, "Important members of the press came in large numbers, and Indians from all over this country flocked to Washington to pay their respects to their first ambassador." It was a gala event. "The many Indian ladies in their lovely saris, the Ambassador and several other Indian gentlemen wearing achkans, and the half dozen bearded and turbaned Sikhs who towered over the crowd, as well as the various army and navy officers with their gold braid, all made a colorful and picturesque gathering in the flower decked main ballroom of the Mayflower Hotel" (*Voice of India*, December 1946, p. 404).

It was a far cry from the meager and often desperate circumstances in which the quest for South Asian civil rights and Indian freedom had begun half a century earlier!

The other event was the selection of Madam Vijayalakshmi Pandit in the fall of 1946, in Kux's words, "an outsider in 1945 at San Francisco," to lead the "official delegation to the UN's first General Assembly session at Lake Success, New York." Her instructions from her brother, Pandit Jawaharlal Nehru, Minister for Foreign Affairs, and soon to become the interim prime minister of India, following Independence, was to "steer clear" of both the democratic and communist power groups (Kux 1993: 51). In her first major speech before the body, on October 25, she declared:

> India holds that the independence of all colonial peoples is the vital concern of freedom-loving peoples everywhere. She looks with confidence to the United Nations to give to the exploited millions of the world faith and hope and the promise that their liberation is at hand (*Voice of India*, November 1946, p. 365).

Mrs Pandit replaced Asaf Ali as Ambassador to the United States in 1950 and then returned to the UN in 1952, where, in 1953, she became the first woman president of the UN General Assembly. Clearly, much water had flowed under the dam in the South Asians' quest for social and political justice!

For all practical purposes, the organizations which had so dauntlessly fought for South Asians' rights began winding down. There was some fight left in them through 1946, however, until India attained full independence the following year. The lobbyists kept up the pressure on the British to implement their withdrawal from India. There was probably more reflex than substance to their concerns, however, since the Attlee government, which had succeeded Churchill and the Tories in London, had actually advanced the withdrawal date from 1948 to 1947. The turmoil surrounding partition was, of course, the principal cause of continuing angst and distrust about British intentions. There persisted a lingering fear throughout 1946 that Hindu–Muslim communal strife in particular might be employed as a pretext for perpetuating colonial rule in some form. But this was a misreading of bottom-line British intentions or, at least, capabilities. Once the process of partition accelerated, and the complexities of disentanglement became frighteningly evident, England's principal preoccupation was not staying on, but what R.J. Moore in the title of his book dramatized as "Escape from Empire!" (Moore 1983)

All the principal actors for the most part went their separate ways. J.J. Singh continued to do some lobbying on the Indian food crisis, but when that abated he eventually returned to India, married, and took up residence in South Delhi. Syud Hossain opted to return to India in 1946 and soon after was appointed India's Ambassador to Egypt, where he passed away in 1949. On March 11, 1946, the National Committee gave him a farewell dinner at the Ceylon-India Inn in New York. Krishnalal Shridharani chaired the gathering. "The restaurant," said the *Voice of India*, "was filled with Dr Hossain's Indian and American friends and admirers." They included Roger Baldwin, Oswald Garrison Villard, James B. Pond (his lecture-manager), Taraknath Das, and many others. Anup Singh read testimonials from Pearl Buck, Norman Thomas, Dr Arthur Upham Pope, Dr J. Holmes Smith, and others who were unable to attend. Hossain made "a brief but exceedingly eloquent address, stressing that India's primary need was independence, even unity coming second; that personally he believed that Pakistan was impractical and that even were it forced on India, as was the partition of Bengal, it would be equally short lived." Hossain was, of course, wrong about this.

Haridas Mazumdar was an American citizen and opted to remain so. In 1946, he left Washington, giving up his position as Assistant Reference Librarian at the Library of Congress and joined the faculty of New Mexico Highlands University in Las Vegas, New Mexico, as a Professor of Sociology.

Krishnalal Shridharani continued his career as a scholar-journalist. The *Voice of India* reported that Shridharani flew to Paris on July 2, 1946, from where he would cover the "Peace Conference" for an Indian newspaper (not named). He returned to the US in September, but eventually he too went back to India and took up an academic position there.

Anup Singh remained on the lecture tour in the United States through 1948 until the *Voice of India* ceased publication. In 1949–1950, he was associated with the UN, as Chief Indian Delegate on the UN Korean Commission, and as Advisor on the Indian Delegation to the Third Session of the General Assembly. He also became a member of the Executive Committee of the Indian Council of World Affairs, the Court of Delhi University and several other bodies, which shows how he was progressively parlaying the credentials garnered in the India Lobby days into a position of prominence in post-independence India. This culminated in his election to the Rajya Sabha in 1952, where he served until 1962. We have already described how his American cohort, Madam Boulter, was left in the backwash of his return to the Indian fold.

Following Indian independence, a new era dawned in US–Indian relations, to which two generations of these South Asian political pioneers had made seminal contributions. They had cleared the way for Indians to legally come to the United States and acquire citizenship here. The rest, as the cliché goes, is history. There were many strains and stresses in the relationship as both countries became swallowed up in the rancor and opportunism of the Cold War. These matters are outside the provenance of this narrative. All that need be said is that by 1964, with the new immigration rules, the gates opened, and South Asians began flooding into the United States. There are now approximately two million persons of South Asian Indian decent in this country and the mark they are making in all walks of its life are everywhere apparent. It is said that the median income of Indian Americans in 2005 is over $60,000 per annum, higher than any other minority group. They have come here on the wings of opportunities, which the energies and the sufferings of Har Dayal, Taraknath Das, Lala Lajpat Rai, Haridas Mazumdar, Syud Hossain, Anup Singh, Krishnalal Shridharani, J.J. Singh, the Sikh leaders on the Pacific Coast, and so many others, including, yes, "Deep Throat" (i.e., Professor Robert E. Crane, to whom this book is dedicated) made possible.

# Glossary

| | |
|---|---|
| *Banians* | Hindustani term for moneylenders and middle-men during the mercantile era |
| *baradari* | extended kin group |
| *bhakti* | intense religious devotion |
| *desh sewak* | service to country/national service |
| *dhoti* | "diaper-like" garment worn by North Indian males |
| *Dubash* | Hindustani term for "broker" during the mercantile era. Derived from *do basha*, meaning "two languages" |
| *Ghadr* | disloyal, revolution. Anglicized version = Gadar |
| *gharwali* | housewife (vernacular) |
| Guru Granth Saheb | the holy book of the Sikhs |
| *gurdwara* | Sikh temple |
| Gurmukhi | script for the Punjabi language |
| *haq* | right (legal) |
| *haq shuda* | right of pre-emption |
| Harijan | Gandhi's term for untouchables: "children of god (Hari)" |
| *izzat* | honor |
| *kachheri* | court (legal) |
| *kafila* | group, batch |
| Kali | goddess of cosmic destruction |
| *khadi* | Hand woven cotton cloth |
| Khalsa | Sikh congregation |
| *kurta* | loose-fitting garment worn as a top by Indian males and females |
| Jat | name of large agricultural caste centered in the undivided Punjab and western Uttar Pradesh |

| | |
|---|---|
| *purdah* | Muslim practice of veiling/secluding women |
| Raj | Hindi word for British rule in India |
| samiti | a society |
| *sloka* | Vedic verse or incantation |
| Swadeshi | political liberation |
| *tahsil* | sub-district administrative unit |
| Satyagraha | Gandhian term for "truth force" |
| Urdu | Persianized Hindustani rendered in Arabic script |
| Vedanta | consummation of the Vedas |
| *zenana* | secluded household space for women and girls |

# Bibliography

Adhikari, G. 1970. "Foreword", in Sohan Singh Josh (ed.), *Baba Sohan Singh Bhakna: Life of the Founder of the Ghadar Party*. New Delhi.

Bajpai, Sir Girja Shankar. 1944. *The United States and India*. Allahabad: Kitabistan.

Barooah, Nirode K. 2004. *Chatto: The Life and Times of an Indian Anti-Imperialist in Europe*. New Delhi: Oxford University Press.

Barrier, N. Gerald and Dusenbery, Verne A. (eds.). 1989. *The Sikh Diaspora: Migrations and Experiences Beyond the Punjab*. Delhi: Chanakya Publications.

Bean, Susan S. 2001. *Yankee India: American Commercial and Cultural Encounters with India in the Age of Sail: 1784–1860*. Salem, MA: Peabody Essex Museum.

Bhagat, G. 1970. *Americans in India*. New York: New York University Press.

Bowles, Chester. 1954. *Ambassador's Report*. London: Victor Gallancz Ltd.

———. 1993. *New Dealer in the Cold War*. Harvard University Press.

Brown, Emily C. 1975. *Har Dayal, Hindu Revolutionary and Reformist*. Delhi: Manohar Books.

———. 1986. "Revolution in India: Made in America", in S. Chandrasekhar (ed.), *From India to America: A Brief History of Immigration, Problems of Discrimination, Admission and Assimilation*. LaJolla, CA.

Bryan, William Jennings. 1907. *The Old World and Its Ways: A Tour Around the World and Journey Through Europe*. St. Louis: The Thompson Publishing Company.

Buchignani, Norman and Indra, Doreen M. (with Ram Srivastava). 1985. *Continuous Journey: A Social History of South Asians in Canada*. Toronto: McClelland and Stewart.

Casey, Dennis. 2004. "Triple-agent Agnes Smedley", *Spokesman Magazine*, February.

Chadney, James G. 1989. "The Formation of Ethnic Communities: Lessons from the Vancouver Sikhs", in N. Gerald Barrier and Verne A. Dusenbery (eds.), *The Sikh Diaspora: Migrations and Experiences Beyond the Punjab*. Delhi: Chanakya Publications.

Chandrasekhar, S. 1944. "Indian Immigration in America", *Far Eastern Survey*, Vol. XIII, No. 15, July 26.

Chang, Gordon H., Mankeskar, Purnima and Gupta, Akhil (eds.). 2002. *Caste and Outcaste* (Reissue of original book by Dhan Gopal Mukerji). Stanford University Press.

Chernow, Ron. 2004. *Alexander Hamilton*. New York: The Penguin Press.

Chirol, Valentine. 1910a. *Indian Unrest*. London: Macmillan.

———. 1910b. "Revolutionary Organizations Outside India", *The Times*, London, August 10.

Coupland, Reginald. *The Cripps Mission*. New York: Doubleday, Doran & Co.

Das, Rajni Kant. 1923. *Hindustani Workers on the Pacific Coast*. Berlin: Walter de Gruyter.

Dhanki, Joginder Singh. 1978. "Introduction", in Lala Lajpat Rai (ed.), *The Story of My Life*. New Delhi: Gitanjali Prakshan.

Drew, Pearson. 1944. "The Washington Merry Go-Round", *Washington Post*, July 23.

Dutt, Girish Chunder. 1868. *A Lecture on the Life of Ramdoolal Dey*. Bellore: Bengalee Press.

*Echoes of Freedom: South Asian Pioneers in California, 1899–1965*. University of California Library, Berkeley. Archival document.

Embree, Ainslie T. (ed.). 1987. *1857 in India: The Revolt Against Foreign Rule*. Delhi: Chanakya Publications

———. 1994. "The Tradition of Mission—Asian Studies in the United States, 1783–1983", *Journal of Asian Studies*, Vol. XLIII, No. 1, p. 12.

Ferling, John. 2004. *Adams and Jefferson: The Tumultuous Election of 1800*. Oxford University Press.

Fischer, Louis. 1942. *A Week With Gandhi*. New York: Duell, Sloan and Pearce.

———. 1950. *The Life of Mahatma Gandhi*. New York: Harper.

Friedman, Thomas L. 2005. *The World is Flat*. New York: Farrar, Straus and Giroux.

Frumkin, David. 1989. *The Peace to End All Peace: The Fall of the Ottoman Empire and the Creation of the Modern Middle East*. New York: Henry Holt.

*FRUS (Foreign Relations of the United States)*. 1994

Furber, Holden. 1938. "The Beginnings of American Trade with India, 1784–1812", *New England Quarterly*, 11, June, pp. 235–65.

Goodrich, L. Carrington. 1951. *A Short History of China*. Revised edition. New York: Harper and Brothers.

Gould, Harold A. 1971. "The Utopian Side of the Indian Uprising (1857)", in David Plath (ed.), *Aware of Utopia*. Urbana, Ill.: The University of Illinois Press.

———. 1994. *Grass-Roots Politics in India: A Century of Political Evolution in Faizabad District*. New Delhi: Oxford and IBH Publishers.

———. 2002. "The Reasons Why", in Ashok Kapur, Y.K. Malik, Harold A. Gould and Arthur G. Rubinoff (eds.), *India and the United States in a Changing World*. New Delhi: Sage Publications.

Gould, Harold A. and Ganguly, Sumit. 1992. *The Hope and the Reality: U.S.-Indian Relations from Roosevelt to Reagan*. Boulder, CO: Westview Press

Gower, Karla K. 1997. "The Hindu-German Conspiracy: An Examination of the Framing of Indian Nationalists in Newspapers from 1915–1918", AEJMC Conference Papers, September 29.

Griswold, Whitney A. 1938. *The Far Eastern Policy of the United States*. New Haven: Yale University Press.

Halifax, Lord. 1974. *Confidential Dispatches: Analyses of America, By the British Ambassador, 1939–1945*. Edited with an Introductory Essay by Thomas E. Hachey. New University Press.

Hardikar, N.S. 1966. *Lala Lajpat Rai in America*. New Delhi: Servants of the People Society.

*Hearings before a Subcommittee on Immigration, United States Senate, 78th Congress, Second Session, United States Senate, on S. 1595*. 1944.

*Hearings, House Committee on Immigration: To Grant Quota to Eastern Hemisphere Indians.* 1945.

Hess, Gary. 1971. *America Encounters India.* Baltimore: Johns Hopkins Press.

Hull, Cordell. 1948. *The Memoirs of Cordell Hull, Vol. 2.* New York. Macmillan.

Jacoby, Harold S. 1958. "Administrative Restriction of Asian-Indian Immigration into the United States, 1907–1917," *Population Review,* Vol. 25, pp. 35–40.

Jensen, Joan M. 1988. *Passage from India: Asian Indian Immigrants in North America.* New Haven: Yale University Press.

Johnston, Hugh. 1979. *The Voyage of the Komagata Maru: The Sikh Challenge to Canada's Colour Bar.* New Delhi: Oxford University Press

Josh, Sohan Singh. 1970. *Baba Sohan Singh Bhakna: Life of the Founder of the Ghadar Party.* New Delhi.

Kamath, M.V. 1998. *The United States and India, 1776–1996: The Bridge Over the River Time.* New Delhi: Indian Council for Cultural Relations.

Kapur, Ashok, Malik, Y.K., Gould, Harold A. and Rubinoff, Arthur G. (eds.). 2002. *India and the United States in a Changing World.* New Delhi: Sage Publications.

Kaye, Sir John and Malleson, G. 1897–1898. *History of the Indian Mutiny* (6 vols.). New York: Longmans Green.

Kopf, David. 1969. *British Orientalism and the Bengal Renaissance: The Dynamics of Indian Modernization, 1773–1835.* Berkeley and Los Angeles: University of California Press.

Kux, Dennis. 1993. *India and the United States: Estranged Democracies.* Washington, DC: National Defense University Press.

LaFeber, Walter 1977. *America in the Cold War: Twenty Years of Revolutions and Response, 1947–1967.* New York: Wiley.

Lal, Chaman. 1945. *British Propaganda in America.* Allahabad: Kitab Mahal.

Leonard, Karen Isaksen. 1997. *The South Asian Americans.* Westport, CN, and London: Greenwood Press.

Lerner, Daniel. 1964. *The Passing of Traditional Society.* New York: Glencoe Free Press.

Macmillan, Margaret. 2001. *Paris, 1919: Six Months that Changed the World.* New York: Random House.

Madan, T.N. 1997. *Modern Myths, Locked Minds: Secularism and Fundamentalism in India.* New Delhi: Oxford University Press.

Manserge, Nicholas and Moon, Penderel. 1944. *Transfer of Power.* London: H.M. Stationer's Office.

Mayo, Katherine. 1928. *Mother India.* New York: Harcourt, Brace & Company.

Mazumdar, Haridas. 1960. *America's Contributions to India's Freedom.* New York: World in Brief.

McIntosh, Elizabeth P. 1998. *Sisterhood of Spies: The Women of the OSS.* New York: Dell.

McMahon, Robert J. 1994. *The Cold War on the Periphery: The United States, India and Pakistan.* New York: Columbia University Press.

Mills, Lennox A. 1945. *British Rule in Eastern Asia.* New York: Russell and Russell.
———. 1970. *Britain and Ceylon.* New York: Longmans, Green and Co.

Mitchell, Kate. 1942a. *India Without Fable: A 1942 Survey.* New York: Alfred A. Knopf.
———. 1942b. *Japan's Industrial Strength.* New York: Alfred A. Knopf.

Mitchell, Kate. 1971. *The Industrialization of the Western Pacific.* New York: Russell and Russell.

Moore, R.J. 1983. *Escape from Empire: The Atlee Government and the Indian Problem.* Oxford: Clarendon Press.

Morris-Jones, W.H. 1964. *The Government and Politics of India.* London: Hutchinson University Library.

Morse, Eric W. n.d. "The Immigration and Status of British East Indians in Canada", Unpublished Master's thesis.

Muir, Peter. 1944. *This is India.* New York: Books Inc.

Mukherjee, Tapan. 1997. *Taraknath Das: Life and Letters of a Revolutionary in Exile.* Calcutta: Jadavpur University.

Nichols, Beverley. 1944. *Verdict on India.* New York: Harcourt Brace & Co.

Pant, Harsh. 2005. "Natural Partners: US and India engaged, no longer estranged", *The Statesman Weekly,* July 30, p. 10.

Parmanand, Bhai. 1982. *The Story of My Life.* New Delhi: S. Chand & Co.

Parsons, Talcott. 1952. *The Social System.* New York: The Free Press.

Phillips, William. 1952. *Ventures in Diplomacy.* Boston: Beacon Hill Press.

Prashad, Vijay. n.d. "PropaGandhi in Black America: The Influence of Gandhi on the American Non-violent Movement", Little India website.

Price, Ruth. 2005. *The Lives of Agnes Smedley.* New York: Oxford University Press.

Puri, Harish K. 1983, *Ghadar Movement: Ideology, Organisation and Strategy.* Amritsar: Guru Nanak University Press.

Rai, Lala Lajpat. 1916. *Young India: An Interpretation and a History of the Nationalist Movement from Within.* New York: B.W. Huebsch.

———. 1978. *The Story of My Life.* New Delhi: Gitanjali Prakashan.

Raman, T.N. 1943. *What Does Gandhi Want?* New York: Oxford University Press.

Rudolph, Lloyd A. and Rudolph, Susanne Hoeber. 1980. *The Regional Imperative: United States Foreign Policy Towards South Asian States.* Atlantic Highlands, NJ: Humanities Press.

Sahai, Hanwant. 1957. "The Ghadar and After", *The Hindustan Times,* August 18.

Sareen, T.R. 1994. *Selected Documents on the Ghadr Party.* New Delhi: Mounto Publishing House.

Schaeffer, Howard. 1993. *Chester Bowles: New Dealer in the Cold War.* Cambridge, Mass.: Harvard University Press.

Selfa, Lance. 2004. "Emma Goldman: A Life of Controversy", *International Socialist Review,* Vol. 34, March–April.

Shaplen, Robert. 1951. "Profiles: One-Man Lobby", *New Yorker Magazine,* March 24.

———. 1969. *Time out of Hand: Revolution and Reaction in Southeast Asia.* New York: Harper Colophon Books.

Sherwood, Robert. 1950. *Roosevelt and Hopkins.* New York: Harper.

Shridharani, Krishnalal. 1939. *War Without Violence.* New York: Harcourt, Brace and Company.

———. 1941. *My India, My America.* New York: Duell, Sloan and Pearce.

Singh, Khushwant. 1966. *A History of the Sikhs, Vol. 2.* Princeton: Princeton University Press.

Singh, Khushwant and Singh, Satindra. 1966. *Ghadar, 1915: India's First Armed Revolution.* New Delhi: R&K Publishing House.

Singh, Malti. 1997. "An Indian American's campaign to 'influence the influencers'", Part 1, *India Abroad*, August 1, 1997. [Part 2 appeared in the August 8 issue.]

Singh, Rashmi Sharma. n.d. "The Adventurous Road to Finding Historical Records of the Thind History", www.Indolink.com.

Singh, Saint Nihal. 1909. "The Triumph of Indians in Canada", *The Modern Review*. Calcutta, August.

Smith, Vincent A., Wheeler, Sir Mortimer, Basham, A.L. and Spear, Percival. 1958. *The Oxford History of India*. Oxford: Clarendon Press.

Venkatraman, M.S. 1983. *Roosevelt, Gandhi Churchill: America and the Last Phase of India's Freedom struggle*. New Delhi: Radiant Publishers.

Venkatraman, M.S. and Srivastava, B.K. 1979. *Quit India: The American Response to the 1942 Struggle*. New Delhi: Vikas Publications.

Verma, Archana B. 2002. *The Making of Little Punjab: Patterns of Immigration*. New Delhi: Sage Publications.

Wilson, Douglas L. and Stanton, Lucia (eds.). 1999. *Jefferson Abroad*. New York: The Modern Library.

Yajnik, Indulal Kanhaiyalal. 1950. *Shymamji Krishnavarma: Life and Times of an Indian Revolutionary*. Bombay: Lakshmi Publication.

Zaehner, R.C. 1960. *Hindu and Muslim Mysticism*. London: London University (Athelone Press).

Zaman, Mustafa. 2003. "Dr Syud Hossain, A Glimpse of his Life, Speeches and Writings", *The Daily Star.net/magazine*. www.thedailystar.net/magazine/2003/11/01/bookr.htm.

# Index

# About the Author

**Harold A. Gould** is Visiting Scholar in South Asian Studies, Center for South Asian Studies, University of Virginia, Charlottesville, USA. He has been Associate Director and Director of the Center for Asian Studies, University of Illinois, and also Professor of anthropology at the same university. He has also held various positions at the Ohio State University, Washington University of St Louis, University of Kansas, and University of Pittsburgh. He has received several grants and fellowships to conduct research in India throughout his distinguished career, including a Fulbright Scholarship to Lucknow University and the Special Research Grants from the National Institute of Mental Health, and the Smithsonian Institution. He also served in the US Navy during World War II, first as a medical corpsman and then as a meteorologist.

Dr Gould has written extensively on India—be it the Hindu caste system, peasant society, social history, elections, or Indian politics. He has authored four books on Indian society and politics: *The Hindu Caste System: The Sacralization of a Social Order*, Vol. 1 (1987); *Caste Adaptation in Modernizing Indian Society*, Vol. 2 (1988); *Caste and Politics*, Vol. 3 (1991); and *Grass-Roots Politics in India: A Century of Political Evolution in Faizabad District* (1994). His co-edited publications include *The Hope and the Reality: US-Indian Relations from Roosevelt to Reagan (1992); India Votes: Alliance Politics: Coalition Government in the 9th and 10th General Elections* (1993); and *India and the United States in a Changing World* (2001).